Consuming Visions

Consuming Visions

MASS CULTURE AND THE LOURDES SHRINE

Suzanne K. Kaufman

CORNELL UNIVERSITY PRESS

Ithaca and London

Publication of this book was supported by Loyola University Chicago.

First published 2005 by Cornell University Press

Printed in the United States of America

Library of Congress Cataloging-in-Publication Data

Kaufman, Suzanne K., 1965–
    Consuming visions : mass culture and the Lourdes shrine / Suzanne K. Kaufman.
        p. cm.
    Includes bibliographical references and index.
    ISBN 0-8014-4248-6 (alk. paper)
    1. Christian shrines—France—Lourdes.   2. Christian pilgrims and pilgrimages—France—
Lourdes.   3. Popular culture—France—Lourdes.   4. Popular culture—Religious aspects—
Christianity.   5. Lourdes (France)—Religious life and customs.   I. Title.
    BT653.K38 2004
    232.91'7'094478—dc22   2004013152

Cloth printing   10   9   8   7   6   5   4   3   2   1

Contents

Illustrations

INTRODUCTION

Religious and Modern

Pilgrimage to Lourdes

The contemporary visitor to Lourdes encounters two remarkable sights: crowds of desperately sick pilgrims drinking, bathing, and praying at the Catholic shrine, and equally large numbers of customers shopping at hundreds of piety shops that line the two major boulevards leading to the pilgrimage site. These two phenomena are commonly understood by devout Catholics and secular observers alike to be unconnected, even diametrically opposed, aspects of popular religious worship. For modern-day visitors, watching attendants care for the sick or witnessing pilgrims pray fervently in front of the grotto where Bernadette Soubirous claimed to have seen the Virgin Mary evokes an image of profound faith. These acts of devotion often inspire committed Catholics even as they unnerve self-proclaimed "secular moderns." Yet the spectacle of countless piety shops selling bottled Lourdes water, mass-produced religious articles, and an enormous variety of novelty items—from shrine T-shirts to Mother-of-God bottle openers—frequently arouses laughter, discomfort, and even revulsion. For many believers and nonbelievers alike, this trade in sacred goods conjures up an image not of profound faith but of religious debasement.

This book challenges these starkly opposed characterizations of Lourdes. Beginning with the contention that the spiritual and the material have always been entwined at sites of pilgrimage, I argue that the interplay of Catholic devotion and commercial culture at Lourdes in the second half of the nineteenth century produced new, exciting expressions of popular religiosity while also generating distinctly modern concerns over the proper relationship between faith and commerce. Commercialization, in other words, was central to the development of the Lourdes pilgrimage site, to its success as an expression of popular religious faith, and to the half century of tumultuous debate over worship at the shrine.

The origins of this religious sanctuary nestled in the foothills of the French Pyrenees are quite recent. On February 11, 1858, a fourteen-year-old peasant girl named Marie-Bernarde Soubirous, known as Bernadette, saw an apparition of the Virgin Mary in a grotto called Massabielle. During the next five months, the young visionary saw the Virgin seventeen more times in front of thousands of witnesses. Bernadette and her visions became objects of popular fascination first for the inhabitants of the Pyrenees and then throughout all of France. By the summer of that year, multitudes of visitors—the devout and the curious— came from as far away as Paris to see the peasant girl who was said to be in mystical contact with the Blessed Virgin. Many came to pray and atone for their sins or to seek out the healing powers of a spring that Bernadette had discovered during one of her visionary encounters. This display of popular religiosity was not extraordinary for the period. Throughout the nineteenth century, women and children claimed to have visions of the Virgin Mary. Popular cults quickly developed around these seers, and the places where their supernatural experiences occurred grew into sites of pilgrimage.[1] What became unusual about Lourdes was the Church's swift approval of the Marian visions and the extraordinary development of the shrine over the final quarter of the nineteenth century. After initially trying to ignore, even discount, Bernadette's visions and the crowds that flocked to see her, the local bishop proclaimed the apparitions to be authentic in 1862.[2] Some ten years later the Augustinian Fathers of the Assumption, a Paris-based religious order, made Lourdes the site of their national pilgrimage. With the help of the railway and the Catholic popular press, the Assumptionists transformed Lourdes into a site of mass pilgrimage, bringing hundreds of thousands of devout Catholics to the shrine each year. By the early 1900s, close to half a million pilgrims, largely women from rural France, were going to Lourdes on church-sponsored national pilgrimages. And what these pilgrims encountered was a monumental shrine that offered highly orchestrated rituals, as well as an economically developed tourist city replete with an abundant variety of religious goods and services.

Lourdes emerged, then, as a modern pilgrimage shrine. Unlike premodern sites of Catholic pilgrimage, which reflected locally based devotional practices, Lourdes relied on methods of industrial development to transform a place of local religiosity into an organized mass spectacle. Church authorities who ran the shrine and institutionalized the pilgrimages took full advantage not only of the railway and the popular press but also of the techniques of contemporary advertising to make Lourdes the center of large-scale religious gatherings. In doing so, they recast devotional practices long associated with the act of pilgrimage within the structures and experiences of a newly commercializing society. Not just the procuring of sacred artifacts but the acts of traveling, seeing, and praying at Lourdes took on new forms. Clerical officials transformed the train into a moving chapel. They encouraged pilgrims to read religious guidebooks and to ship bottled Lourdes water to loved ones at home. Entrepreneurs of religious goods and services marketed newfangled *objets de piété*, such as picture postcards and mini-dioramas of the shrine. They seized on popular entertainments such as wax museums to represent the shrine's miraculous events. This ability of Lourdes to draw on mass cultural forms and new technologies for inspiration became crucial, in turn, to its popularity as a site of pilgrimage.

Church leaders also used modern innovations to refashion traditional healing practices into religious spectacles. New rituals at Lourdes, such as the Procession of the Blessed Sacrament in which the sick were implored to rise and follow the Eucharist before chanting crowds, remade healing into a public exhibition. The shrine not only created a medical bureau at Lourdes to verify the cures but disseminated the scientific findings of its Catholic doctors at publicized medical conferences. Religious newspapers and guidebooks widely circulated these exciting accounts of miraculous healing. Picture postcards displayed images of the pilgrims cured at Lourdes, making these *miraculés* (healed pilgrims) into well-known figures.[3] Taken together, these modern practices produced a new cultural rhetoric of healing, one that focused primarily on ordinary women who had suffered years of devastating illness and ineffective medical treatment only to be healed by the Virgin's love. The miracle cure as routinized spectacle—medically verified and dramatically presented—amazed devout Catholics even as it enraged anticlerical observers.

Thus pilgrimage to Lourdes offered believers unprecedented opportunities to engage with the sacred. Pilgrims drank from and bathed in the grotto's healing waters and then marched in processions at the shrine. They shopped for souvenirs in bustling religious emporiums and frequented entertainment venues in which Bernadette's visions were brought startlingly to life. By purchasing special train tickets to Lourdes that offered excursions to other sacred sites, pilgrims en route to the shrine set out on full-fledged tours of the nation's religious landscape. Melding novelty with reassuring doses of familiarity, these pilgrimage activities infused traditional acts of devotion with the cultural attractions associated with bourgeois tourism and modern commercial life. Pilgrims also encountered—in the figure of the Lourdes miraculée—a new model for imagining a feminine public self. At the turn of the century, when organized mass pilgrimages were at their height, hundreds of laywomen claimed to be healed at Lourdes. These women soon attracted extraordinary attention. Embodied evidence of the miraculous, they marched in special processions at the shrine. Their photographs, along with authenticated accounts of their cures, appeared in religious newspapers and other commercialized media throughout the country. The Lourdes miraculées presented faithful women of humble origins with a female public persona of considerable spiritual authority.

These devotional innovations made for an extraordinarily popular site of Catholic pilgrimage. Yet the public religiosity of Lourdes also became, by the 1890s, a growing problem for believers as well as for secular observers. Catholic critics condemned the shrine's commercialism for debasing religious worship, while anticlerical republicans attacked the marketing of the pilgrimage for corrupting the health of the secular republic. Both sides blamed female pilgrims for the problems of Lourdes, calling the devotional practices of these women crude, superstitious, and injurious to true spirituality. Not only did the material practices of mass pilgrimage generate fierce controversy, so, too, did the hundreds of proclaimed cures at Lourdes. On one side, the Church heralded the shrine's medically verified cures as powerful evidence of the miraculous at work in the modern age. On the other side, anticlerical physicians countered that sick pilgrims were hysterics, their cures mere cases of psychological suggestion. Played out in the pages of popular newspapers, these disputes repeatedly took the form of a sensational war of words in which each side accused the other of factual error, medical incompetence, and calculated exploitation. Much like the Dreyfus affair and other notorious scandals seized on by the press, the debate over Lourdes revealed how publicity and spectacle making were now deeply entangled with questions of truth and proof. Indeed, the determined efforts by clerics and doctors to find out the "truth" of the cure raised disturbing questions about all knowledge claims in the age of the mass press.

Commercialization, then, is central to explaining why the Lourdes shrine became the most popular site of Catholic pilgrimage in fin-de-siècle Europe, and the most controversial. The central aim of this book is to examine how the remaking of Catholic devotional activities within an emerging commercial culture produced distinctly modern forms of popular religiosity, innovative practices that offered new opportunities as well as issues of contention. By framing Lourdes in this fashion, it becomes possible to move beyond certain self-limiting assumptions—that, for example, the intermingling of religion and commerce somehow signifies *debasement*—in order to understand how commercialized worship offered rich possibilities for expressing faith and connecting with the sacred in the modern world. At the same time, such an approach need not minimize the destabilizing elements of new devotional practices or dismiss the powerful standardizing currents set in motion by an increasingly commodified pilgrimage journey. Quite the contrary: religious practice at the shrine, while becoming more democratic in participation, touched off repeated conflicts over the very prearranged rituals, mass-produced goods, and low-cost entertainments that Lourdes provided. As for the shrine's extraordinary reports of miraculous healing, the furious press debates between believers and freethinkers featured sensational accusations and publicity stunts that were much more effective at selling newspapers than at elucidating the ultimate truth about these cures. In the process, however, such conflicts served to lay bare some of the deepest fissures of modern French society, and within modernity itself.

The story of Bernadette Soubirous is well known, having been the conventional starting point for most scholarly work about the Lourdes shrine. While out gathering wood along the shore of the Gave River with her sister and a friend, the visionary saw the Virgin Mary for the first time. Described by Bernadette as a beautiful girl, the apparition carried a rosary, and two golden roses lay at her bare feet. Bernadette referred to the girl in the vision simply as "Aqueró"—"that one" in the local patois. During the course of the serial visions, the beautiful girl called on Bernadette to pray for sinners and told the seer that she would suffer in this world but would be happy in the next. On February 25, 1858, two weeks after the initial vision, the apparition commanded Bernadette to drink from and wash herself in what appeared to be a patch of dry ground near the entrance to the grotto. Bernadette obediently complied and, digging up wet earth, drank from it and smeared mud on her face. Later that day, villagers dug deeper at the spot and unearthed a spring of flowing water, which suggested the presence of the miraculous. At a later visit to the grotto, Bernadette asked the young girl, after much prompting from the local priest, who she was, and received a stunning reply: "I am the Immaculate Conception."

Well before Bernadette's final encounter with the beautiful girl on July 16, the visionary and her apparitions had become objects of fascination throughout France. This asthmatic peasant girl, barely literate, faced a barrage of investigations by clerics and journalists as well as attacks from police officials, government administrators, and doctors. Following orders from the local bishop, church authorities refused to support her while several local newspapers pronounced her mentally feeble and given to hallucinations. Yet she remained resolute and consistent in her story. Such constancy gave Bernadette an air of sincerity and credibility that public officials and journalists, it was said, found difficult to undermine. Moreover, local inhabitants seemed readily prepared to believe that she was in communication with the Virgin Mary, coming by the thousands to witness her in ecstasy and then to pray at the grotto. Sick and disabled believers also came to wash in and drink from the newly unearthed spring, seeking relief from their suffering and, frequently, claiming to be cured. Their assertions of healing confirmed for many devout believers that the grotto was a new site of divine intervention. Even after local bureaucrats outlawed worship at the site, the faithful, often overturning barricades and risking arrest, continued to seek out the grotto for prayer, repentance, and healing. Recognizing the staying power of this new local holy place, Church authorities soon reversed their opposition and eventually transformed the grotto into an official pilgrimage shrine.[4]

For a number of years, historians understood Lourdes as the vestige of a moribund peasant religiosity. The shrine's large-scale pilgrimages and proliferating miracle cures were seen to be largely irrelevant to a broader narrative of modernization that framed the development of French society. This narrative has exerted a strong influence on the writing of modern French history, prompting many scholars to interpret the emergence of new devotional cults in the nineteenth century as momentary diversions from a relentless process of secularization.[5] At the heart of such analyses linking secularism and modernity lurks Émile Durkheim's enormously influential distinction between the *sacred* and the *profane*. In 1912, the French sociologist argued that all religions, whether simple or complex, tend to divide the world into these two mutually opposing categories. Existing quite apart from the familiar and profane order of everyday life, the sacred represents a transcendent realm—the uncanny and magical as well as the sublime and rapturous—that can only be made accessible through a designated set of rites and rituals. For Durkheim, sacred and profane "have always and everywhere been conceived by the human mind as two distinct classes, as two worlds between which there is nothing in common." These two realms "cannot even approach each other and keep their own nature at the same time," and thus, when the sacred and profane do interact, it can only be a sign of growing secularization.[6] This view of the nature of religious life has profoundly influenced still-dominant explanations of modern development. As societies modernize, with scientific rationality emerging hand in hand with capitalist economic development and liberal political democracy, they experience what German sociologist Max Weber labeled the progressive "disenchantment of the world." Thus, the sacred—a belief in magical enchantment—recedes to those ever-smaller spaces left uncolonized by secular society or reemerges, following the logic of Karl Marx's analysis of modern capitalism, as a profane magic of the marketplace in the form of commodity fetishism.[7]

Recently, however, historians of religion have sought to challenge the secularization thesis and, along with it, inherited characterizations of popular Catholic religiosity as archaic vestiges. An important body of literature has shown how the Catholic Church deployed quite effectively the tools of a modernizing, capitalist economy (the railway, the mass press, and new production techniques) to promote a religious revival in the nineteenth century.[8] In the process, the Church often enlisted innovative technologies to construct profoundly conservative, even reactionary, ideologies. In France, these efforts served, in turn, to channel popular faith into political opposition to the Third Republic's campaign to secularize society.[9] Manifestations of popular religiosity were thus a response to the challenges of modernity, providing consolation and comfort to Catholic believers as they tried to make sense of rapid political and economic change. Building on this perspective, historian Ruth Harris has related the extraordinary success of Lourdes not only to the mass circulation press and the railway but also to the Church's adaptation of modern medical science to verify and promote the shrine's miracle cures. Harris further notes that women were instrumental—as lay and clerical workers at the shrine and as fund-raisers for the Church—in shaping a modern therapeutic culture that celebrated female nurturance and a ready surrender to God's will.[10]

These historical approaches dispel views of popular devotions as immutable practices, mere atavistic extensions of traditional ways of life. Focusing on the Church's ability to mobilize masses of Catholics or to create a religious-therapeutic culture, these scholars demonstrate that nineteenth-century expressions of popular faith evolved in relation to key modern developments such as industrialization, urbanization, and the emergence of republican government. Yet, ultimately, the conception of modern religious experience put forth by these historians is unsatisfying precisely because it seeks to reinscribe Catholic devotional practice and belief within a realm of sacred experience that supposedly lies outside the bounds of modern commercial society.[11] For all the discussion of religious experience as "vibrant," "evolving," or "modern," scholars of popular religion continue to accept a sacred/profane dichotomy that limits their understanding of modernity and the modern. Thus, while historians of religion now acknowledge that clerical authorities made use of the technologies of a modernizing economy, recent studies fail to analyze how these tools—especially the emergence of new forms of commercial production, exchange, and spectatorship—have profoundly reshaped religious practice itself. Instead, for many scholars, the "lure of the miraculous" and the "encounter with the supernatural" take place in an arena separate from the marketplace, somehow beyond the reach of secular society.[12]

The notion that real spirituality resides beyond the dross of the marketplace needs to be challenged. Of course, the fact that commerciality has played little visible part in dominant views of modern religious experience and belief is not surprising. Indeed, a scholarly bias against commercialized religion may be one of the most enduring legacies left by sixteenth-century Protestant and Catholic reformers. Historian Colleen McDannell has argued that the Protestant Reformation bequeathed to modern-day scholars a deep suspicion of visual piety, while the Catholic Counter-Reformation handed down its own fears about the devotional excesses of the illiterate masses.[13] These religious concerns furnish important historical antecedents of discomfort with commercialized forms of religiosity. Modern unease with commercialized religious practices also reflects the largely negative assessments of mass culture found in more recent cultural criticism. Twentieth-century theorists Theodor Adorno and Max Horkheimer developed a compelling critique of the modern "culture industry," an interlocking set of capitalist institutions—media, popular arts, entertainment, and fashion—that constitute an apparatus of domination and "mass deception."[14] Such wholly condemnatory assessments of mass culture, combined with enduring prejudices against visual and material forms of piety, have exerted an enormous influence, in turn, on how scholars have approached the subject of popular religion in the modern era. Historians of religion typically disregard links between faith and the marketplace, perhaps from fear of "denigrating" the integrity of their subject matter. The persistence of such concerns helps to explain why historians have dismissed as superficial or inauthentic what might otherwise be recognized as significant characteristics of religious expression. These concerns may also illuminate why scholars of religion still prefer to focus on the experiences of "rural innocents"—female mystics or child visionaries and their devoted followers—as exemplars of nineteenth-century popular religion: these phenomena represent what scholars understand as authentic religious experience. In short, Durkheim's categories still dictate the paradigms of much of today's scholarship on modern popular religiosity.

If the modern opposition between sacred and profane has continued to influence recent writing on religious history, it has also shaped historical work on the emergence of commercial culture. A number of scholars recognize that there is virtually no realm of modern life in which commodities do not influence social identity and cultural meaning. Yet many of these same scholars have all but ignored the interplay between religious practice and modern commerce in the development of mass consumption and new leisure activities.[15] Historians of modern France, in particular, have presented the emerging consumer practices that involve mechanically produced goods as a secularizing phenomenon that arises in cosmopolitan urban centers. Indeed, for many historians, the Parisian department store, with its wondrous display of material goods, represents the quintessentially profane nature of modern enchantment, made possible by the magic of the marketplace.[16] Similarly, recent work on the emergence of organized tourism and mass leisure activities in fin-de-siècle France has presented new forms of travel and urban entertainment as replacements for older, religiously inspired festivals and folk practices.[17] In these analyses, the sacred aura of the relic gives way to the seductive allure of the mass-produced object, while the charisma of the saint is captured by the modern celebrity. Nineteenth-century Parisian exhibitions become "places of pilgrimage to the commodity fetish," as Walter Benjamin put it, whereas religious worship, if visible at all in such analyses, embodies a vestige of the way things used to be.[18]

The weaknesses of scholarship on religion and commercial culture in modern European history, then, are striking. Theories of secularization, insufficiently challenged, continue to wield substantial influence. By providing an appealingly simple notion of modern progressive development, these theories pit the religious against the modern and, in the process, portray religious believers as traditionalists at odds with the forces of industrial growth and liberal democracy. Even historians who reject such views are hobbled by thinly conceptualized notions of modern religious practice. Enduring prejudices against

material forms of lay piety, along with derogatory evalu.
contemporary scholars, have combined to make comme
ject to be dismissed or transcended. Without serious e
have labeled or implicitly treated such expressions of faith
spirituality. In either case, they insist, commercialized for
should not be confused with genuinely sacred experience.

This book offers a different approach to the study of modern Catholic devotion.
By examining the act of pilgrimage as both a spiritual and material experience,
I reposition Lourdes as a crucial site for the emergence of a modern culture of
consumption. The melding of Catholic devotional activities with a developing
commercial culture generated, I contend, innovative and exhilarating manifestations of popular religious faith while also arousing singularly modern anxieties
over the appropriate relationship between belief and the market. The complex
interconnections between faith and commerce at Lourdes were rooted in late
nineteenth-century processes of commercial exchange, commodification, and
spectatorship that accompanied the development of large-scale industrial capitalism in France.[19] Defining features of a modern culture of consumption, such
processes have typically been linked to fin-de-siècle urban society, with its new
shopping venues, low-cost entertainments, and the bustling street life engaged
in by mobile individuals. Yet these elements also defined religious life at Lourdes,
imparting to the shrine a profoundly modern character.

The term "modern" is often seen, like modernity itself, as elusive, multiva-
lent, and contested. I believe it is important to define modern religious experience not only in terms of processes of modernization—that is, the material
social relations connected to capitalist industrialization—but also as a set of representational practices reflecting a new and profound awareness of temporality.
These modes of representation (lithography and photography, popular newspapers, billboards, film) came to shape an emerging cultural consciousness
that embraced, in the words of Charles Baudelaire, "the ephemeral, the fugitive,
the contingent." By taking seriously the central technological innovations of
capitalist development (such as railway construction or techniques of mass
production) as well as the new social and cultural practices that emerge with it—
advertising, *flânerie*, urban spectatorship—this definition of modernity compre-
hends the profound interconnections between a commodity-driven mass culture
and the lived experience of ordinary people.[20] Such a perspective also promises
to shed new light on the ways in which the development of Lourdes as a national
pilgrimage shrine created a mass cultural religious experience that bridged elite
and popular culture, transforming the act of pilgrimage into a modern spectacle.[21] Indeed, the appeal of Lourdes lay precisely in its ability to infuse religious
life with powerful elements of the ephemeral, the contingent, and the spectac-

At the same time, this new religious experience destabilized other, equally modern conceptions of proper faith, setting off repeated conflicts over the commodified nature of modern pilgrimage practices. Lourdes embodied what Marshall Berman has characterized as the key experience of modernity itself: the fraught tension between life's possibilities and perils, a life that "promises us adventure, power, joy, growth, transformation of ourselves and the world—and, at the same time, that threatens to destroy everything we have, everything we know, everything we are."[22] To understand, then, the appeal and the anxiety that Lourdes provoked in fin-de-siècle Europe, one must analyze the commerciality of the shrine within the modernizing processes and representational practices that constituted its inescapably modern identity—and, for that reason, its enduring success.

Over the past twenty years, scholarship has begun to trace a number of developments in nineteenth-century France that paved the way for a modern consumer society. Following the 1840s, the technological innovations of the Industrial Revolution (railways, steamships, the telegraph) began to expand the nation's capacities for production and circulation and, along with them, the availability and affordability of consumer goods. Meanwhile, overhaul of the banking system ensured the growing reliability of the bank check and of credit, laying the basis for a gradual rise in purchasing power among many sectors of French society. A popular, advertising-oriented press, which had sprung up as early as the 1830s, further stimulated the desire for new goods within regional and, increasingly, national markets. Taken together, these economic and technological developments set the stage for an emerging consumer marketplace that altered daily life in much of the country over the second half of the nineteenth century.[23] The initial beneficiary of this transformation was the urban bourgeoisie, whose members enjoyed both the discretionary income and the leisure time needed to take advantage of the new commodity-driven mass culture emerging in most large French cities, especially Paris. These urban dwellers shopped in department stores, dined in restaurants, read newspapers in cafés, and strolled along the city streets. They also sojourned in the French countryside, relaxing in mountain spas and seaside resorts—places that, as a result of growing popularity, were no longer isolated from the impacts of these economic changes. Indeed, "what began as rural resorts," historian Eugen Weber has noted, "eventually turned into showcases of specifically urban lifestyles, propagating a consumer economy long before more normal towns had one."[24] These resort destinations, then, introduced key elements of the new urban mass culture to the provinces.

Lourdes emerged at the forefront of this process of rural modernization. Becoming a site of sanctioned pilgrimage shortly after Bernadette's 1858 visions, the shrine developed much along the lines of secular resort towns, particularly after the success of the annual national pilgrimages in the 1870s. As in Biarritz or Vittel, elites remade Lourdes, pulling down old neighborhoods and building new streets, shops, and hotels to accommodate the city's burgeoning number of visitors. Lourdes increasingly organized itself around new forms of mass consumption—in this case, religious consumption—for the thousands, eventually hundreds of thousands, who visited during the pilgrimage season. Although many travelers to Lourdes were members of the urban middle classes, the site also welcomed large numbers of more humble pilgrims, particularly those from the southwest region but from other rural areas as well. These nonelite visitors, the majority of whom were women, thus found themselves face-to-face—many for the first time—with a vibrant, commercially dynamic pilgrimage town that offered an astonishing variety of religious goods, services, and entertainments.[25]

Religious commerce was not, of course, a phenomenon born of the modern era. One has only to think of *The Canterbury Tales* to recall that pilgrimage sites and religious festivities have long provided money-making opportunities for priest and peddler. Chaucer's Pardoner, for example, who uses counterfeit relics and sham cures to hoodwink gullible believers, proclaims shamelessly his aim to "preach for nothing but for greed of gain."[26] That Chaucer's tale satirically derides such buying and selling reminds us that laments against the commercialization of religion also have a long history. Clearly, the desire to separate religion and commerce, sacred and profane, possesses deep roots. Yet the boundaries between faith and commerce routinely broke down in the daily world of lived religion. Historians of medieval and early-modern Europe have shown that devout Catholics, elites as well as plebeians, interacted with material culture in a variety of ways that expressed their religious faith. This materiality is clearly evident in popular devotions such as pilgrimage.[27] After all, pilgrimage—a religiously inspired journey to visit a holy person or to commemorate a special event that took place at a specific site—has been promoted by the Church at least since the fourth century as an effective means to encourage faith and as a legitimate response to personal religious needs. The physical landscapes, material objects, and personages associated with holy sites became essential intermediaries for pilgrims seeking to receive God's grace. When Catholics went on pilgrimage, they prayed, atoned for past behaviors, and petitioned the saints or the Virgin Mary for aid. They also searched for tangible proof of God's presence by touching the physical site, looking at relics, collecting artifacts, and buying souvenirs. As clerics and lay believers alike sought ways to interact with God, they developed an array of pilgrimage activities that commingled the spiritual and the material, the commercial and the religious, in the course of enacting formal ritual, informal practice, and everyday devotion.

The material practices and rituals associated with premodern Catholic pilgrimage did not disappear with the advent of industrial society, but they were remade in the emerging mass culture of late nineteenth-century France. This

process of re-creation was already in motion before Lourdes became an important religious shrine. Following the cholera epidemic of 1832, for example, the
Miraculous Medal publicized in French religious newspapers was snapped up
by millions of believers eager for its healing powers. During the 1850s, sixty to
eighty thousand Catholics each year were going on pilgrimage to Ars, where the
venerated curé Jean-Marie Vianney, considered by many to be a living saint,
heard their confessions and healed their bodies and souls. By the mid-1870s,
Paray-le-Monial, the site of Marguerite-Marie Alacoque's vision of the Sacred
Heart of Jesus, was drawing some one hundred thousand believers to its
Church-orchestrated pilgrimages of atonement. These emerging signs of large
changes in Catholic popular culture owed much to industrialization, especially
the railway and new forms of communication, and to the rise of a capitalist marketplace.[28] Yet Lourdes, more than any other devotional site, profited from the
developments of a modernizing society, and indeed took them considerably further. Merging older pilgrimage customs with innovative marketing techniques
and a range of new consumer practices, the shrine quickly became the most
popular and successful engine of transformation in French Catholic devotional
culture.

Commercialized forms came to structure devotional life at Lourdes, shaping
religious meanings and identities. For this reason, I take seriously the idea, put
forth by Adorno and Horkheimer, that in modern societies the commodity form
becomes central to the experience of culture. At Lourdes, the orchestration of
mass pilgrimages not only paved the way for an increasingly homogenized and
commodified set of rituals but also created a formulaic yet spectacular account
of miraculous healing. However, simply because the commodity form shaped
the cultural activities and meanings attached to Catholic pilgrimage does not
necessarily mean that mass cultural practices were mere tools of mass deception.
As Benjamin has suggested, mass cultural forms can also furnish moments of
popular agency and even hints of social transformation.[29]

Scholars of religion examining the modern history of the United States have
elaborated on this more open-ended view of mass culture. These historians
demonstrate that the faithful often made sense of the ambiguities of modern life
by incorporating consumer goods, popular entertainments, and advertising
techniques into their devotional practices.[30] Colleen McDannell, for example,
contends that lay believers, even in an era of rapidly growing literacy, do not become less materialist in their worship. Rather, she argues, "word and image often come together" in the devotional acts of Christians, and material expressions
of religiosity become "multimedia events" in which "speech, vision, gesture,
touch and sound combine."[31] Furthermore, McDannell's study, along with
work by historian Robert Orsi, suggest that devotional practices involving religious objects, even mass-produced objects, do not turn the faithful into "weak
Christians," passively dependent on an omnipotent figure for aid or direction.

Rather, such practices provide a means for interacting with powerful forces that, in turn, empower Christians to act in the world. In an analysis of American women's devotion to St. Jude, Orsi found that "the material culture of the devotion—its prayer cards, statues, medals, dashboard figurines—were the media with which women played on their world."[32]

Understanding modern religiosity, then, as a set of practices engaging body and mind, word and image, provides fresh ways to think about the relationship between faith and commerce. The commerciality of Lourdes enlivened the experience of Catholic pilgrimage for many believers. New devotional practices accorded female pilgrims, in particular, unprecedented opportunities for re-imagining their own devotion. When women came to Lourdes, they not only prayed at the grotto but also bought postcards to be sent home to loved ones with descriptions of their pious acts. When these female pilgrims prepared to participate in mass processions at the shrine, they read accounts in the latest guidebooks and purchased votive candles to carry with them—and afterward shopped for souvenirs to remind them of these special experiences. If female attendants nursed sick pilgrims and bathed their diseased bodies in Lourdes water, these helpers also celebrated those who were cured, eagerly shaking their hands, reading thrilling accounts of their triumphs in religious newspapers, and later buying picture postcards that displayed visual images of the blessed miraculées. As participants, consumers, and spectators at Lourdes, female pilgrims asserted their Catholic identities, claiming a measure of authority in the public arena of religious life. This self-assertion is even more evident for the hundreds of women who proclaimed themselves healed at Lourdes. The special processions of healed pilgrims at the shrine, the widespread circulation of healing accounts in religious newspapers, even the process of medical verification carried out by the Lourdes medical bureau—all of these innovations rendered the female miraculées new public figures of great importance, even sacred celebrities.[33]

Church authorities encouraged and supported such activities, capitalizing on the commercial practices associated with mass consumption, bourgeois tourism, and industrialized urban society in order to enhance the experience of pilgrimage. The new practices and rituals of modern pilgrimage—the train travel, the buying and selling of mass-produced goods, the routinized spectacles of prayer, procession, and healing—became integral, compelling characteristics of an emerging mass devotional culture. Yet if Lourdes offered devout Catholic women new possibilities for connecting with the sacred, those possibilities were clearly constrained by the prerogatives of male authorities. The shrine's healing rituals and new practices for celebrating the cured were narrowly defined by nine-teenth-century Catholic culture. Prized for their ability to suffer and surrender fully to God's will, female pilgrims were often praised by male authorities for what was done to them rather than for what they did. Moreover, female miracu-lées who sought the blessings of the Lourdes limelight often experienced only fleeting moments of public recognition. The system of production, circulation, and consumption of healing accounts, while celebrating these women, could also discard them just as quickly when a new cure came into view. In this sense, becoming a Lourdes miraculée was fraught with contradiction and conflict.

Only by examining Lourdes as a modern Catholic shrine embedded within a commercializing society can we begin to appreciate how the site's public expressions of faith generated both excitement and anxiety. The success of mass pilgrimages to Lourdes lay in the shrine's ability to remake the act of pilgrimage and its devotional practices into a meaningful part of contemporary life. Yet it was precisely this merging of religious ritual with modern cultural forms and commercial practices that disturbed Catholic elites as well as anticlerical republicans. If the twinning of faith and commerce that emerged at Lourdes was hardly a new phenomenon, the intensive use of capitalist market practices not only made commercialized pilgrimage appear new—strikingly modern—but also excessive and, potentially, corrupting. In this respect, the public religiosity of Lourdes in late nineteenth-century France presented itself as an urgent problem to be solved. What impacts would such commercialized worship have on religion and society? What might constitute proper religious worship in the modern era? Seeking to pin down answers to these questions, observers began to construct a series of distinctions—between religion and commerce, spirituality and materialism, pilgrimage and tourism—that might bring a reassuring measure of order to these disturbingly interrelated phenomena. Proponents and opponents of mass pilgrimage developed a new way of talking about modern religious life, a discourse of religious debasement that seemed to offer a "fix" to the problem of Lourdes.

Taking this discourse of religious debasement seriously—not as a reflection of some objective historical process but rather as a defining discourse of modernity—enables scholars to denaturalize and historicize Durkheim's opposition between sacred and profane. By seeking to do so, I also challenge historians to move beyond accounts that replicate this opposition, such as those works on Lourdes that treat the figure of Bernadette and her peasant followers as "authentic" expressions of the sacred. At Lourdes, sacred and profane—religious practice and the secular world—never stood in opposition but, rather, commingled in a process of constant cross-fertilization. Although this intermixing and the public diatribes against it had always shaped the experience of pilgrimage, the modern effort to separate religion and commerce at Lourdes involved church authorities, ordinary lay believers, and even anticlerical republicans in a much broader struggle to establish a stable boundary between sacred and profane. More than an extension of age-old concerns, this struggle drew on new techniques of representation that were themselves quite prone to commerciality and spectacle-making. When clerics sought to create the shrine's sacred rituals of healing, they seized on marketplace stratagems to attract the enthusiasm of the crowd. When republicans tried to close the shrine, they were stymied by the sacred site's undeniable importance to the economy of France. And when anticlerical doctors and their Catholic counterparts debated the reality of the Lourdes cures, they found themselves embroiled in sensational public wagers played out in the pages of the mass press. Consequently, the inability to fix a stable boundary between religion and commerce created uneasy, persistent tensions for all parties. In this sense, the "problem" of Lourdes was about much more than religion and its debasement. It was about the unstable, unruly constitution of a modern social order and its commercializing public sphere.[34]

1

Remaking Lourdes

Catholic Pilgrimage
as Modern Spectacle

Lourdes at the moment of Bernadette's apparitions was essentially unknown to the rest of France. When Louis Veuillot, journalist and editor of the Catholic newspaper *L'Univers,* introduced the young visionary and her miraculous grotto to his readers in 1858, he described this unprepossessing town as "more traversed than known." Hidden in the foothills of the Pyrenees, Lourdes was a crossroads for travelers en route to somewhere else, most often the well-known spa towns of Bagnères-de-Bigorre and Cauterets. Yet fewer than ten years later Lourdes, now a sanctioned site of Catholic pilgrimage, was a destination. An 1866 article in *Le Lavedan,* a regional newspaper for the Pyrenees, boasted: "Lourdes has definitely been adopted as one of those places of pilgrimage that each year attracts a considerable crowd of visitors. . . . This privileged situation will confer on our town an unexpected prosperity." The newspaper expected extraordinary bounty to come: "With a population well disposed toward it, all manner of progress is possible and even easy. . . . It is only necessary to wish for it." This blithely optimistic prediction would soon be realized beyond anyone's dreams. By the first decade of the twentieth century, Lourdes had become the best-known and most important site of pilgrimage—apart from Rome and Jerusalem—in the Christian world, welcoming an estimated two hundred thousand visitors annually to a sacred site that had been changed beyond recognition.[1]

A modern Catholic pilgrimage shrine, Lourdes has a different form and content from its predecessors because it is the product of more recent times. Born of the late nineteenth century, pilgrimages to Lourdes were linked to distinctly modern innovations: advancements in railway technology, new advertising techniques, the modern press, and the mass production of religious goods. The scale and scope of capitalist market practices, combined with the development of new forms of visual and written media, created a pilgrimage experience that was dramatically different from premodern pilgrimage—more democratic, but also more homogeneous. On the one hand, capitalist development made the shrine broadly known and highly accessible. A mass public—rich and poor, urban and rural—participated in large-scale pilgrimages to Lourdes and visited the site in huge numbers as tourists. What these visitors found, by the same token, was a pilgrimage shrine that both edified and entertained, providing prearranged rituals, mechanically produced objets de piété, and low-cost attractions that pleased the crowd.

Historians have not ignored the impact of these new technologies and modern market practices on popular Catholic worship. Indeed, they have shown that Church leaders not only adopted such means to promote particular devotions but even embraced them, blessing new technological wonders such as steamships and factories in sermons and at religious processions. Scholarship on nineteenth-century pilgrimage, moreover, has long acknowledged that the railway and the mass press enabled large numbers of pilgrims to reach hitherto-remote holy sites, enriching religious orders and pilgrimage towns alike. Yet while scholars have noted the Church's use of modern technologies and new commercial activities, they have consistently interpreted these innovations as tools in service of the production of an explicitly antimodern religiosity. In effect, they have seen the ritual life of Lourdes as an exemplary instance of the "invention of tradition," a process in which clerical authorities consciously assembled a set of new rituals that evoked an idealized religious past. Thomas Kselman, for example, argued some time ago that "the Church sought an escape from a modern urban France in sentimental images of peasant religiosity and the bourgeois family." Some twenty years later, Ruth Harris has made a similar argument, claiming that the rituals at Lourdes intentionally "associated themselves with a vision of timeless continuity" and "the ancient traditions of rural, aristocratic Catholicism." In short, the Church remade pilgrimages to Lourdes into mass collective endeavors that ultimately sought to reject the secular culture, republican politics, and emerging commercial society of a modernizing France.[2] Although this analysis does well to capture the conservative political sentiments and antimodern tone expressed by key Church leaders connected with Lourdes, it fails to address the vision of Lourdes produced by the shrine's own promotional literature and other popular media used to market the pilgrimage and its products. Even as Church authorities at Lourdes proclaimed that their large-scale gatherings and newfangled rituals were resurrecting a bygone religiosity, the written and visual media used to promote the pilgrimages—popular guidebooks, religious newspapers, mass-produced picture postcards, and advertisements for religious goods and services—were presenting a very different vision of Lourdes. This promotional literature, in both form and content, represented the shrine as a distinctly modern phenomenon. It was precisely this kind of popular literature and imagery that the majority of Catholic pilgrims encountered and came to depend on as they began to see, touch, and interact with the sacred landscapes, objects, and personages of Lourdes.[3]

When the formal rituals and informal practices long associated with the act of pilgrimage—traveling to the holy site, seeing the sacred landscape, buying religious objects, and, of course, praying to and petitioning the Virgin—took on new forms, these activities also took on modern meanings for the Catholics who engaged in them. As early as the 1870s, when the Church decided to make Lourdes a site of national pilgrimages, clerical authorities employed new techniques and commercial practices in a sustained effort to create a mass base of pilgrims for the shrine. These authorities, seeking to accommodate increasingly large numbers of visitors, invested in urban renewal that soon remade Lourdes into a modern tourist city. Even while the Augustinian Fathers of the Assumption who organized the national pilgrimages claimed to be reviving a religiosity that harkened back to the medieval past, these same authorities produced a set of rituals and activities that transformed Lourdes into a modern spectacle in which pilgrims encountered the sacred through a variety of advanced technologies and commercial exchanges. Popular guidebooks, newspaper articles, and mass-produced picture postcards extolled the use of trains, electricity, and other modern marvels. Advertisements praised the value of mechanically reproduced religious goods and promoted novel visual entertainments such as dioramas and wax museums, promising to transform Bernadette's encounter with the Virgin into an affordable yet spectacularly packaged adventure. By reconstituting the material practices of Catholic pilgrimage in late nineteenth-century terms, clerical authorities and local business elites detached Lourdes from its local peasant roots and fashioned a profoundly contemporary shrine, a picture of religious life that looked and felt modern.

It was not simply that the Church incorporated present-day icons into the content of the written and visual depictions of Lourdes, lending the shrine a kind of modern gloss. By deploying new techniques and commercial practices, authorities encouraged pilgrims to interact with the holy site as modern tourists and consumers. Indeed, practices such as reading guidebooks, viewing dioramas, and writing postcards were configured into the devotional life of the pilgrimage, introducing the devout to modern ways of perceiving landscapes, consuming goods, and interacting with other individuals. Going to Lourdes on a pilgrimage gave the faithful access to the modern world even as it made religious worship more exciting and relevant to late nineteenth-century and early twentieth-century believers. Indeed, the very success of Lourdes, I will suggest, depended on erasing its identity as a local holy site and linking the practices of Catholic pilgrimage to the emerging mass culture of urban France. Although in the short term the development of this devotional culture of pilgrimage served to invigorate French Catholic practice during a period of Church instability, its more enduring impact would be to enable rural pilgrims, most of them women, to find an important entrance into the world of mass society and consumer culture.

FROM LOCAL TO MASS PILGRIMAGE: THE FOUNDATIONS OF A MODERN SHRINE

The visions of Bernadette and the grotto of Lourdes gained widespread, even national, attention very quickly. By 4 March 1858, just one month after the first apparition, crowds of up to seven thousand people congregated around the grotto and lined the shores of the Gave River to watch Bernadette in ecstasy. Rich and poor, devout and curious, travelers from neighboring towns and villages arrived to catch a glimpse of the young visionary, to wash in the newly discovered spring, or perhaps even to behold a miracle.[4] Some ten days after Bernadette's final vision, the journalist Veuillot, en route to Bagnères, learned of the apparitions and soon paid a visit to Bernadette and the grotto. Convinced of the visionary's sincerity and moved by the spirituality around him, he began to promote the cause of Lourdes in the pages of *L'Univers*. Other Parisian dailies, such as *La Presse* and *Le Courrier de Paris,* also printed stories of the strange events that had caused such a stir at Lourdes. By the fall of 1858, most of France had heard of Bernadette's visions and the miraculous spring now flowing at the grotto. The attention of influential Parisian Catholics such as Veuillot may have spurred the bishop of Tarbes, Monseigneur Laurence, to begin his episcopal investigation into the visions and cures being proclaimed at the grotto.[5] This kind of attention also helped ease local government opposition to worship at the grotto. In October 1858, the mayor of Lourdes officially allowed access to the site and informal pilgrimages to the grotto began in earnest.

Despite the national attention the visions received, early pilgrimages to the grotto were, for the most part, local in nature and continued to reflect traditional forms of popular religiosity. Even after Bishop Laurence authorized the new cult of the Grotto of Lourdes in 1862, making the site a sanctioned Catholic shrine, the pilgrimages remained regional events. As a rule, the faithful came on foot from areas throughout the southwest of France, sometimes from as far away as Bayonne or Nevers, but more typically from villages and towns near Lourdes. Pilgrims usually stayed no more than a day or two, and arrived as members of a distinct community—a parish, diocese, village, or small town. The bishop of Tarbes led a series of early parish pilgrimages, including a number from the town of Loubajac, located just five kilometers from Lourdes. Of course, even these local pilgrimages could assemble large numbers of faithful Catholics, as was the case with Loubajac, from which thousands came to express gratitude for four miraculous cures. When pilgrims arrived at Lourdes, they petitioned the Virgin

Figure 1. The grotto of Lourdes, June 1858. Archives de l'Œuvre de la Grotte.

for aid or thanked her for graces received. They washed in the grotto spring and often took artifacts—rocks or grass—away from the site. Pilgrims also bought small religious items, such as medallions or statuettes, from the many itinerant peddlers who now converged on the town. These items were brought home or sometimes left within the grotto as small offerings for Mary. A popular cult soon emerged around Bernadette herself. Much to her discomfort, pilgrims sought out the visionary to bless their rosaries or even heal their ills. In short, Lourdes became a thriving site of local pilgrimage and grassroots religiosity.[6]

What stood out during this early period in the life of the shrine was the bishop's ongoing efforts to impose a sense of Catholic orthodoxy on often-heterogeneous rituals and pilgrimage practices. After buying the land encompassing the grotto in 1861, Bishop Laurence erected a small chapel on the site and built a fountain that provided continuous access to the sacred spring. He also constructed a wooden building that housed simple basins for bathing in the water. While acknowledging the importance of the sacred source discovered by Bernadette, the bishop was already trying to direct how the faithful would use the miraculous water in their worship. Laurence also commissioned a statue of the Virgin to be placed inside the grotto, one that aged quite dramatically the apparitional young girl first described by Bernadette. (On seeing the statue, the visionary is supposed to have claimed that its features looked nothing like the "beautiful girl" she had seen). In 1864, the same year that this statue of Mary was erected, the bishop also installed a metal grille to protect the grotto from being continually plundered by pious pilgrims seeking pieces of the terrain to take home with them. While Laurence was concerned to preserve the natural setting of the grotto, he simultaneously wanted to create a shrine that reflected the glory and power of the institutional Church. Hiring Hippolyte Duran, a regional architect, to build a more imposing basilica, Laurence hoped to further rein in the excesses of the grassroots religiosity exhibited by the early followers of Bernadette. Built on the hill above the grotto, the massive neo-Gothic structure dwarfed the sacred site of the grotto. The crypt for this new basilica was completed in 1866. These early efforts to institutionalize popular worship at Lourdes followed a long-standing pattern in which clerical authorities sought to eradicate or at least to domesticate the grassroots devotions that emerged at shrines. These early changes in the physical appearance of the grotto and in its ritual activities were typical of local pilgrimage sites.[7]

During a transitional period between 1866 and 1874, however, an entirely different set of developments—some deliberate and some fortuitous—would begin to transform Lourdes from a local holy site into a national healing shrine of great renown. In 1866, Laurence asked the missionaries of Notre-Dame de Garaison to take over the administration of the shrine. This order of full-time revivalist missionaries, led by Father Pierre-Remy Sempé, harbored ambitious plans to expand the site, a goal made possible later that year when the railway company, la Compagnie des chemins de fer du Midi, decided to build a trunk line linking Lourdes to the departmental capital of Tarbes. In short order, the religious sanctuary became accessible to the rest of France. Seizing on this new mode of transport, the Garaison fathers (who were officially renamed the Missionaries of the Immaculate Conception but were commonly called the Grotto fathers) brought close to fifty thousand pilgrims to the shrine in 1866 for an inauguration of the crypt of the yet-to-be-built basilica. Regional pilgrimages using the railway began almost immediately thereafter.[8] Yet it was more than the fortunate completion of a railway line that shaped the future development of Lourdes. Ironically, Bernadette's departure from her native home advanced the transformation of the grotto into a nationally recognized healing shrine. Her presence had served to distract attention from the sacred grotto as pilgrims continually sought the healing powers that they believed were embodied in the visionary's touch or even in her glance. This kind of popular cult impeded the bishop's efforts to make Lourdes an orthodox shrine. It also made the Church beholden to a visionary whose behavior might prove embarrassing, as had been

NOTRE-DAME DE LOURDES EN 1870 — FAÇADE

Figure 2. Basilica of the Immaculate Conception under construction, Lourdes, 1870. Archives de l'Œuvre de la Grotte.

6 LOURDES. - Grotte et Basilique.

Figure 3. A symbol of Church institutional power: Postcard of the basilica over the grotto, early twentieth century. Author's personal collection.

the case with Mélanie and Maximin, the two visionaries of La Salette.[9] When the visionary departed Lourdes for the Convent of Saint-Gildard in Nevers to join the order of the Sisters of Charity in July 1866, the Grotto fathers became free to develop the shrine in accordance with their own plans. They were also now free to cultivate a safe and acceptable image of Bernadette as an obedient yet stalwart peasant visionary. In a series of carefully crafted photographs, taken shortly before the young woman's departure, Bernadette was dressed in Pyrenean garb and posed holding her rosary. This representation of rustic piety would later be reproduced in numerous postcard series.[10]

The publication of a book by Henri Lasserre in 1869 gave the shrine another "transitional" boost. Lasserre, a devout Catholic journalist, claimed he was healed of an eye ailment during a visit to Lourdes in 1863. In thanksgiving for this cure, he wrote *Notre-Dame de Lourdes,* an "authentic" retelling of Bernadette's apparitions and the early events at the grotto. Focusing on Bernadette's struggle against a skeptical local government bureaucracy out to silence her claims, the book provided a highly sentimentalized account in which the poor yet hardy mountain folk who believed in Bernadette's visions foiled the govern-

Figure 4. Peasant piety: Postcard of Bernadette Soubirous, early twentieth century. Author's personal collection.

ment's attempts to destroy the shrine. Lasserre's melodr
Bernadette story also sought to represent Lourdes as a vi
of peasant spirituality. Reflecting the nostalgic romanticisi
ing learned urbanites to France's fast-disappearing peasant
an immediate best-seller, going through 142 editions in its fi
key to the book's success was the author's vivid retelling of
at the site. These accounts of miraculous healing—depicted
complete with citations from Bishop Laurence's episcopal inʁ   portrayed
the grotto as an ongoing site of supernatural intervention. In effect, *Notre-Dame de Lourdes* combined an idealized vision of Bernadette's peasant religiosity with a novel and compelling story of the power of the miraculous in the modern age. Lasserre's book was instrumental in promoting the shrine to a newly emerging mass audience of readers, though it did so in part by drawing on an image of Lourdes as an unchanging and exotic Pyrenean world.[11] This image would soon change.

The success of Lasserre's book, combined with the town's connection to the railway, sparked interest in the shrine throughout the country and the larger Catholic world. Lourdes was fast becoming a symbol of religious faith in an age of declining church attendance and wavering clerical power, thanks to the wider ambitions of local religious authorities. Yet the idea of capitalizing on the shrine's popularity to create a national pilgrimage (one that would demonstrate to all of France the continuing importance of the Catholic faith) came not from the Grotto fathers or the bishop of Tarbes but from the Augustinian Fathers of the Assumption, a Paris-based religious order. The Assumptionists, as they were commonly called, fought against "the de-Christianization of France" by promoting an explicitly political yet sentimental form of Catholic devotion. Founded in 1843 by Father Emmanuel d'Alzon, this nationwide missionary order came to prominence after the cataclysmic events of 1870–71, *l'année terrible*. Claiming that defeat in the Franco-Prussian War, the emergence of the Paris Commune, and the captivity of the pope were all abominations for which a sinful nation must atone, the religious order hoped its various forms of public prayer and collective ritual would pave the way for a restoration of the Bourbon monarchy and a revitalized Catholic France. The Assumptionists founded the national pilgrimage to Lourdes as part of their political, ultramontane agenda for a penitent Catholicism.[12]

The idea for a national pilgrimage came from Father François Picard, who had succeeded d'Alzon as head of the Assumptionist order. In 1872 Picard chose for its first national pilgrimage of expiation the shrine at La Salette, where apparitions of a weeping Virgin demanding prayer and atonement for a France on the verge of catastrophe seemed to fit the spirit of penance better than Bernadette's more benign visions. Yet the pilgrimage was a resounding failure, in part because La Salette was located in a remote region of the Alps without railway ss. A further problem was that the two visionaries, Maximin and Mélanie, ad failed to gain the legitimacy accorded to Bernadette; certain clergy, in fact, expressed grave doubts as to the truth of their visions. Meanwhile, a large-scale pilgrimage to Lourdes, led by the Abbé Chocarne of Beaune, was carried out that same year with little trouble: this "Pilgrimage of Banners" sent at least twenty thousand and perhaps as many as fifty thousand from regions all over France. Also enacted in a spirit of atonement for the events of 1870–71, the pilgrims marched under regional banners but were constantly reminded of their mission of national expiation.[13]

Seizing on this success, the Assumptionists chose Lourdes as the new site for their own national pilgrimage, to take place the following year. Pilgrims gathered in Paris for the first leg of the trip. They boarded a train scheduled to make several stops at which pilgrims descended together to pray at well-known religious sites. Their stay at Lourdes lasted three days, and pilgrims then returned home by railway. Still a fledgling operation in 1873, the first national pilgrimage gathered only eight bishops, one thousand priests, and fewer than one thousand pilgrims. The following year, the Assumptionists launched a national pilgrimage to transport the sick to Lourdes and that proved more successful. Soon hundreds of sick pilgrims were participating in the event, and the Assumptionists enlisted the help of a Catholic female lay association, the Association de Notre-Dame de Salut, to raise money for the event while recruiting an order of nursing nuns, the Petites-Sœurs de l'Assomption, to help care for these *malades* at the site. From this moment on, ill and infirm pilgrims began to play a central role in the devotional life of the pilgrimage, bringing new attention to the holy grotto as a site of miraculous healing.[14] As Lourdes gained notice for its proliferating miracle cures, large numbers of devout Catholics began to take part in the Church's organized pilgrimages. Within ten years of the first national pilgrimage to Lourdes, an estimated twenty thousand French men and women were participating in the annual three-day religious expeditions. By the first decade of the twentieth century, some two hundred thousand pilgrims and visitors went to the shrine each year, with over one million gathering in 1908 to celebrate the fiftieth anniversary of Bernadette's apparitions.[15]

The remarkable transformation of the Lourdes shrine into a site of mass pilgrimages had much to do with how the Assumptionists capitalized—often in innovative ways—on the railway, the mass press, and other modern developments. Picard, now head of the Assumptionist order, was sufficiently enterprising in his relations with French railway companies to secure reductions of 20 to 30 percent in the cost of third-class train fares to Lourdes. Picard even had a hand in designing special train compartments to transport sick and disabled pilgrims for these guided expeditions. His entrepreneurialism anticipated arrangements that secular tourist associations, such as the Touring Club de France, would later set up to create and expand regional tourism. The coordination of the railway trip, with its scheduled stops to see sacred sites, constructed a new kind of packaged tour of France's religious landscape.[16] Father Vincent de Paul Bailly, another key Assumptionist leader, used the order's emerging press resources to publicize these national pilgrimages. In 1873, he introduced a weekly newsletter, *Le Pèlerin*, that disseminated pilgrimage news to a large audience. Combining spectacular accounts of recent miracle cures with practical information concerning train schedules and registration fees, this journal became a vital tool for promoting the Lourdes pilgrimage. *La Croix*, the Assumptionist daily newspaper perhaps best known for its antirepublican and anti-Semitic diatribes during the Dreyfus affair, devoted itself to promoting upcoming national pilgrimages every July and August. With hundreds of local editions sold throughout France, the paper claimed half a million readers by the 1890s and thus also served as an effective organ of publicity for the three-day pilgrimage event.[17]

While the Assumptionists, often with help from the Grotto fathers, made innovative use of the railway and the mass press to attract growing numbers of pilgrims to Lourdes, parish priests and other religious authorities began to produce specialized guidebooks and manuals for these new religious sojourners. The earliest of the Lourdes guidebooks, which were issued by particular dioceses to publicize the new event to their parishioners, appeared soon after the first national pilgrimage in 1873. Costing as little as thirty centimes or as much as a franc, the small booklets served a variety of functions but were most clearly designed to entice a large audience of Catholics to come to Lourdes.[18] Imitating the style and format of such secular guidebooks as the Guides-Joanne, these little booklets provided a range of practical information about transportation, accommodations, and itineraries for the pilgrimage events. By the 1890s, these pocket-sized manuals—now produced by private entrepreneurs as well—resembled the inexpensive guides used at other regional tourist sites, providing condensed histories of the shrine's sacred past, descriptions of the present-day site, and long lists of lodgings and restaurants for Catholics of varying economic backgrounds.[19]

If these techniques for organizing and promoting travel to Lourdes enabled growing numbers of Catholics to go on national pilgrimages, new forms of economic development and urban renewal remade the town and shrine to accommodate these visitors. The period after 1875 marked the beginning of several important building projects—initiated by Laurence's successor, Bishop Jourdan—that would transform Lourdes into a modern tourist city. Working hand in hand with the Grotto fathers, municipal authorities razed old neighborhoods, constructed new city streets, installed electricity at the sanctuary, and erected large hotels. They also oversaw the building of a tramway and funicular.[20] This urban renewal consciously drew on forms of commerce and urbanization already being carried out in large cities such as Paris. Indeed, these changes were intended to transform Lourdes into an attractive and well-functioning sacred city, one that looked increasingly like other late nineteenth-century resort towns, with its hotels, restaurants, and souvenir shops lining the major boulevards that led pilgrims to the sanctuary.[21] The most important project was the construction of two new avenues, boulevard de la Grotte and rue de la Grotte, that connected the new train station (and national route 21) directly to the shrine without detours through the town. In 1875, the bishop of Tarbes began to purchase significant tracts of real estate in the city of Lourdes in anticipation of building these new thoroughfares as well as a connecting bridge. Many Lourdais, in turn, were happy to sell their properties on the condition that they could retain parcels of land next to the proposed new avenues. Clearly foreseeing the future, these owners encouraged the demolition of existing buildings and were able to profit from the new hotels and piety shops that sprang up along the new route. The municipal council, concerned about crowd control, also contributed funds to the reconstruction project. Working together on these economic development projects encouraged local government officials and the Grotto administration to join forces on other measures, including the policing of the redeveloped site.[22] By creating these kinds of working relationships with the state, shrine authorities once again seemed to anticipate the kinds of public-private partnerships later used by secular tourist associations to help finance the development of regional tourism elsewhere in France.

The Grotto fathers also devoted their considerable resources to building up the site of the shrine. Indeed, if Lourdes was to host an annual public manifestation of faith that involved huge numbers of the nation's Catholics, the infrastructure of the shrine would need to be dramatically expanded. A new residence for the Grotto fathers, a shelter for poor pilgrims, and a larger basilica—the Basilica of the Rosary—were the most important projects. As early as 1871, the Grotto fathers had realized that the recently completed Basilica of the Immaculate Conception was too small to accommodate the pilgrims coming to the site. After the creation of the national pilgrimages, it became imperative to build a second basilica to be used for large-scale church services. Designed in a Romano-Byzantine style with spectacular mosaics painted on the interior, the structure was built underneath the Basilica of the Immaculate Conception, requiring massive excavations and the construction of two large ramps so that pilgrims could still reach the upper basilica. This ambitious project, initiated in 1883, entailed the creation of an enormous esplanade (soon to become the site of large Eucharistic processions)[23] as well as the construction of a bridge that connected the sanctuary to the new boulevard de la Grotte. A huge statue of a crowned Virgin Mary was then placed just before the esplanade, greeting pilgrims as they crossed the bridge. With the completion of these projects in the early 1900s, the physical transformation of Lourdes was more or less complete, resulting in an enormous complex of buildings and public spaces that bore scant resemblance to the original site.[24]

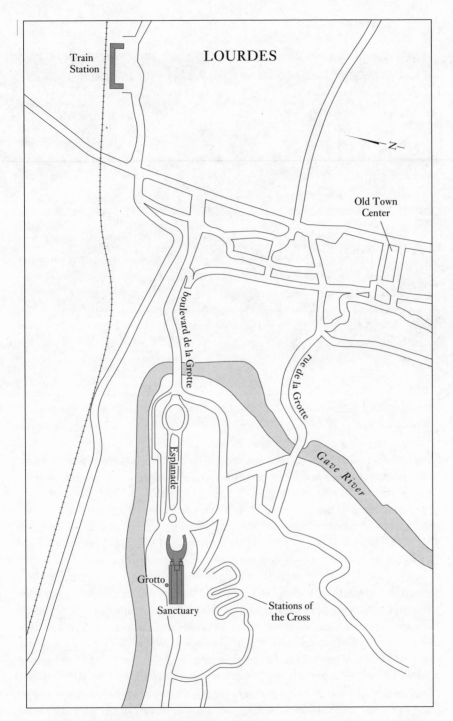

Figure 5. Map of Lourdes, early twentieth century: The two major streets (boulevard de la Grotte and rue de la Grotte) connect the railway station to the shrine.

Figure 6. Rue de la Grotte under renovation, Lourdes, 1912. Musée Pyrénéen, Chateau Fort, Lourdes.

As the Grotto fathers carried out these building projects, they also invested heavily in creating an industrial and commercial infrastructure capable of producing the goods and services needed during the April-to-September pilgrimage season. Among the most important new enterprises developed for the mass pilgrimages to Lourdes were the sanctuary's electrical plant and its printing shop, both housed in a new building completed in 1890. Designed with state-of-the-art equipment, the generating plant served the power needs of the entire sanctuary and kept the shrine illuminated twenty-four hours a day during the national pilgrimages in August. The printing business produced and sold its own pamphlets and guidebooks about Lourdes as well as two important periodicals: the monthly *Annales de Notre-Dame de Lourdes* and the weekly newspaper *Journal de la Grotte de Lourdes.* Sold largely through subscriptions, the *Annales* was oriented to the shrine's wealthier and more educated followers, featuring lengthy articles about life at the grotto as well as broader propagation of the cult of Notre-Dame de Lourdes. The *Journal de la Grotte,* on the other hand, was a popular periodical sold mainly to pilgrims at the shrine for ten centimes an issue. Imitating the simple four-page format of the secular popular press, this new weekly newspaper offered headline stories about newly arriving pilgrimage groups and, of course, accounts of the latest cures. Selling thousands of co[...] during the pilgrimage season, *Journal de la Grotte* printed a weekly program [...] events at the grotto and used its back page to sell advertising space to local en-trepreneurs dealing in pilgrimage-related goods and services, from hotels to re-ligious artifacts. Taken together, the print shop and electrical plant played a vital role in supplying the visual and informational needs of a dynamic, reconstructed shrine.[25]

The Grotto administration also opened its own religious boutique. Located next to the grotto, the shop sold votive candles, medals, scapulars, rosaries, and containers for Lourdes water. Along with selling these traditional articles of de-votion, the Grotto fathers also capitalized on new modes of transport to ship bottled Lourdes water throughout France and the Catholic world. A govern-ment report from 1899 estimated that total shipments of water for that year alone (one hundred thousand bottles) generated some sixty thousand francs in rev-enue for the Grotto administration.[26] These figures pale in comparison to the eight or nine million bottles of mineral water shipped annually at the time from spas such as Vichy, but they do reflect efforts by the Grotto fathers to adopt busi-ness practices already in use at popular thermal resorts to provide larger num-bers of devout Catholics with religious goods and services.[27] These commercial ventures, when combined with the advertising revenue from the shrine's news-papers, suggest that clerical administrators were reshaping the ad hoc forms of sacred commerce traditionally carried out at pilgrimage sites into more stream-lined business enterprises.

By 1900 not even *Le Lavedan,* which a generation earlier had predicted such prosperity for Lourdes, would have recognized the site that emerged. A town of little consequence was now a thriving center of commercial and leisure activity. One measure of the city's vastly expanded economic importance was the tenfold increase in communal revenues—from construction, rents, and the sale of drinking water—between 1860 and 1906. Furthermore, by the early twentieth century, important Parisian-based financial institutions such as Banque de France, Credit Lyonnais, and Société Générale held significant investments in the city of Lourdes. Older thermal stations, such as Gavarnie and Cauterets, were now indebted to the sanctuary for bringing new customers to their spas; in fact, between 1860 and 1906 nearly half the clientele of Pyrenean thermal re-sorts were also on a pilgrimage to Lourdes. The economic importance of these pilgrimages was frankly acknowledged by the prefect of the Hautes-Pyrénées, who noted, in a 1908 government report to the minister of the interior, that the extraordinary movement of pilgrims to the shrine "has had beneficial conse-quences for *the entire region of the Pyrenees* and even beyond."[28]

Yet beyond this striking material prosperity that transformed town, shrine, and region, the new methods used for organizing travel to Lourdes as well as the adoption of modern-style business practices set the stage for dramatic changes

rience itself. As the sanctuary evolved into a site of large-
ges, the Grotto fathers and the Assumptionists adopted
media that not only represented Lourdes as a distinctly
ine but introduced a set of devotional practices that
is encountered the sacred site itself. The creation of this
at Lourdes would be a key to its success, transforming
to the shrine into a meaningful and exciting experience for modern
believers.

SEEING LOURDES

Central to the modern pilgrimage was a new way of seeing the shrine. Beyond the physical and economic transformation of the site, new instruments for re-shaping the visual reality of Lourdes lay in the descriptions and images offered by the profusion of promotional literature. Produced by clerical authorities and local business elites, these guidebooks, mass-produced picture postcards, print advertisements, and assorted visual entertainments all played important roles in directing how the pilgrim might engage with the shrine, its artifacts, and the miraculous events of the Lourdes past. These new visual and written media be-came crucial tools, especially after 1890, for mediating the sacred experience and connecting pilgrims to a larger Catholic community.

This development should not be surprising though it is often overlooked. Historians of tourism and consumer culture have noted that, in the second half of the nineteenth century, visual images became an important element of travel literature and leisure activities. Indeed, the very presence of these new media re-flected a growing culture of visual spectacle often associated with modern urban life and emerging forms of mass consumption. As Rudy Koshar has observed: "Wherever economic and cultural capital accumulated to become an image for mass consumption—in urban spaces, on the stage, in natural environments, in cinema—there one finds evidence for the growing power of the eye in shaping and directing leisure time." The emergence of this new visual culture did not simply replace the written word with visual images. As Vanessa Schwartz has ar-gued, image and text became linked in the production of new forms of "spec-tacular reality" that increasingly defined the mass culture of modern city life.[29] Yet, it was not just secular urban culture that was transformed. A similar set of developments also shaped the culture of Catholic pilgrimage. Lourdes, too, be-came a site of this new kind of spectacular reality, as the Grotto fathers and the Assumptionists relied increasingly on new texts and visual technologies to rep-resent the shrine and pilgrimage itself to a mass audience.

The guidebook became a crucial device for shaping how the pilgrim came to interact with the shrine. Guides to Lourdes appeared as early as 1875, just two years after the site hosted its first national pilgrimage, but these books became especially popular during the 1890s when their prices fell to as low as thirty centimes. Like secular guides of the same period, these texts on Lourdes organized the travel experience for large numbers of visitors who were often of limited means.[30] Yet guidebooks were also intended to be promotional devices used to excite the imagination of tourists, or pilgrims, enticing them to visit a specific site. These texts shaped a visitor's sense of place, determining significant sites to be seen and directing how the visitor should see them.[31] Guidebooks to Lourdes were no different in this respect. What is striking about the Lourdes guides, however, was the strategy to promote the shrine as a new and different place of pilgrimage. Guides to Lourdes employed promotional strategies that emphasized the decidedly modern character of shrine and town.

Guidebook descriptions of Lourdes routinely highlighted the stunning redevelopment of the pilgrimage site. Taking center stage in these depictions were both the newness and the grandeur of the built environment. Guidebooks pointed out the altered state of the grotto, stressing the work involved in pushing back the waters of the Gave River and manicuring the formerly wild state of the cave. An 1888 guidebook claimed that "the Grotto of today is no longer the Grotto of thirty years ago: the thick brambles that covered it have disappeared . . . the shore of the Gave River, long ago strewn with large rocks and other debris . . . has been cleared away, lifted up [and] perfectly leveled off and cemented." Nature had been tamed and replaced by a series of monuments that now dominated the sacred site. An 1896 guidebook by Bernard Dauberive highlighted the newly constructed landscape of statues, monumental buildings, and public spaces that defined the terrain of Lourdes: "Notice, in the middle of the verdant hills, a bronze statue of *Saint Michel* and *the Breton Cross*. Farther away, in the old Savy Meadow, see *the crowned Statue* of the Mother of God . . . to the right, *the pilgrims' shelter,* a vast building that houses an immense room full of benches; to the left, the magnificent *printing works of the Reverend Fathers.*" The sacred landscape was no longer identified with the natural setting of the cave but, rather, with a newly built environment. Similarly, another religious guide depicted the religious ceremonies, especially the evening candlelight processions and Eucharistic celebrations, as modern spectacles in which singing hymns and lighting candles were often merged with less traditional forms of spiritual display: "During the candlelight procession, the sharp radiance of the fireworks, set off in the courtyard of the castle, mingles with the pale glow of the candles, and the roar of the cannons answers the mighty thunder of voices singing the *Ave.*"[32]

Guidebooks also presented Lourdes as a bustling resort town with magnificent hotels and lively forms of commercial activity. In fact, descriptions of the town's delights often overshadowed the grandeur of the grotto itself. An 1893 guide written by the Abbé Martin praised "the new neighborhood adorned with sumptuous hotels of colossal proportions and numerous shops." Using similar language to capture the richness of the sacred city, another guide instructed pilgrims to "stroll down the boulevard and the avenue of the Grotto, admire the sumptuous hotels and magnificent shops selling religious articles." A book from 1888 also highlighted the new public thoroughfare that brought pilgrims directly from the train station to the grotto: "The avenue is lined on both sides with elegant and very beautiful buildings, among them the Continental Hotel, the Sacred Heart Hotel, the Saint Joseph Hotel, the Belgian Hotel, and the Ambassador Hotel." A 1914 guide went so far as to claim that "Lourdes, better than any city in the world, possesses similar marvels capable of attracting, at the same time, the believer, the scientist, and the tourist." Merging the religious and commercial elements of the shrine into one overwhelming spectacle, this guide described Lourdes as a "new city"—a "religious city" that was "full of mystery, prayer, and contemplation, whose striking convents and villas, sumptuous hotels, and piety shops form a white ring around the miraculous Grotto and the Basilica of Notre-Dame de Lourdes." The opulence of the town, then, promised an enticing tourist adventure for pilgrims. Even the countryside around Lourdes was to be seen and experienced as a breathtakingly modern landscape. This same guide, when encouraging pilgrims to visit the nearby Pic du Grand Jer, a 950–meter mountain, urged them to experience "a marvel of modern industry" by taking the new electric funicular to the top. By the early twentieth century, guides were incorporating photographic images that vividly highlighted the lavish shops and hotels of the town as well as the monumental aspect of the shrine.[33]

It is worth contrasting the imagined landscapes found in Lourdes guidebooks with the depictions of rural France found in secular guidebooks of the period. Secular promoters of regional tourism invoked a very different image—one of *la Vieille France* (Old France)—in guidebooks and later in picture postcards. Patrick Young's work on the Touring Club de France, for example, notes that tour organizers consciously deployed a "regional picturesque," portraying a bygone land of quaint villages and traditional peasants engaging in festivals, games, or rapidly vanishing forms of agrarian labor. Images of religious festivals and local shrines were evoked to convey the unique charms of a recognizably rustic France. Young has argued astutely that this regional picturesque cultivated and even presupposed an urban viewer, one who was "fully steeped in the viewing practices of an emergent consumer culture."[34] This marketing of la Vieille France was directed at secularized middle-class men in particular, bourgeois urbanites whose tastes and incomes might dispose them to become tourists of an "unknown France." By playing to male middle-class desires for diverting escapes from the ennui of city life, promoters of secular tourism capitalized on a growing nostalgia for a disappearing world, marketing regional sites as the embodiment of vanishing French traditions.

The marketing of Lourdes, as we have seen, evoked quite different kinds of images. If the regional picturesque was so prominently linked to the urban middle classes, guidebooks to Lourdes were directed to a female and largely rural audience. Pilgrimage organizers and local entrepreneurs, who produced much of the Lourdes promotional literature, presented the site as a reconstructed shrine and a modern town with new hotels and shops. They played on the desires of female pilgrims from small towns and villages to see the wonders of modern urban life—sumptuous hotels, lavish shops, the exciting railway—within a safe and reassuringly devotional environment. Moreover, painting Lourdes as a new kind of religious shrine was crucial to persuade rural pilgrims devoted to local holy sites to embark on a much longer and more expensive journey. This is not to say that religious devotion—the desire to pray for France or to seek out the powers of the Grotto's healing waters for oneself or a family member—was insufficient to justify such a trip. For many devout Catholics, it no doubt was. Nevertheless, guides to Lourdes did evoke forms of festive entertainment and sociability long associated with Catholic pilgrimage, while presenting them in new and exciting ways. In this sense, the Church employed the tools of bourgeois tourism to produce images of travel that spoke to a different and, in key respects, much broader audience.

Marketing Lourdes to a new class of religious tourists meant promoting the pilgrimage journey even to pilgrims of very modest means. To convince Catholics that the three-day visit was financially feasible, most guidebooks emphasized an array of inexpensive accommodations, simple restaurants, and other services for the budget traveler. One of the earliest guides from 1875, written by the Abbé Chaudé, began by reassuring Catholics who might fear they could not afford to make the pilgrimage: "When you arrive at Lourdes, do not be anxious, reader, I speak to you with experience. You will not only find bread but all goods to be the same price that you pay at home." The Abbé estimated that for a four-day trip to Lourdes, a pilgrim could spend as little as seventy francs, including train fare, food, and lodging. He concluded that "this pilgrimage is not only easy for those who are not wealthy but it will almost save you money, not to mention the innumerable spiritual consolations and health benefits that you will receive, too." In a similar vein, another guide, written some twenty-five years later, presented an account from a pilgrim who claimed to have spent a mere five francs per day at Lourdes: 1.50 for his bed, 1.50 for breakfast, and two francs for dinner. This pilgrim hastened to assure readers that while he was known to be hard to please, his accommodations and meals were more than adequate. Other guides advertised rooms for less than two francs a night and listed restaurants charging two to three francs for dinner. If pilgrimage was a modern touristic experience, it offered one that was open to all ranks of society.[35]

Presenting Lourdes as a modern spectacle also involved teaching pilgrims to experience the full panoply of its wonders. Guidebooks thus encouraged the devout to behave like savvy tourists, providing expert advice on how to make the most of short stays. While informal sightseeing had long been a traditional accompaniment of Catholic pilgrimages, Lourdes guidebooks and manuals now sought to simplify and routinize the process for a mass audience. Because "tourists and pilgrims are people in a hurry," one guide knowingly remarked, "the schedule that we recommend will permit them to visit Lourdes in two days, without fear of missing a thing, and even to have time for an outing to the countryside." To encourage efficient use of the pilgrim's time, the guide furnished maps of the town and region as well as lists of principal monuments. Another guide recommended that pilgrims rent bicycles so they could see more of the countryside. Beyond imparting time-saving strategies, however, guidebooks tried to educate pilgrims on how to *see* like modern tourists. One guide, for example, involved pilgrims in the very production of tourist-style photographs. To promote a new edition of *Lourdes en deux jours,* the editors of the guide held a contest in which pilgrims were asked to send three photographs—a happy scene, a sad scene, and a picturesque scene—that they had taken during a Lourdes pilgrimage. The winning photographs would appear in the upcoming edition, with the photographer-pilgrim to be awarded two hundred francs. By encouraging pilgrims to reproduce the conventions of tourist photography, the guide designated certain modern forms of representation as visual templates for regarding the shrine.[36]

Lourdes postcards performed a similar kind of cultural work, directing how pilgrims should see the shrine, the town, and the very act of pilgrimage. As souvenir items intended to memorialize the devotional experience, postcards of Lourdes were instrumental in constructing the recognizable face of the shrine and town. Here, too, the emblematic image of Lourdes was of a strikingly modern religious site. Produced during the first decade of the twentieth century, when postcard collecting was rapidly becoming a craze in France, Lourdes postcards imitated the style and format of popular Parisian postcard series or the cards of well-known resorts.[37] Local photographers developed their own series of postcards while also supplying photographs to companies in Paris and Strasbourg that manufactured postcard sets of Lourdes. Yet whether they were produced regionally or in faraway cities, these cards presented similar images of Lourdes as a reconstructed, modern-looking shrine. The most common postcard image was the panoramic landscape of the shrine itself. This sweeping vista of the physical site portrayed the sanctuary as a monumental structure dominating the horizon. Another popular landscape view depicted the basilica sitting astride the grotto, furnishing the Church with a ready-made image of Catholic orthodoxy. Both views of Lourdes circulated a representation of the shrine that, like guidebooks of the period, highlighted the grandeur of a newly constructed milieu.[38]

Postcard entrepreneurs soon expanded their stock of images to include photographs of the devotional life of pilgrimage.[39] Many postcard series presented a visual narrative of the sacred journey of Catholic pilgrimage by depicting the

17 LOURDES. - La Basilique et le Gave

Figure 7. Panoramic postcard of the Lourdes sanctuary, early twentieth century. Author's personal collection.

arrival of pilgrims, grand processions around the town and shrine, crowds praying at the grotto, and sick pilgrims being carried to the Lourdes baths. Images showing pilgrims drinking water from the fountains or praying before the grotto became quite popular, as did depictions of sick pilgrims lying on stretchers or being wheeled around in elaborate carriages. These images not only captured intimate moments of pilgrims at the site but also reinforced the shrine's own rhetoric of service to the sick. Such images were undoubtedly intended to appeal to women, who came to Lourdes by the hundreds as volunteer helpers, humble pilgrims, and blessed malades. Yet even within these depictions of prayer, ritual, and service, modern technological forms emerged as integral to the scene. The train, in particular, was featured as an icon of the religious landscape. Several postcard series provided close-up views of the special trains designed to transport sick pilgrims to Lourdes. Showing nuns, priests, and lay volunteers helping the sick disembark from compartments of newly arrived trains, these cards effectively linked the shrine's ideals of succor and charity to the industrial power of the railway. The electric tramway system and the funicular, designed to transport sick pilgrims from the town to the grotto, also appeared in numerous postcards. Often juxtaposing these modern marvels of transportation alongside pilgrims marching in traditional peasant costume, the cards asserted the routinized compatibility of traditional religious practice and

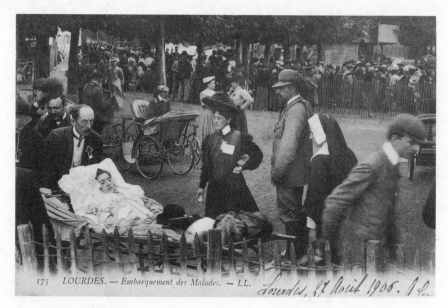

175 LOURDES. — *Embarquement des Malades.* — LL. *Lourdes, 27 Août 1906. 8...*

Figure 8. Brancardiers carry a sick pilgrim to the grotto, early twentieth-century postcard. Archives de l'Œuvre de la Grotte.

Edition F. V.   81. - LOURDES — *Débarquement des malades*

Figure 9. Sick pilgrims descend from the train at Lourdes, early twentieth-century postcard. Archives de l'Œuvre de la Grotte.

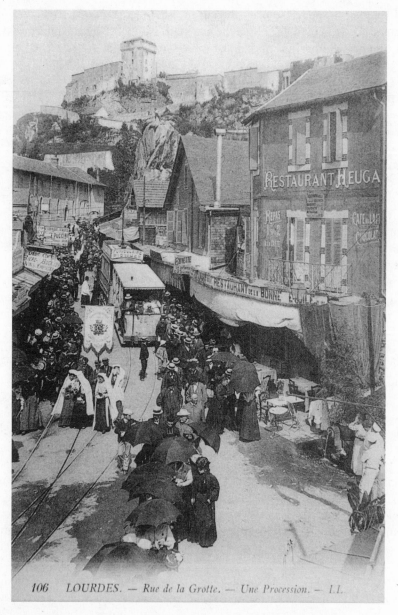

106   LOURDES. — Rue de la Grotte. — Une Procession. — LL.

Figure 10. Pilgrims in traditional dress march alongside funicular: Postcard of the rue de la Grotte, Lourdes, early twentieth century. Archives de l'Œuvre de la Grotte.

modern industrial technology. Even the partaking of Lourdes water became an activity that resembled secular thermalism, as postcards showed women sipping water from tin cups and featured the new stone bathhouses where pilgrims were now immersed in private, individual tubs. Representations of ritualized drinking and bathing mirrored the rituals of the modern-day spa.

Like guidebooks to Lourdes, these postcards also worked to entice a new class of traveler to visit the shrine. Women and rural inhabitants could see themselves captured in moments of prayer, procession, and caregiving. By displaying ordinary pilgrims as visual subjects worthy of postcards, entrepreneurs were effectively making women, peasants, and humble malades an integral part of an extraordinary religious spectacle. The very ordinariness of the pilgrims depicted in these cards served to remind the devout that this monumental event was accessible to them as well. Relying on the verisimilitude of photographic imagery further highlighted this effect by reproducing "real" moments from actual pilgrimages. Several postcard series were devoted to publicized events for which huge crowds had assembled, such as the fiftieth-anniversary celebration of Bernadette's apparitions. As souvenir items mailed to friends and family or proudly displayed in one's home, Lourdes postcards became valued artifacts of a commoner's connection to the sacred. Postcards also depicted bustling street scenes, attesting to the vibrant commercial life of Lourdes. In these imagined urban landscapes, pilgrims stroll along the boulevards like tourists, gazing into shop windows as in any other popular resort town. Indeed, at times the shrine recedes, pushed into the background by the cluster of shops, hotels, tramways and promenading pilgrims. Other postcards captured pilgrims on outings to the countryside. These pictures, like those depicting ordinary pilgrims in acts of prayer or procession, allowed pious women and other humble visitors to imagine themselves in new ways, as flâneurs of the boulevard or modern sightseers in touring cars.

If guidebooks and postcards offered up Lourdes as an inviting modern spectacle for pilgrim-tourists, how did the devout respond to such promotional messages? The question of reception, always difficult to gauge (as historians of tourism and advertising have long acknowledged), is compounded in the case of female pilgrims and visitors of humble circumstances, who seldom left written accounts of their travels to Lourdes. Yet what little evidence does survive (anecdotal accounts, published personal narratives, and church records) suggests that pilgrims, especially women, welcomed the opportunity to discover a modern shrine and to engage in new religious and secular activities. Men who have written about Lourdes have sometimes remarked on the impact that the shrine had on the lives of their female relatives. The memoirs of Marcel Jouhandeau, for example, contend that his grandmother's visit to Lourdes—her only journey outside the region where she was born—introduced her to a larger universe. "She discovered there the world around her, never having suspected its scope

Figure 11. Religious thermalism at the shrine: Female pilgrims sip Lourdes water, early twentieth-century postcard. Author's personal collection.

Figure 12. Interior of the Lourdes bathhouse (with *brancardiers*), early twentieth-century postcard. Archives de l'Œuvre de la Grotte.

LOURDES. — L'Hôtel de la Chapelle: — Rue de la Grotte. — LL.

Figure 13. Pilgrim–tourists stroll along the rue de la Grotte: Promotional postcard for the Hotel de la Chapelle, Lourdes, early twentieth century. Archives de l'Œuvre de la Grotte.

124   LOURDES. — L'Avenue de la Grotte. — LL.

Figure 14. Lourdes as modern resort town: Postcard of the avenue de la Grotte, early twentieth century. Archives de l'Œuvre de la Grotte.

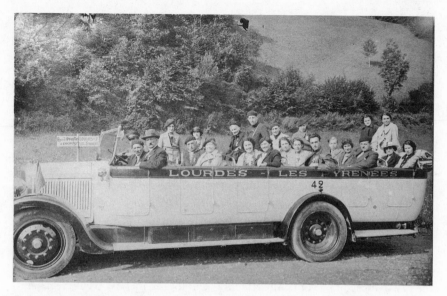

Figure 15. Postcard of Lourdes touring car, ca. 1920s. Archives de l'Œuvre de la Grotte.

and almost having departed the world without knowing it."[40] Such comments, of course, do not really get at how female pilgrims made sense of their momentary immersion in the hustle and bustle of modern Catholic pilgrimage. Accounts of journeys to Lourdes written by educated female pilgrims, however, do shed light on how some women chose to represent the pilgrimage experience. Two women who published such narratives were Bertile Ségalas and Madeleine D.[41] Printed as short popular pamphlets or as articles in such women's journals as *La Femme et la Famille,* their sentimental accounts presented the journey to Lourdes as a type of coming-of-age story in which the two women must overcome fears of making the long trip to the shrine in order to experience spiritual growth and a new intimacy with the Virgin Mary. Although both women presented the pilgrimage as a personal voyage of faith, they did not hesitate to discuss the more spectacular qualities of the pilgrimage experience, often duplicating the very language of Lourdes guidebooks in their descriptions of the train journey, the mass rituals, and the pleasures of the city. Indeed, these conventional, sometimes formulaic narratives are interesting precisely because they were written to inspire other pious women to go on pilgrimage. Examining how these two particular writers adopt the shrine's own rhetoric of touristic spectacle may show why this kind of narrative succeeded in enticing devout women to come to Lourdes. In the process, it may also suggest the ways in which the women helped to translate religious devotion into a thoroughly modern idiom.

Both authors elected to include potentially disruptive modern intrusions in their accounts of religious practice. Madeleine D., a young woman from Blois making her first pilgrimage at age sixteen, and Bertile Ségalas, a bourgeoise from the north of France, each anticipated her railway journey to Lourdes with considerable trepidation. In "Huit jours à Lourdes" ("Eight Days at Lourdes"), published in 1900, Ségalas explained, "I had never really traveled. . . . I spent my whole life close to my mother and she detested traveling." But Ségalas was able to overcome this obstacle when she realized that the train would allow her to encounter the miraculous: "I felt an irresistible desire to travel. It was something of a phenomenon, miraculous, almost supernatural. . . . I wanted to go to Lourdes." The train—the quintessential symbol of France's modernity— became the means for one young woman to experience a much-cherished sacred encounter. In *Mon Pèlerinage de Lourdes* (*My Pilgrimage to Lourdes*), published in 1912, Madeleine D. described her own momentary fear "when the railway- man closed the carriage doors" of the pilgrimage train. She recounted: "I was crying profusely after leaving Mother—and I was not the only one— . . . when the locomotive's whistle announcing our departure startled me. Immediately, the priest-director of our compartment began to sing the 'Ave Maria' . . . [and] I was so happy." In an instant, a threatening encounter with industrial technol- ogy was transformed into a religious act intimately familiar to most women of the era. The train itself became a vehicle for devotional practice.[42]

These published accounts also reveal the women discussing religious worship and more prosaic activities in practically the same breath. Ségalas, in her pil- grimage account, moved seamlessly from a meditation on her time spent in prayer at the grotto to a lively description of an afternoon of strolling and shop- ping along the boulevard de la Grotte—not to mention a side trip to the tourist town of Pau to visit friends.[43] Clearly, Ségalas felt comfortable alluding to such secular activities as sightseeing and people watching while also conveying acts of devotion and prayer. Nor was she the only devout woman to represent the pil- grimage experience as a fluid mix of religious and secular activity. Examining the messages that female pilgrims penned on the backs of surviving Lourdes postcards reveals a similar tendency to blend descriptions of personal piety at the shrine with more prosaic behaviors.[44] One postcard, from 1917, its picture showing two women praying before the grotto, conveyed a written account of a family's entire pilgrimage. Written by a Madame Rousseau to her "dear Mar- cel," the message described the beautiful weather in the Pyrenees, mentioned their one day of rain, and discussed plans to leave Lourdes the following day for Biarritz, where the family hoped the weather would be equally fine. Madame Rousseau also assured Marcel that his mother had said a novena for him, adding that "for all those whom we love, we carried candles [and] flowers to the grotto." She ended the card promising to buy "good things" from Bayonne to bring home for their loved ones. Evidently, pilgrims like Madame Rousseau felt no

discomfort using this new medium to discuss shopping exped
seeing along with sentiments of religious devotion. These acti
an accepted part of the pilgrimage journey. Indeed, a few card
tion the religious aspects of pilgrimage at all, as in one sent by
to her aunt that discussed buying a new hat and sending home r
a blouse.[45]

The postcards mailed by pilgrims remind us that this new visual and written tool was not only the expressive medium of a new kind of religious tourism but also a valued article in its own right. As a souvenir item that was inexpensive to buy and send, the postcard served both as an important means for envisioning Lourdes and as a new kind of objet de piété.[46] Pilgrims could retain postcards as mementos of their own journeys or give them to family and friends as acts of love and devotion. In this same vein, guidebooks also functioned as cherished keepsakes. Indeed, by the early twentieth century, when entrepreneurs began to illustrate their guides with photographs of the sights and rituals of pilgrimage, these publishers explicitly marketed their inexpensive booklets as instruments of inspiration. One guide directed readers to look back through its pages "during long winter nights." Sharing the book with family and friends, it claimed, would "contribute, in a small way, to attracting crowds of believing Catholics and even indifferent observers to the grotto."[47] In this sense, guidebooks and postcards became important commodities in the newly thriving trade of pilgrimage goods and services developing at Lourdes. Furthermore, the promotional strategies used by guidebook entrepreneurs to transform their booklets into "treasured" items would be employed by other merchants to promote a broad array of traditional—and even quite nontraditional—religious articles and services. These marketing techniques and advertisements are themselves worth exploring, not only because they contributed to a vision of Lourdes as a modern religious spectacle but because they stimulated new consumer behaviors that would prove central to the experience of pilgrimage.

CONSUMING THE SACRED

As national pilgrimages took hold at Lourdes, local entrepreneurs, often working with the Grotto fathers, lost no time in seeking out innovative ways to advertise their wares and services to a growing clientele of potential pilgrim-consumers. By the early twentieth century, hundreds of small piety shops lined the two major boulevards leading to the grotto. Major producers of religious articles had established large emporiums along the boulevards to sell their merchandise. Similarly, there were dozens of hotels (grand and small) as well as restaurants that encircled the train station and lined the public thoroughfares near the shrine. To compete successfully for the thousands of pilgrims who came to Lourdes each year needing accommodations and expecting to acquire mementos of their journey, entrepreneurs adopted an array of inventive marketing strategies.

Stiff competition encouraged local merchants and business elites to come up with creative advertising schemes and clever slogans. Although hundreds of thousands of pilgrims converged on Lourdes each year, many were on very limited budgets and not yet accustomed to the material abundance on display. Staying for only a few days, these pilgrims had to be taught to spend their money very quickly, if only on one special item. To do so, businessmen used guidebooks, postcards, and the shrine's own *Journal de la Grotte* to advertise their wares and services. Representing the pilgrimage experience as a distinctly modern religious spectacle, this kind of marketing would profoundly influence how pilgrims approached the sacred site even as these techniques introduced the faithful to a world of mass consumption.

Entrepreneurs of religious goods were among the first merchants to seek out newspapers and guidebooks as new spaces in which to market their wares. These merchants employed the same kinds of slogans and pitches that the secular advertising industry was developing for Parisian department stores such as the Bon Marché.[48] By the early twentieth century, religious emporiums such as Les Grands Magasins des Galeries Catholiques were running newspaper advertisements proclaiming themselves to be "the largest and the most important stores with the best deals." Like any big-city department store, this religious superstore used the latest marketing strategies, such as display catalogs, to show off its wares. Its major competitor, Les Grands Magasins de l'Alliance Catholique, adopted similar tactics, inventing catch phrases—"High volume means low prices / low prices mean high volume!"—for its own catalog of factory-made religious statues, rosaries, medallions, and newfangled items such as postcards.[49] Even smaller piety shops were forced to come up with inventive ways to market their own stock of items. Many religious boutiques imitated secular retailers and their own large-scale religious competitors by incorporating picture postcards into their advertising campaigns.[50] Shops such as Maison Puccini sought to expand their clientele by distributing postcards to pilgrims as they passed by the store. Reproducing a photograph of the shop and its abundant offerings, the portable card enabled the goods to speak for themselves. A simple caption—such as "over 10,000 models of different-sized saints"—sought to assure all pilgrims that they would find something to satisfy their tastes and budgets. Local hotel owners used similar postcards to advertise their establishments, combining a few well-chosen words—"twelve minutes from the grotto" or "across the street from the train station"—with an attractive image of the hotel.

By promoting bountiful goods at affordable prices, this kind of advertising embraced the wonders of industrial development that made possible such consumer abundance. Indeed, the logic of many Lourdes advertisements explicitly

Figure 16. Postcard promotion for Maison Puccini, Lourdes, early twentieth century. Archives de l'Œuvre de la Grotte.

linked the value of their religious goods to new powers of mechanical reproduction. The ability to produce many copies of a desired object was touted by entrepreneurs as a great improvement for the religious world because it provided a larger number of people with greater access to the sacred. To emphasize the ability to fabricate more than ten thousand models of saints in differing sizes, the Maison Puccini displayed the vast array of identical statues that lined the front of the store. The power of this advertisement resided in its image: the vast quantities on display promised that all pilgrims would find a religious keepsake to help recall the experience after they returned home. Similarly, ads for religious emporiums such as Galeries Catholiques drew attention to their gigantic stocks of low-priced goods. In an era marked by the rise of reproducible religious art (the so-called Saint-Sulpice style), the fact that even the smallest figurine and illustration in these stores was typically identical to statues and images found in churches across France visually linked such mass-produced goods to official religious iconography. Indeed, these stores' statuettes of Notre-Dame de Lourdes were direct copies of the statue that stood in the grotto.[51]

The modern-day emphasis on this promotional logic was apparent in the marketing of entirely new kinds of devotional objects as well. A religious wholesaler such as the Alliance Catholique not only touted its ability to manufacture huge stocks of such traditional items as medals and rosaries but also marketed an assortment of new religious articles that the establishment labeled "fabulous novelties." Among these new items were metal cups, napkin holders, and metal-plated stands—all with imprinted images of the shrine, the grotto, and Bernadette's visions—that sold for one-to-two francs apiece. Still more remarkable was a miniature reproduction of the shrine suitable for home display. Lauding this item as a "superb novelty," the Alliance catalog observed, "It is the most beautiful souvenir of Lourdes in existence."[52] Even pilgrims who could not afford to buy such an extraordinary memento (priced at almost ten francs, it was not cheap) were able to browse through the catalog, which they could also keep as a free souvenir.

Yet perhaps the most striking of the new goods being sold at Lourdes were the Pastilles de Lourdes, lozenges made from sugar and the grotto's water. The maker of this novel product, the F. Valette & Company, celebrated its pastilles as a modern marvel of science and industry that would give Catholics greater access to the healing powers of the shrine. As early as 1888, the company's advertising brochures were using such rhetoric. One leaflet praised the factory-made tablets for providing a new and better means for Lourdes water to be carried home: "It is in order to render more easily the transport of the miraculous water and have it arrive, without mishap and without annoyance, to any location, even the most remote countries on the earth, that we have tried to do for the water of Lourdes what doctors have done so well for thermal sources." Touted as a superior and up-to-date alternative to water, the pastilles were lightweight and easy to carry in their own tin, which was beautifully decorated with the imprint of the spring and basilica. The ad further assured pilgrims that the factory was located near the grotto, which, perhaps, was intended to support the proud claim that one single drop of water contained in a tablet was "powerful enough to cure both suffering body and soul." Buying these sugar-coated lozenges would also "enable parents and friends remaining at home to be supplied with perfectly authentic souvenirs of a pilgrimage that the privileged alone can carry out." As the brochure smoothly noted, "Not everyone can come to the waters of the spring . . . but now the waters of the spring can go to everyone."[53]

This type of advertising also showed pilgrims how to behave like modern consumers. To move large stocks of goods quickly and make profits during the pilgrimage season, entrepreneurs strove to make sure that the masses of pilgrims who passed through Lourdes visited their shops. Promoting flashy novelty items was one technique for attracting customers. Another was to produce advertising copy that assured pilgrims the stores were "free to enter" and prices were "fixed." Of course, commercial transactions for religious goods had long been part of the pilgrimage experience, so that many pilgrims arrived at Lourdes expecting to procure sacred souvenirs. Yet this kind of advertising tried to reorient how pilgrims shopped for such goods, touting the benefits of no-haggling

Figure 17. Religious articles for sale: *Cantiques de Lourdes,* advertising catalog for the Alliance Catholique (Lourdes, 1911?), 11. Clugnet Collection, Marian Library, University of Dayton.

Figure 18. Small replica shrine ("superb novelty"): *Cantiques de Lourdes,* advertising catalog for the Alliance Catholique (Lourdes, 1911?), inside back cover. Clugnet Collection, Marian Library, University of Dayton.

exchanges and encouraging such behaviors as "window shopping" and spontaneous consumption that were relatively unfamiliar to visitors from rural parts
of France. Indeed, ads for the Alliance Catholique invited pilgrims to engage in
comparison shopping: "Pilgrims, don't settle on any purchases until *you've visited the Alliance Catholique.*"[54] Guidebooks offered similar advice on shopping
techniques, and asserted that the spiritual value even of inexpensive items would
only grow "as a result of all the pious thoughts they will later evoke." These
guides, like print advertisements, encouraged pilgrims to buy souvenirs for the
well-being of family and friends. One guide instructed pilgrims to "scour the
city for material souvenirs, images, rosaries with all the benedictions and indul-
gences, medals and pretty trinkets and jewelry" because such goods would place
"under the protection of Mary" their parents, friends, and, especially, newborn
babies.[55] Such claims sought to appeal to devout women, who saw themselves
as guardians of religious values and caretakers of their family's salvation. By
linking these products to the shrine's power to heal bodies and save souls, this
promotional literature introduced female pilgrims to new forms of commercial
exchange that became an integral part of women's devotional work.

Certain entrepreneurs found ingenious ways to speak to this female cohort of
faithful pilgrims. While many purveyors of religious goods used new media such
as catalogs to help pilgrims organize their shopping selections, the Alliance
Catholique transformed its catalog into a devotional tool by printing popular
Lourdes hymns on the initial pages of the booklet. The cover of the catalog,
which was labeled, somewhat deceptively, "Hymns of Lourdes, presented by the
stores of the Alliance Catholique," reproduced a full-page image of Bernadette's
visionary encounter. Yet after two pages of popular hymns, the booklet became
a simple advertising brochure, with a printed statement promising customer satisfaction and several pages of displayed goods.[56] Linking the singing of hymns
with the purchase of religious souvenirs, the catalog elevated religious consumption to a species of devotional activity. This catalog's interweaving of faith
and commerce was visually reinforced by an image of two monuments—the
Lourdes shrine and its own religious emporium—presented side by side. Other
entrepreneurs also employed advertising strategies that connected products
with no apparent religious significance to the sacred site. The maker of the perfume Lavande des Pyrénées, for example, linked its product to the pilgrimage
by using an image of Bernadette's visionary experience on the label. Advertised
in the pages of the shrine's *Journal de la Grotte,* this local product of little apparent interest to pilgrims was thereby transformed into a religious good. Producers of a health tonic called La Bernadette similarly capitalized on both the
name and image of the visionary. Such tricks of the ad trade encouraged pilgrims to consider a wider variety of purchases as potential souvenirs.

Just as purveyors of religious goods adopted the modern advertising strategies used in Paris, entrepreneurs at Lourdes also imitated popular entertain-

Figure 19. Religious emporium meets shrine: *Cantiques de Lourdes,* advertising catalog for the Alliance Catholique (Lourdes, 1911?), inside back cover. Clugnet Collection, Marian Library, University of Dayton.

ments that were all the rage in the capital. By the late nineteenth century, an array of local popular attractions—dioramas, panoramas, and, later, wax museums—offered pilgrims the opportunity to encounter the figures of Bernadette and even the Virgin Mary. Lourdes guidebooks promoted these spectacles in much the same way that the Musée Grévin and other Parisian entertainments promoted their own attractions. Dioramas and wax museums, by rendering a physical site and historic personages with extraordinary verisimilitude, provided pilgrims with an "authentic" moment from the past.[57] With admission costing as little as fifty centimes, these attractions enabled a mass audience to witness or engage in such moments within an intensely immediate setting. One guide claimed that the diorama at Lourdes captured the first apparition of the grotto "with such exactitude of detail that one might believe oneself present at the marvelous scene of the Blessed Virgin speaking to Bernadette." The booklet also praised a more elaborate panorama that represented the seventeenth apparition

Figure 20. Advertisement for the perfume Lavande des Pyrénées. From *Journal de la Grotte de Lourdes,* 12 July 1908, back page.

of the Virgin, in which the flame of Bernadette's candle touched her own hand without burning it. This event, taken as a sign that Bernadette was truly in communication with the Virgin Mary, first became a defining theme of the Lourdes story after it was described in great detail in Lasserre's *Notre-Dame de Lourdes.* Now pilgrims could experience this event directly by visiting a local panorama that rendered the scene on rolled-out canvas measuring 126 meters long and 15 meters high. The guidebook proclaimed, "This scene is reproduced by the artists with such an accent of truth that one is defenseless against the emotions it produces."[58] Other guides and manuals also promoted these visual spectacles as must-see attractions, even listing them among the principal monuments of the sanctuary.[59] When the *Journal de la Grotte* printed advertisements for the panorama, the shrine seemed to grant such popular entertainments the stamp of institutional legitimacy.[60]

By the early twentieth century, Lourdes boasted even more visual novelties. The Museum of Bernadette combined pictorial dioramas with wax figures to bring the past vividly to life. Praising this wax museum for "scrupulously reconstituting" all the scenes from Bernadette's life, one guide proclaimed that the wax figures "are so perfectly recreated that the visitor will have under his eyes a real image of the people who played a role in the miraculous apparitions."[61] The Grand Cinematographe, the cinema at Lourdes, also concentrated on historical reconstructions of Bernadette's life. By enabling pilgrims to gain entrance to the wax museum, the cinema, and the panorama for the cost of a single one-franc ticket, entrepreneurs integrated multiple visual entertainments as components of a single spectacle. They also devised ways to market these entertainments to a home audience. Stereoscopic slides, reproducing scenes from the wax museum and cinema, were offered for purchase at Lourdes. Like postcards, these glass slides were portable souvenirs that visually represented the ap-

Figure 21. Bernadette tends her flock, Lourdes Wax Museum, early twentieth-century stereo-scopic slide. Author's personal collection.

paritions of the sacred past as well as the present-day site. Perhaps even more than postcards, though, stereoscopic slides provided the illusion of three-dimensionality, offering believers at home an unrivaled experience of "being there."

Promoting Lourdes to a mass audience, then, created a series of spectacular devotional practices available for purchase. It should be noted, however, that the use of simulations like religious dioramas and panoramas was hardly without precedent. As far back as the late fifteenth century, the Church had commissioned artists to build chapels that housed replicas of famous scenes from the Holy Land. Employing a combination of murals and plaster statuary, these chapels sought to re-create distant places to which most believers could never travel on their own.[62] Yet the dioramas and panoramas at Lourdes re-created the sacred grotto of 1858, along with other local scenes, at Lourdes itself. The faithful thus encountered simultaneously the sacred past and the sacred present of Lourdes. This unusual experience encouraged pilgrims to indulge their fantasies—imagining, perhaps, that they were present when Bernadette saw the Virgin Mary—while still partaking in the mass rituals and spectacles of the modern pilgrimage site. In this sense, entrepreneurs were able to package and sell the shrine's own authorized history to avid consumers of the new. In doing so, they also drew attention to how Lourdes had remade itself to become something exciting and unprecedented, in which the entertainments themselves could be seen as modern technological marvels. Postcard images of Bernadette as the quaint yet exotic Pyrenean seer also performed a similar kind of work, reminding pilgrims of the shrine's origins in a bygone peasant religiosity while simultaneously providing modern souvenir items to enshrine the visionary.

The marketing of sacred goods and entertainments encouraged the Lourdes pilgrim to treat them as central to modern Catholic pilgrimage. There is some evidence that faithful Catholics who incorporated new products and amusements into their devotional practices embraced this new kind of experience. This embrace seems clear in Madeleine D.'s published account of her pilgrimage to Lourdes. Just as the young woman from Blois learned to see the train as a site for prayer and reflection, her personal account suggests how mass-produced religious articles might provide pilgrims with both joy and excitement. The description of her first glimpse of the Lourdes grotto, for example, highlighted a moment of profound recognition: "There stood the statue of Our Lady of Lourdes, just like the one that I have at home atop of my chest of drawers, but much larger." Dropping to her knees, she kissed the ground and stared at the statue as she prayed. It was not simply that Madeleine's first thought on seeing the cave where the Virgin appeared to Bernadette was of her own small statue of the Virgin Mary, one that she had long gazed on while praying at home. For Madeleine, the statuette facilitated a powerfully experienced connection to the sacred site. Similarly enabling was her mad rush, in preparation for the candle-light procession at the sanctuary, to buy "candles wrapped in beautiful paper printed with a blue image of the Blessed Virgin and a reproduction of the Grotto."[63] These seeming digressions imply that these mass-produced goods— the religious articles that surrounded her at home and at Lourdes—were not only treasured objects but aids to worship, fully integrated into devotional practices. For Madeleine D., these articles became valued sources of inspiration, even mediation, in building a relationship with the Virgin of Lourdes. That huge sales revenues were generated during each of these annual pilgrimages suggests that other devout pilgrims were also enthusiastic users of this new material culture at Lourdes.

Catholic believers, to be sure, have always used and interacted with material objects to feel closer to the saints, the Virgin Mary, and God. Activities such as saying the rosary or wearing a scapular represent just two of the many lay practices that have long enabled Catholics to build relationships with God with the benefit of clerical aid. Similarly, buying a small medal, holy card, or amulet at a pilgrimage site became, as far back as the Middle Ages, an accepted practice for devout believers to memorialize their religious journeys and keep nearby a piece of the sacred. Pilgrims at Lourdes were no different in this respect. They, too, relied on material objects to help mediate their relationships with the spiritual world. The point that I wish to emphasize here is that the emergence of mass-produced goods and novel souvenirs did not necessarily diminish such a relationship; in fact, for many Catholics, such objects may have enriched it. The availability of inexpensive votive candles at the shrine, for example, allowed masses of pilgrims to purchase devotional objects that facilitated their participation in the shrine's candlelight processions. The proliferation of inexpensive plaster statuettes of the Virgin of Lourdes, and of the saints, meant that growing numbers of late nineteenth-century Catholics could now buy such objects, imbuing their own homes with the shrine's sacred aura and enhancing (as with Madeleine D.) the spiritual ties between this faraway shrine and their daily lives. In this sense, the mass production of religious articles not only expanded the use of material objects in Catholic devotional practice but also promised, by combining novelty with reassuring familiarity, to integrate pilgrimage and everyday practice in an enhanced religious experience.

Perhaps the use of postcards is an even better example of how devout pilgrims, and the women among them in particular, so ably integrated novel items into their worship at the shrine. Female pilgrims endowed this modern tool of communication with religious meaning in much the same way that clerics remade the railway into a mobile sanctuary. By writing words of prayer and reassurance to family and friends at home, devout women found a new way to provide religious comfort and to affirm their own pious activities at the site.[64] While there was no discernable formula for the messages that writers scrawled on their postcards (or even where they placed these messages), most pilgrims wrote to inspire hope and to convey to the recipient that he or she had not been forgotten at Lourdes. A number of pilgrims penned only a sentence or two; "fond remembrances and prayers" or "I'm thinking of you at Lourdes" were popular phrases. Certain postcard writers, however, wrote lengthy notes, often emphasizing their own diligent work in praying for others. A postcard displaying pilgrims saying the rosary before the grotto, dated 1913, announced: "Dear Madame Lainé, I am thinking affectionately of you. I have not forgotten anyone here, and I am praying especially for you and for those who are dear to you." On another postcard, a pilgrim named Madeleine wrote to Madame and Monsieur Pitre of Paris: "I am thinking very affectionately of you both at the foot of the grotto, where my fervent prayers for you and your wishes are growing." Such messages, sent through the mail, enabled pilgrims at Lourdes to share moments of prayer and devotion with friends and families at home.[65] Exchanging messages of comfort

's of pious women, an established ritual of pilgrimage in-
nagination of believers who were unable directly to see,
h the shrine.

stcards from Lourdes transformed a mass-produced in-
ion into a religious object. In doing so, they also helped
 practice that encapsulated in miniature the spectacle-oriented
 used to promote the shrine. The nature of the postcard itself—its
limited space as well as its very public format and mode of circulation—encouraged pilgrims to limit their narration to the most important moments of the pilgrimage. The postcard celebrates brevity, forcing the writer to efficiently convey
the sights seen, the activities performed, and the emotions experienced during
the course of the journey. Postcard writing spurred many female pilgrims to
adopt a style quite congenial to the presentation of pilgrimage as a series of spectacles that one catalogued for others—the very perspective, in other words, favored by guidebooks and advertisements when promoting the shrine and its
goods. The postcard, then, provided women with a new medium for expressing
their piety, but it also shaped how that piety was reported and represented to the
larger Catholic world.

Spectatorship and the Cinematic

Presenting Lourdes as a series of spectacles helped traditional pilgrims become modern tourists and consumers. In a larger sense, though, the spectacles
of Lourdes—the visual presentation of landscape, goods, and historical personages—also turned pilgrims into modern *spectators*. As this term suggests, a
devotional culture that integrated train travel, sightseeing throughout the town
and countryside, window shopping for religious souvenirs, and viewing visual
attractions of the sacred past encouraged a type of panoramic vision, a mobile
gaze. Pilgrims who came to Lourdes on regional or national pilgrimages watched
the landscape of southwestern France roll by from the window of a speeding
train. They strolled along the boulevard de la Grotte, perusing goods in shop
windows and watching the anonymous crowds pass by. They rented bicycles or
rode the funicular to survey the surrounding countryside. They mailed postcards from the site, and reveled in the virtual reality of the dioramas and panoramas that transported them back in time to the moment when Lourdes became
part of Christian history. Pilgrims not only participated in such sights and experiences, they even helped to produce them, as with the guidebook-sponsored
photography contests that enlisted the talents of readers.

This modern gaze is often assumed to be the product of urban culture. Historians often point to fin-de-siècle Paris as the fountainhead of this type of modern panoramic vision.[66] Although Lourdes was no Paris, it produced a parallel
experience for Catholics, a mass-cultural immersion that urged pilgrims to

adopt the position of the modern spectator. In this subject position, the faithful could enjoy the unfolding religious event of pilgrimage as an exciting excursion to a new monumental shrine and bustling town, a place where they might delight in an artificially rendered, yet religiously authentic, vision of the sacred past and purchase tangible mementos of the experience for future moments of devout contemplation.

The production of this kind of panoramic vision, one that allowed pilgrims to engage with the shrine and its goods as a modern spectacle, made the sacred site an ideal subject for the early cinema. It is not surprising, then, that early filmmakers, such as the Lumière brothers and later Charles Pathé, chose to shoot some of their early *actualités* at Lourdes.[67] These short films consisted of live-action footage of actual events, presenting, in effect, a catalog of images with no narrative structure other than that provided by the events themselves. These "moving pictures" were, as film scholar Miriam Hansen has noted, "presentational rather than representational." They addressed viewers directly, presenting audiences with an array of often-spectacular sights—from speeding trains to exotic images of foreign locales—rather than "enveloping them into an illusion of a fictional narrative." Yet many actualités featured more prosaic depictions of daily street life or landscape panoramas. Film historian Tom Gunning has argued that these early motion pictures created a "cinema of attractions," the type of film that "solicits a highly conscious awareness of the film image engaging the viewer's curiosity." Because the spectator, in the process, "remains aware of the act of looking, the excitement of curiosity and its fulfillment," the popularity of these films rested on their ability to engage the viewer through a series of often discontinuous yet astonishing images.[68] In this sense, Lourdes offered an ideal subject for such films, because the pilgrimage site was already structured around a rich array of visual attractions that merely required presentation to excite the cinematic gaze. Filmmakers at the turn of the century may have been drawn to Lourdes because the shrine embodied a type of panoramic vision of the moment.

The brief actualités of Lourdes made by the Lumières and by Pathé are interesting precisely because the filmmakers seemed to replicate the type of modern imagery already found in postcards, guidebooks, and advertisements. For example, the Lumières, who came to Lourdes in 1895, shot several short actualités that represented ordinary pilgrims engaging in the shrine's carefully orchestrated pilgrimage rituals. In particular, the footage focused on pilgrims marching in processions, candles in hand, and on sick pilgrims being carried on stretchers or wheeled around in carriages to the grotto. The films also presented shots of the faithful strolling about the shrine and exiting from the Basilica of the Rosary. An actualité by Pathé, shot nine years later, covered much the same material. Scenes recorded women praying in the bathhouses, believers moving in procession and praying at the grotto, and pilgrims drinking water at the fountains. Yet, his short film also included other striking shots that, by this later date, had already become typical images of cinematic discourse. Thus, Pathé's actualité opened with a kind of establishing shot, a panoramic view showing the town and basilica with the mountains in the background. He also included scenes of the train's arrival at the Lourdes railway station and of sick pilgrims being carried from their special compartment and loaded into automobiles. These cinematic moments reproduced the shrine's own carefully constructed image of the site as a modern spectacle.[69]

Throughout each actualité, the cinematic audience was reminded of the filmmaker's presence. As the films sought to capture the full range of spectacular elements that made up the pilgrimage experience, there were several moments when pilgrims, suddenly showing their awareness of being filmed, froze in midaction to look directly into the camera's lens. Often looking excited or confused—as is the case in Pathé's film with several women who were sipping Lourdes water from the fountain—these pilgrims appeared to be scrutinizing the audience even as the audience scrutinized them. This actualité also showed photographers at work in the midst of the shrine's elaborate processions, revealing to the audience that these were hardly impromptu events. If the actualités presented the rituals and practices at Lourdes as a documentary-like series of events, the films also suggested that viewers see these spectacles as orchestrated representations involving knowing participants.

Figure 22. Procession: Frame enlargement from Pathé Frères actualité, "Lourdes" (1904?). Library of Congress, AFI—Dorothy Taylor Collection.

Figure 23. Pilgrims drink water at the grotto: Frame enlargement from Pathé Frères actualité, "Lourdes" (1904?). Library of Congress, AFI—Dorothy Taylor Collection.

Figure 24. Procession of the Blessed Sacrament: Frame enlargement from Pathé Frères actualité, "Lourdes" (1904?). Note the photographer at rear left. Library of Congress, AFI—Dorothy Taylor Collection.

These short films, then, introduced to an even larger audience an understanding of the sacred site as a knowable, modern spectacle. Exhibited in music halls, urban theaters, and fairgrounds throughout France, the actualités of the Lumières and Pathé conveyed images of the Lourdes pilgrimage to a public well beyond its devout Catholic participants and even beyond the crowds of curious tourists who routinely visited the site.[70] Surpassing even the intensive efforts of the Grotto fathers and Lourdes entrepreneurs, these films incorporated the spectacles of Lourdes into the emerging mass culture of French society, circulating within the secular world images of the shrine's own modern sacred landscape.

The development of the national pilgrimage to the Lourdes shrine proved to be more successful than either the Assumptionists or the Grotto fathers had ever imagined. By the early twentieth century, the sacred site of the grotto had become the most well-known and most visited pilgrimage site in Europe. The key to its popularity was that Church leaders, in an era of capitalist development and new technological improvements, sought out new visual and written techniques and adopted innovative commercial practices that remade the experience of Catholic pilgrimage. At Lourdes, the religious landscape was no longer identified with the natural setting of the grotto but with a newly built environment. Lourdes water was linked not to the free-flowing spring discovered by Bernadette but, rather, to industrial processes that enabled its distribution in prepackaged bottles and ready-made tablets. The personages of Bernadette and the Virgin Mary were also revised through the visual inventions and constructed settings of popular entertainments. What the Church, entrepreneurs, and pilgrims themselves created at Lourdes was a new popular devotional culture. This culture was distinctly modern because it infused the shrine with the mass-cultural developments of urban life and, more important, because it gave rise to a set of practices and rituals that replicated modern behaviors associated with bourgeois tourism, mass consumption, and even flânerie. This new Catholic pilgrimage provided, in effect, an alternative mass-cultural experience for Catholics, especially rural women, who now experienced the joys of sightseeing, buying, and even people watching in an environment that was sanctioned by religious authorities. By going to Lourdes on pilgrimage, women who were introduced to these practices adopted them simply by engaging in the rituals and informal activities of the shrine.

The market practices and new technologies that became part and parcel of the pilgrimage experience served not merely as instruments for satisfying some pre-existing and unalterable spirituality. These modern forces shaped this spirituality in ways that were entirely consonant with larger trends in cultural development. The devotional culture produced at Lourdes thus modernized the act of pilgrimage, which in turn invigorated French Catholic worship during a period of church instability. The success of this devotional culture enabled religious faith, and the Church itself, to remain a relevant, meaningful, and exciting part of modern life. Rather than interpreting the commercial culture of the Lourdes shrine as a symptom of the demise of "authentic" spirituality or as a superficial distraction that should not be confused with the "real work" of the shrine, the material life of pilgrimage continued to satisfy religious needs, but on terms that made sense for modern society.

2

Commercialized Pilgrimage
and Religious Debasement

The Assumptionists who organized the first national pilgrimage to Lourdes in 1873 hoped to spark a Catholic revival that would transform French society. During these early years of the Third Republic, when a conservative governing alliance reigned as the party of "moral order," the French Catholic Church looked to such public displays of Catholic unity as harbingers of a religious revival powerful enough to topple republican forces and restore a Bourbon king to the throne. After republicans secured their position in government in 1879, however, and the Third Republic began to pursue an aggressively anticlerical program, the mobilization of large crowds at Lourdes took on a different kind of importance.[1] Henceforth, the Church relied on public manifestations of popular religiosity to prove to itself, and to its political opponents, that religion still mattered. The thousands of French men and women who came annually to Lourdes, along with the hundreds of miracle cures proclaimed there, were heralded by clerical authorities as signs of God's continuing intervention in the modern world. In an era of defensive church politics and declining religious worship in many urban areas, Lourdes became, for embattled French Catholics, the symbol of a thriving, popular faith.

Yet with the success of mass pilgrimages came a host of unanticipated problems. As Lourdes became the site of a new public religiosity that was part and parcel of emerging commercial culture, it was swept up in the startling changes often associated with modern urban life. Pilgrims complained of price gouging by slick-talking peddlers and shopkeepers, harassment by the large numbers of beggars, and a disturbing rise in petty crime. More troubling to church leaders were the unpredictable consequences brought about by the mass marketing and advertising of religious goods. Although the Grotto fathers condoned the sell-

ing of new kinds of religious souvenirs such as Pastilles de L
postcards, a number of goods marketed with the Lourdes nam
ligious significance or, even worse, claimed supernatural powe
by the Church. These were not new problems for Catholic autl
appeared more threatening in this new era of mass pilgrimage, be
so difficult to control. In an atmosphere of increasing Church-,   ...sity
marked by vitriolic press debates between anticlerical republicans and Catholic
conservatives, these problems became an enduring source of humiliation for
clerical authorities even as pilgrims grew fearful of having their devotional practices corrupted by swindlers.

Such troubles became important weapons for republicans. During the 1890s
and early 1900s, when anticlerical attacks by the Third Republic reached new
heights, the commercial success of the shrine drew the concern of freethinking
journalists, who worried that the skillful marketing of mass pilgrimage would
bewitch a credulous French populace and threaten the health of the nation. Indeed, the 1894 publication of Émile Zola's *Lourdes,* a novel critical of the shrine,
ignited intense debates about the commercialization of religion. Republican
journalists and legislators connected the "irrational" spending on religious
goods at the holy site with the proliferation of Catholic superstition. They
scorned the shrine and its pilgrimages for propagating a new, dangerous form of
simony. Yet the example of Lourdes also revealed a deeper ambivalence within
the republican camp over the role of economic modernization in secular progress. Confronted with economic dislocation and growing social tensions
throughout the country, many republicans were disturbed by the corrupting effects of the modern marketplace and its commercializing public sphere on a still-
emerging democratic citizenry. Indeed, the very commerce that bourgeois
republicans depended on to secure their own economic positions seemed, at the
same time, to threaten highly prized notions of civic virtue. Republican diatribes
against the Parisian department store and its female shoppers betrayed fears that
the capitalist market might undermine the moral fiber of the republic.[2] Perhaps
even more disturbing were the crowds of largely rural women who flocked to
Lourdes, worshipping devoutly, of course, but also partaking freely of the town's
commercial pleasures. These pilgrims revealed all too clearly the further pene-
tration of a new consumer society into the nation's sacred spaces. Was there no
realm, religious or secular, that was safe from the degrading designs of the marketplace? For many republicans, Lourdes laid bare the ambiguous consequences
of capitalist economic development.

The defining features of mass pilgrimage also furnished the basis for a potent
critique of modern-day popular religiosity by Catholics themselves. The large
crowds that came to the site each year led to overcrowding and rising crime.
Their presence gave Lourdes the appearance of a cosmopolitan city filled with
anonymous and sometimes threatening strangers. The popularity of the pil-

grimages, symbol of France's rejuvenated faith, smacked as well of crass commercialization and the exploitation of naive pilgrims. As Catholic visitors encountered these modern ills within the domain of the sacred shrine, they began
to articulate a critical commentary infused with nostalgic longing for a simpler,
unmediated form of religious worship. Glorifying the pageants and festivals of
the Middle Ages and often idealizing the "humble" piety of the rural peasantry,
certain prominent Catholics recoiled from the glitz and glamour of Lourdes,
lamenting its unrestrained commercialization. Their critique of the shrine, elaborated by male clerics and by such Catholic intellectuals as Joris-Karl Huysmans, did not condemn mass pilgrimages; these critiques expressed, instead,
extraordinary ambivalence toward a devotional culture that ably brought the
masses to worship but depended on modern commercial practices and technologies to do so.

The commerciality of Lourdes, then, tended to throw believers and nonbelievers alike into positions of profound discomfort. While Catholics interpreted
the merging of religion and commerce as a perversion of true spirituality, republicans feared this confluence might further undermine their attempt to create a secular and civic-oriented public sphere. Decrying mass pilgrimage as a
travesty of "proper worship," Catholic critics and their anticlerical opponents
focused on the behavior of female pilgrims as emblematic of much that was
wrong with modern-day religious practice. The result was a newly minted discourse of religious debasement, one embraced, surprisingly, by both Catholic
and republican critics of Lourdes.

THE PROBLEMS OF COMMERCIALIZED PILGRIMAGE

The negative impacts of mass pilgrimage became visible within a few years of
the first Assumptionist-sponsored national pilgrimages to Lourdes. Large-scale
pilgrimages not only brought crowds of devoted Catholics but thieves, beggars,
and peddlers hawking fraudulent religious goods. Clerical authorities were
inundated with complaints by pilgrims who felt harassed and unsafe while visiting the sacred site. Of course, pilgrims who had visited shrines in earlier centuries offered similar complaints of being cheated by phony beggars and
peddlers.[3] At Lourdes, however, these problems seemed magnified because of
the enormous scale of the pilgrimages. The Church responded by using new
tools for dealing with these long-standing abuses that now threatened to spiral
out of control. Employing new techniques of policing and sophisticated public
relations campaigns to discredit those activities it could not regulate, the Church
soon redefined what constituted "normal" economic behavior at pilgrimages. In
the process, such efforts intensified what shrine authorities considered to be the
legitimate commercialization of Lourdes.

The Church cast a wide net in its campaign against crime and fraud at Lourdes.

Any individual who disrupted the smooth running of the shrine became suspect. The large number of beggars made them easy targets, and the Grotto fathers often labeled them "criminals" in the many public warnings issued to pilgrims. Lourdes guidebooks also conflated beggars with petty thieves and pickpockets in special sections about abuses at the site.[4] No longer encouraged to give alms to unfortunate individuals, penitent pilgrims were now assured that such people were unworthy of Christian generosity. Giving money to beggars, claimed one guide, would only encourage their sinful lifestyles: "One cannot emphasize too much that it would be a misguided form of charity and would even encourage vice among these beggars." This same guide claimed that many female beggars, in particular, induced acts of charity by faking blindness and various disabilities, or by using other people's children as their own when begging on the streets. Phony mendicants, the guide insisted, often owned horses, carts, and even homes in nearby towns. Looking for ways to avoid manual labor, they made begging their way of life.[5]

Peddlers hawking their wares near the sanctuary and religious vendors roving through rural France were also labeled charlatans and crooks. The Church issued mandates, published news articles, and used guidebooks to alert Catholics to the problem of fraudulent peddlers. One public mandate, issued by the bishop of Tarbes in 1888, declared that the Church was "compelled to point out and stigmatize certain abuses . . . being committed, in various places, with the name, water, sacred objects . . . of Notre-Dame de Lourdes." The decree specifically condemned "the odious hoaxes of itinerant peddlers, who, with their sacred objects, sell fake *relics of the grotto*," along with "swindlers who demand several sous for the sanctuary to cover the fees of saying a mass celebrated at Lourdes." Labeling such individuals false agents of the grotto, the mandate, sent to dioceses across France, called on clergy and lay Catholics to "help us stop this sacrilegious abuse."[6] Lourdes guidebooks reproduced these church decrees, along with general warnings to pilgrims to be suspicious of all colporteurs selling wares on the streets around the sanctuary. The obedient pilgrim was instructed to buy goods from the boutique run by the Grotto fathers.[7]

The Church also railed against the roving peddlers who hawked religious objects to faithful Catholics far from the shrine. Announcing that "Swindlers Exploit the Cult of Notre-Dame de Lourdes," a front-page article in the *Journal de la Grotte* reproduced a letter from a devout Catholic who wished to know whether a traveling female peddler was really an agent of the grotto. The peddler had displayed a certificate proclaiming herself to have been healed at Lourdes; she also carried a paper with the seal of the Fathers of the Grotto of Lourdes. Reporting that "as soon as I saw her certificate, I trusted her," the letter writer then spent twenty-four francs on "a little reliquary containing grass, several medals, a rosary, [and] a cross." After reproducing the letter in full, the article insisted that the peddler was a swindler and recommended that Catholics alert the police when peddlers—even those with authentic-looking papers—came to town: "It is the best service that you can perform in the name of Lourdes and at the same time for honest people who, after repeated warnings, are still naive enough to let themselves be duped."[8] By providing concrete examples of inappropriate transactions with peddlers, the Church hoped that Catholics would learn to be suspicious, rejecting what was once a commonly accepted commercial practice.

As the Grotto fathers took steps to protect the shrine from crime and fraud, they faced larger difficulties related to the promotion of pilgrimage. Transforming Lourdes into a pilgrimage town that accommodated thousands of visitors at a time resulted in new and complicated economic ties between the Church and private businesses. These ties linked the sanctuary to a vast network of commercial activities that went far beyond the Church's traditional trade in votive candles and other religious articles. Institutionalizing the national pilgrimages involved the sanctuary in financial negotiations with railway companies, while the decision to ship Lourdes water all over France (and eventually around the world) entailed hard bargaining with middlemen who bottled and transported the sacred spring water. Investments by the bishop of Tarbes in the redevelopment of the town meant conducting extensive land deals involving hotels, piety shops, and entertainments. The sanctuary's own newspapers and guidebooks became important venues for new kinds of advertising by independent merchants and industrialists involved in religious commerce. Although these varied business relationships were essential for disseminating the message of pilgrimage and creating a new kind of public worship, they opened the Grotto fathers to charges of simony and exploitation. Shrine authorities learned early on, in fact, that their work to promote the grotto could become the object of strident attacks.

One of the first public attacks came, surprisingly, from a prominent supporter of Lourdes. Henri Lasserre, best-selling author of *Notre-Dame de Lourdes*, assailed the bishop of Tarbes and the Grotto fathers in the 1870s for profiting unfairly from the sale and transport of Lourdes water. Lasserre also complained that these clerics had done nothing to stem the traffic in religious goods and were thus responsible for an unseemly commercialization of the shrine. Singling out the newly constructed boulevard de la Grotte, the author claimed that this redevelopment enriched the shrine at the expense of the town.[9] Lasserre's attack was soon followed by other public accusations. In 1877, the Parisian daily *Le XIXe Siècle* printed an article by a well-known anticlerical journalist, Francisque Sarcey, claiming that the sanctuary was making huge profits from the grotto's spring water. Entitled "Betrayed by Their Own," the story described the author's journey to Lourdes, where he met Brother Henri Soubiat, an employee of the shrine who sold bottled Lourdes water. In confidence, the cleric revealed to Sarcey the large revenues that the sanctuary enjoyed from bottling

water from the sacred source. He also showed Sarcey h⌐
des water by simply placing lead caps bearing the nam⌐
nary bottles of tap water; Soubiat himself, in fact, sold t⌐
a regular basis. Since faith alone healed the sick, the br⌐
matter if the water came from Lourdes or from one's ⌐

These public attacks against Lourdes tarred the Ch⌐
ities as a new form of simony designed to fool the public and enrich ⌐⌐⌐
response, the Grotto fathers claimed that sale of bottled water and other religious objects constituted a traditional church activity. They also insisted that the
shrine did not benefit financially from the shipping of Lourdes water. In January 1876, the Grotto fathers sued *Le XIXe Siècle* for libel and won a settlement
of three thousand francs.[11] Conceding in court their involvement in the commercial trade of religious goods, the Grotto fathers insisted that such trade was
a legitimate service for the devout. They were not making money from this activity but only covering the costs of ensuring that all faithful Catholics might
have access to the grotto's sacred spring. By choosing this line of defense, the
Grotto fathers portrayed their very new engagement in a variety of modern
commercial practices as part of a traditional pilgrimage industry in existence for
centuries.

Yet the charges of exploitation raised other troubling questions for the sanctuary. Even if the Grotto fathers could protect themselves from false accusations,
they came to recognize that an association with embarrassing or inappropriate
religious commerce carried out by independent entrepreneurs tended to undermine their activities. Over time, in fact, such independent commerce grew
quite large. By the early twentieth century, a French court ruled that images of
the Virgin of Lourdes and of the shrine's basilica were appearing on so many regional products that these images were now in the public domain and could no
longer be protected as trademarks.[12] What was the Church's relationship to
these merchants and industrialists who used the Lourdes name to sell their
products? Did the sanctuary profit from these goods? Was the shrine's trade in
religious articles and Lourdes water enriching the Church at the expense of promoting superstition or fleecing naive pilgrims? In response to such questions,
clerical authorities at Lourdes struggled to define more clearly a public stance
toward the role of commerce in the devotional life of the sanctuary. Whereas the
Grotto fathers had unambiguously condemned itinerant peddling, they expressed
greater ambivalence toward other religious commerce that helped sustain the
mass pilgrimages to the shrine. Rather than assail all independent commercial
activity, then, the Grotto fathers tried to distinguish between legitimate and illegitimate forms of religious commerce. Any merchant, peddler, or industrialist
who pretended to work for the shrine or to benefit the grotto financially was
deemed fraudulent. Entrepreneurs who marketed products promising supernatural healing not authorized by the Church were committing sacrilege. The

tto fathers were determined to show that the shrine did not gain direct economic benefit from the elaborate trade in religious goods and services carried
out in the name of Lourdes. By attacking businesses that made false promises or
linked themselves too closely with the sanctuary, the fathers sought to condemn
the worst abuses committed in the name of the shrine while simultaneously protecting the larger commercial culture that had emerged.

The decision to prosecute entrepreneurs for fraudulent use of the Lourdes
name often centered on whether the product disgraced the image of the sanctuary. While the Grotto fathers apparently did nothing to hinder F. Valette &
Co. from selling the Pastilles de Lourdes, they threatened to sue a distiller, La
Maison Victor Sabatier, for launching a new liqueur dedicated to the Virgin of
Lourdes. Typical of many goods being marketed to pilgrims, La Bernadette,
Liqueur de Lourdes was promoted as a "health tonic" that was "indispensable
to pilgrims"; the bottle's label reproduced an image of Bernadette's visionary
encounter with the Virgin. Although this kind of advertising appeal was employed by many entrepreneurs in the region, Monsieur Sabatier-Lavigne, owner
of the company, also began to claim that the liqueur was "sold to benefit the work
of the Grotto." In 1887, Sabatier-Lavigne announced in a letter to the head of
the Grotto fathers that he wished to give a portion of his profits to the grotto
administration in return for backing the product. Sabatier even included an illustration of the label for the new liqueur, with its proud claim to benefit the
grotto. Father Carrère, head of the Grotto fathers, responded with an irate note
warning that "no enterprise of this nature has ever succeeded" and that all such
endeavors "have been and will soon be condemned by the ecclesiastical authority." While Father Carrère made clear in letters to Sabatier-Lavigne that
he was offended by the use of Bernadette's name to sell the liqueur, his full outrage was provoked by the label that linked the product financially to the work
of the grotto. He insisted that these words "must disappear entirely and immediately"; if not, "we will be obliged to resort to the law courts to stop this
scandal." Sabatier-Lavigne responded with a contrite letter that promised to
no longer use the offending phrase. However, he continued to market the product with the name La Bernadette. Father Carrère seemed to treat the matter as
settled.[13] Apparently, the Grotto fathers were prepared to tolerate a product
named after the famed visionary, but drew the line at accepting any revenue from
the business.

The Church worked to educate pilgrims and consumers so that they, too,
could distinguish between legitimate and illegitimate religious commerce. The
numerous public decrees of the bishop of Tarbes, as well as the strident warnings of the shrine's newspapers and Lourdes guidebooks, called on the devout
to protect themselves from specific forms of commercial exploitation, singling
out certain abuses without condemning wholesale the trade in Lourdes products. The bishop of Tarbes's 1888 mandate, for example, listed three types of

Figure 25. Advertising label for La Bernadette, Liqueur de Lourdes, 1887. Archives de l'Œuvre de la Grotte.

commercial exploitation that wreaked havoc on the sanctuary: the "odious hoaxes" of peddlers who sold pretended relics of the shrine; false agents who collected money for masses; and "industrial exploitation that hides behind the appearance of religion (and that can fool the credulous)." The bishop took pains to clarify that it was not wrong to purchase commercially produced religious objects or to buy bottled Lourdes water, so long as Catholics procured these items from the Church alone. The mandate further called on the devout to "regard as false all those individuals who do not bear the signature and the seal of arms of the bishop of Tarbes in an authentic manner."[14] This advice reassured pilgrims that some forms of commerce, particularly goods purchased from the missionaries of the shrine, were approved. Yet the mandate tacitly legitimated the numerous piety shops that lined the main avenues of Lourdes, as did the Grotto fathers when they allowed these stores to advertise in their weekly newspaper.

Sometimes the Church singled out particular industries or products for their desecration of the sacred. Clerical authorities seemed especially concerned when products promised supernatural powers not recognized by the Church; these goods not only constituted fraud but promoted superstitious beliefs. In 1913, the bishop of Tarbes issued a mandate condemning a manufacturer who sold "plastrons hygiéniques de Lourdes," garments said to regenerate both physical health and religious faith. These garments, decorated with an image of Bernadette's apparition of the Virgin Mary, promised to provide the pilgrims who wore them with "relief from their sufferings." The bishop lamented that such items "offended true Christian souls, rendered devotion ridiculous in the eyes of unbelievers, and allowed uneducated believers to maintain superstitious practices and be easily misled." Citing the need to "help defend the honor of religion, in particular the honor of the sanctuary of the Immaculate Virgin," he called on the devotees of Our Lady of Lourdes "to pass on our condemnation against this abuse and other like offenders."[15] Published widely, the decree's core message was intended to insulate the "legitimate" healing powers of the spring water of Lourdes—God's chosen method of supernatural intervention at the shrine—from any damaging association with counterfeit curative aids.

The bishop's pronouncement against the plastrons de Lourdes was just one of a number of his public statements condemning commercial exploitation of the shrine. In a 1913 public communiqué, for instance, the cleric declared that "several times already, the diocesan authority of Tarbes and Lourdes has had to denounce the sacrilegious abuse being made, in diverse places, of the name, water, pious objects, and souvenirs of Our Lady of Lourdes." Why did the ecclesiastic authorities have to make so many of these announcements? In part, clerical officials were engaged in a losing battle to control how the shrine would be commercialized. After the courts declared that the shrine's cherished images were in the public domain, the issuing of public mandates against exploitation became the preferred strategy for fighting fraudulent trade and misuse of the Lourdes name. Mandates also possessed the hypothetical advantage of forcing pilgrims to be responsible for their own behavior. Yet the tone of many of these public decrees also betrays considerable annoyance that the faithful were declining to follow the guidelines. Much to the frustration of the Grotto fathers, Catholics seemed unable to resist such foolish and fraudulent goods.

These admonitions suggest that commercial exploitation was more complicated than church fathers were willing to concede. Beyond nefarious individuals taking advantage of gullible pilgrims, there was also a broader Catholic populace who expected and happily participated in commercial activities associated with the shrine. Church tirades against exploitation and fraud may not have deterred such activities, but these public statements did confuse faithful believers who considered the buying and selling of religious souvenirs to be a normal part of the pilgrimage journey. Church distinctions between legitimate and illegitimate trade flew in the face of long-established customs, and Catholic merchants, far from resembling the criminal elements described in clerical decrees, often believed the sale of their Lourdes products to be advancing the cult of Our Lady of Lourdes. Moreover, pilgrims did not desist from buying suspect goods, but the numerous decrees made them feel more anxious about the articles they acquired. As church leaders attempted to separate the shrine from crass commercialism, their efforts only seemed to further intertwine the religious and commercial realms.

The case of the distiller Sabatier-Lavigne is a telling example of such problems. When the maker of La Bernadette liqueur received Father Carrère's letter threatening to sue for improper marketing, he responded that his product had seemed neither inappropriate nor offensive to the shrine. After apologizing for inadvertently causing the sanctuary any pain or sadness, Sabatier-Lavigne explained: "I did not think, based on precedent, that it was a scandal to mix the things of Lourdes with worldly commerce." He noted that one of his competitors in the nearby town of Pau—a gentlemen appreciably "less Catholic" than himself—had already introduced a liqueur de Lourdes that received "favorable attention from priests and even bishops." Flaunting his own religious credentials, Sabatier-Lavigne asserted: "Brother of a priest and a former editor of a Catholic newspaper . . . I declare that I am incapable of [causing] a Catholic scandal." Rather, it was Carrère, he declared, who mistook for scandal a simple act of good will on behalf of the shrine. Fully intending to share revenue from the sale of La Bernadette, Sabatier-Lavigne could not understand why the Grotto fathers would not want to receive this income. Although he agreed ultimately to change his label in accordance with the wishes of the sanctuary, he could not help but see the product as furthering devotion to the Virgin of Lourdes.[16] Given the numerous products using the name and religious imagery of

Lourdes that were already in circulation by the 1880s, no doubt many entrepreneurs—deeming themselves good Catholics and good businessmen—saw little contradiction in enlisting the market to advance religion.

If entrepreneurs did not always know when they had crossed the line between legitimate and illegitimate commercial activity, pilgrims were also unsure about this ambiguous distinction. Despite the numerous public warnings against fraudulent peddlers selling Lourdes relics and other religious articles, the devout continued to buy from these dealers. The sanctuary received numerous letters from Catholics all over France inquiring about the authenticity of the goods they had purchased. These letters reveal the persistent desires of Catholics to possess religious goods from Lourdes along with growing anxiety about the nature of these commercial transactions. If the goods were too expensive or promised healing powers beyond what was normally expected, believers feared they were being cheated out of their sacred experience. In a letter addressed to the director of the Lourdes sanctuary, Marie Rataboul, a woman from the town of Lauzerte in the department of Tarn-et-Garonne, expressed concern over two individuals who passed through her town selling "reliquaries containing . . . objects having belonged to Bernadette." Although the two peddlers claimed that money made from these sales would be sent to the grotto, she worried because "they were selling these objects at highly inflated prices." The woman's letter concluded with an urgent plea: "As we live in a century where swindlers are everywhere, I beseech you, Director, to tell me if all these things are truthful and, if not, to put a halt to these individuals who would so exploit the faith of worthy people."[17] Marie Rataboul's fears of being swindled seemed to have been, if anything, intensified by repeated warnings that unscrupulous men and women prowled the villages of France looking to dupe innocent Catholics. Yet despite the Church's instruction to distrust all such men and alert the police, Marie Rataboul bought the goods in question and then expected the Grotto fathers to sort out the problem. Another letter to the sanctuary, from Madame Émilie Capelle of Vauvillers par Chaulnes in the Somme, described in detail strategies used by an itinerant peddler she encountered selling "rosaries, medallions, crosses . . . and little pictures . . . of the grotto with Notre-Dame de Lourdes printed on the back." To prove that he was an authentic dealer, the peddler showed papers signed by the bishop of Tarbes and the mayor of Lourdes. After Capelle spent six francs on one item, she decided to write to the sanctuary: "I really believe in him, but I want to be informed if I have been deceived." A note penned by a priest in the margin of the letter concluded that she had been "tricked by a swindler."[18]

Faithful Catholics repeatedly voiced these same concerns in letters to the sanctuary. A man named Jules Roberts inquired "if it is really true that these men are sent by you . . . [to sell] rosaries, statuettes, medals, and other religious objects." A writer from Nantes wrote to warn the Grotto fathers about "a type

of peddling that does not seem to me to be approve
One man wrote to the sanctuary on behalf of his coi.
peddlers who came to his town selling relics of Berna
Lourdes were truly authorized dealers. Despite having bee.
issued by the bishop of Tarbes, community members still worr.
lent vendors had deceived them. This man begged the director of .
ary: "Please respond to me in order to assure us if this is really the
Another writer expressed his outrage over traveling peddlers who "have the
dacity . . . to promise healing by means of . . . medallions." He ended his letter
by urging that the Grotto fathers "put a stop to this state of things, and punish
these brutes that mock the faithful and jeopardize our religion."[19]

Most of the faithful who wrote to the sanctuary had already purchased the articles in question. They clearly desired access to objects with curative powers and hoped that, by buying Lourdes rosaries and statuettes, masses would be said for them at the grotto. These material objects remained a potent source of sacred power for late nineteenth-century Catholics. Yet the devout also feared that these goods might be fakes, and thus worthless, if they came from unauthorized peddlers. Although the Church's response was to condemn all peddlers as exploiters to be avoided, even prosecuted, this position ignored the fact that itinerant vendors still provided Catholics with easy access to the material objects they desired. In this context, the Church's distinctions between legitimate and illegitimate commerce did not solve the problem, nor did they assure faithful Catholics that their devotional practices were safe from corruption.

If some pilgrims were confused by the Church's position, others simply disagreed with it, finding the Church's protection of the industry developing around the shrine to be an affront to the Catholic faith. In 1888, for example, Louis Baron, a pilgrim from Toulouse, wrote to the shrine to complain about the Pastilles de Lourdes: "During my last pilgrimage to Notre-Dame de Lourdes, I was struck by the existence of a steam-works that manufactures, people say, lozenges from *Lourdes water*. My reaction was sorrow and pain." Clearly unpersuaded by the Church's own notion of legitimate commerce, Baron added, "This so-called industry had no other purpose than realizing great profits . . . from a blessed and sacred thing. I was also surprised that . . . you have not gathered all your forces to stop this state of affairs."[20] Other pilgrims complained about the piety shops located near the sanctuary. One woman protested that selling bottled Lourdes water for the "exorbitant" price of five francs per liter "served to destroy the name of Our Mother." The count of Lupel similarly criticized shrine authorities for tolerating business practices that he considered "unchristian." In an 1889 letter to the bishop of Tarbes, he wrote on behalf of a wealthy pious woman who, for one hundred francs, had purchased souvenirs that were probably worth no more than ten francs. The priests at the shrine, he noted, appear to be "tolerating this thievery because they benefit financially in it," adding that one "need not be an enemy of the clergy to have these inner doubts." Yet the count did not call for an end to religious commerce at Lourdes, suggesting instead that all merchandise "should be marked with a number, written visibly and fixed by a member of the clergy."[21] Understanding the importance of such goods for devout Catholics, the count wished to ensure that all businesses at Lourdes were legitimate and well-run operations that did not cheat the faithful. Interestingly, his solution—to employ the same system of fixed pricing used by department stores in Paris—would enlist the Church in taking an even more direct role in the commercial life of the pilgrimage.

These various responses reveal an important moment of transition in the meaning and practice of religious commerce in late nineteenth-century France. New ways of buying and selling religious goods were being introduced at Lourdes even as itinerant peddling, the oldest form of religious commerce in western Europe, remained very common.[22] The shipping of standardized religious articles and bottled water directly from Lourdes to people's homes was fast becoming an accepted practice. Piety shops and producers of religious goods were now using catalogs and advertisements to make themselves known to a national audience of believing Catholics. These practices competed with traditional peddling, which they soon began to replace. Indeed, the fact that letter writers complained about fraudulent peddlers suggests that this restructuring was well underway. Clearly wishing to endow the objects they had purchased with some kind of sacred value, these Catholics nevertheless eyed roving peddlers with suspicion as new ways of buying religious articles emerged. Over time, as itinerant commerce was repeatedly condemned by decrees, it is likely that the artifacts and mass-produced goods ordered from catalogs or from Lourdes appeared a safer form of commercial exchange. After all, bottled water shipped directly from the shrine arrived in church-authorized boxes, while certain piety shops and makers of religious goods such as the Alliance Catholique came to establish themselves as trusted brands. Commercialization itself, assisted by the Church, not only delegitimated peddling but recast large-scale entrepreneurs as authentic bearers of religious commerce.

COMMERCIALIZED PILGRIMAGE UNDER FIRE

The problems of commerce at Lourdes commanded the attention of more than simply clerical authorities and devout pilgrims. As the government of the Third Republic became engaged in a fierce battle with the Catholic Church, Lourdes loomed as a lightning rod in debates throughout the republican press. By the 1890s, anticlerical newspapers were devoting large numbers of articles to presenting the shrine's popularity as a serious problem. Émile Zola was largely responsible for sparking this public debate. While vacationing in the Pyrenees in 1891, the writer had passed through Lourdes during the height of the pilgrimage season. Impressed by "the spectacle of this world of deluded believers," he decided to write a novel about the modern pilgrimage experience and returned the following year to participate in a national pilgrimage. Zola's visit to the shrine, and the subsequent publication of his novel *Lourdes* as part of the *Trois Villes* trilogy, generated enormous publicity, providing anticlerical republicans with an opportunity to scrutinize, debate, and ultimately condemn the development of mass pilgrimage. Harping on the Church's ability to sell Lourdes as a vacation spot and to market religious goods to a mass audience, republican journalists presented Lourdes as a dire threat to the health of the Third Republic. These critics focused on commercialized pilgrimage as an unnatural amalgam of secular society and sacred ritual. Because it combined market huckster-ism with an irrational and backward theology, Lourdes threatened to pollute the secular, civic-oriented public sphere that anticlericalists hoped to create. In the process, Lourdes evoked anxieties harbored by many republicans about the political and social consequences of market capitalism.

When Zola first announced his plans to write a novel about Lourdes, he proclaimed to the Parisian press that, in spite of his history as a religious skeptic and freethinker, he would remain open and impartial toward the events at the sacred site. Yet the writer was clearly no disinterested observer of mass pilgrimage. Responding to a growing interest in mysticism and in Catholicism among Parisian writers and intellectuals, Zola wrote *Lourdes* largely to defend scientific positivism and his own brand of literary naturalism. Anticlerical journalists were less interested in these loftier concerns, seizing on Zola's interest in the shrine as a convenient occasion to attack the Church. Much of their ensuing coverage of Lourdes took the form of bald satire. Yet these anti-Lourdes diatribes also contained a palpable sense of alarm over the successful use of mass pilgrimage to attract and entertain pilgrims with new forms of public religious spectacle.[23]

An 1893 article, "The Virgin for Sale: Scapulars, Cookies, Candies, and Bene-dictions," in the notoriously anticlerical *La Lanterne* resonated with this mock-ing yet worried tone. The author began with ironic praise for the French clergy's ability to profit from religious worship: "The clerics, who invented indul-gences . . . and direct tickets to heaven (round-trip), are savvy salesmen; we must give them their due." Turning his focus to the Lourdes shrine, the jour-nalist described the new commercial activities now undertaken by the Church: "The businesses at Lourdes no longer operate as before, now they have put into action the Blessed Virgin of this country to incorporate a limited company with variable capital from the products of Lourdes." Listing the diverse products sold at the sanctuary, the article moved from traditional objects of piety to more re-cent innovations: "To begin with, there are the scapulars, the rosaries, the medals, etc., then come the Bearnaise waffles, the Saint-Mary vanilla cookies, the Lourdes lozenges, the Virgins, Christs, saints covered in chocolate or barley sugar. All this will be blessed." Casting its critique of commercialization in an appeal to common sense, the article concluded by explicitly condemning the sanctuary's offensive yet highly successful retail trade: "We are not inventing this; our information is authentic. What fate is in store for this kind of enterprise? We will ignore it. But there are so many imbeciles on earth that it is quite possible that it will do a thriving business."[24] The power of the critique lay in presenting the Church's activities as strangely inappropriate because they aped the business practices of the modern corporation. When a religious order began to act like a business, it disgraced itself and the Catholic religion. In another article in *La Lanterne,* a journalist lamented that the Grotto fathers missed no chance to make money for their sanctuary. Even the success of Zola's novel, unwittingly, "has suggested to the clergy the idea of profiting from the publicity created by the author of the Rougon-Macquart series for the grotto of Bernadette Soubirous in order to start up, itself, a little business." Once again the republican daily registered concern over the Church's uncanny ability to use the products of the secular world, this time a novel by one of France's greatest freethinkers, to its own advantage.[25]

It would be easy to overlook the significance of such barbs. Although there was hardly anything new in leveling charges of simony against representatives of the Church, these attacks registered a fresh anxiety about the Church's relationship to commercial life. Republicans were not simply complaining about the ability of clerics to profit from traditional religious practices; these secular journalists were outraged that the Church was luring the public to Lourdes with the aid of modern advertising techniques and the mechanical reproduction of religious goods. What bothered anticlerical journalists about the Church's commercial activities at Lourdes, then, was the explicitly modern nature of the practice. The missionaries ran the sanctuary the way a businessman directed a modern corporation. They engaged in clever marketing of religious items to maximize profits. It was the inappropriateness of using new kinds of commercial practices to promote antimodern religious worship that fueled these tirades.

An article published in *Le Journal* demonstrates this anxiety quite explicitly. Attacking a church booklet called *Lourdes: Yesterday, Today, and Tomorrow* for successfully selling the sanctuary as a vacation spot, the author proclaimed that a religious order was now using a secular publishing house to produce and sell this professionally designed pilgrimage guidebook. Seeking to discredit these promotional tactics, the article observed: "This order begins to manage Lourdes as others might run a seaside resort or a spa." The problem, said the author, was that this brochure "resembles, almost to perfection, those exquisitely illustrated brochures prepared by the railroad companies to excite the tourist." His concern was provoked by schemes to attract the faithful into making the pilgrimage: "It is curious to see the Church . . . using new procedures for calling crowds to its sanctuaries."[26] In effect, religion became more dangerous when it was merged with these new commercial practices. If the Church promoted Lourdes like any other tourist site, then secular-minded citizens might be attracted to the shrine. Republicans feared that this use of modern advertising in the service of Catholic superstition could lure the gullible masses into the hands of the Church. French elites had already discovered that secular businesses, especially the new Parisian department stores, wielded a powerful tool in advertising to dazzle and mislead the populace.[27] In the hands of the Church, such a tool became a destructive weapon against the secularizing policies of the nation.

Republican fears about church-led advertising were directed, not surprisingly, toward the extraordinarily successful merchandising of goods containing Lourdes water. Anticlerical journalists interpreted the array of novel Lourdes products as a sign of the infiltration of Catholic superstition into secular society. A journalist writing for *Le XIXe Siècle* claimed to have investigated one religious shop based in Paris that sold these products. The reporter was outraged to find bottled Lourdes water selling for the inflated price of two francs per liter, and he was even more unnerved to see syrups, soaps, and wines bearing "Notre-Dame de Lourdes" on the label. The shop also sold the famous Pastilles de Lourdes, which prompted the journalist to lament how similar they looked to the fashionable Pastilles de Vichy. It was bad enough that the religious shops overcharged the devout for bottled Lourdes water, but it was worse for them to market products such as soap and wine with the Lourdes name. Such goods confused the public and promoted superstitious beliefs. The author made his contempt for these products known by suggesting that, since the shopkeeper insisted that they had therapeutic powers, such goods needed to be taxed as "pharmaceutical specialties." If religious shops were going to try to sell these kinds of products on the open market, then they should pay the same kind of taxes that any pharmaceutical enterprise would pay.[28]

The depiction of the commercial life of the shrine found in Zola's *Lourdes* represents a particularly vivid example of an ardent republican grappling with his own discomfort with the mixing of religion and commerce. Interestingly, Zola's novel turned out not to be an unabashed attack on Lourdes. Rather, it tried to show why religion still played such an important role in the lives of those who suffered, those without hope. With nearly a hundred characters, the novel traced the journey of pilgrims, priests, doctors, and other curious visitors who came to Lourdes for a national pilgrimage. Zola presented, in effect, two sides of the Lourdes shrine: the extraordinary fervor displayed by pilgrims who prayed, walked in processions, and bathed in the grotto pools and the shopkeepers who lured pilgrims with cheap sacred goods that were consumed in a delirious frenzy.

The religious commerce of Lourdes thus played a central role in the pilgrimage drama that unfolded in Zola's novel. In many ways, writing about Lourdes gave Zola another opportunity to bring together two subjects that had long fascinated him: the crowd and mass consumption.[29] Now, turning his attention to pilgrimage, he examined the impact of mass consumer practices on crowds of fervent Catholics. In an earlier novel, *Au Bonheur des dames,* Zola had registered concern over the "progress" represented by the Parisian department store; his analysis of the religious commerce at Lourdes transformed that concern into a palpable sense of alarm. The use of modern market practices to sell religious goods and services to a mass audience clearly turned progress on its head. The religious crowd was presented as a hysterical mob swept up in the frenzied acquisition of sacred objects:

> The thousands of pilgrims of the national pilgrimage streamed along the thoroughfares and besieged the shops in a final scramble. You would have taken the cries, the jostling, and the sudden rushes for those at some fair just breaking up amidst a ceaseless roll of vehicles. Many, providing themselves with provisions for the journey, cleared the open-air stalls where bread and slices of sausages and ham were sold. . . . But what the crowd more particularly purchased were religious articles, and those hawkers whose barrows were loaded with statuettes and sacred engravings were reaping golden gains.

It is notable that Zola did not resort to satire, as many republican journalists did, but his apparently objective descriptions of the religious commerce nevertheless betray a similar anxiety. Zola seemed unnerved by the desires to buy that were unleashed at Lourdes:

> And the fever of dealing, the pleasure of spending one's money, of returning home with one's pockets crammed with photographs and medals, lit up all the faces with a holiday expression, transforming the radiant gathering into a fair-field crowd with appetites either beyond control or satisfied.[30]

Such depictions of frenzied commercial desires made Lourdes appear not so much a traditional shrine as a religious fairground or holiday getaway. The vision seems to have disturbed Zola in part because this kind of religious site became unduly alluring to a French populace eager for inexpensive forms of recreation. Furthermore, Lourdes was particularly enticing to women and other "weak-willed" individuals, because they were already more susceptible to the lure of mass-produced goods. Incorporating the ideas of the new psychology that claimed women were innately irrational and easily suggestible, the writer portrayed the large crowds of female pilgrims as unwitting victims of the shrine's commercialized religiosity.[31] For Zola, then, the impacts of mass pilgrimage to Lourdes, where consumption and superstition colluded, produced an especially pernicious threat to the health of the republic. He was not the only one to feel this way. Almost ten years later, *La Lanterne* registered similar fears in a more hysterical tone when it blamed "poor stupefied women" and "fanatical imbeciles" for making the shrine so popular.[32]

Yet Zola also worried that the shrine's financial success compromised the republican principles of local politicians. In the writer's personal notes on his trip to Lourdes, he lamented that these town officials had bowed to the power of the sanctuary in order to keep the region economically prosperous.[33] Like the novel, such observations cast Lourdes as a new and dangerous religious phenomenon, one that enlisted modern commercial techniques not only to renovate the Catholic faith but to obscure the clear boundaries between a forward-looking republicanism and religious superstition. More nuanced than the anticlerical diatribes of journalists, Zola's work nevertheless offers a similar critique of the development of mass pilgrimage, depicting the shrine as frenzied, irrational, and antithetical to traditional religious worship. Lourdes, in short, revealed the corrupting influence of a modern market culture.

The attacks on Lourdes by Zola and by journalists pointed up republican discomfort with the shrine's blending of religion and commerce. Whereas this new amalgam made certain pilgrims concerned about the authenticity of sacred experience, such an admixture, for republicans, threatened to compromise the supposedly progressive and secular nature of modern capitalism. Indeed, while many republicans worried about the psychological and moral consequences of the marketplace, they also hoped to rein in its excesses to create a commercial culture that promoted civic-mindedness and other socially responsible values. Yet the example of Lourdes stood as a stern warning that the market served no single master. A powerful new tool, it could even be wielded by old enemies. Thus, the commerciality of Lourdes, often an easy target, also threatened to undermine republicans in their war against an "antimodern" Church. Accustomed to assailing the Church as a bastion of reactionary superstition, the republican press was forced to concede that new technologies and advertising techniques seemed exceptionally well-suited for religious purposes. The determination to keep religion separate from modern commercial life—and thus to distinguish clearly between secular-minded republicans and reactionary Catholics—was becoming more difficult to sustain.

Other factors also help to explain the anticlerical revulsion toward a commercialized Lourdes. Mixing profane commercial practices with the sacred act of pilgrimage not only challenged hopes for a progressive capitalism but also frustrated republican desires to confine religious life within a private sphere, where it could be properly maintained by women and imparted to young children.[34] Historians have often interpreted the anticlerical campaigns of the late nineteenth century as an unambiguous attempt to destroy the Church. Yet while a number of radical republicans were determined to eradicate Catholic influence in all social arenas, many anticlericals held more ambivalent feelings toward religion. Thomas Kselman, in *Death and the Afterlife in Modern France,* has shown that more than a few secular-minded republicans wished to see religion play a significant role in funerals and the mourning of the dead; otherwise, they feared, an emerging professionalized funeral industry would corrupt the sacred rituals surrounding death. In this sense, "the language of anticlericalism and Church-State conflict that shaped" the republican debate over funeral reform "was inadequate to capture and express the sentiments of politicians who desired to preserve the religious dimension of funerals even while they restricted the role of Catholicism."[35] These same concerns to save religious life from the perversions of the market seem apparent in the anticlerical attacks against Lourdes as well. Yet whereas Kselman concludes that the language of anticlericalism inhibited republicans from finding a way to preserve religion, I want to suggest that this anticlerical discourse—in which commercial life and sacred ritual are starkly incompatible—enabled republicans to portray religion as antithetical to modernity. By deploying a rhetoric of religious debasement, then, republicans struggled to reinscribe religion within a private, "traditional" realm and to relegate its practices to the margins of modern political and economic life.

A sense of nostalgia thus pervaded the anticlerical rhetoric of the republican press. Although journalists were clearly mocking the Church when they lampooned newfangled products or modern advertising techniques, these writers also appeared to regret the passing of a peasant religious culture that they perceived as aesthetically pleasing. An article in the moderate republican weekly *L'Illustration* in 1894 encapsulated a strikingly deep suspicion toward a new market culture that appeared to know no bounds. The author, inspired by the publication of Zola's novel that same year, visited the sacred shrine to provide his own journalistic account. Having already visited Lourdes twelve years earlier, the journalist, M. Meys, used his previous experience at the site to gauge how much things had changed. As Meys described the newly bustling atmosphere of the train station, the opulence of the hotels and shops along the main boulevards, and the evident wealth of the Lourdes inhabitants, his narrative account became a searing indictment of commercialized religion. Marveling that Bernadette, "who had unconsciously enriched Lourdes, was soon condemned to disappear completely," Meys declared her "crushed, as it were, under a growing avalanche of freestone churned up by speculation." Making matters worse, Bernadette's own family was participating in this crassly driven operation. Meys complained that each and every family member sought to capitalize on the Soubirous name, noting with scorn the sign that hung from a modest building declaring "Home of the son of the sister of Bernadette Soubirous, wine to go, rooms to rent." Yet the journalist's most biting comments followed a description of his search for a sacred memento, "some figurine as only the artisans of the Middle Ages . . . knew how to make." Frustrated in this quest, Meys lamented that "progress has changed all that. The triumph of machinery, of perfected tools, permits one today to 'create' with notable economy a hundred medals or dozens of statuettes and rosaries." Such commercialism, he concluded ruefully, now inspired some two hundred thousand pilgrims to visit Lourdes each year.[36]

Zola also expressed dismay over the aesthetic dimensions of the changes at Lourdes. In the journal he used to record personal observations during his 1892 visit to the shrine, he remarked that "if Bernadette returned, she would no longer recognize a thing." Development had not only transformed the grotto but robbed the site of its natural beauty: "What is really ugly is the piety shop that stands close by to the left [of the grotto]. Beyond the issue of simony, it destabilizes the frame of the grotto, which would have been worth conserving in its verdant setting. It is truly ugly." He found the basilica, as well, to be an aberrant creation, with its electric lights, hundreds of banners, and bibelots: "The effect is very shimmering but not especially religious." These pointed remarks about the aesthetic aspects of Lourdes also betray Zola's own assumptions about the proper appearance of a religious shrine. Lourdes failed to meet his expectations of what an authentic sacred site should be, suffering in comparison to the majestic shrines of the past or the unadorned local holy sites still dotting the landscape of rural France. The presence of the modern—whether in the form of church design or the bustle of a retail shop—was wholly out of place.[37]

Zola further observed a certain moral decline that resulted from the new pilgrimage industry at Lourdes. Again, many of his complaints focused on the behavior of women, who seemed to be utterly corrupted by the commercialization of religious life. In his journal, he noted with regret that all the local girls adopted loose morals when they began to participate in the religious commerce surrounding the site:

> The town is becoming demoralized as it expands. Mores have completely changed. Formerly, there were no more than five or six low-living women available to young men, who were forced to wait in line, whereas now such women swarm the place. . . . All the young women give themselves over to selling candles and flowers. . . . [They] make a lot of money, and indulge in habits of idleness, doing nothing more for the coming winter. Add to that the transient population, all the coachmen who fill the city, and almost all the girls prostitute themselves.

Conflating women's participation in religious retailing with their entrance into sexual prostitution, Zola seemed to suggest that one form of commerce led seamlessly to the other. The author also appeared to believe that Lourdes sparked immoral behavior in female pilgrims themselves, noting in his journal that "the female volunteers and other women are completely free, coming alone under the pretext of religious devotion. And they can meet with whomever they please." Once again, Zola's expectations for what constituted "proper" religious behavior were confounded by the pilgrimage site.[38] Although Zola was hardly interested in returning to some golden age of religious virtue, he seemed patently distressed by the moral implications of commercial activity at the religious shrine. Mixing two worlds produced dangerous consequences for thousands of pilgrims, mostly women, who came to Lourdes.

THE RHETORIC OF RELIGIOUS DEBASEMENT

Critical response to the modernity of Lourdes, whether offered from inside or outside the Church, centered mostly on the shrine's relationship to modern market practices. Ordinary Catholics, as we saw earlier, voiced diffuse yet palpable concerns over certain commercial activities, while anticlerical republicans betrayed considerable unease over a sacred site that seemed to confound secularist critiques of religion's antimodern essence. Yet more than either group, it was male Catholic intellectuals who transformed these varied anxieties into articulate and highly public condemnations of the problems of modern religious practice. Writers such as Léon Bloy and Joris-Karl Huysmans, well-known contributors to a Catholic literary revival in late nineteenth-century France, delivered the most stinging rebukes.

These authors criticized the Church for its shameless marketing of the shrine but also reproached the "ignorant" masses for embracing commercialized forms of worship. Female pilgrims, once more, were singled out as the root cause of the problems of Lourdes. So easily tempted by the material pleasures that now abounded at the site, these women were said to spend hours buying religious goods or showing off their fancy dresses and ornate rosaries to the crowds around them. French clerics and intellectuals such as Bloy and Huysmans condemned such behavior, combining new scientific ideas about female irrationality with older notions of women's weak morals to epitomize the perversion of religious worship. In doing so, they began to express more fully what had only been implicit in earlier responses to the shrine: a nostalgic longing for a purer spirituality. Their critiques of the Lourdes pilgrimages constructed a discourse of religious debasement. Predicated on an opposition between religion and modernity, such a discourse depicted true devotion as devoid of secular influence. By the early twentieth century, this rhetoric of debasement articulated an idealized vision of the religious past in which peasants had engaged in unadorned worship free from the depredations of commerce.

The first inklings of a Catholic critique linking Lourdes to modern forms of religious debasement can be seen in the writings of French clerics who sought to shield the holy site from public attacks. During the 1890s, when Lourdes had become a target of mounting ridicule in the republican press, members of the French clergy often took it upon themselves to defend the sanctuary from accusations of economic exploitation. Pleading their case primarily to a Catholic audience, they wrote articles for religious journals and published books with church-affiliated presses describing their own experiences at Lourdes. Such accounts typically sought to "normalize" the commercial culture of the sanctuary, either by affirming its place in an established pilgrimage tradition or by drawing attention to its role within the accepted customs of an emerging resort-town tourism. These writers assured Catholics that the trade in religious goods and the commercialized leisure activities surrounding the pilgrimage did not undermine the holiness of the site. Yet even as these clerics defended pilgrimage from charges of exploitation, they were forced to concede that Lourdes was engendering a new form of public religiosity that could not be fully controlled. Listing all sorts of problems, from pickpockets and swindlers to displays of petty vanity and unbridled pleasure-seeking by pilgrims, these clerics revealed their own discomfort with a religious shrine that catered to a mass audience.

One defender of the shrine, the Chanoine Jules Didiot, hoped to refute the republican allegations of exploitation and abuse that followed Zola's visit to Lourdes. Writing for the Catholic *Revue de Lille* in 1893, the cleric granted that the holy site of the grotto had experienced extraordinary commercial development since the apparitions were first recognized by the Church. He acknowledged the multitude of hotels and piety shops, along with other stunning physical changes. Didiot insisted, however, that this kind of commercial life was "very useful to keep and develop" because it stimulated the pilgrimages to Lourdes. This "economic usefulness," he maintained, "finds itself clearly in harmony with Catholic faith and devotion. It makes one think of God easily, sweetly, and almost continually." True, members of Bernadette's family did use the Soubirous name to attract visitors to their shops and hotels, and friends of the visionary now sold photographic prints of Bernadette in ecstasy. Yet these activities were "neither bad, odd, nor indiscreet" because "this advertising, after all, is neither garish nor flashy." As for peddlers and beggars, these questionable types could be seen in any locale. They were simply part of modern life.[39]

The cleric then turned to the real problems of the shrine, "the mocking impiety, the audacious and foolish voluptuousness, the luxury and frivolity without taste or tact" that he had witnessed at Lourdes. Although it is not clear precisely whom Didiot was referring to, one point was unambiguous: Catholics should not be concerned about merchants selling religious goods or poor people begging for alms, but, instead, must seek to "forbid first the pleasure-seekers and pickpockets from coming there."[40] If Didiot meant to reassure his readers, he had done so by revealing a more troubling problem. Blithely asserting that certain forms of religious commerce were a normal part of any pilgrimage, he nevertheless invoked other commercial realities—the visitors who came to Lourdes in search of pleasure, reveling in its luxuries, and the thieves who sought to swindle and steal from the devout—that represented a far less acceptable side of modern pilgrimage.

Didiot was not the only cleric to justify Lourdes in ways that raised questions about the shrine. One year later, in 1894, another member of the French clergy published a defense of the shrine that betrayed a similar feeling of unease over the commercialized culture of pilgrimage. Written by the Abbé Domenech for a Catholic publishing house, *Lourdes, hommes et choses* served as both a manual for pilgrims and a personal meditation on the meaning of the shrine. Like Didiot, Domenech wished to defend Lourdes from what, by now, were common complaints. Many pilgrims, he had heard, felt cheated by Lourdes merchants and hotel owners, who were said routinely to overcharge customers for goods and services during the pilgrimage season. Domenech explained that Lourdes functioned much like any other tourist site. The rise in prices during the summer months of the pilgrimage season was a natural consequence of masses of people descending at once on the holy site. The priest reminded his readers: "One must not forget that in the Pyrenees, just as much as in Switzerland, along the seaside and in the thermal-spa towns, the inhabitants have only three or four months to earn their yearly bread from strangers." Like Didiot, then, Domenech sought to familiarize Catholic pilgrims with the commercial rhythms of the site. After all, Lourdes could hardly be expected to cater to such large numbers—and thereby remain the most important source of divine wonders in the modern world—if it did not follow the business practices of any seasonal trade.[41]

Yet conceding that Lourdes functioned like any modern resort town put Domenech in a difficult position. He did not want to argue that Lourdes was a resort town but, on the contrary, that it was a religious sanctuary. Thus Domenech took pains to assert that the commerce, while legitimate and even beneficial, was separate from the religious life of the shrine. Reminding readers that an ancient fort perched on a large rock separated the city from the grotto, he intoned: "This rock serves as a curtain that providentially separates the dwelling place of men from that of Mary, who came eighteen times to shake up the world, commanding prayer and penance."[42] Despite the resort-like conditions of life in the town, the grotto maintained the holiness of a sacred place.

The abbé could hardly deny, however, that the shrine's popularity had unleashed certain behaviors that profaned the religious site. Complaining bitterly that visitors had transformed the shrine into a place of cosmopolitan people watching, Domenech lamented: "Tourists and curious onlookers sometimes turn the esplanade [of the Basilica] into a picnic area, a gossip beach, a street scene out of the boulevard des Italiens [a fashionable street in Paris]." Still more troubling to the priest was the behavior of the faithful. Exposed to the many pleasures of the city, pilgrims seeking penance too often became tourists on holiday. Although Domenech saw nothing wrong, for example, with the Grotto fathers selling votive candles, rosaries, and other trinkets in a shop near the grotto, he confessed that this shop was "very poorly located," its customers making "a deplorable racket, distracting and disturbing those who pray." Even worse, he said, were the many pious women who dared to "parade their fashions before the good Lord." These bourgeois women "adorn themselves in worldly attire" while praying at the site, their vanity responsible for the rise in petty crime at the grotto: "Thieves, especially female thieves, take advantage of this fashion show to gather an ample harvest of change purses." Thus the "providential" physical separation of sacred and profane at Lourdes failed to prevent even pilgrims themselves from debasing the spirituality of the site. So long as "all were free to watch, sit, eat, drink, and stroll around the rocks of Massabielle," Lourdes remained all too open to the unhealthy influence of the world.[43]

Efforts by French clerics to normalize the commercial culture of Lourdes depended on presenting the realm of religious goods and services as compatible with—but separate from—religious worship at the grotto. Yet even as these authors argued this case they betrayed their own fears that mass pilgrimage produced very unsettling consequences for religious devotion. Lourdes seemed, in fact, to replicate the very ills they associated with modern urban life: the seductions of Parisian boulevard culture, the displays of worldly consumption, the anxieties of the anonymous crowd. As for women, who seemed especially vulnerable to the sins of commercial culture, the clerics feared that female predominance at the shrine might even despoil the grotto itself. Revealing a grave discomfort over the impact of mass pilgrimage, these published defenses of Lourdes were clearly unable to resolve the tensions and doubts over new forms of modern devotional practice.

Ambivalence gave way, at times, to outright critique. It should not come as a surprise that several members of France's Catholic literary elite developed a more explicit condemnation of the Lourdes pilgrimages. The men associated with the Catholic literary revival of the late nineteenth century—Léon Bloy, Joris-Karl Huysmans, Charles Péguy, and Paul Claudel among them—were often harsh critics of the Church, calling for a return to an austere type of Christian worship. Many of these men had embraced Catholicism late in life, converting to the faith after a prolonged period of malaise or crisis. As new converts, they adopted an uncompromising form of Catholicism that rejected the ways and philosophies of the modern world. Condemning French republicanism, capitalist materialism, and scientific positivism, they also disdained the more liberal pontificate of Leo XIII, who reversed the antimodern policies of Pius IX and called on French Catholics to rally to the republic. Although these intellectuals despised the new conciliatory attitude of the papacy, they were equally critical of popular forms of devotion being promoted by religious orders such as the Assumptionists, whose reactionary political views they shared. The Assumptionist order's embrace of new religious practices and aesthetics, especially the vogue for mass-produced religious statues and objects dubbed "l'art sulpicien," made its kind of popular worship objectionable to the Catholic literary elite.[44] This devotional culture, now increasingly linked to Lourdes, too easily accommodated the intrusions of the modern world. Associated most prominently with bourgeois women, it was seen as soft and feminizing, promoting a sentimental theology that denied the spiritual importance of suffering. For these critics, then, rejection of Lourdes was implicated in a nostalgic longing for a strain of Catholic worship that they attributed to the past.[45]

Léon Bloy was an especially acrimonious commentator on the shrine. Best known for his Catholic novels *Le Désespéré* and *La Femme pauvre*, Bloy suggested that Lourdes constituted an example of all that was wrong with the modern Church. Lourdes embodied a religious sentimentalism that Bloy found particularly intolerable, destroying a simple yet heartfelt spirituality that once had sustained the common people. "The sacrilegious stupidity of the Sulpicians," he observed, "has effaced the naive, dusty images of an antique and popular piety, and the suffering poor no longer know where to turn." Lamenting the new forms of worship promoted by the Church, Bloy also raged against a Catholic laity that seemed, by the 1890s, to exhibit an alarming lack of piety. In response to disrespectful behavior that he observed at Montparnasse Cemetery on a particular All Saints' Day, he mused sarcastically on the debased future of religious sites: "Why doesn't an advertising agency use the tombs as they do urinal walls or omnibuses? People could read the ad for a new chocolate or an American toothpaste on the grave slabs."[46] For Bloy, the encroachment of modern market practices was the ultimate sign of a corrupted faith.

Bloy's criticisms of Lourdes also stemmed from his preference for the apparitions that had occurred at La Salette in 1846.[47] There, a weeping Virgin had called on France to repent or bear the brunt of great suffering and pain. The significance of this message, Bloy feared, was being lost as the pilgrimages to Lourdes gained in popularity. Although he never disputed that the Virgin had appeared to Bernadette, Bloy did resent the fact that Bernadette's apparitions received so much attention while the more sobering apparitions of Mélanie and Maximin were increasingly ignored:

> The Church itself appears to have forgotten this extraordinary event [the visions of La Salette]. The Roman missal has, each February 11, a commemorative mass for the Apparitions of Lourdes, which seems all-comforting, neither accusing nor threatening anyone. The Apparition of La Salette . . . has received nothing. The honey of modern devotion found it too bitter.

Bloy attributed La Salette's secondary status to a larger problem: modern Catholics lacked the will to suffer, preferring a theology that consoled and comforted. Linking the Virgin of Lourdes to a sugarcoated religiosity he despised, Bloy openly rejected worship of Our Lady of Lourdes:

> I cannot picture to myself the Mother of the Sorrowing Christ in the kindly light of Lourdes. . . . I feel no attraction toward an Immaculate Conception crowned with roses, robed in white, cinctured in blue, amid sweet music and perfumes. . . . What I require is an Immaculate Conception crowned with thorns, My Lady of La Salette, the Immaculate Conception with the stigmata, blood-drenched, pale and desolate, terrible amid her tears and her chains . . . as all the Middle Ages saw her.

Bloy also blamed the ecclesiastical authorities, though not explicitly, for promoting a corrupted version of Bernadette's apparitions. "By quackery, mediocrity, and avarice," he proclaimed, "the Enemy has tried to desecrate the unique spot where stands affirmed the mystery which he must hold in greatest abhorrence: the Immaculate Conception."[48] The very popularity of the Lourdes pilgrimages symbolized the failures of modern-day Catholicism: a weak clergy more interested in material prosperity than in saving souls, and a laity that embraced a sentimentalized Virgin who promoted mindless prayer. Rejecting Lourdes in favor of La Salette, Bloy turned his back on the institutional Catholicism of his day in order to embrace the notion of an older, harsher religious tradition.

If Bloy articulated an unusually frank Catholic rejection of Lourdes, it was Joris-Karl Huysmans who provided the most sustained yet complicated critique of the shrine from within the faith. Once a disciple of Zola, Huysmans made a name for himself as a Romantic-decadent novelist, before becoming, by the turn of the century, a devout believer interested in using his exacting naturalist style to affirm the presence of the mysterious and supernatural in the modern world.[49] In pursuit of this mission, Huysmans developed, over the final decade of his life, an abiding fascination with the grotto of Lourdes. In his novels *La Cathedrale* (1898) and *Les Foules de Lourdes* (1906), as well as in his personal correspondence, he expressed outrage at the commercialization of the shrine along with a deep affection for the display of public devotion embodied in mass pilgrimage. Like Bloy, Huysmans attacked the burgeoning presence of the market that was so apparent at the Lourdes shrine.[50] Disgusted by the growing commercialization of religion, he was contemptuous of Catholic believers—clergy and laity—who embraced comfort over suffering and compromise over conflict. Yet, unlike Bloy, Huysmans did not simply reject the pilgrimages to Lourdes as a debased manifestation of modern worship. Instead, he struggled to understand the intrusions of the secular world into the religious realm as part of God's divine purpose to re-Christianize France. In *La Cathedrale*, for instance, Huysmans seemed to respond implicitly to Bloy's outright rejection of Lourdes with a more conciliatory attitude, searching for something sublime amid the sacrileges. In the first few pages of the novel, the pious hero, Durtal, muses over the fact that La Salette has "fallen into disrepute," only to be replaced by Lourdes. Durtal is confused by God's seeming preference for a pilgrimage site that is "the exact opposite of La Salette"; even more, he is astounded to find "Jesus condescending to make use of the wretched arts of human commerce, adopting the repulsive tricks which we employ to float a manufacture or a business." Durtal wonders if God is not providing the ultimate lesson in humility by "using our own devices that He may make Himself heard and obeyed." Because of the corruption of modern society, Durtal surmises, God must use the vulgar arts of man—"the American abominations of our day"—to communicate with a fallen people. In *La Cathedrale,* Huysmans struggled to envision such a melding of the material and the spiritual as one of the many mysteries of God.[51]

Huysmans was unable to reconcile himself fully, however, to the view that God was responsible for mixing sacred and profane in the practices of the Church. At the time Huysmans composed *La Cathedrale,* the writer had yet to visit Lourdes. After visiting the pilgrimage site in 1903 and again the following year, he no longer perceived God's mysteries at work in the vulgar trafficking of religious goods. Instead, he blamed the devil, "the Evil One," for "utilising the meanness of man's nature and his lack of faith . . . in the prostitution of the divine" at Lourdes.[52] Nevertheless, Huysmans remained moved by the sacred aura of the grotto itself, and claimed to gain inspiration from witnessing crowds of pilgrims praying day and night for the sick to be healed. His private correspondence reveals the intensity of his conflicted feelings. On the one hand, Lourdes represented the worst aspects of modern Catholicism. He found the sanctuary unbearably ugly, declaring that the basilica created a "religion peculiar to this place, a religion of . . . gold paint and electric light." He also lamented, in a letter to his friend Henry Céard, that the inhabitants of Lourdes had "given up work to sell sausages and rosaries and bleed the pilgrims dry." On the other hand, Lourdes could also inspire. Huysmans claimed, in a letter to the Abbé Mugnier, that the shrine genuinely re-created the religious fervor of the medieval world: "I am walking, eating, and sleeping to the sound of 'Ave Marias' going on day and night. Imagine a town of eight thousand inhabitants with forty thousand pilgrims sleeping, as in the Middle Ages, in the churches, for want of room, and again as in the Middle Ages, astonishing diseases, cases of elephantiasis and leprosy."[53] For Huysmans, who reveled in the most extreme forms of worship and embraced an ethos of suffering and denial, the presence of constant prayers and the extraordinary attention given to the diseased and dying were intensely affecting. These activities made Lourdes an "authentic" site of pilgrimage, resonating with his own vision of a lost piety that he longed to see rekindled.

This tension between the shrine's vile modernity and its capacity to re-create a lost worship from the Middle Ages became the theme of the final novel of Huysmans. Published less than a year before his death, *Les Foules de Lourdes* (*The Crowds of Lourdes*) explored the extremes of worship born of mass pilgrimage, in a work that was not so much a novel as a sustained diatribe. Employing a first-person narrative, Huysmans relied on caustic humor and hyperbole to weave together a history of the shrine's development with his own experiences there. Huysmans saw himself as presenting an unsparing view of the "real" Lourdes, from the heights of religious rapture to the depths of degradation that he had witnessed. He hoped his novel would shatter the sentimentalized myths about Bernadette and the heroic people of Lourdes perpetuated by Lasserre's *Notre-Dame de Lourdes,* while also challenging Zola's one-dimensional depiction of the shrine.[54] Huysmans acknowledged that the religious shrine suffered grievously from crass commercialism and the vulgarity of contemporary design. But Lourdes also brought the faithful together in one place of prayer, reviving worship of an intensity that had not been seen since the medieval world. The tension between religion and modernity set the terms for his view of the site. All that he hated stemmed from the shrine's unfortunate association with contemporary life. All that he found virtuous and sublime was linked to older traditions of Catholic pilgrimage that Lourdes had reinvigorated.

From the first pages of the novel, Huysmans directed particular disgust at the architecture and religious art of the sanctuary. His bitter critique of the shrine's modern appearance was rooted in its failure to resemble a medieval cathedral or a quaint rural pilgrimage site. The offense was more than bad taste; Huysmans was outraged that the basilica reminded him of the urban world he wished to leave behind. When gazing on the new Rosary Basilica, all he could see was "the Hippodrome" or "a religious casino." He compared the structure to a "rotunda for locomotives; only the rails and the central turn-table are wanting, instead of the high altar, to enable the engines to come out of the side-wings and to perform their evolutions on the broad walks of the Esplanade." The interior of the basilica was no better; Huysmans compared it to "the hall of a theatre" and "a bric-a-brac shop." What especially distressed him was the use of electricity inside the church. Lamenting the "hundreds of electric light bulbs lit up at night, with their shattering gleams refracted from the gilding and the marbles of the walls," he insisted that such a scene made "you . . . believe yourself to be anywhere . . . except in a church." For Huysmans, a pilgrimage was supposed to be a retreat, but so much of the sanctuary brought forth vulgar reminders of the modern world. The intrusion of modern technology in a sacred place was particularly distressing, not only because it destroyed the aura of a holy site but because it desecrated the very theology of the Church: "It is, indeed, a real contradiction to make use of inanimate lights where Christ dwells whose living image is light: it also means that the Church is doing away with the indispensable sign of Charity, of which fire is the emblem."[55]

In *The Crowds of Lourdes*, Huysmans was equally disturbed by the built environment of the town. Just a moment's walk from the grotto, one encountered a bustling town that rivaled even Paris in its frenzied street life and urban chaos. From the terrace of a Lourdes café, the "spectacle" of sacred and secular images "to be seen . . . is more entertaining and varied than that which can be viewed from any café on the boulevards." Huysmans continued:

Lourdes in all its cosmopolitanism files past you. . . . Waves from the crowds overflow from the street onto the pavements . . . the trams run past with a metallic sound, unceasingly blowing their horns to clear the rails; a telegraph office . . . is full of invaders: there is a perpetual coming and going of those who are entering and leaving it. All around us floats an odor of dust and vanilla. . . . Street urchins run along shouting "*Le Journal de la Grotte*! The latest miracles!" Bold-eyed little girls try to wheedle passersby out of half pence; nuns file past with downcast eyes, saying their rosaries . . . and now a tram is on its way down, crammed with women.

After this intense urban setting became too much, an attempted escape into the pastoral landscape outside the town was also foiled by intrusions from the modern world. As the writer gazed upon the Pic du Grand Jer, a Pyrenean mountain renowned for its pristine beauty, he was distracted by "what looks like a white worm creeping upwards; it is the funicular railway, climbing sometimes in open daylight, sometimes through the dark tunnels, to the top." At a later point in the novel, as Huysmans wandered about the countryside, he stumbled across a little valley where "you might think you were thousands of miles away from any inhabited region and where nature runs absolutely wild." Yet even here, a moment of serenity was shortly ruined by "the telegraph posts placed here and there amidst the ups and downs of the slopes, and the sound of quarrymen's hammers, which tells you that they are gradually quarrying out hollow gaps in the mountains-sides." Clearly no aspect of the pilgrimage experience was safe from invasion by forces of the modern world.[56]

Huysmans saved his greatest invective for the corrupting role played by modern commerce at the shrine. Vivid descriptions evoke the feverish buying and selling of religious goods, which the novel portrays as a debasement of the true meaning of pilgrimage. How were pilgrims to engage in acts of penance and prayer, as the Virgin had requested, when they were constantly being tempted by the pleasures of the material world? Even worse was the ever-increasing supply of sacred kitsch that engulfed the crowds:

> Not a single shop is without its medals and candles and rosaries and scapulars and pamphlets full of miracles; both old and new Lourdes are crammed with them; even the hotels have them on sale; and that goes on in street after street for miles, starting from old Lourdes with the poor woman who hawks little rosaries with steel chains and crosses and huge characteristic Lourdes rosaries of chocolate-coloured wood . . . and harshly tinted chromos of Bernadette kneeling taper in hand at the Virgin's feet, and Lilliputian statues and medals . . . and all these things grow better and bigger and larger as you get nearer the new town; the statues swarm increasingly and end by becoming, not less ugly, but enormous.

For Huysmans, this never-ending wave of goods seemed to overwhelm the pilgrims. As the crowds became swept up in their desires for religious merchandise, they lost all rational control: "And then begins a frantic competition; you are hooked in at every step by the shops all over the town; and you go to and from and turn this way and that amidst the tumult." Female pilgrims, whose materialistic impulses were the obverse of the Virgin's spiritual purity, appeared to be particularly susceptible to the lure of religious goods: "The shops full of pious trinkets hypnotise the women, and they have to be dragged away by the arm or pushed in the back to get them to move on."[57]

Mass pilgrimage created, for Huysmans, an elaborate commercial life that reduced the shrine to a market bazaar. Although Huysmans had clearly intended to refute Zola's portrait of the shrine as a site of debased piety, his own work reinscribed a similar view of commerce and corruption. As his novel charted manifestations of religious debasement, the theme of commodified spirituality took on a position of central importance. Now that the ordinary person could come to Lourdes, the religious site had been spoiled, its precious aura lost. Instead, masses of pilgrims lined up outside the basilica as if they were waiting for a theater performance, or they treated the esplanade of the sanctuary as their own personal picnic grounds: "returning from the town with bread and sausages and wine . . . families seated on the grass are taking a snack together; it is like a Sunday in the Bois de Vincennes, with the sherds of broken bottles and greasy scraps of paper all around."[58] Such behavior could only have a detrimental effect on the way one worshipped at Lourdes. It became impossible to carry out religious ceremonies with an air of serious meditation amid the festive atmosphere of the shrine. In light of the "regular whirl of Masses at express speed" and the impossibility of getting near the grotto during the high season, "if one wants to pray . . . the best plan is to stay at home." More disturbing, the act of devotion at the site easily became a mere performance without any real sentiment behind it. Here, too, Huysmans seemed to be reinforcing Zola's theme of feminine corruption by focusing on women as the worst culprits of this new and frightening type of modern religious worship. As he described it, female pilgrims "vie with one another as to who will say the most [rosaries], as to who will swill the largest quantity of water, as to who will oftenest make the Stations of the Cross." He witnessed women who "file through the Grotto and touch the rock . . . not only with their rosaries and medals, but even with trinkets that have nothing to do with worship, such as cigar-holders . . . doubtless in order to sanctify the lips of her fortunate husband!" Perhaps this devotional act, he conceded, was "quite natural and, indeed, very good when it is done by some simple person who strikes you as being truly recollected and really devout." Yet such behavior became a desecration when performed by women who "have their face made up with paste and their hair dyed yellow, when they are decorated with jewels and clothed in startling dresses."[59]

Once again, then, Huysmans connected the defilement of Lourdes with the development of a newly commercialized modern world. He was not disturbed by the "superstitious" religiosity of peasant women, because he associated their faith with a simple sincerity. However, the presence of fashionably dressed bourgeois women engaging in similar religious rituals represented an unambiguous debasement of the sacred. Huysmans expressed similar disdain for the Lourdais, who had allowed themselves to be corrupted by their newfound wealth. As these townspeople became hotel keepers and sellers of religious articles, they began to adopt a bourgeois form of worship that was "only part of the window-dressing of the devotional bazaars," one that helps "to hook purchasers" and "contributes towards the increase of cash sales."[60]

In short, a grim pageant of religious debasement parades before readers of *The Crowds of Lourdes*. Despite such corruption, or indeed perhaps because of it, Huysmans seems determined to find something redeeming in this sullied version of Catholic pilgrimage. To do so, the author reimagines the shrine, quite explicitly, to be something it was not. Thus, numerous passages in the novel find Huysmans closing his eyes to envision an alternative Lourdes. On first seeing the grotto, for example, he tried to disregard the "futile statue" of the Virgin Mary from the interior of the grotto so that his soul could begin to "soar freely." At another moment he proclaimed: "If you shut your eyes" during the high Mass on Sunday "when you hear their wailing chant behind the grille, all the false glitter loses its importunity, and Lourdes . . . vanishes away, and you are reminded of that other apparition of the Virgin which took place twelve years previously . . . and you suddenly remember that at Lourdes, too, the Immaculate Conception thrice spoke the word 'penance' to Bernadette." Elsewhere in the book, while trying to understand the reconstruction of the grotto as a necessary step in accommodating the crowds who swarmed the shrine, Huysmans insisted that "one must make a mental effort to think of it as wild and free as it was in the days of Bernadette, when the river bathed its edges, when moss and grass instead of asphalt gladdened its soil."[61] To encounter the sacred aura of the holy site, then, Huysmans simply banished from his mind's eye the commerce and vulgarity of the sanctuary, reinventing Lourdes to fit his own understanding of what proper religious devotion should be.

Only by segregating the profane activities of the modern world from the sacred life of the grotto was Huysmans able to resolve the problem of the Lourdes pilgrimage. As he reimagined a pilgrimage focusing only on the suffering of the sick and the charity of those who cared for them, he was able to reclaim the true spirit of the grotto: "In this city of Our Lady there is a return to the early ages of Christianity, a flowering of loving care that will last as long as people are beneath her spell in this haven of her own." Despite the encroachment of the profane, Huysmans interpreted the faith and charity of the masses at Lourdes as a "return to the resolute confidence of the Middle Ages" and a "fusion of classes mingled together in a single unparalleled love, in a single unparalleled hope."[62] It was an interpretation that depended not only on distinguishing sacred from secular activities of pilgrimage but on labeling the corruption of religion by the profane world as a distinctively modern invention. By doing so, Huysmans could explain why Lourdes, "born only yesterday," was subject to extraordinary forms of desecration. Yet one could save Lourdes from

itself by embracing the suffering of sick pilgrims and by ref
edge the very presence of the secular world.

Huysmans wished for a way to accept mass pilgrimage as a
vine presence in the modern world. It is not surprising to discov
had initially intended to call his novel "The Two Faces of Lou
wanting to reject Lourdes outright, as Léon Bloy had done, nor ⌐   ⌐urch
clerics who tried to justify its commercial culture, Huysmans resolved the contradictions of mass pilgrimage by envisioning a Lourdes that stood outside the
modern world. To do this, he was forced to disconnect the economic life of pilgrimage from the "real" work of the shrine. Dismissing the commercialized
forms of material religiosity as illegitimate and even without substance, Huysmans focused instead on prayer for the sick and the miracle cures brought about
by the Virgin's intercession in order to salvage the spirituality of Lourdes. His
novel participated in an emerging critique of modern religiosity, one that depicted the mixing of secular (especially commercial) and religious activities as an
entirely new and appalling consequence of capitalist development. Nostalgically,
Huysmans closed his eyes to the present, looking instead to an imagined medieval
world in which religious life was purer because it seemed to have no connection
to market practices. Mass pilgrimages, envisioned as a reflection or re-creation of
this older religious reality, could then be taken seriously as worship.

As the Catholic Church developed a new kind of religious worship at Lourdes,
a public rhetoric also emerged for managing the problems that mass pilgrimage
produced. Clerical authorities were determined to protect the shrine and its new
devotional practices from crime, fraud, and the excesses of commercialization.
The Grotto fathers demonized peddlers and attacked entrepreneurs who em-
barrassed Lourdes with false claims. Designed to eradicate the worst abuses,
these tactics nevertheless provoked new levels of public concern over the growing relationship between religion and commerce. Had the development of mass
pilgrimage unleashed forces the Church could not control? Did the pilgrimages
create new desires and behaviors that would undermine devotion to the Virgin
Mary, destroying the sacred atmosphere of the shrine? Church leaders sought
to grapple with these new concerns by distinguishing between legitimate and illegitimate commercial activity, but devout Catholics and anticlerical republicans
alike began to criticize the mass pilgrimages to Lourdes as an aberrant form of
religious worship.

The critiques of Lourdes assailed its potent mix of religion and commerce, as
we have seen, from different angles. For a number of freethinkers and anticlerical republicans, Lourdes loomed not simply as an easily mocked magnet of superstition but as a symptom of modern capitalism gone awry. Its relentlessly
commercial culture suggested that market forces in French society had become

so strong as to permeate even a once-modest religious site in the faraway countryside. Even worse, pilgrimage to Lourdes seemed to spawn a new and dangerous type of religious devotion, one that used the tools of the modern marketplace to lure a secularizing populace back to the Church. For Catholic critics, on the other hand, Lourdes became the symbol of a public religiosity too intimately connected with the pleasures and dangers of the profane world. As clerical authorities focused on fraud and crime as manageable problems of mass pilgrimage, Catholic intellectuals condemned commercial techniques of promoting religious worship that turned Lourdes into a vulgar spectacle. Pilgrims, ensnared by secular entertainments and the enticements of consumer goods, too easily forgot their spiritual goals of penance and expiation.

Both Catholic critics and anticlerical republicans responded to the problems of commercialized pilgrimage by casting Lourdes as a degraded version of religious devotion. Relying on opposing stereotypes of antimodern religiosity and secular modernity, these observers also invoked essentialized tropes of feminine behavior, contrasting frenzied female shoppers with the Immaculate Virgin of Lourdes, to explain the development of this strange form of worship. For Catholic critics as well as republicans, a consensus that women were highly susceptible to the lures of mass consumption, while also being less able to control themselves in public, gave shape to the disturbing impression that devotional life at Lourdes was out of control. Catholics denounced women's unbridled desires to buy religious objects and entertainments for corrupting the spiritual aura of Lourdes, even as republicans blamed women for falling prey to the Church's slick marketing of superstition. By identifying women as the root cause of the problem, Catholics and republicans avoided the uncomfortable reality that all of French society's major institutions—religious, business, and governmental—now had important stakes in the mass pilgrimages to Lourdes. Castigating the debased activities of female believers also pointed toward a more comfortable solution: religious life must be kept out of the public realm in order to protect devout women from the temptations of the modern market.

The notion that pilgrimage should not be contaminated by secular society freed both Catholics and republicans to imagine another Lourdes. This Lourdes, still toiling in the shadows of its commercial counterpart, was one that embodied "true" religious devotion. Reflecting the serious work of pious women, this shadow shrine maintained the properly sacred atmosphere that had flourished in the days of Bernadette's visions. As the commercial culture of the worldly Lourdes became increasingly despised, Catholics also lauded another feature of the shrine: its commitment to care for, comfort, and even heal sick and dying pilgrims. This growing emphasis on rituals of sickness and healing soon became the dominant foil to the commercialized religiosity of the shrine. Yet, as the following chapters will explore, care of the sick and even the miracles cures of Lourdes were hardly isolated from the modern forces of commerce.

3

Scientific Sensationalism and the Miracle Cure

The growing commercialism of Lourdes was widely seen by late nineteenth- and early twentieth-century observers as a deplorable problem. Yet for many Catholic believers, the business of pilgrimage was merely, in the words of Huysmans, one of the "two faces of Lourdes." Beyond the commercialized town, with its souvenir shops and tourist entertainments, lay the sacred domain of the grotto, where ailing pilgrims received tender care and prayers for their recovery. As early as 1874, church authorities had begun to transport groups of suffering and disabled pilgrims, hoping to make "service to the sick" and healing a profound, and very public, display of religious devotion. During the 1880s, an entire infrastructure was assembled to minister to these malades and to authenticate the growing number of miracle cures proclaimed at Lourdes, including the Bureau of Medical Verifications (Bureau des Constatations Médicales), which was set up on the premises of the holy site. Meanwhile, the Assumptionist order created new healing rituals, such as the Procession of the Blessed Sacrament, in which the sick were implored, before chanting crowds, to rise and follow the Eucharist. By the final decade of the nineteenth century, these new rites dominated the spiritual life of the shrine, guiding how sick pilgrims made use of Lourdes water and shaping the very meaning of the miraculous healing experience. Disseminated to the larger Catholic world through the religious press, pamphlets, and guidebooks, the national pilgrimage of the sick made tending the sick and praying for miracles the principal focus, the core meaning, of the Lourdes shrine.

The centrality of the pilgrimage of the sick has not been lost on scholars interested in Lourdes. A number of historians have interpreted the ritual life of the shrine as a kind of invention of tradition, an attempt by clerical authoriti

evoke an idealized religious past. For Thomas Ksel-
optation of local healing practices that established
worship of suffering and redemption in defiance
Ruth Harris has shown that women, who became
hrine, played a key role in creating a culture of
..atural" and "God-given" gifts for nurturance.
needs of sick pilgrims, women offered their own willing
others as a model of female spiritual authority, a public display
.r that defied the secularism of France's new republic.[2]

These interpretations are important because they show how both male clerics and female lay believers helped to shape the national pilgrimage of the sick
and the meaning of miracles at Lourdes. Yet both accounts of the shrine's development reproduce the nineteenth-century contention that the sacred domain
of the grotto lay beyond the influence of the profane Lourdes. Furthermore,
these interpretations view church authorities and female believers as largely defensive actors, creating a spiritual realm of suffering bodies and miraculous
cures that offered refuge from the modern world. This chapter proposes a different interpretation. I argue that the new rituals of healing and care of the sick
were themselves the products of a commercializing and modernizing world. By
examining how the healing rituals at Lourdes grew out of innovative technologies and modern cultural forms, I show that the pilgrimage of the sick enacted
new forms of sacralization, bringing into being a distinctly modern kind of healing experience.

The Lourdes medical bureau played a pivotal role in making the pilgrimage
of the sick a modern experience. More than any other new practice adopted by
the shrine, the verification of cures by medical professionals had a transforming, and standardizing, effect on miracle making at Lourdes. As the bureau's
doctors assumed a more visible role in authenticating cures at the shrine, modern medicine gained a new level of authority over popular and official under-
standings of miraculous healing.[3] Indeed, the bureau's widely circulated case
studies of miracle cures—reproduced not only in scientific studies but also in
the religious press, guidebooks, and even on postcards—became a new and influential literature of devotion in its own right. Yet it would be a mistake to view
this development only in terms of a Foucaultian "medicalization" of the miraculous, or as simply an effort by the Church to expunge what it now deemed "su-
~rstition."[4] For even though the newly standardized accounts of the cure,
d of local variation and couched in a language of medical objectivity, did
d regulate popular beliefs about the miraculous, these medical narra-
le the cures themselves more spectacular. Indeed, these accounts
~avily steeped in the formulas of nineteenth-century fictional
'ical history provided for each cure reproduced faithfully
.s popular form of storytelling: a suffering woman of

virtue contends with grievous physical misfortune; her hardship is compounded by an ineffective, often coldhearted doctor; her cure is sudden and instantaneous, defying all natural explanation. This melodramatic account of suffering and redemption was offered up, at the same time, with painstakingly rendered clinical detail.[5] The result was a routinized healing narrative possessing both medical authority and emotional drama, a kind of "scientific sensationalism" that was well crafted to dramatize and publicize the remarkable cures at Lourdes.

The Church, of course, had long used medical experts to help verify miracles, just as it had relied on older genres of dramatic storytelling—from oral folktales to medieval morality plays—to spread the word of extraordinary healing.[6] What was innovative about this new healing account at Lourdes was not so much the recourse to medical verification or popular dissemination but, rather, the bringing together of these two kinds of storytelling—medical case study and melodrama—and their reconfiguration within an emerging consumer society. In a context of mass pilgrimage, church authorities turned to new cultural forms from medicine and secular entertainment to create a miracle-cure narrative that catered to a mass audience and spoke to modern concerns. The accounts of healing produced at Lourdes drew on a language of medical fact and physical detail to conjure up realistic depictions of authentic suffering. These narratives often made new diseases such as hysteria or social problems such as drug addition central components of the story, thus demonstrating the relevance of Lourdes to contemporary medical issues. Even while the accounts enlisted scientific knowledge in support of the cures, they also borrowed popular conventions of storytelling—from the patient testimonials used in patent-medicine advertising to the stock characterizations of melodrama—to facilitate narrative excitement and offer compelling resolution to the afflictions of the modern world. Produced to be distributed to a mass audience, this new discourse of the cure resulted in narratives of healing that were authentic as well as extraordinary, standardized yet spectacular.

The rhetoric of scientific sensationalism also dictated the shape of public ritual at Lourdes. As examining the sick and celebrating the cured grew central to the life of the shrine, the new rites of national pilgrimage became, for devout Catholics, the spiritual focus of Lourdes. Yet the spiritual importance of these rites was not connected to an antimodern revival of the world of medieval miracles but, rather, to a new sacred drama that invoked contemporary storytelling and spectacle making to give the Lourdes cures a thoroughly modern look and feel. This innovative religious melodrama almost always focused on a female pilgrim whose claims to being healed made her into a new kind of sacred protagonist. Indeed, the female miraculée came to represent the shrine's service to the sick, her body itself the powerful evidence of divine intervention in the modern age. As such, the female miraculée was publicly displayed, scrutinized, and even celebrated before the assembled masses at Lourdes. Circulation of her story and image throughout the Catholic world taught devout believers everywhere to see the cured woman as a central figure within the newly commercialized religious landscape.

MANAGING THE MIRACULOUS

Miraculous healing at Lourdes predated the national pilgrimage of the sick. Indeed, miracle cures were associated with the grotto of Lourdes almost from the start of Bernadette's visions. Soon after the young visionary discovered the hidden spring of water during the ninth apparition on February 25, 1858, local inhabitants began to seek out the grotto for curative purposes. Invoking the intercessory powers of the Virgin Mary and the saints through the use of natural substances such as spring water was long integral to Pyrenean religious traditions. These traditions were core elements of a premodern, and often locally defined, devotional culture in which sacred sites and healing shrines were linked to local topography, usually landmarks such as springs and caves.[7] Thus, for many villagers already caught up in Bernadette's serial visions, the sudden appearance of a spring at the site of the grotto confirmed the presence of the divine. When dozens of sick and disabled pilgrims claimed to be cured after using the water of the spring, local inhabitants became convinced that the grotto was a new site of healing.[8]

The Church soon responded to this outpouring of popular faith. In July of that same year, Bishop Laurence of Tarbes established an episcopal commission to investigate Bernadette's visions and the numerous cures being claimed at the grotto. The bishop called on "specialists versed in the sciences of mystical theology, medicine, physics, chemistry, [and] geology" to help determine whether events at the grotto were of divine origin.[9] Such a step was not particularly unusual for a cleric in Laurence's position. Apparitions and miracle cures often provided dramatic proof of supernatural activity, but they also could be the product of fraud, hallucination, or, even worse, diabolical influence. Experts were needed to evaluate the physical and spiritual evidence. The charge of Laurence's commission, following the guidelines set up during the Council of Trent, was to investigate, document, and prove that claims of private revelation and miraculous healing were true before the bishop could authorize a new cult devoted to the Virgin Mary. Once the commission passed favorable judgment on Bernadette's visions in 1862, Bishop Laurence quickly proclaimed the new cult of the grotto of Lourdes. He also announced that seven of the many proclaimed cures were of divine origin.[10] These pronouncements served to confirm an already strong popular faith in the healing powers of the grotto and ensured that customary rituals around the spring water would now become part of the official devotional life of the new shrine. In this sense, both popular customs and official church procedures shaped the early beliefs and healing practices at Lourdes.

After authorizing the new cult of the grotto, Laurence moved to regulate worship at the site. He erected a wooden building to house primitive baths and put up a permanent fountain with taps to provide a constant flow of water. Serving to recognize the efficacy of drinking from and bathing in the grotto spring, these new structures also legitimated local customs for seeking the Virgin's intercession. When the Grotto fathers took over the administration of the holy site in 1866, they continued this process of institutionalizing the miraculous. They oversaw the diocesan pilgrimages to the site and began to catalog the miracle cures that were regularly proclaimed at such events; they even began to track down new information about past cures that had escaped the notice of the 1858 episcopal commission.[11] This important work was fairly typical of church management of any local holy site. Expected to record the supernatural life of the shrine, the Grotto fathers kept a journal to document the growing number of claims of miraculous healing. Recording biographical information about cured individuals and providing brief accounts of their healing experiences, these reports were early and predictable efforts by the Church to establish a new shrine.[12]

Yet these clerical reports also attest to the largely informal and heterogeneous practices that still, in this early period, made up the miraculous healing experience. In these years before the onset of the national pilgrimage to Lourdes, the devout came to the shrine on regional pilgrimages, engaging in an array of practices and customs. Those in search of healing drank the grotto water, rubbed it on the bodies, or bathed their ailing parts in the spring. Believers also experienced moments of divine intervention in differing ways. Some found themselves healed immediately, while others were cured over a period of several weeks and even months after multiple applications of the water. Although Lourdes water almost always triggered the curing process, the experience of healing fit no single pattern. The accounts, which were sometimes written by those claiming to be cured but more often were told to clerics who later transcribed them into the official reports, suggest that lay believers as well as clerical authorities found a wide range of healing scenarios possible.[13] Ruth Harris has suggested that class differences and varying degrees of religious education among the cured explain the diversity of practices reflected in these early accounts.[14] Yet another reason for this heterogeneity lies in the Grotto fathers' initial reliance on oral storytelling for authenticating miraculous experiences. The conventions of oral storytelling did not depend on uniformity of plot or a linear recounting of events for assembling a compelling rendition of an experience.[15] Local variations and idiosyncratic practices of recitation were typically accepted and simply incorporated into official reports. The miraculous at Lourdes remained embedded in the local religiosity of the Pyrenees, even as the shrine became an authorized site of Catholic pilgrimage.

Henri Lasserre, in his *Notre-Dame de Lourdes,* captured elements of this distinctive religious world. Yet Lasserre's work, published in 1869, also attempted to reach a mass audience of readers, and the author deliberately reworked oral tales of the miraculous. Neither mythic nor rigidly moralizing, Lasserre's version of the cures read like the popular fiction of his day. He presented the miraculés as suffering protagonists in dramatic narratives that climaxed with the use of Lourdes water. This new narrative style was important not only because it attracted such an enormous audience but because it removed the Lourdes cures from the realm of local devotional culture and began to imagine them as a form of modern melodrama.

Lasserre relied on transcripts of the 1858 episcopal commission to tell the story of the first cures. While retaining the basic facts, he dramatized these first cures by telescoping the time frame of the event or by citing medical testimony to prove the supernatural nature of the healing process. The cure of Louis Bourriette provides a good example of his approach. Bourriette, a stonecutter who injured his eye in a quarry accident, sought out Lourdes water to regain his vision and then was cured. Although Bourriette subsequently told the bishop's commission that he had used the water for some fifteen days before experiencing a complete recovery, Lasserre's account emphasized an immediate transformation when he washed his eye for the very first time:

> [Bourriette] cried out, his emotions so strong that he began to tremble. His eyesight underwent a sudden miracle. Already, all around him, everything was becoming bright again and bathed in light. . . . The fog remained, but no longer black as it had been the last twenty years. . . . Bourriette continued to pray and wash his right eye in this beneficial water. The daylight grew little by little under his gaze and he discerned objects clearly.

In other cases, the facts did not permit Lasserre to present so sudden a cure. Yet, as in the case of Marianne Garrot, he cited the commission's detailed medical explanation of the disease's pathology to support his own assertion that a week-long process of recovery still constituted a miracle. Garrot suffered from a skin infection that covered her face. Such an infection

> might not necessarily be terribly grave. . . . However, the one that afflicted Madame Garrot would be marked by its extensive duration, its resistance to all medications prescribed and faithfully applied, its continual and progressive growth; to eradicate this pronounced malignancy, the infection . . . of a deeply rooted virus, would require a prolonged course of treatment.

Given this medical assessment, any cure now became remarkable: "The disappearance of the milky scabs on Madame Garrot's face, while not instantaneous, was rapid—very different from the usual action of chemical preparations." Although she required several applications of the water to be fully healed, the cure was nevertheless caused by "an action both strange and superior to natural agents." Documentary evidence reminded readers that these were "real" accounts, not fiction, while they further dramatized the extraordinary nature of the cure.[16]

Lasserre humanized his main characters, adding personal details to their accounts. At times, he inserted family members into the stories or situated his protagonists within a larger community. In the case of Bourriette, the author contributed a compelling episode in which the stonecutter's daughter rushed to the grotto for water. In another healing account, Lasserre has a neighbor preparing a special funeral shroud for a dying child, while the boy's mother runs to the grotto, frantically searching for a cure.[17] The presence of these supporting characters served vital narrative functions, heightening the gravity of an illness or the emotional pitch of a moment of crisis. By helping to flesh out the drama of the cure, these details made the commission's report into a kind of domestic fiction. Much more than folktales or a clerical catalog of healings, Lasserre's renderings of the early miracles were fully realized narratives of religious melodrama. And yet his book also remained tied to the local world of the Pyrenees. Paying careful attention to the personal details of each curing experience, he highlighted its distinctive qualities, noting how each person used the water and how long it took to take effect. By providing small details about the social backgrounds and customary behaviors of the various miraculés, Lasserre not only personalized these healing narratives but reminded readers of the peasant culture that defined life at Lourdes. In this sense, Lasserre's book straddled two different ways of talking about the miraculous. His book was steeped in the world of oral storytelling, but he sought to make these tales more compelling and realistic by combining melodramatic narration with medical testimony.

Lasserre's best-selling work introduced new narrative possibilities for talking about miracles. It was only with the creation of the national pilgrimage of the sick in 1874, however, that these new narrative techniques became linked to authorized church worship. In this sense, the modern identity of Lourdes only emerged after the Assumptionists, working with the Grotto fathers, set in place an infrastructure to make "service to the sick" the devotional focus of pilgrimage activities at the grotto. The building of such an infrastructure tied miraculous healing to newly created rituals and practices centered on the care of suffering pilgrims. This development altered the meaning of healing at Lourdes: formerly heralded as proof of Bernadette's divine visions, the miracle cures now became a sign of the Church's new commitment to healing the sick of

France. As church authorities created a set of highly stylized public exhibitions focused on tending the sick and celebrating the cured, the Lourdes cures themselves became more homogeneous, more orthodox, and yet simultaneously also more astonishing.

The rapid growth of a national pilgrimage directed toward the sick was remarkable. Whereas scarcely fifty sick pilgrims registered for the event in 1875, over nine hundred malades left for the national pilgrimage to Lourdes five years later. By 1892 the Assumptionists counted well over one thousand sick pilgrims among the thirty thousand devout Catholics registered for the annual event, and these numbers continued to rise over the following decades. The Assumptionists quickly developed institutional networks to help support the care of this mass of needy pilgrims. The order sought out the skills and energies of the devout women who belonged to the Association de Notre-Dame de Salut, a female lay organization dedicated to evangelization of the poor. Father François Picard, the Assumptionist leader, increasingly directed the efforts of these laywomen, who were mostly from aristocratic backgrounds, to focus on fund-raising for the national pilgrimage. Also vital to Picard's new pilgrimage of the sick were the Petites-Sœurs de l'Assomption. This female religious order, dedicated to the care of the poor, was recruited to nurse sick pilgrims, but it soon became clear that the small order was overmatched. In 1880, the Hospitalité de Notre-Dame de Salut was created to oversee the national pilgrimages of the sick. The lay organization, an extension of the Association of Notre-Dame de Salut, enlisted the help of male and female volunteers who worked with the Petites-Sœurs in taking care of sick and disabled pilgrims.[18]

Dramatic changes in the spiritual life of the grotto were soon evident, as caregiving and healing rituals became church-run affairs. By 1881, sick pilgrims no longer lodged with family and friends but at the newly completed Hospital of Notre-Dame des Douleurs. When visiting the grotto to pray or bathe in the pools, the sick pilgrims were helped by *brancardiers,* male volunteers, who carried them around the shrine on stretchers or pushed them in wheelchairs. At the grotto, they were assisted by nuns or by female lay volunteers called *dames hospitalières,* who bathed them, fed them, and tended to their needs throughout the day. The Hospitalité de Notre-Dame de Salut carried out all these tasks with a military-like discipline that dismayed a number of ailing pilgrims and their families, who resented these strangers and their imposition of a new code of discipline on long-held customs.[19]

The Assumptionists not only established the institutional framework for the care of large numbers of sick pilgrims at the shrine, they also used their mass-circulation periodicals to promote the new national pilgrimages. From early on, the weekly pilgrimage newsletter, *Le Pèlerin,* devoted intensive coverage to care of the ailing and to episodes of healing at Lourdes. For the Assumptionists, service to the sick was intimately tied to hopes for a cure. Demonstrating to the world,

Figure 26. Postcard of the Hospital of Notre-Dame des Douleurs, Lourdes, early twentieth century. Archives de l'Œuvre de la Grotte.

especially anticlerical republicans, the extraordinary power of God to heal diseased pilgrims at Lourdes became a major theme of the Assumptionist press. No longer simply proof of Bernadette's divine encounter with the Virgin Mary, the cures became signs of the extraordinary devotional work being performed at the shrine. As such, the cures needed to be presented as grand events. *Le Pèlerin* and the sanctuary's own *Annales de Notre-Dame de Lourdes* began to fashion a curing drama that adopted many of the narrative techniques that Henri Lasserre had used so effectively. Yet while Lasserre took pains to capture Bernadette's world of Pyrenean religiosity, the Assumptionists and Grotto fathers positioned their own newly created rituals surrounding the care of sick pilgrims at center stage.

An 1877 issue of *Le Pèlerin* exemplified many of the elements of this new ritualized culture of healing. The arduousness of the railway journey, the striking exhibitions of piety from suffering pilgrims, the painstaking rituals of bathing—these details were the focus of typical journalistic accounts. One article began with a grueling trip by some 150 sick pilgrims. Several of these malades "were in a situation so extreme that we hesitated to let them continue the journey," claimed the narrator; "three required absolution en route." These pilgrims' mere survival was presented as the first of many miracles. The article then emphasized the atmosphere of prayer and consolation at the shrine: "At the grotto and the pools, the recitation of the rosary and the singing of hymns were a constant refrain." The ailing pilgrims "were praying with fervor, rosary in hand." It was these conditions, then, that produced the cures of Lourdes, and the article reported some thirty cures and ameliorations emerging from this particular pilgrimage. *Le Pèlerin* then presented the stories of seven cured pilgrims in greater detail, infusing the intimate accounts of the life of each miraculé with a careful dose of realism. Providing their names, the histories of their illnesses, and the diagnoses of their doctors (if available), these stories described sudden and miraculous recoveries in the grotto pools.[20]

Two other developments in the spiritual life of the shrine emerged as key supports of the new national pilgrimage of the sick. The first was the opening of the Bureau des Constatations Médicales in 1884. With growing multitudes of sick pilgrims coming to the shrine each year, the number of proclaimed miracle cures also started to mushroom.[21] A simple cataloguing of cures was no longer deemed sufficient to document such extraordinary—and highly public—events. Miracle cures of such magnitude demanded more authoritative methods. Seeking to proclaim to the world that astonishing events were occurring at Lourdes, the Assumptionists and Grotto fathers enlisted medical science to help them in their campaign. Although medical examinations of cured pilgrims had been an informal part of the grotto's religious life since the time of the episcopal commission, they had never been systematic or formalized. The medical bureau institutionalized new procedures for verifying the extraordinary nature of the proliferating number of cures.[22] The bureau's first president, Dr. Georges-Fernand Dunot de Saint-Maclou, recruited devout physicians to come to the shrine during the national pilgrimages. These doctors conducted medical examinations of all pilgrims claiming to be healed, and their findings were routinely cited in the religious press as proof of the numerous cures occurring at the site.

Nevertheless, it was only after Dr. Gustave Boissarie succeeded Saint-Maclou as president of the bureau in 1891 that the shrine began to adopt the latest medical techniques and procedures for judging miraculous cures. Born in the southwest of France, Boissarie had received his medical training in Paris, where he was schooled in the scientific theories and practices of the nineteenth-century medical world. Despite his immersion in the secular culture of Parisian hospital medicine, he remained a fervent Catholic and a believer in miracles. His impeccable medical credentials and ardent faith made him a perfect successor to Saint-Maclou. Dedicated to employing scientific methods to prove the existence of the miraculous, Boissarie's agenda meshed neatly with the desires of the Assumptionists, who wished to make the supernatural events of the shrine known and respected throughout the world.[23] At Lourdes, the pious doctor enacted new policies for streamlining the verification process. He insisted that sick pilgrims have their medical conditions certified by expert diagnosis before their arrival at the shrine. Pilgrims needed a doctor to declare, in writing, that their illnesses were organic and were regarded as incurable. Boissarie also insisted that

the bureau conduct its own ongoing examinations to verify that cu
spontaneous and, second, enduring in nature.[24] In effect, these c
serted the norms of professional medicine into the process of mir;
ing, while also ensuring that the bureau would remain an indispen
the curing experience.

The doctor created new symbols at the shrine to represent his imposing medical authority. Inheriting a simple wooden building where Saint-Maclou had
conducted the first medical examinations of the cured, Boissarie saw this humble shed as woefully inadequate for a new scientific center for the study of the
miraculous. He soon undertook the construction of a new medical bureau to accommodate the numerous doctors he hoped to attract to the shrine. The digni-
fied stone building was constructed under the right ramp of the Basilica of the
Rosary, making it quite literally part of the sanctuary's foundation. With the
medical bureau now prominently located and looking out onto a newly created
esplanade, it conveyed to all pilgrims coming to Lourdes the message that modern medicine now determined the truth of the cure. In this way, too, the medical bureau was clearly established as integral to the healing rituals of the
shrine.[25]

LOURDES — L'ANCIEN BUREAU MÉDICAL

Figure 27. Old Bureau of Medical Verifications, located near the grotto. From Gustave Boissarie,
Lourdes: Les Guérisons, series 1 (Paris, 1911), 2.

LE NOUVEAU BUREAU DES CONSTATATIONS AVEC LA STATUE DE SAINT LUC

Figure 28. New Bureau of Medical Verifications, Lourdes. From Gustave Boissarie, *Lourdes: Les Guérisons*, series 1 (Paris, 1911), 3.

A second important innovation to emerge out of the national pilgrimage of the sick was the Procession of the Blessed Sacrament. Introduced by Father Picard in 1888, this procession was led by clerical officials who carried the consecrated host in its monstrance. Able-bodied pilgrims followed the procession, or observed it from the sides, as the Blessed Sacrament was paraded along the newly constructed esplanade. Crying out to be cured, sick pilgrims lined up on either side of the basilica on stretchers or in wheelchairs and waited for the Blessed Sacrament to pass before them. (Initially, they had waited at the grotto and pools, but Picard soon made the vast esplanade the site for this moment of public prayer.) After offering a special benediction, a priest shouted the Invocations, imploring God to heal the sick.[26] The litany was chanted back by the crowds, who watched in rapt anticipation of a cure. The sick were then urged to rise and follow the holy Sacrament. Soon taking place daily, these processions became the most important, and most watched, public ritual at Lourdes.[27]

The significance of the new Eucharistic celebrations at the shrine can hardly be overestimated. By making the Procession of the Blessed Sacrament the devotional focus of worship for the sick, the Assumptionists connected the cures,

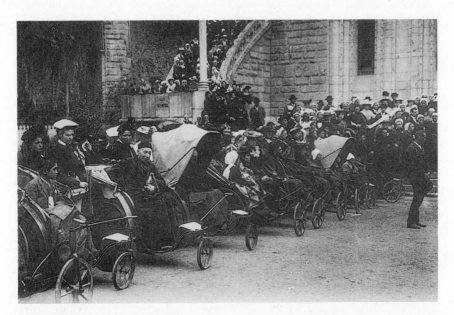

Figure 29. Sick pilgrims await the Procession of the Blessed Sacrament, Lourdes, early twentieth century. Archives de l'Œuvre de la Grotte.

as Thomas Kselman has pointed out, to the doctrine of transubstantiation. The most important and mysterious doctrine of the Church—the belief in the real presence of Christ in the consecrated host—became tied to the cures at Lourdes. Picard thus inscribed a new level of Catholic orthodoxy within the ritual healing of the sick even as he created a public event that would appeal to large numbers of pilgrims. And, over time, more and more of the shrine's moments of miraculous healing began to occur at the procession itself: whereas only six of forty-two verified cures in 1888 took place during the first Procession of the Blessed Sacrament, more than half of the verified cures happened there by 1894, a margin that continued for the rest of the decade.[28]

Ultimately, the national pilgrimage of the sick signaled a rupture with the earlier healing rituals of the grotto. A fresh set of practices—in which men carried the sick around the shrine, female volunteers bathed them in the pools, doctors examined the cured, and masses of assembled pilgrims participated in spectacular processions—came to define the spiritual life of the shrine. Although these innovative activities clearly reined in popular healing practices and beliefs, they also created a new public religiosity dependent on grand spectacles. It is tempting to see in these new rituals an effort by the Church to invent a "timeless" tradition, and thus establish an air of legitimacy for a pilgrimage barely two decades old. Indeed, Picard claimed that his Eucharistic processions were an attempt to re-create the Corpus Christi processions of the medieval world. Yet, the shrine's new rituals around sickness and healing are better understood as the expression of a distinctly modern religiosity. The late nineteenth-century pilgrimage of the sick was not focused on the medieval past but directed toward and shaped by the idioms of a newly emerging mass culture. Even though the Assumptionists claimed to be resurrecting an older form of religious pageantry, a careful look at how miraculous healing was enacted—at the shrine and away from it—suggests a religious encounter that increasingly was imagined and experienced as a form of modern spectacle. To understand how this new aesthetic and practice of miracle making evolved at Lourdes, it is useful to examine more closely the extraordinary influence of Boissarie's Bureau of Medical Verifications on fin-de-siècle rituals of healing.

SCIENTIFIC SENSATIONALISM

The rise to prominence of Gustave Boissarie brought about dramatic developments in the pilgrimage of the sick and the miraculous healing experience at Lourdes. The most obvious impacts were the new rigor and unprecedented stature of medical authority that the doctor contributed to the verification of cures. Not only did Boissarie formalize scientific criteria for authenticating cures but he also published a series of important medical studies and held regular medical conferences to discuss the most astounding cases of healing. Even though Boissarie always acknowledged that only a bishop could decide whether a cure constituted a genuine miracle, his numerous scholarly reports and public appearances made the work of doctors essential for determining the miraculous at Lourdes. Yet these medical studies and conferences did more than bring the new regulatory power of science to the shrine. Boissarie's presentations and written texts also brought the medical bureau and its practices, as well as the miracle cures themselves, into the world of modern spectacle. In doing so, the doctor helped to invent a new way to talk about miracle cures, a rhetoric that became an important part of the modern culture of mass pilgrimage.

A close examination of Boissarie's first major medical study, *Lourdes: Histoire médicale, 1858–1891,* makes clear how the doctor's merging of modern medical discourse with popular forms of storytelling transformed the miracle cures into fin-de-siècle spectacles. Published in 1891, shortly before he took over as head of the bureau, this four-hundred-page medical study was both a theoretical treatise on miraculous healing and a compilation of individual case studies. In the work, Boissarie sought to illuminate the mechanisms underpinning the healing process in order to demonstrate that the cures at Lourdes defied the natural laws of science. Although the doctor spent several hundred pages detailing the prevailing theories that comprised the medical profession's understanding of sickness and recovery, the real power of the work lay in its thousands of case studies of extraordinary cures that had transpired at Lourdes. These cases presented the reader with overwhelming evidence that nonnatural cures were occurring at the shrine. A model for all of Boissarie's later medical studies, *Lourdes: Histoire médicale* was the first published work about the Lourdes miracles to reach beyond a strictly religious audience. In its first year alone, the book went through four editions, helping to bring large numbers of curious doctors, many of them nonbelievers, to the shrine.[29]

Boissarie's pathbreaking volume seized the attention of believers and nonbelievers alike precisely because of the doctor's insistent claims to medical objectivity. The work appeared to offer a powerful new interpretation of the miracle-cure experience. Avoiding all discussion of religious belief or devotional practice, the doctor provided a sober-minded analysis of the cures alone. Emphasizing his rigorous medical objectivity and his own credentials as a former intern at a Parisian hospital, Boissarie presented himself as a scientist gathering facts at the shrine. He recounted his own personal observations from the point of view of a trained physician. In the preface to *Lourdes: Histoire médicale,* he referred to his study as "less a personal memoir than a critical work and compilation." He asserted with pride that he had waited several years before publishing the book in order to verify his findings, evidence that he was in no way tainted by the "demands of the crowd." By using the medical case-study format to reexamine past cures as well as document present-day ones, Boissarie rewrote the divine history of the grotto in terms of modern medical theory. What was new in this analysis was Boissarie's attempt to categorize past cures—including the first cures from the 1858 episcopal reports as well as later accounts of healing found in the sanctuary's *Annales de Notre-Dame de Lourdes*—in light of modern definitions of disease. Several chapters were devoted to the study of specific diseases that had been healed at Lourdes, ranging from tuberculosis, paralysis, and stomach ailments to various maladies of the eye and ear. This approach allowed the doctor to explain in detail the etiology of a particular disease and the failure of traditional medicine to cure it. By providing such detailed information about the nature of illness and healing, Boissarie presented the truth of the miracle cures as scientific facts. Such an approach was intended to make the medical bureau a respected site for the scientific study of the miraculous as well as to publicize the cures to the larger secular world. Yet this method also effectively severed the Lourdes cures from their roots in oral folktale. While this process had been already under way by the 1870s, when the pilgrimages of the sick became headline news in the Assumptionist press, Boissarie's scientific study accelerated the transition, relating accounts as a series of facts that proved nonnatural healing mechanisms to be at work at the site.[30]

Yet Boissarie's *Lourdes: Histoire médicale* was not simply a dry theoretical treatise written for specialists. Despite his sometimes complicated medical discussions of illness and healing, the doctor's recitation of numerous case studies made the book read like a compelling collection of stories. Even the most complicated medical cases became engaging mini-dramas of suffering heroines seeking divine intervention. In this sense, Boissarie's book owed a considerable debt to nineteenth-century popular melodramas, or what Thomas Laqueur has labeled the new "humanitarian narratives" of the era. Such narratives elicited feelings of sympathy from readers by focusing on personal details of pain and hardship in the lives of ordinary people. Present not only in fiction of the period but also in the newspapers and the writings of social and political reformers, this narrative strategy relied on graphic and intentionally shocking depictions to motivate readers to intervene in the lives of the poor and the suffering. Boissarie's medical study employed this kind of formula to present the case history of each sick pilgrim. Melodramatic narration lent credibility to religious tales that might otherwise have seemed like antiquated folktales or peasant superstition, while it also enabled readers to connect personally with the suffering protagonists. In short, the medical case study as narrative of healing transformed the story of the cure, reframing the drama and spectacle long associated with miracle tales in modern terms.[31]

The account of Léontine Chartron's 1872 cure exemplified this new kind of healing narrative. As Boissarie's *Lourdes: Histoire médicale* presented it, the case began with a medical diagnosis of the patient. Suffering from Pott's disease, "a grave affliction of the spine," for over five years, Chartron's medical condition was serious: she had no appetite, her body was emaciated, and she suffered from continual fevers and insomnia. Her doctor concluded that "death was imminent." With these medical facts clearly established and authenticated by a reproduction of the doctor's certificate, the story of her miraculous encounter unfolded. Chartron made the difficult and painful journey to Lourdes from her home in Lormes in one of the special trains for sick pilgrims that were chartered for the national pilgrimage. At the shrine, she was bathed in the grotto pools and immediately found herself cured. The curvature in her spine disappeared, and she was able to walk without assistance. She regained her strength and appetite. At this point in the case study, Boissarie interjected his own medical insights, explaining that a case of Pott's disease "of seven or eight years' duration cannot heal in an instant without leaving any trace of the physical lesions that characterize this illness." Given the absence of such lesions, Boissarie could only concur, then, with her doctor that the incident was "absolutely inexplicable."[32]

Following this medical analysis came the words of the miraculée herself. After thirty years of good health, Chartron had begun to experience a malaise that she was unable to explain. Her health rapidly disintegrated: "I was seized by a little fever, my breathing becoming difficult; my legs refused to support me; I was unable to make any movement without pain; and I was forced to take to my bed." After consulting numerous physicians, she was diagnosed with Pott's disease. Here, her story of pain and suffering intensified, for while these medical experts were able to diagnose the malady, they were unable to cure it. Indeed,

Chartron seemed only to suffer at the hands of these doctors. Sent to Paris, she was forced to wear "a supported corset" and endured "moxas, iodized plaster treatments, and cauterizations." For over three years, she submitted to "these tortures." In the end, she claimed: "My poor back was so lacerated and burned that I could not longer endure these extreme treatments, despite my willingness to undergo them." During this painful period of treatment, the only relief she experienced came during a novena she recited to Our Lady of Lourdes. Convinced that only the Virgin of Lourdes might help her, she heard the voice of Mary calling her to the shrine and the Virgin's gentle hand pulling her toward the cure. Chartron then recounted the difficult journey on the train, the hours devoted to prayer at the sanctuary, and the ritual bathing in the pools, where she was instantly cured. The case history then returned to the terrain of medical observation, with Boissarie concluding the account by citing her doctor's affirmation of the extraordinary nature of the cure.[33]

A series of vignettes like this one, bracketed on both sides by dispassionate medical analysis, was typical of the most dramatic and compelling moments in Boissarie's study. Drawing on a device also common to the patent-medicine promotions of the day, the doctor employed the patient testimonial to great effect.[34] The device enabled the sentimental moralism and sheer excitement of melodrama to enter the story directly through the voice of the female pilgrim. While Boissarie explained the facts of the case, the woman recounted the emotional side of the story. This division of labor served a vital function, enabling Boissarie to relate an emotionally dramatic miracle tale without jeopardizing his own scientific legitimacy. Making effective use of the gender conventions of the period, the doctor merged medical discourse with popular entertainment to produce a modern rhetoric of miraculous healing, a story of the cure that was at once objective and compelling. In doing so, he repositioned his sacred protagonists as the central figures of this new narrative. Objects of medical investigation when male doctors scrutinized their bodies, these women also became subjects of an unfolding melodrama narrated by themselves. The female miraculée, both subject and object of the new medico–miracle tale, was in this sense a flexible symbol that could appeal to multiple audiences. While male readers encountered the familiar figure of the sick female in need of medical investigation, devout female readers found a familiar heroine, one who suffered at the hands of men only to be saved by the Virgin's powers of intercession. This versatile figure, then, was indispensable to Boissarie's groundbreaking rhetoric of scientific sensationalism.

One final section of Boissarie's *Lourdes: Histoire médicale* deserves extended attention. The concluding three chapters of the book, a discussion of hysteria and suggestion at Lourdes, brought together the key elements—medical scrutiny, melodrama, and the repositioning of women—that now defined a new discourse of the cure. The emerging psychological theories of hysteria, in fact, were potentially troublesome for the bureau's verification of miracles. Yet Boissarie's skillful handling of these theories solidified his scientific work while capitalizing on the current vogue for the ideas of such celebrated medical authorities as Jean-Martin Charcot and his rival Dr. Hippolyte Bernheim. The doctor began his discussion, rather ingeniously, by freely admitting that large numbers of hysterics were among the sick at the shrine. Rather than denying their presence, Boissarie discussed it candidly, even noting that many experienced relief and full recovery from their illnesses while at Lourdes. Yet Boissarie insisted that these cures were not counted among the extraordinary graces attributed to the Virgin. Emphasizing his own keen understanding of the theories of Charcot and Bernheim—both of whose ideas on suggestion, hypnotism, and hysteria he discussed at length—Boissarie and his crew of doctors claimed to be able to distinguish hysterical cures from cases of divine healing. He asserted proudly: "We observe at Lourdes the disappearance of nervous attacks just as one does at the Salpê-trière and other hospitals, but we treat these facts with the greatest reserve. We never rely on them to prove supernatural intervention." Explaining in detail what hysterical illnesses were and how healing by suggestion worked, Boissarie deftly neutralized the most threatening arguments against the Lourdes cures by incorporating them into his own explanations.[35]

Boissarie's ability to integrate the latest medical theories into the study of miracles accomplished several goals at once. The doctor legitimated his scientific investigations of the miraculous. Examining systematically every possible explanation for the Lourdes cures, he engaged the secular medical community on its own terms, demonstrating his own rigor and scientific impartiality. Yet by openly acknowledging that hysteria and suggestion played a role in recovery at the shrine, he was also placing Lourdes at the center of late nineteenth-century debates that had moved beyond the medical world. By the time *Lourdes: Histoire médicale* was published in 1891, Charcot's weekly lessons on hysteria at the Salpêtrière hospital were already high-profile events well known to educated Parisians. Courts and newspapers regularly debated the role of suggestion and hypnotism in scandalous crimes of passion. Novels, plays, and music hall productions showcased these new psychological theories.[36] Boissarie's treatment of the controversial topic could only catapult the Lourdes cures into the arenas of public debate and cultural spectacle. In many ways, then, the doctor's approach to hysteria and suggestion was positioned to excite and entertain his readers as much as to validate his scientific investigations.

Boissarie's dispassionate discussion of such contemporary medical issues as hysteria enlarged the terrain of the miraculous. For even as the doctor clearly differentiated the truly inexplicable organic cures at Lourdes from those that were merely hysterical, he did not want to dismiss the many nervous disorders that were healed at the shrine. In the concluding chapters of the book, he insisted, in fact, that it would be foolhardy for medical science to ignore cures from hysteria and other kinds of mental pathology, not only because they provided important insights into the nature of healing and treatment but because these cures were a type of divine grace as well: "Doctors who only want to see the cures of Lourdes as cures from nervous illnesses have committed an obvious error, as we prove each day. Those who reject all illnesses in which the nervous element plays a more or less preponderant role cast aside what are often very important facts that well merit inclusion in our *Annales*." Thus Boissarie presented numerous case studies of women suffering from nervous complaints (some so severe as to carry them to the brink of death) that modern medicine had failed to cure. These women, sometimes patients from the Salpêtrière or other well-known medical establishments, came to Lourdes as a last resort and found themselves, said Boissarie, cured immediately of their ailments. Take, for example, the case of Céleste Mériel. Diagnosed as a hysteric (and suffering from paralysis as well as deaf-muteness), she first was sent to the Salpêtrière. After six years of failed treatments, Mériel came to Lourdes and was cured. She regained her speech, her hearing, and her ability to walk. Boissarie noted with amusement that the Salpêtrière would have claimed a medical miracle if its own doctors had enacted such a remarkable transformation, but the doctors at Lourdes were more cautious: there simply was insufficient proof to call the cure "a supernatural act." Boissarie nevertheless did not shy away from labeling it a grace from God. Similarly, a second example, this one involving a woman who recovered from a morphine addiction, did not constitute an inexplicable cure, either, but rather "a special grace from God made manifest through a natural phenomenon."[37]

Giving such cases a place of importance on the terrain of the miraculous effectively engaged with the emerging problems of the day. Within a new framework of analysis, Boissarie reimagined religious healing in terms of modern experience. Such accounts revealed to the world that Lourdes was a site of divine intervention where contemporary problems, such as drug addiction or hysterical illness, could be cured. Moreover, Boissarie's use of a melodramatic narrative formula transformed these complicated social and medical problems into easy-to-follow scenarios of good versus evil. Thus, the hysterical illness of Céleste Mérial became a story of emotional abuse, her illness erupting only after her husband had abandoned her, taking their child with him. Or, in the case of the addict, we learn that a heedless doctor had initiated her dependency by treating her neuralgia with morphine. Stark dramas of moral women undone by nefarious men (usually husbands or doctors), these cases of healing provided dramatic resolutions to some of the most pressing social ills. The pilgrimage of the sick, therefore, was relevant to the modern world, offering hope and healing. By conveying this kind of story in the terms of religious melodrama, Boissarie's *Lourdes: Histoire médicale* created accounts of divine intervention that were compelling for a mass audience.

The doctor soon sought to make his medical work even more visible to the secular world. In 1894, Boissarie organized a medical conference in response to the recent publication of Émile Zola's *Lourdes.* The purpose of the conference, to be held in Paris, was to refute the novelist's presentation of the Lourdes cures as mere cases of psychological suggestion. Boissarie also sought a measure of personal revenge, as the famed novelist had depicted the Lourdes medical bureau as little more than a ramshackle hut where dithering, superstitious doctors mistook hysterical healing for miracles. The appearance of Zola's work, in fact, had been the most damaging event in the three-decade history of the shrine, but Boissarie now hoped to turn it to his own advantage. If Zola was an expert in seeking publicity for his novels, Boissarie would fight fire with fire. The doctor had previously held medical conferences at Lourdes and elsewhere, but they had been small-scale affairs. Seeking a grand public forum where he could display to the world Zola's blatant distortion of the reality of the cures, Boissarie ensured that the Paris conference, held at the Cercle du Luxembourg, would be a major media event from start to finish. "All desirable publicity was given to the conference," the official proceedings from the conference later noted, "and from the start, one sensed that there would be an enormous crowd at rue Luxembourg on the twenty-first of November." Indeed, not only did a huge crowd pack the conference auditorium but the event was covered by such important Parisian dailies as *Le Temps* and *Le Débat,* along with major Catholic newspapers.[38]

Boissarie's public presentation at the conference struck a stridently polemical tone. Accusing Zola of slander, the director of the medical bureau claimed that the novelist was woefully unfit to judge medical phenomena. Criticizing the author's superficial understanding of the theories of Charcot and Bernheim, Boissarie went on to attack, one by one, the novel's fictionalized presentation of the cures. By basing two of his characters on cured pilgrims he saw during his 1892 visit to Lourdes, Zola unwittingly furnished Boissarie with ample ammunition. The character of Elise Rouquet, for example, was taken from the case of Marie Lemarchand, a young woman who had arrived at Lourdes with a tubercular lupus that covered her face. Zola altered certain facts about Lemarchand, and Boissarie seized on these changes to undermine the writer's dramatization of her cure. Whereas Zola portrayed the woman's ghastly affliction as a hysterical ulcer that gradually disappeared after the young woman repeatedly washed her face in the Lourdes water, Boissarie insisted, citing Charcot himself, that no lupus this serious could ever be of hysterical origin. Even more egregious, insisted Boissarie, was Zola's retelling of the case of Marie Lebranchu, a woman who had arrived at Lourdes suffering from consumption and was later healed in the grotto pools. Zola presented this woman, called La Grivotte in the novel, as a case of temporary cure; the result merely of a short-term reprieve of her physical symptoms, La Grivotte's newfound health had faded by novel's end to the point that she was near death. Yet, Boissarie exclaimed, the real La Grivotte,

Marie Lebranchu, was alive and well! That Zola had fabricated for her a relapse and imminent death, continued the doctor, was surely a sign of the ultimate weakness of his case. Finally, Boissarie drew attention to Zola's heroine, Marie de Guersaint, whom the novel presents as a textbook hysteric who found herself cured during the Procession of the Blessed Sacrament. A character invented by Zola, Guersaint was, Boissarie assured his audience, the type of case that never passed the rigorous investigations that he oversaw at Lourdes.[39]

Boissarie's tirade against Zola was only part of the public spectacle at the Cercle du Luxembourg. The real climax came when the doctor presented several Lourdes miraculées to the cheering audience. He began with a short summary of their cures—"enthusiastic applause greeted each miracle as it was described by Dr. Boissarie," noted *Le Temps*—and then asked each woman to stand so the audience could see her. When Boissarie asked Marie Lemarchand (Zola's infamous Elise Rouquet) to stand up and show her healed face to the public, he nearly brought the house down. Further intensifying the drama, the doctor then read Zola's horrifying description of the lupus that once had disfigured her face, then pointed to the attractive woman before him. At this point, it was said, Marie Lemarchand began to cry, never having read Zola's description of her sore and overcome by a sense of fear and shame at hearing it described in such graphic terms. Boissarie, apparently overcome with emotion, quickly regained his composure and denounced Zola for his heartlessness. Speaking directly to the novelist, he shouted:

> Here is Marie Lemarchand! She is cured and beautiful to look at. . . . As you lingered over the descriptions of her sores, you forgot one thing, that this poor child worked—and how she worked! . . .—to provide for her father and her mother, that she was the eldest of five children and their sole support. . . . What am I saying? This interior beauty, you did not even think of looking for it!

As in his *Lourdes: Histoire médicale,* but in a more overtly theatrical setting, Boissarie was relying on the entrance of a female miraculée to transform medical investigation into religious melodrama of the highest order. By bringing Marie Lemarchand into public view, the doctor shifted the terrain of authentication from Zola's understanding of modern medical theory to his moral bankruptcy as a human being. The roles were, again, stark and compelling: Lemarchand became the suffering heroine, Zola the black-hearted villain. Meanwhile, Boissarie retained his demeanor as impartial scientist even as he orchestrated a spectacle worthy of P. T. Barnum.[40]

Boissarie's concluding verdict was that Zola had come to Lourdes "looking for a scandal" and, not finding it there, manufactured a fictional one in the pages of his book.[41] Yet Boissarie's own efforts of the early 1890s involved something very similar, making medical verification of the miraculous into a respectable

CONFÉRENCE DU DOCTEUR BOISSARIE
AU CERCLE CATHOLIQUE DU LUXEMBOURG

Figure 30. Presentation of miraculées by Boissarie at the Cercle du Luxembourg, Paris, 1894. From *Le Pèlerin,* 9 December 1894, reproduced in Gustave Boissarie, *Lourdes: Les Guérisons,* series 2 (Paris, 1911), 24.

scientific enterprise while transforming the Lourdes cures into dramatic spectacles. His success in doing so places the pious doctor on a par with other spectacle makers in fin-de-siècle France. Like Zola and Charcot, his anticlerical enemies, Boissarie exploited for his own purposes the aesthetic practices of the mass press and the theater, enterprises that historian Mary Louise Roberts has labeled "the two most powerful cultural commodities of the era."[42] His subsequent efforts continued to combine the spectacular qualities of late nineteenth-century popular journalism and stage performance with the rhetoric of objective science, keeping the name of Lourdes, the miracle cures, and his own bureau in the headlines of the mass press.

The media attention given to the 1894 conference encouraged Boissarie to mount a series of medical conferences featuring public presentations of Lourdes miraculés. What had begun as a polemical attack against the Church's anticlerical enemies became integrated into the ritual life of the phenomenon of Lourdes. Each year, Boissarie organized an open conference to discuss the cures that had transpired during the preceding pilgrimage season. These conferences, usually held in Paris, assembled the most recent Lourdes miraculés to be interviewed by panels of medical and religious experts before a public audience. The cured pilgrims who sought the verification of their cures had no choice but to appear at this dramatic gathering, which, by the early 1900s, took place at a Paris theater. Although such events were invariably presented as the culminating stages of the medical bureau's rigorous investigations, they were also inextricably tied to Boissarie's flair for the spectacular. Indeed, the doctor seemed all too aware that his orchestrated exhibitions of miraculés might be seen as a form of popular entertainment. As he wrote in one of his last published works: "A miracle does not present itself like a tableau, like a stage set; we are not in a theater and we cannot place before the eyes of spectators the scene shifting that they demand of us."[43] Yet Boissarie had done precisely that. He employed a public arena—a theater, no less—to exhibit cured pilgrims, who served as his physical evidence of divine intervention into the lives of ordinary people. Translating the melodrama of his written case histories into live performance, his public forums became a type of fin-de-siècle theater designed to delight, surprise, disarm, and even titillate his audience.

Once again, then, Boissarie repositioned the female miraculée to be the subject and object of a modern religio-medical spectacle. Because the doctor's promotional tactics depended on the physical evidence of the cured pilgrim's body, he made seeing "real" miraculées a central moment of the curing drama for the devout as well as for doctors. Yet to wield this scientific evidence effectively, Boissarie needed to demonstrate to devout Catholics and anticlerical adversaries alike that it was acceptable, even necessary, to gaze at these women's bodies in public. He did so by trying to assuage fears that it might be improper for these women to be publicly displayed:

LA SÉANCE DU RÉCIT DES GUÉRISONS A PARIS EN 1898

Figure 31. Public examination of Lourdes cures, Paris, 1898. From Gustave Boissarie, *Lourdes: Les Guérisons,* series 1 (Paris, 1911), 5.

> Just seeing on stage these simple people of modest, almost timid appearance, often poorly dressed, one understands immediately that there is something serious going on there which has nothing to do with the theater or theatrical production, and that the need to demonstrate the truth in a peremptory manner has alone inspired the chronicler of the grotto.[44]

Respectable servants of God, then, were appearing in public for the good of the Church. Given the investigator's scientific motives as well as the humble demeanor of the miraculées, Boissarie insisted it was impossible to see any resemblance between these women and the dissolute actresses performing on the theatrical stage.

Boissarie's later medical studies evinced a similar concern to entertain and educate his readers through the figure of the female miraculée. These works incorporated photographic evidence of the cures to convey the supernatural events occurring at Lourdes. *Les Grandes Guérisons de Lourdes* (1900) and *Lourdes: Les Guérisons* (1911), for example, avoided the more complicated medical discussions found in Boissarie's earlier book, presenting instead a series of case histories with "before" and "after" photographs of the miraculées. These works displayed shocking images of half-naked, often-emaciated women to underscore

LA SALLE DU « BON THÉATRE », A PARIS, OU CHAQUE ANNÉE LE DOCTEUR BOISSARIE PRÉSIDAIT
LES RÉUNIONS CONSACRÉES AUX GUÉRISONS DE LOURDES

Figure 32. Paris theater for presenting cured pilgrims. From Gustave Boissarie, *Lourdes: Les Guérisons*, series 4 (Paris, 1922), 88.

the dramatic transformation from sickness to health. Only by reading the physical evidence written on the sick body—oozing sores, twisted limbs, wasted figures—could the world understand the miraculous nature of the recovery. Wrapping himself in the mantle of science, Boissarie again assured his readers that his studies were beyond reproach. These graphic, sometimes appalling photographs were legitimate, scientifically authorized depictions of healed women. Yet they were also stunning images that shocked and excited. Extending the rhetoric of scientific sensationalism to the photographic medium, Boissarie thus made peering at images that might otherwise be considered lurid, grotesque, or at the very least inappropriate, into a respectable, even vital, activity, a type of sacred voyeurism for the Catholic community. Whether gazing at real women, often young and single, at Boissarie's conferences or staring at their photographic portraits in medical books, devout believers were learning to see the female miraculée as a significant public figure in the Catholic world.

Boissarie was no less astute at making effective use of the practices of the new

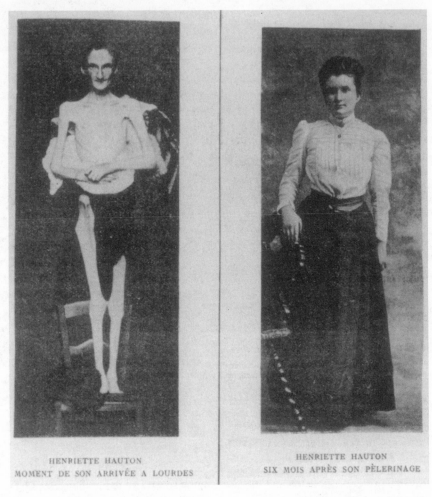

HENRIETTE HAUTON
MOMENT DE SON ARRIVÉE A LOURDES

HENRIETTE HAUTON
SIX MOIS APRÈS SON PÈLERINAGE

Figure 33. "Before" and "after": Photographs of a Lourdes miraculée. From Gustave Boissarie, *Lourdes: Les Guérisons,* series 3 (Paris, 1912), 15.

journalism. As he freely admitted, he allowed the religious press access to the findings of his medical investigations before he had fully verified the cures. In defense of this practice, he claimed that publication of incomplete results served to "spark discussion of all the various facts," stimulating a "free dialogue" in which all witnesses might participate and all opinions could be heard. Boissarie insisted, "It is not in the isolation of the doctor's office that one can build a body of work that requires the light of day and rests only on testimonial evidence." Rather, it was crucial to surrender one's findings to "open criticism, to the press, to the thousand papers [*milles feuilles*] that reproduce them while often distorting them. . . . It is in capturing again, in twenty different forms, the account of the same facts, it is in compiling a bundle of all the proofs that we can give an indisputable consecration of these events."[45] Of course, this spirit of open dialogue and eagerness for public debate also yielded a great deal of useful promotion, one might even say unpaid advertising, for the cures and for the doctor's scientific work at the shrine.

Boissarie's theatricality and shrewd use of the press made him a legendary figure at the shrine. By the end of his life, he was lionized for the scientific rigor and impartiality that he brought to the Lourdes medical bureau. Devotional pamphlets, guidebooks, and religious newspapers all lavished attention on his scientific endeavors and on the careful role played by medical verification at the shrine. The iconic status of Boissarie and his bureau is perhaps best exemplified by the multiple series of Boissarie postcards for sale at Lourdes at the turn of the century. Pilgrims could purchase striking images of the great doctor, stern-looking colleagues at his side, as he interviewed a female pilgrim claiming to be cured. These mass-circulated images captured the seriousness of the medical verification process, even as their appearance on postcards also made the doctor and the bureau available as objets de piété. Their sale as religious articles confirmed that the bureau was a shrine institution, and by the time of Boissarie's death in 1917 he had become a celebrity in his own right. As an obituary (later reproduced as an appendix to one of the doctor's own books) put it: "All the pil-

158   LOURDES. — Le Docteur Boissarie au Bureau des Constatations. — ND Phot.

Figure 34. Postcard of Dr. Boissarie at the Bureau of Medical Verifications, early twentieth century. Archives de l'Œuvre de la Grotte.

grims wanted to see him and desired to hear him. Around his name, an extraordinary renown had developed." In the ultimate tribute, the obituary noted that physicians from all over the world came to see him at the bureau, only to be shocked by the great doctor's dogged skepticism. This valediction ended with a much-told story: a devout woman, after watching Boissarie interrogate a female pilgrim, concluded that he must be a "famous freethinker," because "he is the only one who does not believe in miracles."[46]

Marketing the Cures

Boissarie developed a healing narrative that was both authentic and compelling. Whether exhibiting a healed pilgrim to an eager crowd or recounting the minute details of a cure in a report, the pious doctor invoked the rhetoric of scientific objectivity to fashion an exciting story of miraculous intervention. The Church seized on these techniques to promote the national pilgrimage of the sick and its related rituals of healing. The Grotto fathers and the Assumptionists soon incorporated Boissarie's case-study melodrama into many kinds of devotional literature, adapting this accessible and dynamic narrative form for ready use in religious newspapers, guidebooks, and even picture postcards. Clerical authorities at Lourdes, already marketing Lourdes water, souvenir goods, and religious services for a mass audience, now employed these commercial vehicles to promote the medical case-history as miracle tale. Drawing on Boissarie's theatrical innovations, they also began to develop their own pageants of cured pilgrims. These efforts would raise to new levels the spectacle-oriented commercial culture of Lourdes.

The religious press was a ready-made venue for promoting Boissarie's medical case histories. Both the Assumptionist press and the sanctuary's own newspapers enjoyed large and devoted readerships by the early 1890s. The affordable price of the Assumptionist daily, *La Croix*, ensured that stories of healing would quickly reach a mass audience of Catholic believers. The sanctuary's weekly *Journal de la Grotte*, official voice of the Grotto fathers, was the recognized source for all important news during the national pilgrimages to Lourdes. Boissarie's investigations became regular features in the pages of both papers, and as early as the 1890s *La Croix* began to publish regular accounts of the medical bureau's findings. Appearing throughout the pilgrimage season, these brief articles recounted in quick succession the many proclaimed cures that had recently transpired. While adopting the dispassionate language of the medical bureau, these newspapers aimed for realistic accounts of supernatural events that nevertheless provided engrossing stories. An 1891 article in *La Croix*, for example, began:

Today we had some joyous cures: *Louise Merlet*, eighteen years old, suffered for two years with severe pain in her spine and swelling on her left side; after two months of constant bed rest she was able to sit up, but could walk only slightly with the aid of a cane. At three o'clock she was immersed in the grotto pool and found herself cured on leaving it. She is now able to walk alone.

The article continued with the story of Clémentine Trouvé (later immortalized in Zola's *Lourdes* as Sophie Couteau), who suffered "for three years from osteo-peritonitis . . . of the heel." After this succinct diagnosis, the article focused on the drama of her cure: "She plunged the foot into the pool, the wound healed instantly; there is no trace of the abscess. The ladies saw the bloody linen bandage at the moment when the foot was immersed."[47] Such journalistic reenactments of the cures made the extraordinary a regular part of the everyday news for devout readers. In many ways, these accounts can be read as the religious equivalent of the *faits divers* of the secular press, a new journalistic genre that became all the rage in late nineteenth-century France. The faits divers worked to attract readers by presenting "true accounts" of extraordinary and shocking events that happened to ordinary people. Newspaper publishers hoped to capture a growing, literate mass audience by making the daily life of the city and its people the subject of sensational, often bizarre and violent, reports.[48] By adapting Boissarie's medical case histories to the innovations of fin-de-siècle journalism, the Assumptionists of *La Croix* were able to develop their own kind of counter-faits divers—one might even call this type of story the *foi divers*. In this religious subgenre, the Church amazed and delighted its readers with daily reminders that extraordinary things did happen to ordinary people, that is, to devout women from all walks of life. A counter to the blood and gore often prominent in the typical fait divers of the secular press, the foi divers found extraordinary moments of God's grace occurring regularly in the lives of pious Catholics.

The sanctuary's *Journal de la Grotte* presented more in-depth coverage of the cures. Making certain cures into headline news, the weekly drew on a medical-case format to retell the events in intimate detail, highlighting the emotional drama along with the scientific facts. A 1901 article covered the cure of Hermine Viel. Reminding readers that its information was culled from "an investigation as rigorous and well-documented as possible," the article provided subheadings that elucidated each phase of the healing story. Beginning with "Medical Observation," the story recounted Viel's descent into illness: Suffering from "serious pains . . . in the stomach and the back, especially on the left side," she sought care from several doctors. They diagnosed her with "tuberculosis of the spine" (Pott's disease) and forced her to endure several painful, and useless, treatments. Section two, titled "Diagnostic," reproduced the medical certificates of the doctors who treated Viel, providing the authentic proof of the illness. "Prognostic" featured a letter from a doctor who discussed her unlikely prospects for a full recovery. A fourth section presented this same doctor's reluctance to let the pa-

'mage; but Viel, insisting the Virgin would cure her, braved
Lourdes. The fifth section, "The Cure," captured the pre-
..ing in Viel's own words: "'It was as if my blood, now very
.o circulate vigorously throughout my body.'" Cured so suddenly
.rst her own stretcher-bearer refused to believe her, Viel was subjected
. a week of surveillance at her home; only after that, the article assured its readers, were church officials certain of the lasting nature of the cure. In a section
labeled "Personal Observations," the physician who wrote the article then
stepped forward to provide some expert opinion. Rebutting the possibility that
the cure might be a form of autosuggestion, the doctor excluded the relevance
of "nervous maladies" and reemphasized the "spontaneity" of the cure. A final
section, "Moral Lesson," added that a freethinker who witnessed the cure was
so dumbfounded that he duly converted.[49] By the early twentieth century, when
photography became an affordable medium for the mass-circulation press, these
stories were accented with photos of the cured pilgrims, sometimes on the front
page.

Turn-of-the-century guidebooks also took up the findings of the Lourdes
medical bureau, further disseminating the new rhetoric of the cure. Produced
by the Church or by independent businessmen, these religious guidebooks devoted large sections to recounting the miracle cures. Eschewing the stories of
healing made famous by Henri Lasserre, these guides focused instead on the
most recent cures documented by Boissarie's bureau. An 1896 publication by
Bernard Dauberive, for instance, provided succinct accounts of every proclaimed cure of the preceding year. The guide furnished the name, age, and
hometown of each healed pilgrim, transforming a list of anonymous pilgrims
into "real life" individuals. Following the medical bureau's case-history format,
the guide offered a medical diagnosis as well as a short summary of where and
when each cure took place. Another guide, this one from 1900, reproduced the
"official summary" of the cures of that year. Listing over fifty accounts of healing from the national pilgrimage alone, this guide-almanac provided documented proof of the ongoing occurrence of contemporary miracles.[50] This kind
of promotional literature, then, portrayed Lourdes as a modern holy place where
miracles happened on a regular basis. Presentation of the latest cures also underscored the very ordinariness of these newest recipients of divine grace. They
came from towns, cities, and villages all over France, suffering in obscurity until pilgrimage and recovery transformed their lives. In presenting proof that ordinary people could be touched by divine events, the guidebooks and other
Lourdes publications translated Boissarie's new rhetoric of the cure into a mass-
produced and increasingly standardized narrative. The cures remained unique
and extraordinary events, of course, but they were made accessible to a mass audience through these newly affordable commercial media.

The circulation of the story and image of the female miraculée marked an im-

DIMANCHE, 10 DÉCEMBRE 1911   Le Numéro : 10 Centimes   63ᵐᵉ ANNÉE. — N° 50

JOURNAL DE LA GROTTE
DE
LOURDES
HEBDOMADAIRE
PUBLIÉ PAR LES CHAPELAINS DU SANCTUAIRE

ABONNEMENTS			
Ville	5'	3° »	1'50
France (dép. limit.)	6	3 50	2 »

ABONNEMENTS			
France (d e. limit.)	7'	4'	2 »
Étranger	8	4 50	2 55

ÉCHOS DE LA RÉUNION DES « MIRACULÉS » DE LOURDES
DE 1911

ALLOCUTION PRONONCÉE PAR M. LE Dʳ BOISSARIE
au début de cette Séance, tenue, le 26 novembre dernier, au Théâtre Chrétien de Paris

RAPPORT DE M. LE Dʳ E. VINCENT, PROFESSEUR AGRÉGÉ, ANCIEN CHIRURGIEN DE L'HOPITAL DE LA CHARITÉ A LYON, SUR LA GUÉRISON DE Mᵉˡˡᵉ VERZIER
(FRACTURE COMPLÈTE DU FÉMUR)

REMERCIEMENTS ADRESSÉS PAR SON ÉMINENCE LE CARDINAL DE ROVERIÉ DE CABRIÈRES A SES DIOCÉSAINS
AU RETOUR DE LEUR PÈLERINAGE A LOURDES (SUITE & FIN)

Le Part proposé par M. l'Abbé Dupierny à M. Chide, Professeur de Philosophie au Lycée de Nap. au sujet des Miracles de Lourdes— (Suite)
Lettres à M. Chide, Professeur en activité et l'auteur en retraite — Première Lettre : Les Faits à côté

Nouveaux Pèlerinages annoncés : Le Pèlerinage National Français de 1912 — Le Pèlerinage Diocésain de Paris

---

Échos de la Réunion des « Miraculés » de Lourdes
DE 1911
TENUE AU THÉATRE CHRÉTIEN DE PARIS
le Dimanche 26 Novembre dernier

ALLOCUTION DE M. LE Dʳ BOISSARIE

Au début de la séance, M. le Docteur Boissarie a prononcé l'allocution suivante, que nous sommes heureux de reproduire en tête de nos colonnes :

Mesdames et Messieurs,

Nos Réunions de Paris sont entrées désormais dans le cadre de nos études habituelles. A Lourdes, au milieu du mouvement des Pèlerinages, du tumulte des foules, de l'émotion des malades, il nous est bien difficile de faire des enquêtes suivies, des enquêtes complètes. Nous devons les reprendre ici, en faisant appel au jugement de nos Confrères qui veulent nous prêter leur appui. Cependant, à Lourdes, le concours des médecins grandit chaque année. Nous avons eu, en 1911, cinq cent trente-quatre médecins qui ont inscrit leur nom sur nos registres : c'est à peu près notre moyenne depuis quatre ans. Et, si nous y ajoutions les 100 ou 150 qui ne nous laissent pas leur nom, nous arriverions ainsi à 600 ou 700 médecins par année. Parmi ces médecins, un tiers environ sont des étrangers. La France a médecins de tous pays qui suivent les Pèlerinages, médecins allemands : de Berlin, de Cologne, de Munich, de toute la Bavière ; médecins des provinces annexées : de Strasbourg et de Metz. Nous avons en grand intérêt les médecins de l'Italie, de l'Espagne, qui étudient nos guérisons avec un très grand intérêt.

Si la France étonne les étrangers par ses persécutions religieuses, elle conserve cependant un foyer assez puissant pour éclairer de ses rayons les Catholiques du monde entier. La France est encore le berceau et le centre de la civilisation chrétienne.

Mais, à côté des médecins étrangers, nous avons des Professeurs, des Agrégés, des médecins des Hôpitaux. Nous en avons compté 40 cette année, et, parmi eux, plusieurs ont pris une part importante à nos travaux. Nous avons eu 14 Professeurs qui ont fait des études sur des guérisons de Lourdes.

Lorsque les médecins allemands nous ont attaqués, en disant que les phtisies guéries à Lourdes n'étaient que des phtisies nerveuses, trois Professeurs de Paris sont venus affirmer que les phtisies nerveuses n'existaient pas, et que les cavernes creusées au sein des poumons ne pouvaient guérir par le simple jeu des nerfs. Du reste, cette question s'est précisée beaucoup plus dans ces derniers temps. Nous avons eu dans notre Bureau le Professeur Renon, dont le nom fait autorité dans l'étude des maladies de poitrine. Il nous a dit que les phtisies nerveuses étaient très souvent un rêve. « J'en ai vu très peu, » dit-il ; « un jour pourtant, j'ai cru me trouver en face d'un cas intéressant ; je l'ai examiné avec beaucoup de soins, et, lorsque la maladie a été morte et que nous avons fait l'autopsie, nous avons trouvé dans les deux poumons des tubercules. Nous nous étions donc trompés. »

En comparant le sommaire de cette Réunion, reportez à l'Univers, à paru dans le Journal de la Grotte du 3 Décembre 1911.

Il ajoutait : « Il n'est pas possible, aujourd'hui, même avec tous les moyens dont la médecine dispose, de cicatriser des cavernes, de guérir la tuberculose, lorsqu'elle est arrivée à ses dernières limites ; et si, à Lourdes, nous observons la cicatrisation de ces cavernes, si nous sommes témoins de ces résurrections, nous pouvons bien déclarer que, tous les moyens de la médecine disposent, on ne peuvent obtenir ces résultats.

Le Professeur de Tours nous a donné un grand exemple d'indépendance ; il est venu au milieu de nous étudier une guérison dont vous avez entendu le récit l'année dernière, celle de Mme Travaillard. On l'avait traitée longtemps pour un cancer ; sa vie n'était qu'une question de jours ; en quelques instants, à Lourdes, elle fut guérie, et, le lendemain, sa convalescence s'était complète.

Le Docteur Barnsby est venu reconnaître franchement

Photo. Viron, 73, rue de la Clarté, Lourdes.

MADEMOISELLE MARGUERITE VERZIER

Cliché d'une fracture complète du fémur, le 9 juillet 1907, après dix-neuf mois de traitement, à la suite d'une fracture complète du fémur ...

au Bureau des Constatations, qu'il n'était pas possible, de ne pas voir là une résurrection au-dessus des lois naturelles. »

Au sujet de la guérison de Mme Travaillard, voir le Journal de la Grotte, n°ᵉ des 31 juillet, 4 Décembre 1910, 12 mars, 25 août et 1ᵉʳ octobre 1911. C'est dans ce dernier numéro qu'a paru une lettre adressée par M. le Professeur Barnsby à M. le Dʳ Boissarie à propos de cette guérison.

Le Docteur Babinski, — le Professeur le plus compétent dans l'étude des maladies nerveuses — a bien voulu me recevoir et m'a dit : Je ne sais pas ce que vous observez à Lourdes ; vous n'avez peut-être que des guérisons de troubles nerveux, mais, si vous avez des guérisons de phénomènes obtenues en un instant, je déclare ne pas pouvoir les expliquer ; et, si vous me donnez des exemples, je n'ai aucune raison de douter de votre parole. »

Je lui ai raconté la guérison de Marie Borel. La malheureuse femme avait des fistules, par lesquelles s'écoulaient continuellement toutes les matières ; son intestin était perforé ; elle était à bout de toute résistance.

L'éminent Professeur m'écouta avec beaucoup d'attention, et, quand j'eus fini, il me dit : « Ces cicatrisations ne sont plus dans nos moyens ! Peut-être l'avenir nous donnera-t-il une explication ; pour le moment, nous n'en avons pas ! »

Voilà la réponse d'un homme dont personne ne peut contester la haute compétence.

Vous allez entendre des faits bien extraordinaires : D'abord le Professeur Vincent, de Lyon, vous racontera la guérison instantanée d'une fracture de cuisse ; c'est un fait qui nous rappelle la guérison de De Rudder. La jeune fille qui a été l'objet de cette guérison est là, devant vous. Vous la verrez marcher ; elle ne conserve aucune trace de son accident.

Vous entendrez aussi le récit de guérisons de maladies de poitrine sous toutes les formes.

Un Pasteur protestant converti, qui a mérité par sa piété et sa sincérité la guérison de son fils, va vous le présenter. Ce dernier avait une série osseuse de l'oreille ; on voulait lui faire la trépanation du crâne, et sa vie était menacée. A la Sainte Messe, pendant l'élévation, au moment où le prêtre élevait la Sainte Hostie, il fut instantanément guéri. Vous entendrez le récit du père avec beaucoup d'intérêt. [1]

J'ai vu M. Boothman, il y a quelques mois, à Lourdes, où il fut témoin et acteur dans la conversion d'une protestante. Il lui dit devant nous : « Je ne peux pas vous donner la foi, mais je vais vous raconter la guérison de mon fils. Priez, et le bon Dieu fera le reste ». Et le bon Dieu a fait le reste, et la protestante est aujourd'hui convertie.

Nous devrions entendre aussi une protestante de Berlin, qui a trouvé la foi, quelques jours après le Pèlerinage national, pendant le Pèlerinage bordelais. Elle m'écrit : « Je ne puis pas venir assister à votre Réunion. Le 26 août, je me trouvais à Lourdes, je ne croyais à rien ; Lourdes ne me disait rien ; la Grotte ne me disait rien. Je m'éloignais de la Procession. Et voilà que, le soir du 31, vers 5 heures, je vois, à la Procession, se lever devant moi une malade de Bordeaux qui avait pas marché depuis 14 ans. La foi que je n'avais pas me jusqu'à ce jour vint brusquement éclairer mon âme. Depuis ce moment, tous mes doutes se sont évanouis ».

Cette femme se convertit, en effet, à Lourdes, abjura la

[1] Au sujet de la guérison du jeune Boothman, voir le Journal de la Grotte, n°ᵉ des 12 et 19 juin 1910, et 1911, ainsi qu'au l'a imprimé par erreur dans un autre numéro ancien.

Photo. Viron, 73, rue de la Grotte, Lourdes.

MADEMOISELLE MARGUERITE VERZIER

Guérie d'une fracture complète du fémur, le 9 juillet 1909, après avoir
communié, à la fin d'une Neuvaine en l'honneur de N.-D. de Lourdes
(Photographie prise à Lourdes en 1910).

Figure 36. The miraculée as celebrity.
From *Journal de la Grotte de Lourdes*, 10
December 1911.

portant development in the repositioning of women in French Catholic culture.
Boissarie's medical studies and conferences had initiated this process by remaking the miraculées into established figures whose bodies served as vital evidence in proving the truth of the cure. For Boissarie, this meant cultivating a
"proper" image of a demure woman, one who willingly showed her oozing sores
or crippled body for the greater glory of God. It also meant encouraging the
cured female pilgrim to parade her newfound health at public conferences and
other organized spectacles. An object of medical scrutiny and investigation, the
female miraculée was now a legitimate public figure. The mass circulation of
Boissarie's cases, by church officials and secular businessmen, took public
scrutiny one step further as the women became figures of renown. In this sense,
the female miraculées took on the status of fin-de-siècle religious celebrities. Of
course, these blessed women did not gain the type of fame or "star power" of
other nineteenth-century female notables. They did not look or act, for exam-

ple, like the celebrated actresses of the Paris theatrical stage. Nor d
the sacred authority or popular recognition garnered by female sai
aries of the day.[51] However, the Church's promotion and circul
women's stories and photographs made the process of seeing the miraculée in
commercialized public venues a central part of the devotional work of mass pilgrimage. Her account of suffering and triumph—bought, read, and shared by
thousands of devout believers—transformed the female miraculée into a prominent public figure whose fame now spread well beyond the borders of her own
town or village.

These cured pilgrims, usually women but sometimes men, too, soon became
celebrities at the sanctuary itself. By instituting in the 1880s a variety of large-
scale pageants focusing on sick pilgrims at Lourdes, the shrine's leaders had already demonstrated a special flair for making spectacles. Ten years after creating
the Procession of the Blessed Sacrament, Assumptionist leader Picard devised
a new procession that focused directly on cured pilgrims. This spectacle, part of
the shrine's 1897 jubilee celebration of twenty-five years of national pilgrimages
to Lourdes, explicitly tied the public figure of the miraculé—female and male
alike—to the shrine's ritual care of the sick. The scrutiny and celebration of the
cured pilgrim, first fully developed by Boissarie at his 1894 Paris conference,
was now shifted to the terrain of the shrine and orchestrated for an even larger
crowd of devout believers. The culmination of three days of prayer, penance, and
celebration, this procession was so successful that it would be repeated for the
fiftieth-anniversary celebration of the apparitions in 1908, an event that would
bring over one million visitors and pilgrims to Lourdes.[52]

Every aspect of the 1897 jubilee pageant treated the Lourdes miraculés as sacred celebrities. Clerical authorities consistently used the language of celebration, even adoration, to talk about these blessed individuals. To recruit cured
pilgrims from past national pilgrimages to participate in the jubilee, the Association de Notre-Dame de Salut promised them a privileged role, including special insignia to wear throughout the three-day celebration to mark their status
as miraculés. They were also asked to write accounts of their cures, to be kept at
the sanctuary as a public record. Recruiting efforts proved highly successful, as
some 350 cured pilgrims (mostly women) participated; wearing their badges,
these special attendees were honored in stirring pageants. At the final procession, they marched before the many thousands of cheering spectators. As the
miraculés paraded past the hundreds of sick pilgrims, themselves hoping to be
cured, Father Picard shouted to the crowds, "Behold, your friends, your models. . . . They were once like you, now do as they did. They lay on stretchers,
they got up. What is stopping you? . . . Get up!" In response, over forty sick pilgrims rose from their stretchers and chairs to follow the procession as it passed
by. Once ordinary believers, cured pilgrims had become extraordinary because
they were healed, and now their presence continued to project a remarkable aura

of healing. After the jubilee ended, they were further memorialized in the devotional literature of the shrine. As one pamphlet proclaimed, "One can truly call them 'the heroes of the Jubilee,' those whom Mary so wanted to cure and whose cures have been scientifically verified."[53]

Church-sanctioned adulation effectively merged the shrine's "service to the sick of France" with this more joyous celebration of the cured. Indeed, by the early twentieth century, the cured pilgrim as public figure may have eclipsed the suffering malade. This transformation from ailing pilgrim to object of divine grace was especially dramatic for the hundreds of nonelite women who participated in these processions. Through their stories in the mass-circulated devotional literature and their presence at the shrine, female miraculées became the symbol of the "true meaning" of Lourdes, the adored objects of a new spectacular religiosity. For the ordinary devout pilgrim, who came to Lourdes longing to see, touch, and talk with blessed miraculées, these women were recognized as sacred celebrities. Memoirs and other published accounts written by pilgrims of the period invariably focus on the witnessing of a cure as the highlight of the pilgrimage journey. More than that, these personal narratives reveal the intense desire to establish physical contact with the female miraculée herself. An American who participated in the 1903 national pilgrimage to Lourdes described such a moment in *Catholic World:*

> A voice cried aloud that a miracle had taken place. We were pressed in. . . . There before us was a lady who had been paralyzed and unable to walk for the past eight years—unable in fact to put her foot to the ground without great pain. And now she walked with ease and was cured. The people pressed around her, kissed her hands, deluged her with questions.

In a similar vein, the memoir of Madeleine D. from Blois described her own passionate response to seeing several cures at Lourdes: "It was stronger than me, I wanted to see, I cried with all my tears." She then recounted how she and several other women followed the newly cured pilgrims to the medical bureau, waiting outside until the doctors were finished examining them. As a blessed miraculée emerged, the young woman reached out to shake her hand, declaring to her readers: "We had the good fortune to be able to shake the hand of Mlle. Sylvie Bienaime, cured that evening." In another account, Bertile Ségalas described her ecstatic reaction to meeting a young woman whom she had earlier seen healed at the Procession of the Blessed Sacrament: "I offered her my chair and shook her hand, then I shook the hand of her father, who in turn obliged me to shake his daughter's hand again—O sweet obligation!"[54]

Women were not alone in seeking this kind of personal contact with the cured pilgrims of Lourdes. Male pilgrims were also anxious to touch or speak with the cured. In a letter written to the Association de Notre-Dame de Salut, one man reported that he had been lucky enough, after observing the cure of a Sister Marie-Eugène, to obtain her autograph for his family. He asserted proudly: "I presented my wife and my little girl to her. She gave them some pictures and signed her name on them." He also described the extraordinary moment of crowd adulation after Sister Marie-Eugène had called out that she was cured. Along with hospital attendants present at the scene, he struggled to protect the nun from the overwhelming rush of the devout.[55] A further, quite suggestive example of celebrity-making was captured by a photograph from one of Boissarie's medical studies. Here, a crowd of onlookers congratulated a female miraculée as she was being escorted by two brancardiers to the medical bureau. Although the brancardiers may have been merely supporting the newly cured woman as she struggled to regain her footing, a closer look suggests they were also protecting her from an admiring crowd on the verge of public rapture. From shaking hands with the cured to collecting physical mementos such as autographs and photos, devout pilgrims sought some kind of personal or physical connection with these blessed public figures. The cured pilgrim, acclaimed for being healed at Lourdes, was now admired and congratulated by strangers.

The female miraculée, in particular, became the object of a type of mass adulation characteristic of modern celebrity. Reports that pilgrims, on seeing a cure unfold before their eyes, lost all control and converged on the recipient—male or female—were not at all unusual. The Church's devotional literature often commented on the overzealous behavior of Lourdes pilgrims in the presence of a miracle cure. A pamphlet proclaiming the extraordinary cure of Gabriel Gargam, a male postal worker healed at the 1901 national pilgrimage, noted, almost in passing, that his medical examination could not be completed because of the riotous demeanor of pilgrims: "Outside, an enthusiastic and impatient crowd laid siege to the Bureau; the pushing against the doors was threatening. It was necessary to postpone the medical examination until the following day." Such frenzied curiosity from the crowd seemed to become an issue of greater concern when it was directed toward a female miraculée. Robert Triger, a devout Catholic who participated in the 1908 national pilgrimage, expressed in a published memoir his own reservations about this outpouring of excitement: "In effect, 'seeing the miracles' is, for certain Lourdes pilgrims, a violent passion; some of them are so eager that they see miracles where there are not any to see." Meanwhile, pilgrims claiming to be cured, he lamented, had to be smuggled in and out of the Lourdes medical bureau to avoid the riotous attentions of the crowd.[56]

Certain cured pilgrims seemed to attract a special kind of public adulation, with a select few becoming household names among the devout. Triger, for example, delighted in pointing out the most well-known as they marched by in the 1908 procession. Singling out Marie Lebranchu (La Grivotte from Zola's novel) and Gabriel Gargam (the injured postal worker) as "the most famous" marchers

UNE MALADE GUÉRIE ESCORTÉE A LOURDES

Figure 37. Cured pilgrim and the admiring crowd. From Gustave Boissarie, *Lourdes: Les Guérisons,* series 1 (Paris, 1911), 52.

at the event, Triger declared that seeing them walk by was a "spectacle without precedent."[57] Indeed, his ability to recognize these individuals—pilgrims cured many years earlier—attests to the enduring fame that certain of them achieved within the Catholic community. Other "stars" included Marie Lemarchand and Clémentine Trouvé, who had first emerged in the public spotlight as a result of

Boissarie's campaign against Zola. By the early twentieth century, th
experiences of these celebrities were told and retold so many times in
publications that strangers were able to recognize them when they retu
Lourdes to participate in the shrine's processions and anniversary events.

One of the most interesting venues of celebrity recognition took the form of
the picture postcard. By the early 1920s, a Parisian company, the Edition Spès,
was producing a postcard series featuring the cured pilgrims of Lourdes. Here,
the focus on the female miraculée as the embodiment of divine intervention is
especially striking. In a series comprising twelve different cards of cured pilgrims, eleven were dedicated to women. Printed with a photograph of the miraculée and a short narrative of the cure, these postcards drew on Boissarie's own
rhetoric of scientific sensationalism.[58] Each photograph presented an unsur-
prising image of respectable female piety: women clothed in somber dress,
hands clasped together as if in prayer. A few portraits depicted women of distinctly humble origins. Blanche Pontier, injured while working in the fields of
her native Puyricard, appeared as a common peasant woman; the pastoral setting of her photograph evoked an aura of rural simplicity. The very ordinariness
of these women is emphasized; plain looking and sober in expression, they came
from villages, towns, and cities from every region of France. They often engaged
in difficult and debilitating manual work. They lived unexceptional lives of toil
and suffering, until they went to Lourdes and were cured. The postcards also
reproduced condensed versions of the medical bureau's corresponding case histories. Beginning with a biographical sketch of a seemingly ordinary woman,
each card told a succinct story highlighting the rapid onset of disease, years of
suffering, the pilgrimage journey, and miraculous recovery. Recapitulating all
the elements of Boissarie's case studies, these terse narratives—in which doctors fail to cure diseases, sick pilgrims travel to Lourdes and are cured, and
physicians attest to the cures—summoned the legitimacy of the scientific world,
in concentrated form, to establish the validity of these commercially produced
accounts of miraculous healing.

Although the cured pilgrims on the postcards gained a certain type of noto-
riety, lasting renown was probably not the norm. Most experienced a more fleeting form of public attention that came with being a given week's headline story
in the religious press. Even this more transient visibility, however, was still quite
different from premodern experiences of miraculous healing. Miracle cures in
earlier periods had also guaranteed a certain type of recognition, but this status
was inevitably tied to one's membership in a particular community; public
renown for cured pilgrims was both local and personal. In the new setting of the
Lourdes pilgrimage of the sick, by contrast, renown for the cured was typically
national in scope and tied to the widespread dissemination of their accounts in
commercialized media. This kind of public attention and even celebration was
therefore broader but, paradoxically, more temporary. For the female pilgrims

Les Guérisons de Lourdes

MADELEINE ROUXEL

Madeleine ROUXEL, de Cherbourg, a été admise au Pèlerinage National de 1922, munie d'un certificat d'un médecin du sanatorium de Villepinte, où elle se trouvait en traitement, qui attestait que sa malade était atteinte de *lésions pulmonaires* en voie de ramollissement et que cette *tuberculose* avait débuté par d'abondantes hémoptysies. Au moment de son arrivée à Lourdes, la fièvre était très élevée, l'état général très mauvais.

C'est pendant la procession du Très-Saint-Sacrement que la jeune fille a été guérie, le lundi 21 août 1922.

Cinq docteurs en médecine, désignés comme experts, au Bureau médical, ont constaté la disparition de tous les symptômes de la tuberculose, et les quarante médecins présents à Lourdes ce jour-là, ont déclaré que cette guérison, qui a été complète en quarante-huit heures, ne pouvait être attribuée à un processus naturel.

AVE MARIA

Nº 2

Figure 38. Postcard: "The Cures of Lourdes," Madeleine Rouxel, 1920s. Archives de l'Œuvre de la Grotte.

Les Guérisons de Lourdes

BLANCHE PONTIER

Blanche PONTIER, 25 ans, de Puyricard (Bouches-du-Rhône) a fait une chute à la renverse, en travaillant aux champs, en décembre 1919. Hospitalisée à Aix, le 1er octobre 1920, l'épreuve radiographique révéla des lésions de quatre vertèbres. Cette carie vertébrale a été soignée depuis au moyen de corsets plâtrés.

C'est couchée sur un brancard, dont chaque mouvement lui faisait pousser des cris de douleur, que la malade est arrivée à Lourdes le 12 septembre 1920. Au cours de la procession Eucharistique, Blanche a ressenti une secousse générale, en même temps que toute douleur cessait aussitôt. Amenée au bureau médical, les docteurs Gicquel, de Gheldère et Boudani, constatèrent que la colonne vertébrale avait recouvré son intégrité parfaite et conclurent, d'accord avec tous leurs confrères présents, que la guérison si soudaine d'un mal de Pott ne pouvait s'expliquer en dehors d'une intervention extra-naturelle.

AVE MARIA

Figure 39. Postcard: "The Cures of Lourdes," Blanche Pontier, 1920s. Archives de l'Œuvre de la Grotte.

healed at Lourdes, such exposure involved a dramatic kind of public acclaim, one to which most ordinary women had no access. But, of course, these women had little control over this attention. Mass circulation of the story of a female miraculée meant that anonymous strangers now read about the intimate details of her healing experience. These readers of the cure could revel in this act of divine intervention, perhaps even feeling a personal connection with the cured pilgrim because her story was so familiar. Yet the audience would probably also forget about her rather quickly when an equally extraordinary miraculous cure appeared the following week. It is in this sense that female miraculées, as mostly interchangeable figures, became distinctly modern celebrities.

Adoration that was similarly spectacular but fleeting also became evident at the shrine's own anniversary celebrations and processions. What made these pageants so compelling was the number of cured pilgrims brought together in one place. To see hundreds of devout Catholics claiming to be touched by the intercessory power of the Virgin, marching in unison, was an extraordinary sight. It provided believing Catholics with tangible proof of the limitless power of the divine in the modern world. Nevertheless, these gatherings ultimately were temporary affairs. After three days of celebration, the cured dispersed to their homes in towns and villages across France. Most of them did not become household names; indeed, they might easily be replaced at future processions by new recipients of cures. Thus their very status as celebrity figures did not rest on the singularity of their individual experiences but rather on the continual process of miracle making at Lourdes. In this large-scale operation, involving the production, circulation, and consumption of melodramatic case histories, the female miraculée may have been a sacred celebrity, but she was also—like any fetishized commodity—a reproducible, and disposable, public figure.[59]

The creation of the national pilgrimage of the sick irrevocably altered the devotional life of the Lourdes shrine. Serving the suffering believers of France and praying for their cures became the central purpose of the Lourdes pilgrimage. For devout Catholics such as Joris-Karl Huysmans, this devotional work alone represented sacred experience and true spirituality at Lourdes, redeeming the profane commercialism of the site. Present-day scholars who have written about Lourdes have tended to reproduce that approach, looking beyond the seeming corruption of the marketplace to locate the spiritual worth of pilgrimage. Yet the shrine's new religious rituals of healing were products of a modern and commercializing society, and pilgrims experienced them as such. Almost from the first national pilgrimage, the powerful Assumptionist order sought to make service to the sick and prayer for miracles into a set of spectacular events packaged and promoted for a mass audience. With the institution of the Lourdes medical bureau, the miracle experience became linked to modern medical practice and new forms of popular entertainment. Boissarie's medical studies and his media-savvy conferences effectively merged scientific investigation with melodramatic storytelling, producing a rhetoric of scientific sensationalism. The doctor's focus on distinctly modern maladies, such as hysteria and drug addiction, enabled him to construct a new healing narrative that was both socially relevant and emotionally compelling to believers. In his public examinations of the healed bodies of the Lourdes miraculés, Boissarie used the legitimating power of science to dazzle and delight the devout with "proof" of the miraculous in the modern age. In this way, Boissarie gave an old tale new life. The mass marketing of these verified cures—in such commercialized forms as the foi divers or picture postcards—not only disseminated a new rhetoric of healing but transformed the Lourdes miracles into recognizably modern events. With the triumphant institutionalization of national pilgrimages of the sick, the Lourdes cures—such compelling and exciting enactments of miracles—became mass cultural spectacles that were meaningful in modern terms.

The figure of the female miraculée, positioned at the center of these mass cultural events, suggests new ways to interpret the feminized religiosity of nineteenth-century pilgrimage. More than a site of feminine succor for women, Lourdes became a place of public performance and celebration. In processions of cured female pilgrims at the shrine, and through the mass circulation of their pictures and stories in religious publications, women played crucial roles. As both participants in and spectators of the Lourdes cures, female pilgrims learned to see themselves as subjects of extraordinary drama and spectacle. When devout women tended to the sick and prayed for cures, they were not seeking to escape the modern world or create a feminized culture of surrender and self-denial. As producers and consumers, they were participating in an unfolding drama that made ordinary devout women into celebrated figures, even sacred celebrities. Witnessing an extraordinary cure, touching one of the blessed miraculées, and taking home a small memento of the event (a newspaper article, postcard, or photograph) became crucial to the experience of modern pilgrimage. That the central protagonist of this extraordinary event was so often a woman only enhanced the excitement of female pilgrims who read about or participated in the pilgrimage of the sick. Indeed, it is hardly surprising that the new public role of the female miraculée made the Lourdes miracle cures so compelling for large numbers of ordinary women. What, however, did those who had been touched directly by the miraculous think of these new events? How did the women cured at Lourdes make sense of their own healing experiences and respond to their new public status as miraculées?

4

Female Pilgrims and Spiritual Authority

The 1897 jubilee pilgrimage to Lourdes marked a key moment in the life of the shrine. Commemorating twenty-five years of national pilgrimages to the holy grotto, the jubilee saluted the shrine's long commitment to serving the sick and celebrated two and a half decades of the Virgin's intercessory powers of healing. In organizing the three-day jubilee, the Assumptionist order was honoring the work of the grotto with a special celebration, one even more spectacular than the typical national pilgrimage. Having a procession of Lourdes miraculés met their needs perfectly. Bringing hundreds of previously cured pilgrims back to Lourdes to march together in an elaborate procession would serve as the ultimate symbol of God's power and grace on earth. For the faithful, this collective body of cured pilgrims was intended to reaffirm faith and provide hope that they, too, might become recipients of divine blessings. For those who doubted or scorned the work of Lourdes, the procession was meant to provide undeniable proof of the miraculous healing powers present at the shrine. In preparation for the event, the miraculés, most of them women, were asked to write a "succinct account" of their healing experiences. Not surprisingly, they responded with enthusiasm, their "succinct" accounts—often several pages long and written in minute handwriting—retelling events of horrendous sickness and miraculous healing in extraordinary detail. These handwritten testimonials provide a unique opportunity to analyze laywomen's relationship to the miraculous at Lourdes.[1]

It is tempting, at first glance, to treat these healing accounts as a direct window into women's real experiences of healing at the shrine. But it is important to consider the circumstances under which the accounts were written. The request for a personal testimonial, either written or dictated by the cured pilgrims themselves, was part of an elaborate recruitment and selection process by the Association de Notre-Dame de Salut (for the Assumptionists) to seek out pilgrims who were recognized as cured by the Lourdes medical bureau or the association itself. The women who responded and wrote accounts for the jubilee procession, then, had not only been previously authenticated but also were involved in a long process of interaction with church authorities in which their claims of miraculous healing were solicited, scrutinized, and (in fortunate cases) eventually rewarded with acceptance in the jubilee procession. Moreover, when read en masse, the healing accounts share a strikingly formulaic quality in their narrative structure and language. The shrine's own production of miraculous healing as mass spectacle—with its concern for medical verification and its public celebration of the cured—was clearly implicated, therefore, in the writing of these testimonials. It remains possible, of course, to attempt, as Ruth Harris has done, to read beyond the "conventionalized language" of the shrine's healing script to find the real voices of these women writers.[2] Yet it would be naive to assume that *real* experience and identity are recoverable through reading these accounts. After all, the voice of direct experience, with its confessional tone, that pervades the testimonials was itself a rhetorical strategy designed to evoke an acceptable impression of authenticity.

My approach is to treat these healing testimonials as literary performances in which the women drew on and combined multiple discourses to assert the truth of the cure and thereby articulate a public identity for themselves.[3] Indeed, the healing accounts are interesting precisely because the women who wrote them were seeking public recognition for their healing experiences. The fact that these testimonials were written for the jubilee pilgrimage allows us to see how ordinary women chose, within certain limitations, to produce a public record and to take on the persona of the Lourdes miraculée. The jubilee pilgrimage provided these women with an opportunity to write themselves into Christian history as important religious figures. In doing so, however, these writers also revealed certain tensions within the shrine's rhetoric of the cure.

By treating these accounts as literary performances, framed by traditional and more recent types of Catholic devotional literature, we can see how the women writers drew on multiple narratives of the miraculous to testify to the extraordinary nature of the events that had transformed their lives. As modern-day miracle tales, the testimonials relied on the shrine's own rules for authenticating cures. In all the accounts, doctors played a large role, as did names of diseases and diagnoses of physical suffering. The women also called on the shrine's rhetoric of mass spectacle by including descriptions of crowd reactions to their cures or by noting articles about themselves that had appeared in religious publications. By incorporating the shrine's two key arbiters of truth—medical experts and the mass press—the women reproduced crucial conventions of the official rhetoric of the cure. Yet these accounts also harkened back to older Christian narratives that connected suffering with sanctity. Echoing familiar rhetorical strategies found in popular devotional works such as *The Golden Legend* or other collections of saints' lives, the testimonials replayed a well-known story of the martyred saint who undergoes a time of personal trial followed by a time of public glorification.[4] As in such accounts, abundant and even excessive suffering proved the subject's worthiness; triumph over adversity became, in turn, a sign of God's grace.[5] Of course, the testimonials differed from legendary accounts of saints in one crucial respect: each of these women did not die a martyr's death but, rather, received the blessing of a cure. Nevertheless, the cured women of Lourdes appropriated this older rhetoric of suffering and sanctity to impart a similar logic to their own narratives and to represent their own experiences of sickness and healing as part of God's divine plan.

By assimilating the shrine's new rhetoric of healing into preexisting narratives of Christian martyrdom, the writers reimagined older miracle tales within a modern idiom. In these modern-day miracle accounts, doctors were now villainous persecutors, medical treatment was a torture to be endured, and the roar of the crowd (or recognition by the religious press) signified the triumph of God's will. Women rewrote popular tales of miracles as up-to-date melodramas, casting themselves as protagonists in a battle for their lives. Their triumphant recovery secured their position as heroines, even celebrities, touched by the sacred. What emerged from these testimonials of miraculous healing, then, was a public figure—the Lourdes miraculée—who was recognizable and worthy of celebration. By fashioning an account that was emotionally compelling to themselves and acceptable to clerical authorities, these women were able to imagine themselves as important religious figures. Martyr-like heroines who became objects of grace, they were modern-day Christians who endured personal trials so that others would venerate Our Lady of Lourdes.

In this sense, these women became exemplary public figures who served as undeniable proof of God's grace on earth. Claiming such a position might bring the tangible benefit of being selected to participate in the jubilee procession. It also offered the spiritual comfort that came with knowing one was part of God's divine plan. Beyond such rewards, becoming a Lourdes miraculée enabled these women to remake a very traditional feminine role into a position of spiritual authority. Despite the skill of many of these women writers, however, the testimonial accounts often drew on multiple discourses that failed to blend successfully into an entirely compelling narrative. Problems of dramatic overkill, contradictory figures of authority, and narrative moments of uncertainty and ambivalence all tended to point up the far-from-seamless qualities of the shrine's rhetoric of the cure—and, in the process, destabilized the persona of the individual miraculée under conditions of routinized miracle making.

WOMEN AND WRITERS

In early July 1897 the Assumptionist leader Father François Picard announced that a procession of Lourdes miraculés would take place at the upcoming jubilee pilgrimage in late August.[6] Immediately, the organizers of the Lourdes national pilgrimage, in particular the female volunteers of the Association de Notre-Dame de Salut, began to track down cured pilgrims and invite them to take part. Before being selected, however, interested pilgrims had to undergo a lengthy examination of their cures by the Assumptionist General Council of Pilgrimages. The pilgrims had to respond to a questionnaire; submit very short accounts of their cures (either written or dictated by the pilgrims themselves); and provide medical certificates confirming the reality of their illnesses and sudden recoveries. In addition, they were required to present certificates from priests who authenticated their accounts and vouched for their piety. Candidates who needed financial assistance to make the pilgrimage were also expected to submit an attestation of poverty confirmed by a cleric or a volunteer of Notre-Dame de Salut who had visited them at home.[7] Thus the initial request for the pilgrim's own account of the cure was part of a much larger application process in which potential participants were screened, weeded out, and selected. The narratives that survived this winnowing were those that conformed to the shrine's own rules for authenticating cures, an imposition of orthodoxy that, as previous chapters have shown, promoted miracle making as public spectacle.

Those cured pilgrims who were chosen were treated as important individuals worthy of celebration. The council sent several letters to these "special pilgrims" to prepare them for the event, along with identity cards that gave them permanent access to the grotto and a red cross made of cloth to wear on their clothing during the three-day pilgrimage. Both items distinguished the chosen pilgrims as Lourdes miraculés. They were also sent copies of the pilgrimage council's dossier on them, which they were asked to review while preparing final accounts of their healing experiences—accounts they should expect to leave at the shrine as ex-votos of their cures. The testimonials henceforth preserved in the shrine's archives were almost all written either in the final week before the jubilee event began or several days after its conclusion. Composed as the pilgrims were preparing to be (or had just experienced being) the center of attention at an elaborate celebration, these testimonial accounts were an opportunity for women cured at Lourdes to tell their own stories of healing for the public record. These accounts should be seen as part of the miracle-making practices of the shrine, in which the women themselves were able to retell their healing experiences with the hope of contributing to the work of Lourdes. And indeed, excerpts from these accounts were later reproduced in official devotional literature.[8]

Based on what little information the Church recorded, the 117 women whose accounts remain in the shrine's archives were, in many ways, typical Lourdes pilgrims. Primarily single women from lower-middle-class or working-class backgrounds, these pilgrims were, on average, thirty-one years old when they were healed. More than two-thirds were unmarried at the time of their cures; only four were nuns. Quite a few lived in the Midi-Pyrenees, Provence, and Languedoc regions, areas that brought large numbers of pilgrims to Lourdes; but most were from Paris or regions near the capital, including the Centre, the Nord, Normandie, and Picardie.[9] Although this preponderance of pilgrims from the Paris area may seem noteworthy, it probably reflected the fact that Notre-Dame de Salut was located in the capital and that the national pilgrimage was especially well organized in the surrounding regions. A number of these Parisian miraculées may have been recent arrivals to the city, products of an ongoing rural exodus that was transforming late nineteenth-century France. At least one woman, Rosalie Gouhier, noted her rural origins: daughter of a poor farmer, she moved to Paris, where she worked as a cook. The social backgrounds of many of the other women are harder to determine, but it seems likely that a large number of them also had modest origins. Hermine Jumeau noted that she worked as a seamstress for a local convent, while Mme. Le Compte simply described herself as a "worker." Two other women identified themselves as the wives of masonry workers. Many writers also stated that they could not afford a pilgrimage to Lourdes and needed assistance from Notre-Dame de Salut. Others received financial support from parish priests, wealthy patrons, religious orders, or charitable organizations. Elisa Fichelle, for example, thanked the Sisters of Charity for defraying the cost of her pilgrimage. Despite their modest means, many women had received rudimentary educations, or at least were sufficiently literate to have written their own testimonials or signed their names to dictated accounts.[10]

This group of 117 female miraculées might be seen as unusual, even unconventional, women, insofar as they sought wider recognition for their healing experiences. They had been selected for the event, whereas others failed to pass muster or refused to submit to such an examination. Simply by seeking to participate in the jubilee procession and inviting public scrutiny of their cures, such women were venturing beyond the confines of the private sphere to court the limelight of Lourdes. In this respect, they defied certain codes of nineteenth-century feminine behavior. Yet, in another sense, the group of female miraculées was remarkably conventional. As nonelite women, they often labored in female-defined occupations. They were seamstresses, cooks, or caretakers of young children. They were very devout and often belonged to religious confraternities such as the Children of Mary sodality. Although their prolonged illnesses may have relegated many of them to the margins of their communities, they often relied on networks of family and friends to care for them. They were devout women who had chosen to abide by the norms of feminine behavior for much of their lives. What makes these women interesting, then, is how they used the jubilee pilgrimage to recast their personal dramas of sickness and healing into public events, thereby transforming themselves into figures of celebration.

Personal Dramas, Public Spectacles

The testimonial accounts were first and foremost stories of physical suffering. The writers devoted several pages to recounting the graphic details of their ailments. Merely naming the illness was not sufficient to convey the full meaning of their pain. Female miraculées detailed the ways in which long-term illness ravaged their bodies and destroyed any semblance of normal life. The testimonial of Mlle. Elzire Gronnier provides a vivid example of this kind of narrative. Gronnier, who said she suffered from hysteria and a chronic urinary ailment, claimed the status of "martyr" because of the extraordinary suffering she endured. Her testimonial letter is worth citing at length for its compelling account of unbearable suffering. The letter began with the sudden appearance of illness: "I became sick following a sudden chill. I was no longer able to eat or walk for almost eight years—a real martyr, I suffered throughout my entire body." The letter continued:

> The doctor gave me medication after medication and nothing ever succeeded in giving me any relief; on the contrary, the pain increased day after day. He gave me three to four bottles of morphine to drink to make me sleep, but never did I have any sleep. The doctor himself said that all the medications did the opposite of what he expected.

In addition to this devastating attack, Gronnier described in detail a urinary ailment that left her bedridden:

> I had serious pains in my back and sides, and could digest nothing anymore—sometimes only an egg for a whole day, sometimes nothing at all; a drop of broth stayed in my stomach for three days and would not digest. My urine was clayey, like blood with little grains of red sand throughout; they were putting me on the bedpan every minute up to fifty or sixty times an hour, but nothing would happen. . . . With the pain increasing more and more, I was no longer able to leave my bed.

Using heightened language and dramatic flourishes—"my urine was clayey, like blood," "never did I have any sleep," "they were putting me on the bedpan every minute up to fifty or sixty times an hour"—Gronnier reveled in portraying herself as a type of modern-day martyr, a suffering victim of devastating illness.[11]

Elzire Gronnier's portrayal of personal suffering, even her exaggerated prose, was not unusual. Many female miraculées seemed to welcome the opportunity to detail every aspect of their pain. Mlle. Léotine Aubain, a thirty-five-year Parisian woman, described each stage of a spinal illness as it progressively vaded her body:

> The illness began in the month of August 1875 with an inflammation of the roots of the nails of the hands, which necessitated in the following months the removal of the ten fingernails; at the same time, an internal abscess and an inflammation of the exterior of the spinal marrow put my life in danger. When, after ten months of cruel suffering, they wanted to lift me, they discovered that the left foot was twisted, and that the hip and the leg were immobile.

Aubain claimed that for seven years she was unable to walk without crutches, suffering daily from "violent pains in the back" that made "all movement very painful." Another *miraculée*, Constance Piquet, described in detail how breast cancer quickly transformed her life into a living hell: "The pain was very great and I was no longer able to eat, slept badly, and had continual diarrhea which sapped my energy." As her condition worsened, she realized that she was dying: "I lost much weight. My complexion was yellow; I was aware that the end was approaching and I spoke of it often. The doctor said he could do nothing." It was at this point that Piquet decided to go to Lourdes, where she claimed she was cured on her third immersion in the grotto pools.[12]

Historian Robert Orsi has argued, in his work on twentieth-century Catholic devotional writing, that "Catholics thrilled to describe the body in pain. . . . There was always an excess in devotional accounts of pain and suffering of a certain kind of sensuous detail, a delicious lingering over and savoring of other people's pain." In this kind of devotional writing, "pain had the character of a sacrament, offering the sufferer a uniquely immediate and intimate experience of Jesus' presence." Such attention to the body in pain has had a very long history in Catholic devotional literature, going back to early narratives of Christ's passion as well as Christian stories of the lives of the saints and martyrs. In these hagiographic narratives, the body in pain was not only a path to saintliness for the afflicted; it was also a source of wonder and astonishment for the devout listener or reader. The saint's body in pain—the tortures endured and the sacrifices willingly made—guaranteed that his or her eventual triumph would inspire a sense of awe at this exemplary person's holiness as well as at God's grace.[13]

For nineteenth-century French Catholics, this kind of devotional writing was both popular and pervasive. Devout women, in particular, were reared on popular religious works that dwelled on pain and suffering as the path to spiritual redemption and knowledge of God. Young middle-class girls were often introduced to collections of saints' lives as well as to popular biographies of female saints such as Teresa of Ávila and Saint Cécile or the martyred Mary, Queen of Scots, as part of a proper female Catholic upbringing and education. Peasant

us collections of the lives of the saints and were equally
y accounts of suffering Christian martyrs. The female
dly introduced (or reintroduced) to these works dur-
es, when nursing nuns often became their primary
ut—clergy and lay believers alike—often encour-
comfort in the idea that their intense pain and anguish
closer to Christ. To suffer like Jesus on the cross was presented
to the chronically ill, the disabled, and the dying of Catholic France as a sign of
sanctity.[14] Given the importance of physical pain in Catholic popular religious
culture, then, it is not surprising that descriptions of horrific suffering played
such a large role in the handwritten testimonials crafted by female miraculées.
The women appropriated the familiar discourse of suffering and sanctity to
make sense of their own experiences of protracted illness. This narrative allowed
them to envision themselves as heroic victims or modern-day martyrs (as with
Elzire Gronnier) in an unfolding drama that ended in triumph over adversity.
In these accounts, then, the more horrendous the physical suffering endured by
the women, the more magnificent the cure. Their graphic descriptions of pain
and affliction served to inspire a sense of awe and wonder toward themselves as
Lourdes miraculées, new kinds of exemplary figures.

Yet while the women presented their pain as horrific, excessive, and en-
nobling, they were also careful to provide specific facts and details about their
physical illnesses. A general preference for historical accuracy had developed as
early as the sixteenth century, with the Council of Trent, and was reflected in
subsequent scholarly histories of saints. Yet the nineteenth-century Church introduced a renewed emphasis on scholarly erudition over uncritical hagiography, and with the emergence of Gustave Boissarie's medical case studies of
cures, this concern was translated into a popular idiom at Lourdes.[15] The testimonials also suggest an acute awareness of the need to provide a credible account
of the illness to clerical authorities in order to prove the miraculous nature of
the recovery. Thus it is not surprising to find female miraculées interweaving the
shrine's rules for authenticating sickness and healing into their own accounts.
Dramatic descriptions of wasting bodies and agonizing afflictions were invariably supplemented with medical explanations or doctors' diagnoses. Pain, never
inexplicable, was presented as a set of symptoms attached to a particular disease
or illness. In Léotine Aubain's testimonial, for example, the miraculée first provided a frightening description of disease ravaging her body, and then calmly
noted the doctor's diagnosis, an "inflammation of the exterior of the spinal marrow" and an abscess that "profoundly attacked the motor nerves." Marguerite
Lecherpin Descoutures began her account with the diagnosis of her doctor:
"Acute coxalgia [pain] of the right hip, the foot distorted and contraction of the
leg, twelve centimeters." After this recitation of medical facts, she shifted to a
description of the terrible suffering she endured while bedridden for thirty-

three months. Jeanne Delesalle also began her letter with a medical diagnosis—tubercular arthritis of the knee, hip, and ankle—before exclaiming that she had braved all sorts of pain to make a pilgrimage to Lourdes. Eugénie Hanceaux reported that her doctor had confirmed "a disease of the spinal marrow," reciting dispassionately the symptoms of the disease—"the body was swollen, the muscles were atrophied, the legs were paralyzed, the spinal column was deviated"—before bursting out that she was in a state of constant affliction. These testimonials named diseases and carefully established symptoms while giving voice to an excruciating descent into incapacitating illness.[16]

Writers carefully noted the dates and times of key events or listed medical facts with extraordinary exactitude to substantiate their claims to horrific suffering. Léotine Aubain cited the month and year her illness commenced, while Elzire Gronnier stated that she needed two to three bottles of morphine a day to soothe her pain. Marguerite Lecherpin Descoutures noted, as we have seen, that her leg had contracted exactly twelve centimeters. By providing these details, the women wielded the shrine's rhetorical strategies for mobilizing authenticity to their own advantage. The recitation of historical and medical detail, a type of personalized and self-executed case study, allowed the miraculées to present their extraordinary suffering as medical fact. In this sense, the body in pain was also established as a source of evidence that would validate the claim of miraculous healing.[17]

What emerged from this blending of older tales of suffering and sanctity with newer church-authorized case studies of healing was a very modern miracle-cure account that read like popular melodrama. In these testimonials, the narrative of suffering served to shock, maintain suspense, and garner sympathy for heroic victims. Not simply exemplary figures to be admired or evidence to be scrutinized, such victims were also objects of pity, ordinary women struggling for existence. Shunted from normal lives of good health and productive labor to death's door, these women emphasized the tragedy and hardship of their circumstances. While the extraordinary nature of their suffering transformed them into exemplary Christian martyrs, their constant ruminations on their misfortunes made them into rather stock melodramatic heroines. Take the account of Hermine Jumeau, the young seamstress, who worked in an atelier run by a convent in Chartres. She described herself as possessing relatively good health until, on January 11, 1895, she was "suddenly seized by fits of vomiting blood":

The doctor who was brought in immediately judged the gravity of my illness. . . . In vain the excellent sisters of Saint-Vincent de Paul who oversaw the convent workroom lavished on me the most attentive care; the illness was making such rapid progress that nothing could impede it. After eight months at the convent I was judged incurable and, as such, was admitted to the hospital in Chartres.

She was eventually sent to Villepinte, a well-known sanitarium, where she was diagnosed with a stomach ulcer and pulmonary tuberculosis. "I was immediately classified with the girls most gravely afflicted." During her nine-month stay at Villepinte, she experienced relentless bouts of vomiting blood and slowly wasted away from an inability to eat. So weak that "the doctor and my parents considered me at death's door," Jumeau decided to seek her cure at Lourdes.[18]

The melodramatic tone of these testimonials is even more pronounced in the lengthy discussions of ineffectual care that the women received from their doctors. These descriptions of failed medical intervention served as evidence that appropriate medical means had been attempted before turning to Our Lady of Lourdes for help. The shrine demanded such proof to show that the illnesses could not have been cured with standard medical treatment. Yet, in the hands of the writers, fulfilling the rules of the shrine also became a means for portraying themselves as sympathetic heroines. The women were not merely victims of disease but of incompetent doctors, whose failed remedies only served to exacerbate their conditions. Marie Havard, who suffered from paralysis complicated by nervous attacks, discussed her doctor's therapies in some detail. Both her arms and legs were paralyzed, and she suffered from five to six nervous attacks a day. At first, her doctor suggested bed rest and fresh air. After being bedridden for six months and still suffering from nervous attacks, her doctor prescribed "vesicants on the stomach, on the back, [and] on the sides," without any improvement.[19] He also ordered "baths of warm seawater" and other immersions. Havard described this hydrotherapy as ineffective and exhausting: "Each summer, I took from thirty to forty cold showers, which resulted only in an even greater fatigue." Discontinuing the treatment, her doctor then tried a variety of potions, granules, ointments, and boiling water poured over her body. These therapies only made her feel worse. Eventually her doctor lost all hope of a cure, stating that there was nothing left to try. Havard declared that she endured both illness and ineffectual medical care for some fifteen years before going to Lourdes, where she was cured.[20]

Many female writers presented medical treatment as a kind of torture they endured until their doctors finally gave up, lost interest, or abandoned them. Eugénie Hanceaux stated that she had been "subjected to the application of fourteen consecutive vesicants" to treat her stomach problems and anemia. She also took potions and morphine injections to soothe the intense pain. After a year, her doctor "abandoned" her "under the pretext that there was nothing left to do." At this point, her condition worsened and new doctors were called in. They diagnosed her condition as a spinal cord disorder. She was then subjected to a new round of torturous treatments consisting of "points of fire, injections of Doctor Brown-Séquat, electric charges, cold lotions, damp cloths, plasters of hemlock and belladonna, all endured without any appreciable result." Another writer, Marguerite Ménard, who suffered from a stomach ulcer, was sent to the

Villepinte sanitarium for treatment. While there, she subm
treatments, from "points of fire" and "injections" to "a mo
the stomach." All these treatments, she declared, were unab
condition or even soothe her pain. Eugénie Sédilère, sufferi
spinal cord disease, described her painful experience with ...
sion: "My doctor made me wear a plaster corset, which, proving inadequate, was
replaced with one made of metal; yet the pain was always getting worse." She
could not bend down or walk without pain. Her doctor then ordered her to endure a round of sulfur baths, but she refused, instead "putting all my hope in
the baths of the [grotto] pool."[21]

Medical treatment as torture was an especially prominent theme for Elzire
Gronnier, who portrayed her doctor as a tormentor. After subjecting her to numerous medications that had no ameliorative effect on her worsening hysterical
attacks and urinary ailment, Gronnier's physician declared that he no longer
wanted to see her; she and her parents had become an annoyance. She noted with
scorn that he had even suggested that she go to Lourdes, but only "to get rid of
me," for he "was not at all a believer." When she took the suggestion seriously,
he then forbade her to go, saying she was too weak to survive the trip. Beyond
incompetent, her doctor was outright cruel, calling her attention to Lourdes
only to deny her the possibility of making the journey. She went anyway and was
cured in the grotto pools.[22] As in all these accounts, the medical profession—
its doctors and battery of treatments—played a vital role in the narrative of suffering and sanctity. Whether as incompetent practitioner or sadistic villain, the
doctor and his arduous treatment became a crucial motif, part of the long period of personal trial that the female miraculée had to brave on her road to
grace.[23]

The climax of this narrative of suffering and sanctity was, of course, the cure.
Writers often depicted the cure—whether it was in the grotto pools or at the
Procession of the Blessed Sacrament—as a final moment of crisis, one involving intense physical pain that tested the body and soul. The women described
being internally ripped apart or feeling a complete physical disruption of the
body at the moment of healing. They often feared that they were not being
healed but were dying instead. Suddenly, they experienced a sense of inner peace
or well-being, and they knew they were healed. They could walk, had new energy, or felt a strong desire to eat. In narrating this climactic trial of faith, the
women evoked moods of suspense, then fear, and finally jubilant triumph as they
cried out that they were cured. This was melodrama of the highest order. Marguerite Ménard, healed in the grotto pools, described her cure in this fashion:
"I felt terrible pain in my entrails and especially in my stomach; i
that something inside of me ruptured." As she rose from the poo
appeared: "I experienced a soothing warmth and a well-being tl
explain and an unbelievable hunger, which made me see that my

had given me back my health." She recalled sitting down to a meal of soup and veal: "I ate all of it with an appetite impossible to describe, but which is understandable considering the number of years that I had passed without being able to eat."[24]

The experience of a final moment of crisis before the cure was commonly reported by the faithful. One woman, Elise Delahaye, even claimed that, in the midst of her intense suffering, she remembered that all those who had been healed at Lourdes experienced intense pain right before the cure. Taking comfort in this knowledge, she rose to follow the Procession of the Blessed Sacrament. Most female miraculées were less self-conscious than Delahaye in narrating the events of their healing experiences. Yet they nonetheless presented their cures as the final trial in the unfolding drama of the cure. Eugénie Hanceaux's cure took place at the Procession of the Blessed Sacrament as the Sacrament passed before her. Using the present tense to capture the force of the moment, she recounted: "Suddenly I feel a violent shock all over my body; it appears to me that I am going to die, but at the same time I experience the desire to take a few steps behind the Blessed Sacrament." She asked her attendant to help her to her feet when, suddenly, a second shock jolted her spine, and she called out: "Lord, I believe in you, but bolster my faith! Lord, cure the others!" She began to follow the procession, walking without assistance, and realized that she was cured. For Jeanne Delesalle, her unwavering faith in the Virgin's healing powers gave her a presentiment of her own imminent cure. Praying before the grotto as the Procession of the Blessed Sacrament passed by, she recalled her growing confidence that she would be cured: "It seemed impossible to me that the Immaculate Virgin, who had placed in my heart such unshakable confidence that I defied everyone to come implore her at her favored sanctuary, would disappoint my hopes." Then suddenly, the healing began: "I felt electrified, an interior force pushed me to get up." She rose from her wheelchair and walked toward the grotto with the help of her sister and a friend. Blanche Meurant, suffering from a pulmonary disease that caused repeated vomiting of blood, described her sudden cure before the sacred grotto as a final trial. Just minutes after receiving Holy Communion, she began to experience intense pain: "I felt an enormous shudder and a cracking throughout my being. Thinking I was dying rather than being healed, I said this short prayer: 'Good Blessed Virgin Mary, if I am still useful on this earth, heal me, since I am your child, and if I am no longer useful: Take me! I am yours.'" At that moment, she looked up and saw a vision of the Virgin smiling and telling her that she was cured. She hesitated to rise, but "an invincible force" pushed her forward. She knew then that she was cured and went to the Lourdes medical bureau to be examined.[25]

Descriptions of healing, like those of physical illness, needed to be verified by outside observers if the women were to claim effectively the status of Lourdes miraculée. Beyond the rhetoric of suffering and sanctity, factual detail, in conformity with the shrine's guidelines for authenticating cures, was also necessary. Thus many writers mentioned the required visit to the Lourdes medical bureau and provided the names of their doctors or witnesses to the healing event. Other women sought to make their dramatic healing experiences fit a precise chronology. Blanche Meurant did both, taking pains to note the exact date and time of her cure and then recounting her visit to the medical bureau. Marie de Saint Sacrement, who later became a nun, provided a daily and even hourly account of her activities. Arriving at Lourdes on August 21, 1891, she was taken to the grotto pools at two in the afternoon. At four o'clock, she was brought to the Procession of the Blessed Sacrament, where she was healed. Fifteen days after the cure, she took her religious vows. Still other women inserted prosaic details about their newfound health, such as the reappearance of a hearty appetite, as factual evidence of the miraculous. Typical demonstrations of a miraculée's renewed desire to eat might include the listing of the contents of her first postcure meal. Like Marguerite Ménard, who reported her first meal consisted of "soup with vermicelli, [and] veal with macaroni," many female writers seemed to take delight in providing such details, perhaps not only because such prosaic facts established the reality of the cure but because they signified, in very concrete terms, that the period of personal trial was now over. In short, the matter-of-fact recitation of the mundane represented the women's reintegration into society. For Marie Favraux, the fact that she ate salad the day after she was healed "was proof of the cure, because before I was not able to tolerate even the most basic foods." Louise Leroux declared that she knew she was cured when she was able to consume and digest hard-boiled eggs and sausage. Hermine Jumeau, who claimed to be cured two hours before departing from Lourdes, described her desire to eat on the train journey home as a sign of full recovery: "Since I was dying of hunger, I descended at each station café to drink and eat." Since that moment, she said, "I feel wonderfully well, and I have experienced no symptom of my former illness."[26]

Such exactitude suggests these women adopted the Church's concern with outside verification but also sought to turn this requirement to their own advantage. In the hands of the testimonial writers, the attention to historical exactitude—from chronologies to the mundane references to food—became a key ingredient in the production of a very modern melodrama of the cure. Constructing accounts of healing that portrayed themselves as ordinary individuals touched by the miraculous, these women were suffering victims who became objects of grace. The cure meant more than simply their reintegration into society; it represented the triumph of the Virgin's intercessory powers and thereby validated the work of the Lourdes shrine. By providing the prosaic details of their regained health, these women were putting behind them the period of trial to embrace a period of public thanksgiving and celebration. In this sense, the cure also became the grounds for establishing their new public status as

Lourdes miraculées. Presenting oneself as an object of God's blessing—as a special pilgrim deserving of public attention—took on the importance of a sweet obligation, one's very duty as a devout Catholic. These conventional narratives of sickness and healing, then, had become vehicles for making far-reaching claims.

CLAIMING SPIRITUAL AUTHORITY

To be selected for the jubilee procession and entered their stories in the public record, the women writers needed to portray themselves as exemplary figures deserving of God's grace. To this end, the story of the martyred saint whose personal suffering is publicly vindicated seemed to provide a ready model.[27] The narrative of suffering and sanctity was probably the most accessible discourse of spiritual authority familiar to the lay Catholic women of nineteenth-century France. By invoking this tale of martyrdom in their own stories, the women became more than suffering victims. They were defiant actors, even heroines, who challenged the authority of doctors by making a pilgrimage to Lourdes. Adapting such a tale also enabled the writers to envision their years of suffering as part of a larger divine plan, and to recognize themselves as messengers of truth who understood the spiritual significance of the cure. As both heroines and messengers, these women were able to see, in turn, their postcure lives as something more than a return to normal existence as ordinary women. From descriptions of cheering crowds to references to newspaper articles about themselves, the testimonial writers claimed recognition in terms that equated cultural authority with public attention from anonymous strangers. In this way, their stories, steeped though they were in long-standing narrative models of suffering and sanctity, also employed a very modern notion of celebrity.[28]

The first rhetorical device for establishing spiritual authority as a Lourdes miraculée involved the depiction of the period of trial. Lengthy description of physical suffering and ineffectual medical treatment set the stage for the presentation of the decision to go to Lourdes, a small act of defiance that utterly transformed the woman's life from suffering victim to determined actor. Elzire Gronnier's account of her resolve to visit Lourdes against her doctor's wishes illustrates this remarkable transformation. Presenting her doctor as a cruel scoundrel for suggesting, in jest, that she go to Lourdes and then forbidding her to make the journey, she went anyway and was cured in the grotto pools. Other women also portrayed their doctors as obstacles to overcome. Mélanie Herrman, who suffered for sixteen years with chronic gastritis, stated that she was "tired of asking men for help," declaring "I resolved to implore Our Lady of Lourdes." Applying to be admitted as a sick pilgrim for a diocesan pilgrimage, she set out for Lourdes in 1882 "with the firm confidence of returning from there healed." Marie Favraux announced: "I have seen too many doctors" and insisted that her

family take her to Lourdes. Hermine Jumeau decided to go t
hearing about the extraordinary cures occurring there. She rem
terior voice" telling her, "Go to Lourdes, you will be cured the
to convince her reluctant doctor to authorize the pilgrimage. A
who suffered from a chronic colon disorder, lied to her doctor ꜱᴏ ᴛʜᴀᴛ ꜱʜᴇ ᴄᴏᴜ
go to Lourdes. She explained her dilemma: "I had my doctor called—he who
had abandoned me three months earlier—for a last consultation. He found me
very tired and told me to leave without delay for Montpellier. Since he was a
Protestant, I hid from him my true intentions. Thus I left the seventh of May"
for Lourdes. Her act of defiance was later rewarded when she found herself
cured after being bathed in the grotto pools.[29]

Other women writers presented anxious family members and friends as bar-
riers to surmount. Worried parents, siblings, or even priests often refused to let
the women go on pilgrimage for fear that they would die en route. When financial hardship proved a problem, benefactors miraculously appeared to sponsor
the pilgrimage. Yet it was usually the persistent demands of the women themselves—their prayers and steadfast faith in Our Lady of Lourdes—that proved
the deciding factor in enabling them to go on pilgrimage. As passive suffering
gave way to decisive action in these narratives, the women were transformed
from hopeless cases into active heroines. By recounting these determined acts
of defiance, framed though they were in conventional terms of female piety, the
women portrayed themselves as initiating their own cures. This initiative, fueled
by their indomitable faith in the Virgin of Lourdes, foreshadowed their future
transformation into objects of divine grace.

In a second rhetorical move, the testimonial writers tended to position themselves as messengers of truth. Their healing accounts often introduced key medical and spiritual facts about the sickness or the cure that helped to endow their
long bouts of physical suffering with a larger religious purpose. In pragmatic
terms, of course, this information was necessary for constructing an authentic
and acceptable account of the cure. Yet the women also provided these facts to
show that the cure entailed broader religious contributions beyond their own recoveries of health, bringing glory to Lourdes by converting wayward souls back
to the faith. In this way, the writers presented themselves as spiritual authorities who understood that their individual dramas of illness and recovery served
a divine purpose.

Nor were the women shy about proclaiming this larger purpose. Léotine Aubain's testimony is a good example. Aubain first described the progressive decline of her health, which began with the removal of ten fingernails and ended
with the paralysis of her legs. At Lourdes, she immediately went to the ᴏᴛ
where she was cured after taking communion. Aubain then a˙
that seem intended to substantiate her claim of divine interveɪ
declared that she did not want her recovery to be confused witl

by hydrotherapy, a treatment to which doctors had subjected her numerous times without success. She stated emphatically: "No doubt the Blessed Virgin, . . . not wanting anyone to be able to attribute my cure to the physical qualities of the water of the grotto pool, allowed me to be cured before the Grotto one hour after my arrival, without even having touched the water of the pool." Aubain then added that she had said many novenas before deciding to go to Lourdes, but they had failed to help her. Only when her entire town became interested in her pursuit of a cure, participating in a novena for the pilgrimage as she departed for Lourdes, did the Blessed Virgin hear her prayers. She concluded that the Virgin had "wanted to cure me at Lourdes, and only at Lourdes, to give more grandeur to her work and thus bring about many conversions, which have been considerable as a consequence of my cure." By emphasizing these two additional points, then, Aubain drew on both medical and religious knowledge to explicitly characterize her own cure: unconnected to any known form of medical therapy, her cure had happened without any intermediary agent such as Lourdes water and was therefore truly extraordinary. Furthermore, her long period of suffering and imploring the Virgin made sense only when connected to a larger spiritual purpose: the veneration of Lourdes and the conversion of souls. As the recipient of an extraordinary cure, Aubain took seriously her role as messenger of truth. She had a responsibility to present assiduously the full facts to the public in order to bring greater glory to the Virgin of Lourdes. Indeed, her story simply had to be told for the work of Lourdes to continue.[30]

Many miraculées sought to link their personal dramas of illness and recovery to larger divine purposes. Marie Havard declared that her fifteen years of continuous illness was a spiritual test of her faith. Whereas she, her sister, and her mother had made numerous novenas to the Virgin, she was cured only after she prayed to the Virgin to take her life in exchange for allowing her brother, who was gravely ill from meningitis, to live long enough to take his first communion. He did make this first communion, and she interpreted her cure at Lourdes as a celestial reward for her noble gesture. Eugénie Ghisolfi declared at the conclusion of her account that she was certain that the Virgin had cured her at Lourdes in order to spur the conversion of her family. A writer who identified herself as Mme. Hugot, in a similar vein, claimed that the Virgin had wanted to cure her to bring about the conversion of her husband. And indeed, after hearing that she was healed at the shrine, he "knelt down to thank the blessed Virgin" and has remained a devout Catholic. Hugot also claimed that, as word spread of her miraculous recovery, others in her neighborhood rediscovered their faith. By finding a larger spiritual purpose in their sickness and sudden recovery, these women were able to transform years of seemingly incomprehensible suffering into God's work. In doing so, they portrayed themselves as holy agents of divine intervention.[31]

This type of narrative implication meant that many female miraculées saw

their personal dramas of sickness and healing as public events of great importance. As signs of God's grace, they spurred conversions and brought attention
to the work of Lourdes. They were the "evidence of the miraculous" that Dr.
Boissarie and other authorities at the shrine trumpeted for all the world to see.
It is not surprising, therefore, that the accounts of these miraculées called attention to the excited clamor of the crowd that witnessed the cure. This invoking of public celebration clearly served to legitimate further the extraordinary
nature of the cure, showing that others, usually male observers, took their cases
seriously. Yet the claim to public glory also enabled female miraculées to envision themselves as celebrated figures in their own right. As such, they were worthy of public adulation and were eager to recount their own experiences as sacred
celebrities at Lourdes. Aline Desrumaux, for example, concluded her testimonial with a description of the crowd's rush to see and touch her after she walked,
unaided, from the shrine's bathhouse: "An immense crowd swarmed around me,
because everyone had indeed noticed my former inability to walk." She went in
search of the doctor to confirm her cure, after which "everyone then sang the
Magnificat." She noted, "I was presented to Monseigneur Dennel, the bishop
of Arras; seeing me cured, he had them sing it a second time."[32] By highlighting the crowd's effusive reaction, Desrumaux marshaled further proof of the
truth of her miraculous cure. She also affirmed herself as someone special, worthy of being introduced to a bishop and honored with song.

Although the healing experience was often described as an intensely personal
moment for most miraculées, it was also a public spectacle that they clearly enjoyed. Many women recounted with delight the attention they received from
strangers. Marie Favraux noted that those who had seen her at death's door on
the train to Lourdes were now, on the train journey home, "thrilled to see me
cured." Some miraculées, in fact, seemed to go out of their way to appear in public after being cured. Blanche Sergheraert reported that she deliberately walked
to the grotto with her brancardiers to show the other pilgrims that she had been
cured in the grotto pools. On seeing the miraculée, the crowd went wild: "Everyone began to cry out 'Miracle! Miracle!' and to sing the Magnificat in honor of
Jesus and Mary." Mme. Hugot wrote that after she was cured she telegraphed
the good news to her family in Paris. When her train arrived in the capital, "half
of the city was at the station to see me, not being able to believe it, my doctor
completely shocked not knowing at all what to say." Mme. Quiriel recalled that,
after she arrived home, numerous people not only came out to look at her but to
shake her hand. Those blessed days, she said, were "the happiest days of my
life."[33] Such comments suggest that cured pilgrims did more than tolerate their
newly acquired fame as Lourdes miraculées. Some wanted people to know about
their cures and deliberately sought the attention of the crowd. Others held to
their memories of being the center of attention, even if it was only for a brief
moment.

A testimonial by Elise Delahaye, cured of a liver ailment in 1893, provides yet another example of a female pilgrim eager to take up the mantle of her newfound public status. Cured at the Procession of the Blessed Sacrament, Delahaye rose and walked toward the basilica, where she found herself deluged by questions. People wanted to know her name and where she was from. She wrote: "I had to give them my name." Interestingly, Delahaye had claimed earlier in her account that she had chosen to register for the pilgrimage under a false name; she wanted to remain anonymous. However, after being healed, she understood that it was her duty to become an object of public celebration. She knew that her cure brought joy to other pilgrims at Lourdes: the "ladies were happy to see such cures in their hospital because there were so few miracles" that year. Recounting the train ride home, she again described being the center of attention for the devout: "Everyone was asking to see me." For Delahaye, the transformation from obscurity to sacred celebrity was a duty that seemed to have become a pleasure.[34]

As a number of miraculées readily complied with the new demands of public scrutiny thrust upon them at Lourdes, others welcomed being objects of attention for a still larger public: the readers of the popular religious press. Constance Piquet, one such miraculée, even boasted about being the focus of articles in newspapers and magazines. An account of her miracle cure had appeared in the religious weekly *Le Pèlerin* and was later reprinted in other religious newspapers; her story and photograph had also appeared in a newly published religious almanac. She ended her testimonial by declaring: "I was one of the cured pilgrims selected for presentation at Dr. Boissarie's medical conference held in Paris in 1895." This kind of media attention, like the roar of the crowd at the shrine, helped to substantiate the authenticity of the cure. Piquet clearly understood that such public recognition would be helpful in securing a position in the procession of miraculés at the jubilee pilgrimage. By asserting her new status as object of grace—displayed in the public realm and circulated in the commercial arena of the modern press—she could portray herself as an exceptional figure. In this respect, Constance Piquet's behavior as a Lourdes miraculée contrasted dramatically with the actions of the earliest pilgrims to the grotto. Many of these women, whose cures had taken place before the Lourdes national pilgrimage, insisted on remaining anonymous even when the shrine wished to publish their stories in its monthly periodical, *Annales de Notre-Dame de Lourdes*. The shrine's registry of cures for the period 1866–1868 listed numerous female pilgrims who allowed their stories to be published on condition that their full names be withheld. By the turn of the century, such modesty and discretion had become obsolete, an impediment to the important work of the shrine. Cured pilgrims were now told that it was their duty as signs of God's grace to leave behind their humility and embrace their public role as Lourdes miraculées. Many women, Constance Piquet among them, went even further, eagerly claiming celebrity status for themselves.[35]

Cured female pilgrims ably exploited the shrine's own spectacle-making discourse to present themselves as exceptional individuals. The public attention that they received at Lourdes or through the religious press became, for them, a mark of distinction as well as further proof of divine grace in a life formerly marked by suffering and despair. Although most other female miraculées could not claim the same degree of media attention as Contance Piquet, they, too, were careful to mention that accounts of their cures had been previously published in religious newspapers or other kinds of devotional literature. Marie Aiglehoux, after noting that the Lourdes medical bureau had found her to be radically cured, declared that "the newspaper *Le Pèlerin* has mentioned it in its issue of September 27, 1879." Louise Reutenam also noted the exact date that news of her cure appeared in *Le Pèlerin;* and even Elise Delahaye, who had come to Lourdes under a pseudonym, boasted of an account of her cure that appeared in an 1893 issue of the paper. Angèle Lesbrossart, rather than submitting a full account for the jubilee, chose simply to send a published pamphlet describing her cure. She claimed that the brochure, written by a cleric, "is completely exact." For these cured pilgrims, calling attention to the publication and circulation of newspaper accounts of their healing experiences was tantamount to saying that their cures were real. The appearance of the miracle account in the religious press both secured authenticity for the cure and conferred on the miraculée a certain sacred authority.[36]

Establishing this public persona of the Lourdes miraculée involved a circular logic that proved to be indispensable to celebrity making in the modern age. To be worthy of selection for the procession of miraculés—to be seen as an object of grace—one had to be recognized not only by clerical officials and doctors but also by a larger public sphere defined by anonymous crowds and the mass press. And as the women described their experiences of sickness and healing, they seemed careful to construct precisely such an image for themselves. Objects of God's grace, they were exceptional figures, revered by anonymous pilgrims at Lourdes and featured by Catholic newspapers. By invoking this public recognition, then, they claimed to be integral participants, key protagonists, in the unfolding saga of the miraculous at Lourdes. As Marie Demontés declared in the concluding words of her account: "By attending this magnificent procession, I hope to add a floret to the splendid wreath of flowers offered with gratitude to Immaculate Mary, Our Lady of Lourdes."[37] Demontés projected herself as a natural participant in this celebration of the miraculous, a flower whose presence would enhance the splendor of the Virgin of Lourdes. This was no small claim for an ordinary lay believer, a woman of humble origins who had spent most of her life suffering in obscurity.

To claim the status of Lourdes miraculée was to assert oneself as a sacred celebrity within a public realm. I would not want to exaggerate this celebrity status, for, as I suggested in the preceding chapter, one's moment in the spotlight was often brief and the public sphere was limited to the Catholic devout. Celebrity through Lourdes was not celebrity in Paris. Nevertheless, Lourdes may have felt like Paris for those blessed miraculées, often from modest backgrounds, who experienced fame (however fleeting) in a bustling commercial city amid crowds of cheering strangers. Perhaps more important, these women, by claiming the status of Lourdes miraculées, were fashioning a public identity for themselves that reached well beyond their traditional roles as domestic caretakers or humble workers. I would even suggest that they were invoking a model of the self based on personal achievement. In the context of mass pilgrimage to Lourdes, where healing had become a public spectacle, ordinary laywomen found opportunities to write themselves into Christian history as actors, spiritual authorities, and objects of grace. This was no small achievement in late nineteenth-century French society, where nonelite women still enjoyed few opportunities for recognition and self-expression in the public sphere.

THE FRAGILE MIRACULÉE

The women's testimonial accounts mobilized rhetorical strategies that did not always blend smoothly. By merging traditional Christian narratives of suffering and sanctity with the shrine's discourse of medical verification as well as the triumphant voice of the Catholic press, the women produced modern-style melodramas in which they heroically vanquished both disease and villainous doctors. In doing so, they cast themselves as legitimate public figures—visible evidence of divine intercession and adored objects of God's grace—in the ongoing drama of the miraculous at Lourdes. Yet the women's efforts to reconcile very different notions of legitimacy resulted in unavoidable tensions and inconsistencies within their testimonial accounts. What made for an "authentic" experience of healing, for example, now that healing was a mass spectacle observed by thousands of onlookers yet verified by only a few experts? Which of the three key elements of the healing narrative—the woman's abundant suffering, the doctor's objective diagnosis, or the commercial media's record of the cure—was most important to establishing the "true" Lourdes miraculée? Although the women's accounts never posed these questions directly, such uncertainties did raise problems within the narratives. Writers often seemed heedless, for instance, of the diagnoses they cited to describe their years of pain. As a result, the logic of extravagant suffering was not always compatible with the shrine's call for medical verification. Similarly, a woman's claim to have experienced a radical and singular moment of divine intervention sometimes sat at odds with her description of the healing experience. The desire to include intimate details, to leave out no supportive piece of information, served to make these inconsistencies even more apparent. Furthermore, the women typically portrayed their doctors in a contradictory light. Ineffective healers, even malicious torturers, physicians and their expertise were nevertheless required to confirm the truth of illness and recovery. One historian has argued that such contradictions emerged because the women chose to ignore, or were simply oblivious to, the objective definitions of medical science.[38] Yet this interpretation fails to engage with the very contradictory conditions of miracle making at Lourdes, where multiple rhetorics were blended together and *individual* claims of divine intervention were now *mass* produced as spectacles. It was not easy to claim the status of authentic miraculée in an age of medical scrutiny and commercial reproduction, and it is not surprising that, in their accounts, some women expressed moments of doubt when they were unable to fulfill the shrine's many requirements for effectively narrating the emergence of a cure. These rhetorical tensions are worth exploring because they reveal the fragility of the public persona of the Lourdes miraculée.

One needed both prolonged, extreme pain and a doctor's diagnosis to be a legitimate miraculée. A rhetoric of suffering and sanctity enabled the women to claim spiritual authority as believers who suffered for the healing work of Lourdes and were rewarded with the blessing of a cure. A rhetoric of medical authority ensured, in turn, that the extraordinary suffering and the miraculous cure would be seen as real. Both discourses were crucial for fashioning the public persona of the Lourdes miraculée. Yet the language of Christian martyrdom and the shrine's rules for medical verification were not always easily reconciled in these narratives of the miraculous. While the women writers routinely cited a medical diagnosis for their complaints, their accounts of prolonged and excessive pain often followed a dramatic logic that had little to do with contemporary medical analysis. Thus, all ailments were presented as life-threatening, whether they were tuberculosis, cancer, or simply chronic gastritis. Mme. Hugot's testimonial of suffering is a case in point. Declaring that her long bout with muteness had put her life in jeopardy, she asserted that she feared dying en route to Lourdes because her physical pain was so great.[39]

Other women presented their descent into illness as an attack on their body that caused the breakdown of all normal functions. In these cases, medical diagnosis played a crucial yet contradictory role. Presenting a medical diagnosis was clearly an attempt to shore up the authenticity of a claim to unbearable suffering. Yet it also seemed to give the women license to list numerous diseases or to describe an array of frightening symptoms that had little to do with the stated disease. Léotine Aubain, for example, connected an assortment of unrelated health problems to her medically diagnosed spinal cord disease. She described an infection of the ten fingernails that led to their removal, an internal abscess, swelling on the spine, and a twisted leg that made her an invalid for seven years. Aubain presented all these problems as one terrifying illness that was suddenly and miraculously cured at Lourdes. Eugénie Hanceaux presented a similar account of slow bodily decay resulting from a congeries of unrelated ailments. She

endured chronic vomiting and spitting up of blood associated with chloro-ane-
mia as well as paralysis from a malady of the spinal cord, finally becoming mute
after a bout of influenza. Marie Dout also presented a disparate set of afflictions,
declaring: "I cannot describe all the illnesses that I had and all the suffering that
I experienced during eight-and-a-half years . . .—it would take pages and
pages." But she then proceeded to list a grave case of gastritis, a tumor in her
heart, and a disease of the spinal cord.[40] Although these writers attempted to
meet the shrine's new verification requirements by employing the vocabulary of
medical experts, the effort often collided with their own attachments to an older
vision of spiritual legitimacy rooted in Christian martyrdom. Indeed, this well-
established language of suffering and sanctity, so familiar and accessible to these
women, frequently overshadowed the validating power of science. By mobilizing two very different rhetorical strategies to bolster their claims to being "true"
Lourdes miraculées—one focused on extraordinary suffering and the other
grounded in medical exactitude—the women sometimes called those same
claims into question.

The conflicting role of the doctor within these healing accounts could also
destabilize the women's claims. For while the writers relied on a newly powerful medical profession to guarantee the truth of illnesses as well as extraordinary
recoveries, they portrayed these medical experts at the same time as blundering
incompetents who failed to heal them. As we have seen, the women cited diagnoses by the very doctors who had forced them to undergo useless treatments
and even, in certain cases, had conceded their own medical inadequacies. For all
his glaring impotence, the doctor's diagnosis remained the arbiter of truth, providing the crucial evidence of disease and suffering. Many women even returned
to these same doctors to confirm their cures. Marie Pilot, who decided to go to
Lourdes only after her doctor had "abandoned" her, reported that she went back
to him to verify her cure. She quoted his exact words: "'You are completely
cured. You had an open sore on your chest, [and] it has absolutely healed.'"[41]
Thus the doctor, an ineffectual practitioner who was unable to cure disease, was
also a skilled expert whose diagnosis was authoritative. Furthermore, his expert
eye was needed to recognize a true moment of inexplicable healing: submitting
medical verification in the form of a doctor's certificate of the cure was an essential part of the screening process for participation in the jubilee procession.
It is not surprising that almost all of the selected miraculées enclosed short notes
or certificates written by doctors attesting that traces of disease had completely
disappeared. In a few cases, the women simply listed the names and addresses
of their physicians for confirmation. The doctor, then, occupied a paradoxical
position, verifying the miraculous from the grounds of his own failure.

The doctor's suspect moral position in these narratives further complicated
his role as medical authority of the miraculous. His torturous treatments and
callous behavior, for example, cast him as the villain of the story. The cruelty of

the doctor helped to shape the melodrama of the narrative, allowing
to depict themselves as suffering heroines. Yet his reprehensible beh...
made him morally fit to judge moments of divine intervention. Certain women
drew attention to this problem when they discussed their doctors' refusals to
acknowledge the cure. For Elise Delahaye, description of a return visit to her
doctor to seek out the needed medical certificate served to underscore his unscrupulous character. She declared that when the physician learned about her
cure, "he was furious, [and] he no longer wanted to see me." She explained that
he had wanted her to undergo an operation at all costs, but instead she had
prayed to the Virgin of Lourdes to heal her. Refusing to verify the cure or give
her the needed certificate, this physician forced her to find another doctor. In
such instances, the narrative logic of suffering and sanctity that positioned the
doctor as villain undermined the doctor's other role as adjudicator of miraculous recovery.[42] Thus the rhetoric of Christian martyrdom could be a double-
edged sword. By employing a discourse of the excessive and extraordinary, in
which pain knew no boundaries and doctors were villains, the women told awe-
inspiring stories that strengthened their claims to legitimacy as sacred heroines.
Yet when overdrawn, such discourse could have the opposite effect, drawing
attention to narrative inconsistencies that exposed the instability of the public
persona of the miraculée.

This problem of dramatic overkill was equally apparent in the women's descriptions of the cure. At certain moments, the effort to invoke a sense of awe toward the cure was undermined by an evident desire to prolong or intensify the
climactic moment of divine grace. Some women, for example, claimed to be recipients of multiple cures. Often penned as postscripts to the principal stories
of healing, these reports of additional cures seemed intended to confirm the
original moment of healing while also enlarging the writer's claims. By directing attention to the Virgin's continuing interest in them, the women apparently
hoped to magnify their own special positions as figures of grace. Yet citing
additional cures, often for minor physical ailments, could also displace the
core moment of healing. Rather than enhancing the emotional impact of the account, the presence of supplementary cures dissipated the affective force of the
drama.[43] Following a detailed account of her miraculous cure at Lourdes, Elzire
Gronnier described a second moment of extraordinary healing at her home, after she had pricked her finger and suffered from a painful infection. She applied
Lourdes water and the oil of Saint Martin to the infected sore, at which point
her finger was completely cured. Gronnier observed that her neighbors had
wanted to fetch a doctor, but that she insisted on using Lourdes water because
she knew that the Virgin would cure her. Gronnier ended her account by thanking the Virgin for this "double cure." Marie Favraux also ended her testimonial
by describing a second moment of divine grace. After her initial cure from paralysis and a stomach malady at Lourdes, she reported, two small cysts developed

on her leg; through constant prayer to the Virgin Mary, both cysts soon disappeared. Favraux proclaimed this second cure to be "a visible proof of the protection of the Blessed Virgin." Rosalie Gouhier followed up an account of miraculous healing from a hernia with three additional cures from a variety of ailments including a cold and a fall down the stairs. She concluded her testimonial by thanking the Virgin for never abandoning her in times of need.[44]

Introducing multiple cures into the narratives suggested that truly exceptional individuals attracted ongoing divine intervention. For these Lourdes miraculées, additional healing experiences were used to claim positions of importance that transcended their initial cures. Indeed, additional cures even distinguished such women from other Lourdes miraculées. Yet these supplemental cures exacted a price, their narrative function as postscripts serving to diminish the suspense and drama of the primary cure. Instead of concluding with an extraordinary recovery from the very brink of death, multiple-cure accounts put forth minor healing events as serial encounters with the Virgin Mary. Did every ailment, even minor ones, require a miracle cure? Dramatic overkill not only subverted the force of the narrative but potentially cheapened the value of the miraculous. This multiplication of miracles also pointed to a deeper problem with the singularity of the miraculée. When hundreds of cured pilgrims were lauded in the Catholic press and celebrated at the shrine, how were these women to distinguish themselves as exceptional figures of grace? The citing of multiple cures, like exaggerated accounts of physical suffering, seemed intended to make vivid this public persona so routinely reproduced at the shrine. Yet it was not easy for these women to fashion effective public roles for themselves as Lourdes miraculées when conflicting forms of authenticity were required to prove the truth of their cures.

In fact, at particular moments in their testimonials, the writers betrayed a certain anxiety, perhaps even doubt, about the miraculous nature of the cure. These moments of uncertainty usually surfaced when the woman's effort to inspire awe was compromised by her need to comply with the shrine's rules for medical proof and factual accuracy. Thus, while dramatic overkill, propelled by the rhetoric of Christian martyrdom, could undercut the validating power of medical claims, the reverse was also possible: the requirements of historical accuracy and medical detail often worked against the effort to inspire awe. The women routinely declared, for example, that moments of healing were "instantaneous" and "permanent," thereby invoking the shrine's own definition of an extraordinary cure. Yet their attempts to provide historically exact depictions of events often resulted in healing experiences that were obviously gradual or even incomplete. Jeanne Delesalle described an interior force that electrified her body and pushed her to her feet during the Procession of the Blessed Sacrament. She was able to walk and immediately regained her appetite. Delesalle's dramatic description of the cure, however, was quickly undercut by further details. Her

arthritic leg was still stiff for a time, and her foot remai
following day, after bathing in the grotto pools, did s'
foot, and even then she was forced to walk with a ca
she experienced a relapse of arthritis, but was fi
through the use of Lourdes water and constant praye
gin. Perhaps realizing that this account did not fully comply
understanding of a radical cure, Delesalle added an explanation for tie
it could only be a final "test" of faith by the Virgin to allow her entire family
participate in the cure. Other miraculées faced a more difficult time squaring
the medical facts of their cases with claims of divine intervention. Euphrasie
Bourgault affirmed that the Virgin healed her from a hip disorder (coxalgia) in
1890 and she had since enjoyed excellent health. Yet she noted that one leg remained shorter than the other. Despite this disability, she considered herself the
beneficiary of an extraordinary cure, asserting with pride: "All my companions
who saw me so infirm, and now walking so well, say that it is truly a great miracle."[45] In each of these accounts, then, the need to provide a detailed and medically accurate account of the cure complicated the woman's ability to evoke a
radical, singular moment of healing.

The writers sometimes expressed ambivalence toward the multiple requirements for authentication. In rare instances, this ambivalence could turn into outright hostility toward clerical officials. The testimonial of Rosalie Gouhier
provides an interesting example of how the need to comply with the shrine's
rules of verification could produce both confusion and anger. Before her cure in
1888, when Gouhier had first attempted to go to Lourdes, the Association de
Notre-Dame de Lourdes refused to admit her as one of its chosen malades (registered sick pilgrims) because she would not submit to a medical exam. Later, in
her testimonial, she noted with scorn, "You know how one is received at rue
François 1er, No. 8 [the association's address] when one wants nothing to do
with medicine." Claiming that a pious woman then took pity on her and bought
her a train ticket to the shrine, Gouhier was cured en route to the grotto. Yet
even as Gouhier subsequently criticized the shrine's insistence on medical verification, she seemed impressed—and even a bit starstruck—by women who did
undergo the now ritualized process of seeking authentication. Thus she gushed
that on the train to Lourdes she "sat next to Mlle. Celestine Dubois, the miraculée from 1887 who had been to the Bureau of Verification."[46]

Gouhier's comments reveal a deeply ambivalent atti
spectacle of the Lourdes cure. On the one hand, Gouhie
medical verification as an obstacle to her own pursuit c
hand, she approved of other women who willingly e
scrutiny, treating Celestine Dubois as a "true" miraculé
Furthermore, her anger at the Notre-Dame de Salut f
thority to control access to the shrine did not stop her,

account, from routinely procuring Lourdes water from the charitable or-
nization at its office in Paris. This water, in fact, cured her of three subsequent
ilments. Gouhier's account suggests that certain female miraculées bridled at
the shrine's call for public scrutiny to prove the truth of the cure; she even referred to the many cures she reported as her "secrets." Yet even as Gouhier refused to become an object of grace by following the rules of the shrine, she
seemed to accept and delight in the women who did. This apparent contradiction suggests how impossible it was to reject completely the shrine's new discourse of the cure and still participate in the spectacle of miracle making at
Lourdes. After all, Gouhier chose to make her "secrets" known by writing an
account of her cures for the very association she criticized. And even though
Gouhier did not play by the shrine's rules, she nonetheless found a way to write
herself into Christian history. Rosalie Gouhier's testimonial reminds us that the
public spectacle of the cure, for all its paradoxicality, provided extraordinary opportunities for ordinary women.

Women who participated in the jubilee pilgrimage of 1897 responded to an
invitation to contribute to the shrine's official record by transforming their personal dramas of sickness and healing into public events. Treating these testimonials as public documents—literary performances that required both skill and
imagination to compose—enables us to appreciate the extraordinary possibilities for self-representation that Lourdes offered devout women. Although women
cured at Lourdes did not control the conventions defining the healing experience at the shrine, they used those conventions to create a model of female
spiritual authority in the figure of the Lourdes miraculée. By fashioning this religious persona, the women drew on popular models of Christian martyrdom—
derived from such works as *The Golden Legend* and, more generally, a religious
rhetoric of the body in pain—to make themselves into virtuous heroines. They
combined this familiar narrative of suffering and sanctity with the shrine's rules
for authenticating cures, which had already merged other modern discourses of
the spectacular (ranging from popular melodrama to the reportage of the mass
press), in order to present themselves as female icons of spiritual authority. As
suffering heroines, messengers of truth, and objects of grace, they became important religious figures, worthy of adulation from the crowd and deserving of
permanent commemoration in the annals of the shrine. That the women were
able to write themselves into Christian history not just as suffering heroines or
humble servants of God but also as beloved public figures, even sacred celebrities, attests to their abilities at reworking conventional models of femininity into
new role models for devout women in the public sphere.

The jubilee pilgrimage to Lourdes, with its triumphant procession of cured
ims, provides a new perspective on the possibilities and constraints that

mass culture offered ordinary women. The female miraculée represented a distinctly modern figure. Inextricably linked to the late nineteenth-century commercialization of female images, she was a product of the social spaces—the mass press, the theater, and print advertising—opened up by a modernizing society. Like her secular sisters—the female journalist, the Parisian actress, and, more generally, the New Woman—the Lourdes miraculée offered a new model for imagining a feminine public self. The miraculée presented an enticing public persona for Catholic women because she transgressed traditional models of womanhood based on modesty and self-abnegation, embracing instead an assertive and achieving feminine subject. Humble servants of God who acted only for the good of the faith, these women nevertheless became public performers, writers of their own life stories, and, ultimately, sacred celebrities at the shrine. In fact, it was precisely the combination of tradition and transgression that made the figure of the miraculée so compelling for many devout Catholic women. Thus did the conditions of mass pilgrimage, which provided large numbers of nonelite laywomen access to the rituals and practices of miraculous healing, make these various public identities possible.

The conditions of miracle making at Lourdes, while democratizing the figure of the miraculée, also produced a public feminine self that was inherently unstable. Making this persona persuasive depended on mobilizing multiple and competing strategies of legitimacy. To claim the status of miraculée, one had to invoke the rhetoric of medical objectivity as well as the spectacle-making power of the mass press. Combining these discourses within a narrative of Christian suffering enabled these women to proclaim themselves exceptional figures of grace. Yet the often uneasy juxtaposition of quite different discourses yielded an unstable amalgam of claims. Ultimately, the miraculées of Lourdes struggled to reconcile the miraculous experience as a singular moment of divine intervention with the fact that such an event was now routinely reproduced at the shrine. Indeed, the very claim to be an exceptional figure—an authentic miraculée—hinged on the shrine's ability to reproduce rituals of healing as mass spectacles. Thus while the production of miraculous healing enabled ordinary women to fashion a new public identity, this routinized process served to question, by its very operation, the authenticity of such a self. In this way, the women healed at Lourdes were forced to struggle with the problem of authenticity in the modern age.

5

Public Wager

Publicity and the Truth
of the Cure

In 1871 the Catholic daily newspaper *L'Univers* published a challenge to all free-thinkers. A devout Catholic, E. Artus, offered ten thousand francs to anyone who could disprove one of the Lourdes cures. Outlining the terms of his public wager, Artus proposed two specific cures recounted in Henri Lasserre's *Notre-Dame de Lourdes* as best suited for the bet, but he was confident enough to let opponents select other cures from Lasserre's book if they wished: "I do not have a preference." He added, "I have no hesitation in putting up my money!" Claiming to have already deposited the large sum with his lawyer, Artus declared, "We will see what the freethinkers will put up." In response, critics of Lourdes dismissed Artus as a publicity hound or pronounced the cures to be products of autosuggestion and other forms of "mind cure." Enormous quantities of ink were spilled over this public wager, yet not a single freethinker accepted the bet. A series of would-be opponents vowed to take up the contest, but each one withdrew amid disputes over the terms for judging the cures, declaring that the understanding of proof was too "elastic" and that no one could possibly win a bet to prove the cures were *not* "miracles."[1]

Although the public wager of Artus, on its face, was very effective, the cause of Lourdes did not escape unscarred. One problem was that the skeptics' interpretation of the Lourdes miracles as mind cures would not go away. Perhaps more troubling was that the accusations of publicity seeking leveled at Artus would also envelop subsequent promoters of the cures. Following the Artus incident, the miracle cures engaged church supporters and anticlerics in a series of public challenges and counterchallenges that regularly became headline news over the course of four decades. Pulling in clerics, doctors, journalists, and men of letters such as Émile Zola, these disputes over the nature of healing at

Lourdes often took the form of wagers to prove, once and for ai
the cure. Both sides relied on the popular press to convey their cha.
reading public, hoping to make their cases by winning the battle of ɪ.
ion. Such a strategy led proponents and opponents alike not only tɔ
tensively on the evidence of the cures—scrutinizing medical ce
eyewitness accounts, and the bodies of healed pilgrims—but also to eɪ.gage in
attention-getting exposés and scathing denunciations of each other's competence, credibility, and motives. Indeed, the increasing recourse to sensationalist
rhetoric and ad hominem attacks suggests the need to pay as much attention to
the forms and venues of debate as to the substance of the views exchanged.

The fin-de-siècle disputes over the Lourdes cures engaged old antagonists on
a new battlefield: the pages of an emerging mass press. These disputes cannot
be separated, of course, from the broader sweep of nineteenth-century exchanges between science and religion. The Church's first line of defense against
materialist explanations of seemingly supernatural events had been outright rejection of the beliefs and practices of positivism. By the 1880s, however, the
Church found itself responding to the epistemological sovereignty of positivism
by adopting the methods and metaphors of modern science to legitimate its own
claims about the miraculous.[2] At Lourdes, as we have seen, clerics and devout
Catholic doctors joined together to create a medical bureau that ingeniously
wielded the tools of medical science to prove the reality of the shrine's miracle
cures. Although the bureau's case studies and public examinations of cured pilgrims may have convinced few anticlerical doctors that the cures were truly
miraculous, they did inspire a new recognition among at least some physicians
of the therapeutic value of Lourdes and of faith healing in general. As recent
scholarship has pointed out, a number of doctors who interpreted the cases as
instances of mind cure nevertheless looked to Lourdes for insights about hysteria and the power of suggestion to heal the body.[3] Yet approaches that have focused on questions of antagonism versus dialogue have too often ignored the
very terrain on which the debates were fought out.

The emerging mass press furnished not only the arena but the implements
and audience for the contest over healing at Lourdes. Framed as a series of public challenges—wagers, lawsuits, and back-and-forth personal attacks—these
debates were never simply intellectual arguments among experts but battles to
sway public opinion. Moreover, the public wager of Artus showed early on that
attention-getting gimmicks were highly valuable weapons in these contests. Although rhetorical stunts did not necessarily prove the contentions of Lourdes
supporters, such tactics sold newspapers, spread word of the cause, and, perhaps most tellingly, impugned the character and credibility of anticlerical detractors. Not surprisingly, opponents of the miracle cures also found such
gimmicks difficult to resist. Indeed, even as both camps claimed to be searching
for the truth of the cure (embodied in the findings of their "rigorous" investi-

gations) the two sides increasingly enlisted the tactics of a sensationalist press to make their cases to the reading public. In this respect, the fin-de-siècle newspaper debates over the Lourdes cures came to resemble, as historian Jason Szabo has perceptively noted, the coterminous press wars over the Dreyfus affair.[4]

This parallel between the Dreyfus affair and the Lourdes debates is more than circumstantial. The two controversies, in fact, shared many of the same protagonists—the journalists of the Assumptionist *La Croix,* the republican press, and Zola himself—along with a similar sense that the relative influence of anticlericals and devout Catholics over French political life hung in the balance. Yet more than common actors and an overlapping context, these two fin-de-siècle conflicts were united by a similar logic of progression. Supporters and detractors of the Lourdes cures, like the Dreyfussards and anti-Dreyfussards, soon found themselves trapped by their chosen rhetorical terrain. As a result, the two sides in each conflict sought to exploit the spectacle-making tactics of the mass press even as they blamed this institution for its sensationalizing tendencies.[5] In the Dreyfus affair, the growing resort to invective, innuendo, and shocking exposés made clear that, regardless of the guilt or innocence of Alfred Dreyfus, mass politics as scandalous spectacle would become a central feature of modern social life.[6] For Lourdes, the dawning realization that all knowledge claims (religious as well as medical) were now embedded within a modern commercial public sphere served to deepen the insecurities of supporters and adversaries alike, making efforts to establish an objective or untainted "truth of the cure" increasingly difficult. Perhaps more than the conflict over Dreyfus, the Lourdes debates showed with startling clarity how questions of truth and proof were entangled not merely with political commitments but with the commercial interests of the modern popular press. In this way, the debates about the cures can be read as a key instance of a broader transformation in late nineteenth-century France, one in which authority was now established in part through truth claims advanced and "demonstrated" through modern publicity.

The many public challenges to prove and disprove the Lourdes cures ensnared supporters and critics, clerics and doctors, in an intractable conflict. This fruitless contest not only failed to resolve the truth of the cure but also raised disturbing questions about the status, competence, and character of the authority figures involved. The challenges to establish the nature of healing at Lourdes gave rise to a seemingly stark set of oppositions—truth versus falsehood, reality versus appearance, authenticity versus deception—that were erected upon the slippery terrain of an emerging commercial public sphere.[7] By the 1890s, these same issues reemerged following the publicity-saturated visit to Lourdes by Zola, whose subsequent interviews and published novel set the terms for a series of sensational but inconclusive exchanges with Lourdes supporters over the reality of "mind cure." These dramatic contests resurfaced in the first decade of the twentieth century, when supporters of Lourdes seized on a "perfectly objective" miracle cure—the exhaustively documented case of Pierre de Rudder—to reassert the incontrovertible truth of miraculous healing. Yet, once again, debate led to further challenges, to revelations of fraud and incompetence, and, ultimately, to the mutual embarrassment and disrepute of both sides. In short, nearly half a century of claims and counterclaims, spectacles and counterspectacles, not only failed to resolve the bitter disputes over the Lourdes miracles but also laid bare the commercial entanglements that beset both religious and scientific claims to knowledge.

THE PUBLIC CHALLENGE OF MONSIEUR ARTUS

Why did Artus choose the tactic of a public wager to challenge the freethinkers of France to take seriously the miracles of Lourdes? Some years later, the devout Catholic explained that, following the enormous success of Lasserre's book, scores of counterattacks emerged to deny a priori the very possibility of miracles. Refusing to examine the cured pilgrims in person or even to interview their doctors or other eyewitnesses, these unbelievers passed off mere philosophical speculation ("des thèses philosophiques") as evidence that miracles did not exist.

What upset Artus most of all, however, was that these theories were routinely reproduced in the popular press and that "the masses who read the newspapers . . . take seriously all these printed stupidities, these arguments a hundred times refuted but still given as evidence, all these shameless denials of the most incontestable and solidly established facts." He explained further:

> The masses, who cannot conduct an investigation themselves, who have neither the time nor the money for doing so, rely on their newspapers. They imagine, in all their decency, that the writer who speaks to them has carried out a conscientious investigation. They suppose, naively, that behind the peremptory assertion of the publicist or his disdainful denial stands a serious examination, some sort of study of the issue, a certain respect for the truth, a certain good faith, a certain intellectual integrity. . . . But, one must say that, in supposing all this, the masses are almost always mistaken.[8]

On the contrary, the press—"these educators of the masses"—had failed to carry out any systematic investigation of the cures, passing off prejudice and passion as the unvarnished truth. Concerned that the untutored reader was being taken in by such lies, Artus felt compelled to expose these false accounts in the most public way possible. In short, he had to fight fire with fire. If the freethinkers were so confident of their position, they should be willing to wager on its veracity. This kind of public challenge, played out in what Artus saw as his adversaries' own arena, would reveal the real truth.

The public wager of Artus may be dismissed as the overeager gesture of a devotee or as a crassly sensationalistic ploy. Yet his rationale, along with the evident appeal of the public wager itself, makes quite clear that the popular press quickly became the proving ground—and money the agent of proof—in the battle over the Lourdes cures. Under these conditions, any challenger willing to accept a wager would have to accept its premises, and yet these very premises could soon become recipes for consternation and even ridicule. For both sides, the willingness to engage in a wager demonstrated aggressive confidence in their own positions. Yet such a wager introduced money into the process of adjudicating the cures, a situation that threatened the credibility of the participants as impartial seekers of the truth. This dilemma becomes especially vivid if we follow the exchanges between Artus and the editor of *Le Progrès de l'Est,* a provincial newspaper from Nancy that responded to his challenge. The heated exchanges between Artus and the paper over several months in 1873 reveal an increasing similarity in rhetorical maneuvers to camouflage the reality that neither side could "prove" its case.

On January 6, 1873, *Le Progrès de l'Est* responded to the challenge of Artus. Questioning whether Artus even possessed sufficient funds to cover his bet, the paper demanded the name and address of the supposed lawyer said to be in possession of the ten-thousand-franc stake. The editor also noted a striking similarity between this wager and the infamous challenge launched by a Monsieur Mangin, an industrialist and maker of pencils who once had offered to pay 33,333 francs and thirty-three centimes to anyone who could prove that his pencils were not the best. Artus and his ultramontane friends, the editor noted, were not even as generous as Mangin, betting a measly ten thousand francs on the Lourdes cures. Dismissing Artus as a publicity-seeking huckster, the paper reminded its readers that no one had ever accepted the Mangin challenge "because the word *prove* is an elastic term, because Mangin was free to judge and reject all proof." Artus, the paper argued, enjoyed a similar advantage, because "he can always resort to saying that he does not accept the evidence." Although Artus had promised to assemble an "impartial" commission to judge the evidence presented to him, the newspaper concluded that such a commission would make a mockery of objective scientific inquiry: the money involved surely jeopardized all pretense to impartiality. Yet even as the article mocked the public wager of Artus, it concluded by countering with one of its own. Pretending to up the ante, *Le Progrès de l'Est* grandly offered one hundred thousand francs to anyone who could prove the truth of a single Lourdes miracle cure.[9]

The newspaper soon regretted issuing this mock challenge when Artus wrote back with a letter of acceptance. Claiming that the newspaper's counterwager was merely a cheap publicity stunt intended to sell newspapers, Artus nevertheless responded point by point to the charges against him. He provided a long list of "impartial" judges for the commission, including reputable historians, doctors, and scientists belonging to academies of medicine and science, and even well-known adversaries of Lourdes. He also suggested a specific cure to investigate, one especially suitable because the cured woman was still alive and could be examined by all involved. The serious tone taken by Artus—a striking contrast to the playful sarcasm of *Le Progrès de l'Est*—and his apparently reasonable conditions for pursuing the bet now tended to cast the freethinkers in the role of hucksters. Under his precisely established conditions, Artus claimed, proof was hardly "elastic" and the wager could be carried out in good faith.[10]

Yet Artus was not above questioning the integrity of his opponents or invoking the supposed authority of wagered money. Asserting that he had already put up his stake, he asked whether the newspaper would dare to do the same—or would it back down, like all prior challengers who had dared not "venture a bet or risk a crown?" Such failures of nerve, in fact, "judged them definitively, taking the measure of their good faith and its value." After this affirmation of the wager as a moral standard, Artus concluded his letter by retaking the high road. Enjoining the press to be the bearer of truth and honesty, he cautioned that otherwise "it warps the consciousness of those countless classes who do not have the time or ability to carry out by themselves a similar investigation, and who, in their ignorance and their honesty, rely on others who claim the mission to instruct them." *Le Progrès de l'Est*, he implied, had not lived up to this duty.[11]

The newspaper responded with a short but firmly worded defense. The tone of this new article, no longer one of ridicule, wavered between angry and defensive as the paper tried to expose the wager by Artus and his impartial commission as cunning deceptions. First, the editor noted the careful wording of the wager, which invited opponents to prove as false a single cure that had taken place at Lourdes. Yet "we have never denied," the editor countered, "that there have been cures at Lourdes. What we have denied is that these cures have been the result of the intervention of a supernatural power." Noting that inexplicable cures had also occurred at the Salpêtrière hospital in Paris, the paper dismissed the Lourdes miracles as similar cases of mind cure. Artus, charged the editor, was playing a game of words with his public wager, but it was a game that could have serious consequences. What would happen, the editor asked, if this public commission concluded that the cures were real? He feared that "the Catholic press will claim, as soon as the commission has sanctioned the miracles of Lourdes, that scientists . . . have recognized the reality of the intervention of the Virgin." Acknowledging that the press had the power to make the truth because people believed what they read, *Le Progrès de l'Est* worried that miracle cures would be given a new legitimacy. To make matters worse, the list of so-called impartial scientists and physicians submitted by Artus failed to include, the editor claimed, a single freethinker: "M. Artus fashions an ultramontane deck of cards, then graciously bids us: choose one. Under these conditions, the wager is a fraud."[12]

Clearly, *Le Progrès de l'Est* had no intention of following through with the bet, but it did not want to appear to be backing out. In a shrewd move, the editor demanded a change in wording, insisting that the question for the commission should not be whether the cures were real or false but rather whether "it is true that the Virgin of Lourdes had cured Mlle. X . . . or Y." "All other questions," he claimed, "are a sham." Artus, of course, could never agree to this kind of an investigative inquiry; only a bishop had the authority to determine if a cure was miraculous in nature. Yet Artus remained undaunted. Responding to the accusation that his impartial jury was a sham, he noted that his list included even Protestant doctors, who were known for their open-mindedness. Of course, he refused to invite ardent positivists such as Ernest Renan and Émile Littré, who denied a priori the very existence of miracles, because such intellectuals could be neither "unbiased" nor "objective." Accusing the editor of "playing with the facts," Artus pointed out that the newspaper had agreed to the terms of the commission's inquiry when first pushing its own one-hundred-thousand-franc wager. The paper had no right now to try to change the wording of the challenge, and was simply afraid, he charged, to follow through with its own bet. *Le Progrès de l'Est* printed a curt, final answer: "We do not reply to such letters. We simply hand them over to the court of public opinion."[13]

Thus did the public wager of Artus conclude without any clear resolution. Although the bet was never accepted nor was any commission formally convened, each side claimed victory in the arena of public debate. The anticlerical newspaper crowed that it had successfully unmasked the fraudulent nature of the wager of Artus; playing with a loaded deck, the Catholic was exposed as nothing more than a hustler. Artus claimed victory as well, because the newspaper had been so quick to back down from its own grandiose challenge.

For all this posturing and grandstanding, the public wager of Artus was in many respects a small event in the life of Lourdes. Involving a single lay Catholic promoter of the shrine, a few undistinguished doctors, and a provincial press, the incident was played out on the margins of French public life. Yet the charges and countercharges launched by Artus and *Le Progrès de l'Est* raised an issue that grew in importance as French society struggled with the problems of a mass press in a democratic society. Should both sides fear the growing power of the press to manufacture the truth and to manipulate a naive reading public?

The Artus incident revealed a set of emerging contradictions that bedeviled subsequent higher-profile clashes over the Lourdes cures. Could the commercial press be a mirror of the truth *and* a reflection of the people's interests? At different moments, Artus and *Le Progrès de l'Est* had championed both images of the press, and each protagonist took up the cause of proving or debunking cures with these idealized images in mind. Yet each side also engaged in character assassination, suppression of evidence, and blatant exaggeration. Attacking one another for undermining the noble principles of the press in order to advance political agendas, the two sides became similarly vulnerable to charges of pursuing economic interests—such as the desire to sell newspapers or to win large sums—in order to generate publicity. The two sides, by engaging in a shared set of rhetorical maneuvers, convincingly demonstrated that it was difficult to launch a modern press campaign without tainting one's own cause. They also tended to undermine the intellectual power of religious and scientific authorities, whose ideas about the nature of healing seemed so easily twisted by the press to win over a vulnerable public. Indeed, if the Artus wager failed to attract the spotlight of national attention, the issues it raised soon moved to the center of French public life.

COUNTERCHALLENGE: ZOLA AND THE SUGGESTION THESIS

The newspaper furor surrounding the publication of Zola's *Lourdes* in 1894 became the catalyst for a new round of debates over the truth of the Lourdes cures. The impact of this coverage, as with the publication of "J'Accuse" four years later, was to bring a still-nascent controversy to the notice of French society. In both instances, the mass press enabled Zola to ignite sensational debate by issuing a dramatic challenge to orthodox opinion. In the case of Lourdes, Zola's bold intervention was to declare in a flurry of interviews with Parisian newspapers (given before he had completed his novel) that the Lourdes miracles were cases of mind cure.

These assertions were good publicity for the forthcoming novel, and they certainly did not go unnoticed. First, the famed doctor Jean-Martin Charcot entered the public discussion, offering his own "scientific" interpretation of the cures as cases of suggestion. Soon afterward, Gustave Boissarie launched a counterattack to materialist explanations of healing at his 1894 conference in Paris. This new wave of debate over Lourdes, like the Artus episode, soon saw charges of incompetence and dishonorable conduct take center stage. Although the manifest subject of the debate focused on whether the cures were natural or unnatural, cases of suggestion or of divine intervention, the polemics that erupted on both sides revealed a growing preoccupation with questions of character and credibility. The debates also pointed up the role of the press as both purveyor and arbiter of knowledge claims, in this case over the truth of the cure.

Zola's proclamations set the terms for this extended series of disputes over suggestion. If the author had found Lourdes compelling (as we saw in chapter 2) for its admixture of crowds and commerce, he was equally fascinated by the shrine's claims of miraculous healing. Yet it was clear from the start that Zola found nothing very miraculous about these cures. After his visit to Lourdes in 1892 to gather material for the forthcoming novel, he was already convinced that the cases of healing were triggered by suggestion. In an interview with *Le Temps,* Zola described several cures that he had witnessed while visiting the shrine: "Before the grotto, the enthusiasm [élan] of the crowd is extraordinary; the elation of the pilgrims . . . is there, at its height. And so, I saw people who could not move suddenly get up and walk. But the same results are obtained in hospitals by suggestion." He further maintained that religious faith could heal where medical suggestion could not. Invoking Charcot, who referred patients to the sanctuary when his own techniques failed, Zola noted: "No doctor denies that cures of this nature occur before the grotto, and Charcot sends to Lourdes those of his sick patients who are believers." Zola concluded that "certainly nervous illnesses are cured at Lourdes."[14] Without contributing new scientific insight to the phenomenon, such interviews nevertheless were largely responsible for producing a clear and powerful presentation of the suggestion thesis to French literate society.

Zola's interviews also foreshadowed the stinging critique of the shrine's Bureau of Medical Verifications that would later appear in his novel. In the interview with *Le Temps*, he insinuated that the bureau's goal in verifying the illnesses of the pilgrims cured at Lourdes—to prove that organic diseases were indeed healed at the shrine—was a pipedream at best. Noting that medical science was, in fact, often unable to judge accurately the true nature of any organic disorder, Zola asked aloud:

> How does one diagnose the cure of an organic illness like a lesion on the heart or a phthisis, for example? With these sorts of conditions, the diagnoses are always uncertain. One doctor certifies a cavity in the right lung, while another will never discern it. . . . Under these conditions, it is well-nigh impossible to establish the cure of an organic illness.

If the nature of organic lesions was impossible to determine for medical practitioners under the best circumstances, how did the shrine's bureau expect to carry out this complicated task during a three-day pilgrimage?[15] Zola hoped to show how absurd it was for the shrine to use modern medical techniques to legitimate its miracle cures when even medical experts could not always agree on a diagnosis. Yet these comments cut both ways: though directed against the Lourdes doctors, they could also be used to criticize the secular medical profession more generally. That physicians, including specialists, could not always determine the difference between organic and hysterical illnesses suggested the presence of larger problems. How might the public ever really know the truth of the cure? Who was fit to judge?

Zola's provocative remarks sparked an immediate response. One of those who joined the public discussion was Charcot himself. Some months after Zola's trip to the shrine, the *New Review*, a British literary journal, asked Charcot to provide a medical perspective on the novelist's findings. Charcot responded with an essay entitled "La Foi qui guérit" ("The Faith Cure"), which soon came out in popular journals in both France and Great Britain.[16] Although the essay did not mention Lourdes by name or discuss specific cures, Charcot argued that all healing shrines throughout recorded history—whether Muslim, pagan, or Christian—worked in the same way: their cures were the product of autosuggestion or contagious suggestion provoked by such outside stimuli as group prayer, mass processions, and rituals involving sacred water. Suggestion allowed the mind to heal the body. Written for a literate but popular reading audience, Charcot's essay quickly became the authoritative medical work on the Lourdes cures, and his explanation was eagerly taken up by critics of the shrine. Zola himself relied on its ideas for his own presentation of miraculous healing in his novel, which appeared one year later.[17]

Zola's *Lourdes* gave life to abstract theories of suggestion by providing a dramatic rendering of miraculous healing as religious therapeutics. Focusing on the travails of two main characters, Marie de Guersaint and Pierre Fromment, Zola fashioned a narrative that highlighted key elements of the suggestion thesis. Once childhood sweethearts, Marie is now an invalid (after falling from a horse) and Pierre a priest who has lost his faith. They decide to go on a national pilgrimage in the hope that Marie will be cured and Pierre will regain his spiritual commitment. To travel to Lourdes as a registered sick pilgrim, Marie must acquire at least two doctors' certificates verifying that her illness is incurable. Three doctors are summoned to examine her; two diagnose an organic lesion and declare the young woman beyond medical aid. The third, however, tells Pierre in confidence that Marie suffers from a nervous disorder that can be easily cured at the sacred shrine: "The girl ought to be taken to Lourdes and . . . would assuredly be cured there, if she herself were convinced of it." This doctor explains that because Marie's illness is a "simple case of autosuggestion," it would only resolve itself through a "sudden determination to throw off the false notion she had formed of her complaint." This kind of cure could only happen through "the lash of some intense emotion," which Lourdes might be able to generate.[18]

Zola further prepared readers for precisely this type of cure by presenting the rituals and processions at the shrine as suggestive forces in the production of a miracle. The novel portrays the three-day pilgrimage as a mind-altering experience that prepares those suffering from nervous illnesses to be cured: "There had been the fever of the journey, the besetting influence of the same endlessly repeated hymns, and the stubborn continuation of the same religious exercises; and ever and ever the conversation had been turned on miracles, and the mind fixed on the divine illumination of the Grotto." At the climax of the book—the Procession of the Blessed Sacrament on the final day of the pilgrimage—Marie and other sick pilgrims are cured, and Pierre realizes that the bewitching atmosphere of the shrine is the curative agent at work. Musing over the scenes of healing that he has just witnessed at the procession, Pierre asks himself: "Ought one to believe that a multitude became a single being . . . able to increase the power

of auto-suggestion tenfold upon itself? Might one admit that, under certain circumstances of extreme exaltation, a multitude became an agent of sovereign will
compelling the obedience of matter?" He then answers his own question: "That
would have explained how sudden cures fell at times upon the most sincerely
excited of the throng." Pierre's revelation cements his own loss of faith, though
he takes solace in Marie's newfound health and steadfast faith in the Virgin of
Lourdes.[19]

This work by Zola, along with the publicity that accompanied it, gave vivid
expression to the theory of mind cure. Not unexpectedly, publication of the
novel (first issued as a *roman feuilleton* in *Le Gil Blas* from April to August 1894)
prompted an immediate, violent reaction from clergy and lay Catholics. After
the Catholic press denounced the novel, heated exchanges between Zola and
Monseigneur Antoine Ricard, a high church official from Aix-en-Provence, appeared in the pages of *Le Gaulois* and *Le Figaro*. The pope placed the novel on
the Index of Forbidden Books within weeks, and two months later Gustave Boissarie staged a spirited counterattack at a public conference in Paris (detailed in
chapter 3) that was extensively reported in the press. Lambasting Zola's pretense to literary naturalism, the Catholic doctor asserted that Zola had not only
altered the facts of real cures to suit his novelistic purposes but also betrayed his
own misunderstanding of the scientific mechanisms that ruled hysterical illnesses. After all, Zola was no doctor, and his presentation of this complicated
and perplexing disease simply could not convince genuine medical experts!
Such shortcomings were ultimately traceable, Boissarie concluded, to Zola's
moral failures as a man. Other supporters of the shrine, clerics as well as doctors, soon published similar attacks on Zola and his apparent misunderstanding
of suggestion.[20] Adversaries of Lourdes followed suit with rousing defenses of
the author and his novel. Mainstream Parisian dailies, such as *Le Matin* and *Le
Temps*, followed the uproar over the novel in great detail and continued to hound
Zola for interviews, which he readily granted.[21]

Zola's *Lourdes* thus set in motion a powerful counterchallenge to the spectacular assertions of miracles at Lourdes. Despite Boissarie's skillful use of public
theatrics and the popular press to attack the well-known author, the suggestion
thesis became a ready source of bad publicity. On one level, the enemies of
Lourdes simply used the notion of suggestion to lampoon the shrine, presenting devout pilgrims as unconscious hysterics or naive fools. The anticlerical popular press had a field day with such depictions, but even serious medical journals
could not resist using satire when it came to discussing the Lourdes miracles.
During the excitement over Zola's trip, the prominent (and generally serious)
medical journal *Le Progrès Médical* reproduced a short article from a Parisian
daily, *L'Écho de Paris*, for its readers' amusement. Entitled "The Miracle of
Lourdes," the article reported that a group of sick and disabled pilgrims arriving at Lourdes received a frightful scare after being helped off the train. Bran-

cardiers had gently lowered these beloved malades onto the adjoining track without realizing that an express train was rapidly pulling into the station. Upon seeing the train's approach, the sick and disabled pilgrims quickly dashed out of the way, leaving their wheelchairs and crutches behind. The article ended by noting that the few skeptics present at the scene had enjoyed a good laugh at seeing "this somewhat premature intervention of the Blessed Virgin." Versions of this account were told and retold so often by anticlerical journalists and doctors that it became a kind of urban legend. The satirical illustrated journal *L'Assiette au Beurre* also found the suggestion thesis grist for the mill. In a 1901 issue devoted to mocking the shrine, the magazine presented the figure of a charlatan priest who tries to pass off a phony cure to a faithful and dim-witted pilgrim, himself a helpless invalid. The implication was not subtle: the Grotto fathers were using their great powers of suggestion to convince naive Catholics that miracles were occurring before their eyes.[22]

Yet the suggestion thesis was more than just a tool for mocking gullible pilgrims and crafty priests. At another level, suggestion provided adversaries of Lourdes with a powerful means for discrediting the shrine's use of medical science and its doctors who verified the cures. This tactic had already become evident in 1892, when Zola pointed out, in his interview with *Le Temps*, how difficult it was to diagnose properly any organic illness. Charcot's essay "La Foi qui

Figure 40. Satirical cartoon: "Miracle!" "You see that lady: She arrived with laryngitis . . . and yesterday, she walked in the procession!" From *L'Assiette au Beurre*, 29 August 1901.

guérit" complicated the matter further by suggesting that organic conditions such as tumors and ulcers, which he had formerly believed to be beyond the reach of hysteria, could indeed be "born under the influence of neurosis." For Charcot, hysteria was a "capricious" disease that could simulate almost any illness, thereby leading even the best medical practitioner to confuse a typical hysteric with someone suffering from an organic condition. This understanding of hysteria meant that eyewitness testimony from pilgrims, clerics, or any respected laymen was essentially useless, and that even the claims of physicians were open for debate. Clearly, the most convincing cures were suspect.[23]

An article in *Le Progrès Médical* adopted such an argument in its effort to discredit the Lourdes medical bureau and its findings. Responding to the media attention surrounding Zola's trip, the article "Science and Miracles," by journalist Marcel Baudouin, challenged the shrine's ostensibly objective and rigorous methods of verification. After reminding his readers how difficult it was to diagnose hysteria, Baudouin took up the case of Clémentine Trouvé, whose cure had recently been trumpeted in the religious press, to demonstrate the flimsy standards of proof used by the medical bureau at Lourdes. The shrine asserted that a degenerative "bone disease" in the abscessed heel of the young girl's foot, verified by her doctor, was suddenly cured at Lourdes. Witnesses who attested to seeing the foot before and after the cure claimed that the lesion had disappeared with simple immersion in the grotto pools. Boissarie confirmed the case. Yet Baudouin noted that there was not a single photograph of the foot, either before or after the cure. He remarked further that all the witnesses were untrained laymen whose testimony lacked any credibility. Finally, he observed that the lone medical certificate verifying the existence of the lesion came from an unknown doctor. Baudouin concluded: "It is not the guarantee furnished by the sash of a mayor or the seal of a rural constable that we are asking for. It is not a banal certificate, composed in haste without sufficient precision, that we would like to see. It is a serious inquiry, a scientific investigation with material proof." Despite such slight and superficial evidence, Baudouin marveled, Boissarie had declared the case an extraordinary cure.[24]

Scathing criticisms and bald satires were only part of the problem for the shrine. The media uproar over Zola's novel and the ongoing debate over suggestion at Lourdes also made the medical bureau a ready target for all sorts of tricks and medical hoaxes. Boissarie received letters from Catholics warning him of impending plots by anticlerical doctors to send hysterics to Lourdes with false medical certificates in order to humiliate the shrine. One instance, in particular, led to considerable public embarrassment, and nearly a lawsuit, when it became clear that Boissarie had mistakenly authenticated one of these falsified cures and even published an account of the healing event. The incident is worth exploring in some detail, because it shows how public rivalries over proving the truth of the cure became further complicated by questions of economic interest for both sides in the debate over Lourdes.

What became known as the "Dubois deception" began in April 1901, when Boissarie received an angry letter from a Dr. Dubois. Claiming there was "a deplorable error" in the bureau director's latest work on Lourdes, Dubois expressed outrage that the name of his brother (also a medical doctor who was presently out of the country) appeared within the pages of Boissarie's medical study.[25] The work apparently claimed that the brother had once verified the astonishing case of a young girl healed with the use of Lourdes water. Dubois asserted that this was simply impossible because his brother, an ardent freethinker, would never have confirmed such a cure. His own Masonic lodge, in turn, was now threatening to sue Boissarie unless he released a public retraction clearing his brother's name.

Not surprisingly, this letter set off a heated exchange between the two doctors. Boissarie declared that the brother must be a scoundrel who was perpetrating a hoax against the shrine. Claiming that this brother had sought him out at a medical conference in Reims in 1897, Boissarie insisted that the man had discussed the cure of the young girl before a roomful of seven to eight hundred people. The brother had even exhibited before-and-after photographs of the girl as part of a convincing account of the cure. When Boissarie decided to include this account in his next book, he wrote to the man asking for permission to print his name and version of the cure but did not receive a reply, hearing subsequently that the doctor had gone to America. Boissarie chose to print the story without releasing the girl's name or address. It was now obvious, Boissarie maintained, that this doctor had tricked him, and under these conditions the pious doctor flatly refused to print a public retraction.[26]

The affair escalated from here. Enraged by Boissarie's unwillingness to concede error or retract the slanderous accusations against his brother, Dubois threatened to go to the press and turn the incident into a public scandal. He also leveled a series of countercharges against the pious doctor. Asserting that his brother had declared the cure in question "a banal case of psychosis," Dubois marveled at the decision to print an account of the cure when his brother had never responded to requests for permission. Clearly, Boissarie's reputation for cautious and rigorous inquiry was severely inflated! Boissarie's sharp reply reminded Dubois of his brother's activities in Reims and further claimed that this same man had visited the medical bureau two years later to give an official account of the cure for the shrine's records. Yet Boissarie also concluded his letter with a surprising admission of vulnerability. Declaring that he had truly believed in the sincerity of this Dr. Dubois, he insisted that "if I made a mistake, Lourdes has nothing to do with it. I do not claim to be infallible." He continued: "Amid the hundreds of cases that I report on, errors are bound to slip by.

For it to be otherwise is impossible. It is not a question of the number that I bring up, but a question of principle; one single well-demonstrated case is enough for my argument." Forced to admit that he had probably made a mistake, Boissarie nevertheless maintained such an error did not damage Lourdes itself because one miraculous cure was enough to prove the healing power of the shrine.[27]

The Dubois deception dealt a blow, all the same, to Boissarie's reputation as a medical expert and a man of integrity. He had obviously confused a case of hysteria with an organic illness and then published the account by Dubois without his permission. It was on this second issue that the brother now demanded twenty thousand francs as just compensation. Boissarie's book, he claimed, had been written with a "financial goal" in mind and only a financial settlement would resolve the conflict. Once again, money had become the agent of truth in disputes over the cure. Yet it was precisely on this question of economic remuneration that the claim pressed by Dubois soon foundered. Boissarie, with his reputation and now a large sum of money at risk, began to look into the matter more seriously and discovered that the brother whose honor was at stake was in fact a well-known confidence man. A priest from the diocese of Reims wrote to Boissarie confirming that "the famous Dr. Dubois" was nothing more than a wheeler-dealer (*un chevalier d'industrie*): "The general opinion is that he demanded to speak [at your conference] in order to attract attention to himself and build up a Catholic clientele." The doctor had tried subsequently to establish a special clinic that used electricity to treat the sick, but when the clinic failed he secretly left town without paying his debts. The priest, after noting that an amusing caricature depicting the doctor trying to peddle a serum made of horse manure had become a great source of laughter around town, estimated that at least twenty people (doctors, pharmacists, and priests) would gladly testify to the disreputable character of Dubois. With such damaging information at hand, the priest assured Boissarie that the brother would give up the suit. The absence of further correspondence on the matter seems to confirm the prediction.[28]

The Dubois deception underscored the vulnerability of the shrine to Charcot's suggestion thesis, along with the negative publicity incurred by efforts to combat it. Patients "cured" of hysteria might pass for authentic cures, while the rigorous Boissarie was revealed as all too fallible. The insinuation that Boissarie might cut corners to promote the miracles—and personally profit from them—was especially damaging. Such revelations endangered more than personal reputations, however. The debate over faith healing and suggestion triggered by Zola's novel, and the interested agendas this dispute brought to light, generated concern over the verification process and ultimately over the authenticity of the miracle cures themselves. The suggestion thesis, in this sense, sowed doubt over whether the truth of the cure would ever be fully revealed. And not merely for supporters of Lourdes: the suspicions raised about the competence and character of the shrine's medical experts could be directed toward anticlerical doctors as well. The suggestion thesis, in fact, was a double-edged sword for the secular medical community, as campaigns against the miracles betrayed the uncomfortable reality that secular doctors were not immune from the lure of money and publicity that the shrine provided. Certain doctors, like Dubois, tried to capitalize on the cures for their own profit. Medical authorities such as Charcot and Hippolyte Bernheim, while certainly much more respectable, had also exploited the fame of the holy grotto to promote their own theories of hysteria and suggestion.[29] Anticlerical doctors could hardly declare themselves to be impartial observers when they, too, depended on publicity stunts, lawsuits, and a sensationalist press to make names for themselves or to assert their own professional claims. In this way, the seemingly ideal rhetorical cudgel of the suggestion thesis opened up new vulnerabilities for the doctors who wielded it.

Catholic doctors were quick to undermine the very credibility of the suggestion thesis by attacking the expertise of Charcot and others. For example, Dr. A. Vourch, in a critical response to "La Foi qui guérit," drew attention to Charcot's own lack of evidence to support his theories. Vourch observed that Charcot had never examined a single cured pilgrim, preferring instead to conduct a kind of "retrospective diagnosis" leading always "to the most contradictory results." As Vourch commented, "To diagnose illnesses from figures in a painting or to search for insights in old authors, ignoring issues of precision, of language, and modern ideas . . . this only creates a sort of scientific novel." In this respect, Charcot's famous essay on faith healing was scarcely better than Zola's fiction, as it was not based on hard scientific evidence but on speculation and unreliable anecdotes from the past. Vourch also capitalized on the rivalry between Bernheim and Charcot, as well as new disagreements among neurologists over the nature of hysteria, by highlighting the striking lack of consensus on questions of suggestion and hysteria among prominent medical experts.[30] Such arguments may not have convinced ardent freethinkers and anticlerical doctors that the miracle cures were the work of divine intervention, but they did raise doubts over the capacity of the suggestion thesis to provide a valid, scientific explanation for the cures.[31]

More effectively, perhaps, defenders of the cures also drew attention to the large number of doctors who attested, in writing, that their own patients had been healed at Lourdes. These physicians willingly signed the shrine's medical certificates, in spite of the apparently widespread influence of the suggestion thesis. Catholic supporters of Lourdes asked their readers: Could all these medical professionals be wrong? Did every single instance of healing represent a hysterical illness mistakenly diagnosed as organic? By posing these rhetorical questions, Catholic doctors and clerics were appealing to readers' common sense that hundreds of physicians could hardly be in error.[32] Yet for anticlerical observers familiar with the world of medicine, such questions, ironically, led precisely to the opposite conclusion: significant numbers of practitioners were indeed prone to being mistaken when they declared their patients inexplicably cured on returning from Lourdes. After all, so many doctors lacked the specialized knowledge and skill to diagnose hysteria properly—not to mention those who, like Dubois, committed fraud for personal gain. Zola had raised precisely these issues in his 1892 interview with *Le Temps,* when he noted that even the best medical experts found it difficult to determine the difference between organic and hysterical illnesses. By the early twentieth century, the problem of medical competence and credibility was becoming even more apparent to anticlerical doctors, because Lourdes was now trumpeting such a large number of "certified" cures in the pages of the religious press. Indeed, as anticlerical doctors increasingly relied on the suggestion thesis to label Lourdes miracles as ordinary cases of mind cure, supporters of the shrine countered by publishing close to four thousand accounts of extraordinary cures complete with certificates from physicians attesting to both the reality of the illness and the radical nature of the recovery. To prove that these seemingly inexplicable cures were nothing more than instances of suggestion, then, freethinking doctors were forced to focus on the seemingly intractable problems of ignorance, incompetence, and outright fraud among their own peers.[33]

A 1901 article published in *Le Progrès Médical,* in which the physician-author concedes his own medical blunder, provides a telling case in point. The writer, a Dr. Terrien, recounted the story of his attempt to provide a natural explanation for the cure of one of his patients who returned from Lourdes fully recovered from a supposedly hopeless case of tuberculosis. After providing the case history of the young woman, he noted that his original diagnosis—a case of consumption—had led to his complete stupefaction on witnessing the woman's apparent cure. His own skepticism, Terrien recounted, spurred further research into the nature of hysteria, at which point he discovered his error. He declared, "I had made a gross diagnostic error: my consumptive was only a vulgar hysteric." Eagerly confessing his own mistake, the doctor was determined to show how suggestion worked at Lourdes and to prove conclusively that its cures were natural and susceptible to scientific explanation. Yet he also cited this example "in order to shed light on the errors that hysteria often perpetrates even on doctors who believe themselves well versed in the study of neuropathology."[34]

The problem of medical incompetence was raised again, and even more forcefully, in a virulently anticlerical attack on the Lourdes miracles published in 1910. *La Vérité sur Lourdes,* an in-depth medical study of hundreds of Lourdes cures, written by a Dr. Rouby, attempted to prove beyond any doubt that these recoveries were either cases of hysteria cured by suggestion or instances of outright fraud. Examining the most famous healing events cited by key promoters (Lasserre, Boissarie, l'Abbé Bertrin) as well as accounts found in the shrine's *Journal de la Grotte,* Rouby was compelled to acknowledge that his own secular colleagues were a significant part of the problem: "It is regrettable that doctors, ignoring the diverse manifestations of hysteria, give certificates of incurability so easily because they have not known how to recognize or cure these maladies." Rouby lamented that not only medical incompetence but financial hardship often explained the willingness of doctors to sign the shrine's medical certificates and thereby to shore up the very spectacle of the cure that anticlerical professionals wished to dismantle. As Rouby saw the problem, "It also happens, unfortunately, that certain colleagues are too often subjected to moral blackmail by their sanctimonious clients; if one signs the certificates one keeps them, if not one loses them." Doctors, especially rural practitioners, had little choice in the matter: "The needy doctor must comply if he wants to earn his bread and that of his children." Rouby's discussion of the suggestion thesis led to a striking conclusion: physician ignorance and economic dependency were making the medical profession complicit in the shrine's spectacle of the cure. He ended his analysis with a plea to doctors to become better informed about the true nature of hysteria so that henceforth they "will no longer sign the certificates on which the bureau of verifications depends for establishing cures as miraculous events." No task facing the medical community was more important, insisted Rouby, because only knowledge would allow doctors to separate themselves, once and for all, from the shrine's use of medical science.[35] In this sense, the long-standing debate over faith healing and suggestion at Lourdes jeopardized the secular medical community's own expertise and authority as much as it damaged the credibility of the shrine.

As the two camps came to recognize the precariousness of their own positions, each side sought to direct blame toward a convenient scapegoat. Both proponents and adversaries of Lourdes condemned a sensationalist press for compromising their efforts to determine the truth of the cure. Such was the contention of anticlerical journalist Baudouin, who declared, at the height of the Zola affair, that the press was "endangering Medicine and Science, Doctors and Scientists" with its uncritical, even histrionic coverage of the Lourdes cures. Writing in *Le Progrès Médical*, Baudouin bracketed his attack on the shrine's "false" methods of verification with resounding denunciations of both the religious and secular wings of the popular press. Beginning with the claim that a sensationalist press was jeopardizing the very core of science by publishing undiscriminating accounts of miraculous cures, he ended by calling for a dramatic departure from journalism-as-usual:

> If I were director of an important newspaper, rolling in gold as some of them are, it's by this route that I would finish off Lourdes: I would have the heart to send to these blessed places one or two medical journalists . . . to take scientific notes at the moment of the great pilgrimages. I would then publish numerous documents that they would have brought back from their long voyage in search of the Truth.

Sending well-trained and serious journalists to Lourdes to reveal the actual truth of the cures, Baudouin asserted, would be a noble act—both a "Scientific Mission" and a "social duty." Yet the journalist doubted that any such newspaper director was up to the task: "Unfortunately, until this new Messiah arises, the daily newspapers will record plenty of miracles."[36] Astonishing cures, after all, were precisely the kinds of stories that spun newspapers' "gold."

Blaming the popular press directed attention away from the poor skills and financial interests of doctors. Indeed, Baudouin had found an ideal scapegoat, because few would deny that the popular press was trivial, corrupt, and prone to misrepresent the truth. That the press was inescapably tied to the demands of a commercializing public sphere, with its profit-making pressures to satisfy the desires of large numbers of readers, made the news a suspect commodity.[37] If the press perverted science with sensationalized accounts of the cures, then perhaps doctors could reestablish the truth and redeem medical science by committing themselves to dispassionate observation and rigorous investigation. Yet even as Baudouin was demanding a "critical" medico-journalism to replace the uncritical reporting of the press, *Le Progrès Médical* (not a scandal sheet by any standard) was choosing less high-minded methods for responding to the threat of Lourdes. One week after publishing Baudouin's commentary, the medical journal chose to reprint the well-worn satirical account of paralytic pilgrims running from a speeding train. Hardly an exemplary piece of detached scientific reporting, this article furnished ample evidence that neither side in the debate on Lourdes could resist "popular" tactics in its bid to win over public opinion. In this sense, blaming the press for sensationalism only hid a deeper concern that medical authorities were themselves dependent on a commercializing public realm in order to assert and prove their own claims as experts.

Religious authorities found themselves in a similar position. They, too, made the press a frequent target of attack in their efforts to reestablish the credibility of the Lourdes medical bureau along with its confirmed cures. In a parallel rhetorical move, supporters of the shrine criticized the religious press for printing unverified accounts of healing. The Abbé Domenech, writing during the Zola affair, took this approach when he complained that Catholic journalists "spoke only of cures." He continued:

> Unfortunately, the press often spoke of cures without checking the facts, without realizing their nature, their character, and with a warmth inspired by piety and gratitude. The word *miracle* was thrown about in such a manner that even the most religious souls were becoming skeptical toward the miracles of Lourdes.[38]

Domenech was careful not to criticize the commercial needs of the religious press; to do so might have highlighted the uncomfortable similarities between secular and Catholic newspapers.[39] Instead, by scolding the pious enthusiasm of Catholic journalists, the cleric shifted attention away from the shrine's doctors—clearly overmatched by cases of suggestion—to the overzealousness of well-meaning journalists, whose faith predisposed them to uncertain judgment. Joris-Karl Huysmans, in his work *The Crowds of Lourdes* (published some ten years after Domenech's commentary), continued to blame the religious press for spreading false rumors of prodigious cures and proclaiming miracles without the slightest evidence. Like Domenech, he hoped to reestablish the credibility of the shrine's medical bureau by juxtaposing the "extreme caution" of its doctors with the complete "lack of prudence" exhibited by Catholic journalists. Huysmans noted, in his typically caustic tone, that if the accounts reported in the religious press were all true then "the uncured would be the exception, and the miraculously healed would be no exception at all."[40]

In this tendency to blame the sensationalist messenger, then, supporters of Lourdes were not so different from their anticlerical adversaries. Both camps insisted on separating medical authority, and science itself, from the contaminating influence of a commercializing society so clearly embodied by the modern mass press. For Catholics such as Huysmans, it was not only the authority of science that was at stake but the miraculous itself. The religious press, with its exaggerated accounts of proliferating marvels, debased the genuine miracles of Lourdes. By shoring up the shrine's medical bureau and its rigorous methods of verification, Huysmans sought to save the cures from the corrupting influence of the press, thereby enabling the devout to have faith in them once again. Yet even Huysmans was forced to admit that the baleful pull of the press was not easily countered. Indeed, given the presence of the editor of the *Journal de la Grotte* within the walls of the medical bureau—begging for exciting news from a Dr. Boissarie only too eager to comply—it was hard for a sober observer to be optimistic. Even clerics at Lourdes, complained Huysmans, fell prey to embellished accounts printed in the press, believing that all who left the bureau walking on their own must be true objects of divine intervention: "I have seen some of them [priests] fling themselves upon women, who were being carried out from the medical clinic and supposed to be cured, to get them to touch their rosaries, and these women were mere cases of hysteria."[41]

Two decades of debate over suggestion and faith healing, then, ended up bringing both camps nearly full circle. First gaining wide prominence in the early 1890s as a seemingly devastating critique of miraculous healing, the suggestion thesis soon cast disrepute not only on the doctors at Lourdes but on the entire French medical profession as well. As all such experts, religious and secular, fell victim to insisting on a truth of the cure they could not prove, authorities on both sides were forced to confront—within embarrassingly public arenas—the rampant propensity within their own ranks for making claims based on fraud, incompetence, and economic self-interest. Seeking to cope with such revelations by scapegoating an irresponsible press, the two camps merely succeeded in drawing further attention to the pervasively commercial entanglements of religion, medicine, and media. The suggestion thesis had become, in effect, a net that ensnared all parties. To extricate itself, the Church, seizing the offensive, pinned its hopes on a single indisputable miracle cure.

THE INCONTROVERTIBLE MIRACLE OF PIERRE DE RUDDER

The astonishing case of Pierre de Rudder seemed to be the perfect cure for the credibility problems of the Lourdes miracles. In the first half-decade of the twentieth century, supporters of the shrine launched a major campaign to publicize the stirring account of de Rudder, a peasant man whose fractured leg was healed through prayer to the Virgin of Lourdes. Presented as a direct challenge to the secular medical community, the de Rudder cure set off a new round of acrimonious debates that soon captured national and even European-wide attention. Like the recent events of the Dreyfus affair, debates over de Rudder inflamed the raw political tensions between anticlerics and devout Catholics at the turn of the century. However, the bitter polemics that surrounded the case of de Rudder, even after the 1905 separation between Church and state was supposed to have diffused such antagonisms, suggest that more than politics was at stake. This final set of debates, even more than previous exchanges over the cures, revealed the extent to which both faith and science were made vulnerable by their dependency on sensational forms of publicly constituted knowledge.

Every aspect of Pierre de Rudder's case, from the initial injury to the cure, was remarkable. Crippled when a tree fell on his leg in 1867, de Rudder, a Belgian agricultural laborer from the Flemish-speaking town of Jabbeke, suffered for eight years with a fractured leg and an open wound that refused to heal. On April 7, 1875, he made a difficult and painful pilgrimage to a replica shrine of Lourdes in Oostakker, Belgium, where he was miraculously cured while praying before a re-created grotto.[42] The de Rudder miracle—an "organic" case of healing far from the intoxicating crowds of Lourdes—seemed invulnerable to the usual accusations made by anticlerical doctors, especially charges of suggestion. Extraordinarily well documented, the cure was supported by expert medical testimony and even by de Rudder's leg bones themselves, exhumed from his grave in 1899 and made available for the world to see. The case was heralded by its supporters as simply beyond all dispute. But was it? After the Church declared the cure a miracle in 1908, anticlerical doctors and journalists devoted extraordinary efforts to demolishing the evidence that supported this ultimate testament to the wonders of Lourdes. In the process, the de Rudder case became a compressed recapitulation—in exaggerated, almost comic form—of all the themes of earlier public challenges.

The roots of the Church's ultimate offensive extended back before the turn

LA GROTTE DE LOURDES A OOSTACKER-LEZ-GAND

Figure 41. Replica grotto: The Lourdes shrine in Oostakker, Belgium. From Gustave Boissarie, *Lourdes: Les Guérisons,* series 1 (Paris, 1911), 40.

of the century. As early as 1892, Boissarie had recognized the potential value of the de Rudder cure for Lourdes. At that time the pious doctor was wrestling with the damaging fallout from Zola's visit and from the publication of Charcot's "La Foi qui guérit." Boissarie seized on the de Rudder cure as an ideal disproof of the suggestion thesis. Just days after Charcot's essay appeared in the *Revue Hebdomadaire,* Boissarie asked a prominent Belgian physician, Dr. Royer, to go to Jabbeke to investigate the case. Writing to Royer, he disclosed his fervent hope: "This example will be the basis of our argument; I will present it in response to Charcot. There must be no possible doubt." If Boissarie held any lingering doubts over the merits of the case, those reservations were put to rest with the autopsy of de Rudder's bones in 1899. By the following year, Boissarie was publicly proclaiming the irrefutable truth of the cure. At a Catholic congress in Paris, he announced: "This autopsy of a miracle is the most astonishing thing that we possess. All objections made against the cures of Lourdes—nervous lesions, the faith that heals, the effects of suggestion—will fall before the facts of such evidence." Indeed, Boissarie confidently predicted that "the efforts of the impious will be dashed to pieces" by the de Rudder case.[43] Henceforth, this particular cure gained increasing attention in the Catholic press and in various popular and medical works about the Lourdes miracles. The figure of the deceased

Figure 42. Postcard of Pierre de Rudder, early twentieth century. Author's personal collection.

de Rudder soon became something of a sacred icon, his image appearing on postcards sold at pilgrimage shrines (Lourdes as well as Oostakker), while plaster copies of his bones were displayed in a special glass case for all at Lourdes to see.[44] Almost like relics, these replica bones served as powerful evidence of the authenticity of the cure.

The de Rudder cure stood out, in part, because the case so clearly defied any connection to the suggestion thesis. After all, de Rudder was a man, and thus by definition less susceptible to hysteria. Healed in the relative quiet of an obscure replica shrine, far from the beguiling atmosphere of the real Lourdes, de Rudder's illness had been organic in nature and could not be confused with a nervous malady. Moreover, the basic facts of the case seemed to be verified by a wealth of evidence. Doctors who had treated the injured man testified that the leg was broken in two places and that a gangrenous wound located near one of the fractures refused to heal, revealing a three-centimeter gap between the two broken bones. Declaring the leg impossible to set, physicians recommended amputation, but de Rudder refused, enduring eight years in great pain. Lay witnesses testified to having seen the putrid wound on the morning of the man's departure for Oostakker; they attested as well that on de Rudder's return the wound had vanished without a trace. De Rudder lived for another twenty-three years in good health, his newfound vigor and ability to work a testament to the fullness of the cure, his sincere piety a confirmation that the cure was indeed a grace from God. Yet the ultimate triumph of proof came only after the man's death, when Dr. Van Hoestenberghe (the physician who had treated de Rudder) and the Jesuit Alfred Deschamps (also a medical doctor) exhumed the body of de Rudder and amputated the two legs. An autopsy of the bones found them to be of equal length (despite the three-centimeter gap in the bones of the fractured leg!), revealing only the thin line of a scar where the fracture once had existed.[45]

Despite this surfeit of evidence, or perhaps because of it, controversy erupted almost at once. In response to the publication of the autopsy by Deschamps, a host of freethinking doctors began to investigate the case. One of the earliest critics of the de Rudder case was the respected Belgian physician Dr. Logie (later an inspector general of health for the Belgian army), who declared the cure was "rare, interesting, but not miraculous." Presenting his findings at a conference on the de Rudder case in 1903, he claimed to see no sign of deliberate fraud but merely an honest mistake by well-intentioned but incompetent doctors. After looking over the evidence, Logie concluded that de Rudder's fracture and wound indeed were real, but "the fragments of the tibia were not separated from one another, they were touching one another. And their relative position was precisely that which had been preserved by their having definitively healed." Logie claimed that Van Hoestenberghe had made a serious error in taking "for a gap between the fragments what was actually a gap between a bone splinter and the lower fragment." He also noted that Van Hoestenberghe had last examined de Rudder some three months before the voyage to Oostakker, by which time the leg had probably healed on its own. De Rudder's ongoing inability to walk, he postulated, was due to the bone splinter lodged in his flesh, which continued to infect the wound and cause the man great pain. Finally, Logie dismissed the testimony of the lay witnesses as lacking all credibility, untrained as they were to interpret the evidence they saw. Hoping for a miracle, these well-meaning folk mistook a rare but natural cure for a supernatural event.[46]

By the time Monseigneur Waffelaert, Bishop of Bruges, began his own official investigation into the case, medical debate over the de Rudder cure had grown wider and considerably more hostile. Anticlerical doctors in Germany, Holland, France, England, and Italy all took interest in the case, and many were much less charitable than Dr. Logie in their assessments of the various witnesses involved.[47] A German doctor, Dr. Julien Marcuse, for example, writing in the pages of the *Berliner Tageblatt* in 1902, accused the Church of blatant fraud. Calling the cure "a sophisticated hoax *ad majorem Dei gloriam* [for the greater glory of God]," he noted with suspicion that clerics only began to promote the cure after de Rudder was dead and it was impossible to verify properly the facts of the case.[48] A nearly yearlong debate in the pages of the French medical journal, *La Chronique Médicale,* unleashed similarly hostile responses, with one doctor insinuating that photographs of de Rudder's bones were doctored and that the Church may have coerced its witnesses into giving false testimony.[49] It was becoming increasingly clear that the shrine's perfect cure was no longer beyond dispute. Indeed, the growing number of accusations of fraud and ineptitude raised anew suspicions about the authenticity of the cure. Yet the proliferating attacks against the de Rudder cure also began to hurt the anticlerical physicians who launched them, for they revealed the inability of medical experts to provide a unified or coherent counterinterpretation of the event. The reality that doctors so quickly resorted to personal diatribe and outright mockery only emphasized their own sense of fear and frustration that the case could not be won on the firm terrain of scientific facts.

Nowhere was this more apparent than at a 1910 medical conference held in Milan, at which anticlerical doctors seemed unable to establish any clear criteria for how to judge the merits of the de Rudder case. The Medical Society of Milan, which sponsored the conference, invited one of its own members, Franciscan priest and medical doctor R. P. Gemelli, to present a scientific defense of the de Rudder miracle.[50] In presenting the facts of the case, Gemelli argued that the cure defied all accepted laws of science. In response to Gemelli's presentation, doctors supplied a plethora of "natural" explanations for the cure, but their own arguments revealed an astonishing lack of consensus. One doctor simply argued that there had been no three-centimeter space between the bones and that the leg healed naturally over time. He hypothesized that because de Rudder had remained under a delusion of still being crippled—a type of autosuggestion—he failed to realize his own recovery. A second doctor suggested that unknown forces were at work, while a third claimed that de Rudder was a hysteric and his famous fracture a nervous ailment.[51] With such disparate (and in some cases laughable) explanations being advanced, it is not surprising that doctors quickly moved from discussing the facts of the case to attacking the character and credibility of the individuals involved. Doctors could agree, for example, that the lay witnesses were suspect because these simple folk were, in the words of a Dr. Sigurta, "strangers to medicine." Physicians also rallied around the criticism that not a single one of de Rudder's doctors had followed the invalid systematically during his eight years of incapacitation. These maligned doctors, moreover, were "nobodies" in the profession, prone to making serious errors in their diagnoses. Comparing such incompetents to charlatans and dealers in patent medicines, a Dr. Bayla snorted that accepting their accounts of de Rudder's cure would be like taking seriously the "advertisements on page four of the newspapers, extolling their own cure-all remedies."[52]

The conference in Milan soon took on a carnival-like atmosphere. Supporters of the cure, trying to take the podium to defend Father Gemelli and his evidence, were hooted off the stage. Yet beneath the raucous, almost festive, tone of the proceedings, a sense of anxiety permeated the air. One defender of the cure, a Dr. Louis Necchi, put his finger on the source of this disquiet. He pointed out that while opponents of Lourdes had poked several holes in the de Rudder case, they had failed to provide a convincing alternative explanation. Indeed, he noted with evident satisfaction that his adversaries "have mutually destroyed their own arguments." Musing over why the de Rudder case had provoked such violent reactions from the detractors of Lourdes, Necchi concluded with his own set of accusations: "You are afraid that if you were to accept one single cure, you would have to renounce your faith—the positivist faith. You are afraid of becoming clericals." He noted the striking contrast in demeanor between these rabid anticlerics and his own fellow supporters of Lourdes: "We remain calm and are able to speak dispassionately, as doctors, [admitting] that we do not know how to provide an explanation. And we are not bothered by it." Even if all the cures of Lourdes were proved false, the Catholic doctor concluded, their supporters would not be troubled because the cures were not the basis of their faith.[53]

Necchi's remarks turned the tables on his anticlerical enemies. Freethinking doctors had lost their composure and were behaving not like impartial scientists but like religious fanatics. Necchi was not alone in making this observation; the newspapers that covered the conference similarly presented the detractors of Lourdes as unthinking dogmatists. Even opponents of the cures seemed aware that their conflicting theories and personal insults failed to advance their cause, and one such physician, a Dr. Filippetti, urged his freethinking colleagues to return to the terrain of scientific fact to refute the de Rudder miracle.[54] Yet what emerged all too clearly from the medical debate in Italy, and from those elsewhere, was that scientific arguments were not enough to discredit this perfect cure. With the Church appropriating the terrain of forensic medicine (the autopsy of the bones) and anticlerical doctors unable to provide their own coherent counterexplanation, the medical debates over de Rudder only intensified anxieties as to the proficiency and status of secular experts and their ability to make legitimate claims to knowledge.

In this atmosphere of growing doubt and uncertainty, it is not surprising that freethinkers and anticlerical doctors unleashed increasingly sensational allegations of fraud and deception. Freethinkers began to speak of an elaborate conspiracy within the Church, as the de Rudder debate became a battle for public opinion in which scandal, innuendo, and even paranoia displaced scientific arguments. Rouby's *La Vérité sur Lourdes*, for example, went so far as to insist that de Rudder had undergone a clandestine operation that healed the injured leg just weeks before his pilgrimage.[55] A writer using the pseudonym P. Saintyves, in a work entitled *La Simulation du merveilleux,* went even further by implicating the bishop responsible for investigating the cure in an elaborate cover-up of incriminating evidence.[56] The greatest revelations of fraud and conspiracy, however, came from journalist F. Verhas, who, in 1911, published an exposé of the de Rudder case that claimed to present irrefutable proof that the exalted miraculé was nothing more than an impostor and that a host of religious and medical authorities had falsified evidence to transform the phony cure into a divine miracle.[57]

The Verhas account, like many great tales of conspiracy, seemed to contain a grain of truth, one that made it especially difficult for the Church to refute. The journalist began by alleging that de Rudder's fracture had healed naturally years before he made his pilgrimage, but that the man continued to simulate the injury in order to collect a pension that his patron, the Vicomte du Bus, had established for him. In July 1874, when the generous patron died, the pension was suspended. Threatened with sudden poverty, de Rudder decided—or so Verhas alleged—to go to Oostakker where he would stage a miraculous recovery. To evade the problem posed by the scar that remained visible on his formerly fractured left leg, de Rudder showed to all the world his "miraculously" healed right leg, which in fact had never been injured. To substantiate these shocking accusations, Verhas pointed to a striking inconsistency that he had discovered in the church-sanctioned accounts of the cure. After carefully perusing all the key texts (from the earliest report by the Abbé Scheerlinck to the study by Deschamps of de Rudder's amputated bones), Verhas found that the three earliest publications all noted that the right leg had been healed while later works reported the left leg. A discrepancy of such magnitude, Verhas asserted, could only be evidence of an elaborate hoax. That none of the pious doctors involved with the case had ever remarked on this strange reversal was a sign of gross incompetence or, more likely, of secret complicity. Indeed, Verhas charged prominent religious and medical authorities with a massive cover-up.[58]

Like a popular detective story, with the journalist playing the intrepid sleuth, Verhas unveiled his evidence piece by piece, with drama and suspense, to build an overwhelming case against the cure. In 1875, the Abbé Scheerlinck, author of the first work on de Rudder, had recorded that Pierre's right leg was caught between two trees and cruelly maimed. The following year, a French cleric, the Chanoine Le Couvreur, also noted that de Rudder's right leg was crippled, then miraculously cured. An 1892 letter written to Boissarie from Van Hoestenberghe, the doctor who treated de Rudder during his eight-year ordeal, again confirmed that the right leg had been injured and cured. Yet one year later, Dr. Royer examined de Rudder and found that it was now the left leg that bore the scar of the fracture, as did all subsequent accounts of the miracle cure. "What can we conclude?" asked Verhas. "After the pilgrimage, de Rudder showed the first three observers his right leg, which had never been injured!" Verhas also charged that other signs of a cover-up abounded, from shifts in Van Hoesten-berghe's testimony to the emergence of "newly discovered" witnesses with sud-denly vivid recollections of long-ago events. Even the authoritative study by Deschamps of de Rudder's amputated bones glossed over these glaring incon-sistencies. Verhas concluded that "the history of de Rudder's cure proves that one cannot trust the assertions of Catholic doctors in questions where faith ap-pears to be at stake." He added: "Some consciously, others unconsciously, alter the simplest facts in order to be able to impart a meaning that the facts do not have on their own."[59]

Not surprisingly, shrine supporters fought back, with Deschamps leading a counterattack that challenged the journalist's own character. Deschamps asked why Verhas was so intent on proving conscious fraud and not simple error. Why had the journalist chosen ad hominem attacks and insinuations—the "least hon-orable weapons"—to fight this battle? Quoting the words of Saint Gregory of Nazianzus, Deschamps concluded: "We are the mirror in which we see others." Verhas, in short, called the cure's defenders liars and impostors because he was one himself. Not a physician but a Belgian engineer who lived in Saint Peters-burg, Russia, Verhas apparently did not even speak Flemish and thus was unable to read any of the original documents. Verhas, noted another defender of the cure, was not even his real name. Indeed, this fellow was an unscrupulous no-body who had tried to capitalize on the very public de Rudder case to make a name for himself.[60]

Under attack, the Church brandished an old weapon. At the height of the de Rudder debate, clerics across Europe challenged all skeptics in a series of pub-lic wagers to prove their scandalous accusations. Just as doctors had recognized that this debate could not be won on the terrain of hard fact alone, so the Church seemed to appreciate that scientific arguments were not sufficient to refute the accusations of fraud and conspiracy unleashed by the likes of Verhas. By re-launching the public wager, church authorities could use popular tools, even lowbrow tactics, to appeal directly to the masses and win over public opinion. Deschamps conceded as much in his own defense of the public wager as a legit-imate approach to fighting what had become a dirty war. He admitted that "the best refutation of these [anticlerical] works is to confront them with proven facts." Indeed, he and other defenders of the cure had tried, he said, to use ra-tional, scientific arguments to prove the cure. "But the anticlerical press feeds itself so avidly on these anti-Lourdes publications; in the presence of the noisy publicity that surrounds such works, there is only one way to show the people— who do not read the pro and the con—that their newspapers deceive them: it is by resorting to that popular argument par excellence, the offer of a wager."[61] This rationale for the public wager echoed the words spoken some forty years earlier by Artus, who also had asserted that only a public, spectacular challenge could demonstrate, once and for all, that opponents of Lourdes were liars and scandalmongers. Once again, supporters of Lourdes hoped to discredit their enemies by making money the final arbiter of truth in the battle over the miracles. And once again, the tactic succeeded, in the sense that all those who initially seemed poised to accept a bet backed out. Yet, as we saw in the case of the Artus wager, a price would be paid for such success.

The most famous public wager over Pierre de Rudder emerged in France in 1911. A cleric, the Abbé Ebrard, reissued the original Artus challenge in response to allegations made by a professor of philosophy named P. Chide. When it was discovered that the ten thousand francs put up by Artus was no longer available, the Abbé Duplessy stepped forward with five thousand francs to bet that Chide, who had raised his charges at a conference held in the French town of Gap, could not disprove the miracle of Pierre de Rudder. Chide accepted the wager, and the two men then negotiated the criteria to be used for judging the cure in a series of letters reprinted in local newspapers, in the Catholic daily *La Croix*, and in the pages of *La Réponse*, a popular religious journal directed by Duplessy. Negotiations soon broke down, predictably, over the issue of "proof." Accused of looking for a way out, Chide proposed an alternative wager over a "future cure," one that could be studied from the start by both sides. If it was an attempt to save face, this call to change the bet was a shrewd tactic. Chide knew that Duplessy could never agree to such a wager because it would be presumptuous, indeed offensive, to anticipate in advance God's impending intervention in the world.[62]

Thus the public wager, once again, demonstrated itself to be both asset and liability for the Church. The tactic certainly proved successful in making Chide, like others before him, appear defensive and cowardly in refusing to take up the bet. If this kind of maneuver did not prove the truth of the cure, at least it raised serious doubts about the integrity of the shrine's critics. The wager against Chide was successful enough, in fact, that it was used against Verhas the following year, when Dr. Royer bet Verhas five thousand francs that the latter could not prove his accusations of intentional fraud and cover-up. Claiming that it was impossible to *prove* intentional fraud, Verhas proposed instead a wager over whether the facts of the de Rudder case were sufficient to declare a miracle. Royer and his supporters, refusing to change the terms of the bet, pointed out that it was expressly on the issue of fraud that Verhas had pitched his exposé. When Verhas declined to take up the bet with these conditions, Royer claimed vindication for the cure.[63]

Yet the public wager was not without cost for the Church even when its defenders did not lose a bet. While the tactic ably impugned the credibility of de Rudder's critics, it also risked discrediting his supporters for resorting to such low-road gambits. This seems especially apparent in Duplessy's challenge to Chide. At one point, for example, Duplessy recounted a popular anecdote about a lion tamer who offered five thousand francs to anyone brave enough to stand in his lion's cage; a seemingly courageous man accepted the wager but then, like Chide, tried to change its conditions—insisting that the lion tamer first remove the beast from the cage. The cleric's anecdote, while intended to mock Chide as a hustler, unwittingly drew attention to the vulgar, commercial nature of the public wager itself. If Chide was little more than a con man, then Duplessy cast himself as a kind of carnival performer looking to promote his sideshow act. Was the public wager, after all, nothing more than a cheap publicity stunt used by circus performers and unscrupulous hucksters to promote themselves and make money? Deschamps seemed to concede that it was when he apologized for clerics having to "resort" to such "popular" stratagems to defend themselves against the lies routinely published in the anticlerical press. And then, of course, there was always the risk that the public wager might backfire. In Germany, for example, a priest who issued a wager to disprove de Rudder's cure found himself being sued for defamation of character. The priest was found guilty and forced to pay damages to a doctor who had reneged on the bet. Although the judge in the case made it clear that he was ruling not on the miracle but only on a case of libel, supporters of Lourdes still ended up looking compromised and defeated.[64] If money, indeed, was now the agent of truth, then did the damages paid to this doctor "prove" the supporters of de Rudder to be liars and frauds?

Public wagers bracketed nearly a half century of contentious, often raucous debate over the meaning of the miraculous at Lourdes. Effective publicity for the cures, the initial wager by Artus had helped to establish the issuing of challenges within the popular press as an expedient technique for persuading an emerging mass readership of the miraculous nature of the Lourdes shrine. That the critics of Artus were quick to respond with grandiose promises to disprove the cures in the pages of anticlerical newspapers only further foreshadowed the powerful role that the modern press would come to play for freethinking republicans and religious authorities alike. The Artus incident showed early on, in fact, that gimmicks such as wagers, accompanied by sensational attacks in public forums, could be tempting weapons in the battle for popular opinion, even when they failed to prove the contentions of either side.

Two decades later, the full fruit of this pattern of challenge and counterchallenge was abundantly on display. After Zola, a publicity-savvy intellectual, visited Lourdes and soon thereafter published his controversial novel about the shrine, low-road rhetorical strategies flourished in the contentious debates over suggestion, faith healing, and hysteria that gripped the final decade of the nineteenth century. Indeed, as these debates made it increasingly clear that scientific examinations of the cures could yield only ambiguous and contradictory findings, recourse by both camps to new wagers, lawsuits, ad hominem attacks, and outrageous accusations proved to be almost irresistible—not simply to discredit the enemy but to divert attention away from the failure to prove or disprove miraculous healing.

Yet there was a price to be paid for depending so heavily on publicity to establish the truth of the cure. After another two decades of bitter disputes over the miracles at Lourdes, both doctors and clerics had become badly tarnished by mutual charges of incompetence, fraud, and financial motivation. Even as supporters and opponents of Lourdes blamed a sensationalist press for corrupting their serious efforts to investigate the cures, each camp only further implicated itself in a commercializing public sphere that offered no solid ground on which to stand. Indeed, what made proving the truth of the cure so important for these professionals—and what perhaps also explains why both camps refused to back down—was that their own expertise and integrity seemed to hinge on the outcome. In short, it was not simply the reality of the cure that was at stake in the debates over Lourdes but the legitimacy of religious and medical authority.

Both supporters and opponents eventually came to see the debates over the cures as unwinnable and even injurious to their own reputations. Accordingly, each side sought to reposition its claims. In an effort to insulate the medical profession from further revelations of physician ineptitude and economic self-interest, anticlerical doctors separated themselves from an unprovable suggestion thesis and searched for other theories to explain cases of healing at the shrine. Church supporters, too, shifted their own positions, seeking to avoid further problems with fraudulent cures and incompetent diagnoses by focusing on a select number of unassailable miracles in order to reestablish their authority and the credibility of Lourdes. Even as both sides sought to reconfigure their positions on healing, the bitter disputes over Pierre de Rudder demonstrated all too clearly that these maneuvers had simply generated an even more unruly round of polemics. Trapped on a terrain defined by the sensational practices of the mass press, the debate could not be settled by a fine-tuning of claims. That each side so insistently resorted to insulting accusations, renewed wagers, and lengthy libel suits only pointed to the debate's most certain winner: the popular press, in fact, had now displaced both religious and medical authorities as the ultimate public arbiter of truth. In this sense, the recurring debates over the Lourdes cures—like the shorter-term press scandals that also engrossed readers in turn-of-the-century France—provided a very extended lesson in the power and pitfalls involved in demonstrating public authority through publicity. Supporters and opponents of Lourdes claimed to be striving to educate a new, and often-naive, mass reading public. Indeed, each camp, promising to shed light on the truth of the cure, portrayed itself as engaging in the noble pursuit of dispelling false rumors and outright lies in service of the moral well-being of French and European society. Yet as, time and again, debate over the cures took the form of a newspaper scandal, edification gave way fully to entertainment.

What stands out from nearly fifty years of debate over the Lourdes cures is neither careful scrutiny of medical facts nor serious discussion of theological issues but a practically endless stream of entertaining incident: stories of paralytic pilgrims running from speeding trains; a blockbuster novel and its scandalous inaccuracies; confidence men and investigative exposés; bickering doctors shouting one another down at public medical conferences; the melodramatic tale of de Rudder's tragic accident and astonishing cure; and the public wagers themselves. Recast as press reportage, roman feuilleton, and fait divers for a popular audience, these believe-it-or-not stories and "real-life" incidents became part and parcel of the very spectacle of Lourdes, furnishing a constant supply of drama, suspense, and even comic relief for Catholic readers and their anticlerical enemies.

Recognizing the debate itself as entertainment may also explain why religious and medical authorities adopted an increasingly bitter, even hysterical tone as the public battles over Lourdes unfolded. Not only did both camps find themselves locked in an unwinnable war of words but even genuinely serious efforts to enhance knowledge about the cures soon became the stuff of modern press scandal, simply more fuel for a new kind of mass entertainment. This particular "truth," then, was the ultimate revelation of the disputes over Lourdes: the debate itself became the vehicle for tying religion and science inextricably to the logic of a modern commercializing society.

Politics and Mass Culture

Representing Lourdes
in the Twentieth Century

In 1903 republican legislators in Paris tried to close down Lourdes. For ardent anticlericals in the capital, such a step was long overdue. A bastion of superstition and reactionary clericalism, the holy grotto and its miracle cures stood in the way of secularizing modern France. The religious sanctuary and its pilgrimages, however, appeared quite differently to businessmen and government officials in the Pyrenees, who immediately protested that closing Lourdes would plunge the entire region into economic ruin. Sending a flurry of petitions and letters to Paris, business elites and politicians, many of them republicans, pleaded with Prime Minister Émile Combes not to close the pilgrimage site. Contentious debate ensued as many Parisian newspapers took up the anticlerical battle cry to suppress this last-remaining bulwark of religious deception. Yet Lourdes was never closed. Instead, the Combes government placed the shrine under the jurisdiction of the bishop of Tarbes, and the Grotto fathers were quietly replaced with secular (diocesan) clergy. In effect, the state authorized the religious site.

The failed campaign to close Lourdes raises still-unresolved questions about religion and politics in French society. Historians of the Third Republic continue to characterize the period following 1890 as an era of polarizing struggle between Catholics and republicans, one that culminated, with the passage of the 1905 law separating Church and state, in the triumph of a secular, republican vision.[1] Such an interpretation mirrors the very rhetoric of nineteenth-century republicanism. Depending on a strict opposition between religion and modernity, this rhetoric has defined the public sphere as a uniquely secular arena while confining questions of faith and religiosity to a diminished, private realm of personal practice. Indeed, it may be tempting to read into the survival of Lourdes

a striking manifestation of how faith succeeds in carving out for itself an enduring and significant niche (sometimes defined as liminal space) within a largely
secular social order. Yet this sort of narrative ignores the ways in which faith and
religious practice remained embedded in public life. If Lourdes had been simply a reactionary political project—a platform for clerical rearguard actions
against rising secularism—or solely an expression of personal hopes and needs,
then the site probably would not have outlived the early twentieth century as
a religious shrine. Instead, Lourdes not only survived but thrived, drawing
huge numbers and spreading its cultural influence globally throughout the re-
mainder of the century.[2] Success on this scale suggests that the resolution of the
1903–1905 conflicts represented more than an expedient political compromise
between encroaching secularization and embattled faith. Indeed, even a brief examination of Lourdes at the moment of separation between Church and state
reveals how this "final" effort to fix a coherent boundary between sacred and
secular was marked by the longstanding economic entanglements of both faith
and politics. Not only do such entanglements make clear why the shrine was
never closed but they also suggest why subsequent forms of popular religiosity
would be enshrined not in the politics of the nation-state but in the mass culture of modern society.

The political conditions for closing Lourdes became especially propitious in the
first years of the twentieth century. In 1903, the Combes government proclaimed that the Missionaries of the Immaculate Conception (the official name
of the Grotto fathers) were an unauthorized congregation and would have to be
disbanded, putting the future of their shrine in question. The vehicle for
launching this threat was the 1901 Law on Associations. Brainchild of Prime
Minister René Waldeck-Rousseau and the coalition of republicans that came to
power after the Dreyfus affair, the bill initially called for the Conseil d'État to
authorize the numerous religious congregations that had sprung up during the
nineteenth century but had never received official recognition.[3] A moderate republican, Waldeck-Rousseau hoped to use this law to maintain better control
over potentially subversive religious orders. Yet a parliament with large numbers
of newly elected radical republicans and socialists soon altered the bill so that it
could be used to suppress all unapproved religious associations. Passed in July
1901, the Law on Associations gave unapproved religious orders three months
to apply for authorization from parliament, or face dissolution. When Combes,
a medical doctor and an ardent anticleric, became prime minister of France the
following year, the law was ruthlessly applied throughout the country to disband
religious orders that were seen as promoting antirepublican sentiments.[4] By
April 1903, legislative supporters of the law were turning their attention to the
Grotto fathers who administered the Lourdes shrine.

Yet what should have been a routine process of dismantling an unapproved religious order and its illegal shrine soon turned into a highly contentious issue. A resistance movement sprang up, as businessmen, shopkeepers, and republican politicians in the Pyrenees took action to stop the shrine from being suppressed. Meeting just five days after the announcement to dissolve the Grotto fathers was issued, the municipal council of Lourdes stated its case plainly in a petition to Paris: "The cessation or abatement of the flow of pilgrimages to Lourdes would produce the complete ruin of the entire region and would throw almost all of its inhabitants into the most profound misery." The mayor of Lourdes, in a separate letter, pointedly reminded the Combes government that national economic interests were at stake because "important institutions of credit" had lent money to the city to develop the site. Electric tramway and railway companies were also heavily invested in the pilgrimages. The municipal council of Lourdes called on Combes to take all measures necessary to "safeguard such numerous and considerable interests." They also mobilized local republican officials, whereupon chambers of commerce, municipal councils, and village communes throughout the Pyrenees sent similar petitions to Paris, all conjuring up the prospect of economic catastrophe if the government was to suppress the shrine.[5]

Combes responded quickly to the outcry. After meeting with Archille Fould, deputy of the Hautes-Pyrénées, the prime minister promised not to close the sanctuary, and a compromise was soon reached. On May 1, 1903, the bishop of Tarbes was instructed to replace the Grotto fathers with members of the secular clergy. Combes also insisted that the shrine become the legal property of the bishop of Tarbes, thereby ending its status as an independent religious sanctuary. This transfer of ownership took effect officially on February 27, 1904, when the court of appeals at Pau confirmed the judgment of the tribunal of Bagnères-de-Bigorre, declaring that the grotto of Lourdes and its dependencies now belonged to the bishop.[6] Not surprisingly, ardent republicans in Paris were outraged. The anticlerical press labeled Combes a coward who had betrayed his principles. A number of journalists lamented that an impotent Third Republic had been defeated by the economic prosperity of Lourdes. Even such moderate newspapers as *Le Temps* took note of one implicit, and disturbing, consequence of this supposed compromise: "the republican and secular consecration of the Lourdes miracles."[7]

The enactment of a legal separation between Church and state in 1905 seemed to offer a renewed opportunity for anticlerical action against Lourdes. After breaking off diplomatic relations with the Vatican the preceding year, the Combes government had nullified the Concordat, the set of principles governing Church-state relations ever since the Napoleonic era.[8] According to the separation law that followed, all ties between Church and state were severed, and the government soon confiscated the Lourdes sanctuary and its property from

the bishop of Tarbes, placing the site in the hands of private citizens. Not surprisingly, devout Catholics loudly condemned these actions, but ardent anticlericals also continued to clamor for the outright suppression of the shrine. The
following year, journalist Jean de Bonnefon led still another campaign to close
Lourdes, this time on the grounds that it represented a threat to public health.
Yet, once again, public debates soon degenerated into an inconclusive war of
words.[9] Meanwhile, the attention surrounding these campaigns to close the
shrine appeared to have generated ever-growing public interest in seeing the
famed grotto of Lourdes. Only two years after Bonnefon's energetic attack,
the shrine celebrated, in August 1908, the fiftieth anniversary of Bernadette's
visions with a massive celebration, including a new procession of Lourdes
miraculés. The event attracted over a million visitors to the site and brought
record profits to the region.[10] Finally, in 1910, the government put the sanctuary under the jurisdiction of the city of Lourdes as a sort of public charity, a decision carried out with the apparent approval of the bishop of Tarbes.
Recognizing the sanctuary as an "inviolable trust," the city thus gave the bishop
de-facto control over all affairs at the shrine.

The campaigns to close Lourdes, and the ways in which these conflicts were
resolved, revealed a complex set of ties that bound mass pilgrimage to the public life of France. As the mayor of Lourdes had reminded Prime Minister
Combes in 1903, railway companies, banks, and other investors were deeply involved in the pilgrimages as well as in the ongoing commercial life of the town.
The prefect of the Hautes-Pyrénées, in his 1908 report to the minister of the interior in Paris, also underscored the ties between shrine and state, estimating that
the sale of stamps alone had generated one hundred thousand francs during the
1907 pilgrimage season and roughly double that amount the following year, with
its special anniversary celebration. As the prefect noted, the pilgrimages had
considerable economic impacts "not only on the town of Lourdes but also on
the region and even the entire country."[11] State revenues of this magnitude
could scarcely be ignored, and putting Lourdes in the nominal hands of private
citizens did nothing to jeopardize this bounty. Quite the contrary: the 1910 settlement ensured that shrine and state would henceforth be intertwined.

The case of Lourdes provides new ways to think about the 1905 law of separation between Church and state. This watershed moment was not an unambiguous triumph for the secular nation-state. Yet neither was the law simply a
grudging compromise between warring forces that enabled religion to flourish,
if only in the realm of private life. The separation law enacted a convenient fiction that religious worship, as a matter of private practice, was no longer tied to
the public life of the French republic. The language of "separation" enabled republicans and Catholics alike to deny the realities of public religious practice in
the modern era. In the case of Lourdes, the law inscribed a new private status
on the sanctuary that effectively legislated the desires of republicans as well as

Catholics, both of whom wished to envision religion as safely beyond the realm of modern economic affairs. By legally defining religion as outside the purview of the state, it became easier to think of Lourdes as something different from what it really was. For devout Catholics, the shrine might be more comfortably imagined as the expression of a bygone world of simple peasant religiosity. For republicans, the pilgrimages could now be seen as acts of private religious worship with no bearing on the political or economic life of modern France. Catholics could ignore the commercial realities of Lourdes, focusing instead on the shrine's "pure" commitment to tending the sick, while republicans could close their eyes to the economic ties that linked shrine and state. The law separating Church and state thus provided a solution to the problem of modern religiosity that was not so different from the one concurrently offered by Huysmans in *The Crowds of Lourdes* (1906) or by Durkheim in *The Elementary Forms of the Religious Life* (1912): it drew a line between the religious and the modern. In this sense, anticlerical republicans and devout Catholics were both instrumental in defining Catholic pilgrimage as a traditional, premodern act. Seeking to differentiate religious practice from commercial activity, pilgrimage from tourism, the two sides helped to forge, together, the modern opposition between sacred and profane. And, in the process, the shared commercial terrain that made such an accommodation possible was obscured.

It is not surprising, then, that over the course of the twentieth century Lourdes lost the status of a political cause célèbre even as it gained in stature as an international site of pilgrimage and miraculous healing. There were occasional attempts to resurrect Lourdes as a site of reactionary politics. In the aftermath of the French defeat of 1940, Marshal Pétain even sought to secure the blessings of the Church for the Vichy regime by traveling to Lourdes in a symbolic act of national forgiveness and healing.[12] Yet such opportunistic efforts were largely transitory, and they were overshadowed by the ever-growing integration of Lourdes into the mass culture of modern democratic society. In this sense, it is a quite different event from the World War II years—the making of the Hollywood film *The Song of Bernadette* (1943)—that may provide the clearest indication of the legacy of Lourdes: the integration of religion and commerce, along with its effacement.

Lourdes became a pivotal site of popular Catholic worship because it developed, as we have seen, in concert with a newly commercializing French society. Although the shrine's enduring popularity over subsequent decades suggests how successfully popular religious devotion has merged with the thriving commercial culture of contemporary Western society, this integration is not only evident at the physical site. Adapted from Franz Werfel's best-selling novel of the

same name, *The Song of Bernadette* retells the story of Bernadette's visionary experience and the early struggles to make the grotto a Catholic holy place.[13] The
Twentieth Century–Fox production won several Academy Awards, including
one for best actress by Jennifer Jones, who played the peasant seer. The film's
popularity and success were no doubt related, in part, to the wartime context of
its release. A stark melodrama in which Bernadette struggles against the skeptical and often unscrupulous government officials of Lourdes, the motion picture
presents the story of the innocent visionary as a triumphant tale of pure-hearted
resistance against immoral and corrupt forces. Its message that ordinary individuals—humble French peasants—can persevere and succeed, even in the face
of overwhelming odds, is easily read as a story of occupied France resisting Nazi
domination.

Yet what is most interesting about the film is its direct appropriation of the
shrine's own historical narrative and visual imagery to tell the story of the
holy grotto. The film reproduces a highly sentimental vision of Lourdes, one
that strongly echoes the tone and content of the shrine's devotional literature.
Like Henri Lasserre's classic nineteenth-century work *Notre-Dame de Lourdes,*
the film presents an account of good peasant folk seeking to assert the truth
of Lourdes against evil government bureaucrats. It focuses on a humble Bernadette—ignorant of theology yet pure in faith—who must do battle with a
scornful imperial prosecutor (played by Vincent Price) along with other schem-
ing government administrators. Not unlike Lasserre's own telescoping of key
events, the film collapses time and space to compress its narrative and heighten
the drama of miraculous healing. Bernadette's spring begins to flow, and miracle cures suddenly abound, as the events of several months are made into a series of dramatic moments through the use of montage. What becomes clear,
then, is that the shrine's story of Bernadette was a tale ready-made for Hollywood adaptation, as the German social critics Max Horkheimer and Theodor
Adorno observed at the time of the film's release. In their well-known discussion of the culture industry, the Frankfurt School critics offered *The Song of
Bernadette* as an exemplary instance of the industry's tendency to impose a universal—homogenized and commodified—style on all its cultural products. Yet
they also noted that the film's Hollywood producer was hardly doing violence to
the original. "Even before Zanuck [*sic*] acquired her," they pointed out, "Saint
Bernadette was regarded by her latter-day hagiographer [Werfel] as brilliant
propaganda for all interested parties. That is what became of the emotions of the
character." Horkheimer and Adorno invoked the film not so much to show the
culture industry's ability to mold any subject into one of its nearly indistin-
guishable products (though they believed it could) but, rather, to show that "the
thing itself [Bernadette]" had been "essentially objectified and made viable before the established authorities began to argue about it." In short, the image of

Bernadette had been produced, reproduced, and transformed into a ready-made commodity long before Hollywood producers got their hands on the humble peasant.[14]

The incorporation of the shrine's own narrative and aesthetics also enabled the Hollywood film to represent Lourdes as a tale of timeless peasant spirituality at odds with the forces of the modern world. This opposition is quickly manifested in the movie's storyline when, shortly after Bernadette begins going to the grotto, government bureaucrats meet to discuss how best to stop the large crowds converging at the site to observe the visionary in her trance-like ecstasies. What most concerns these men, who pride themselves on their secular and modern view of the world, is that the "imbecilic" girl and her superstitious followers might ruin an impending railway deal, the town's most promising chance to benefit from the "progress" of their century. Juxtaposing the secular interests of government officials with the pure faith of Bernadette and her peasant supporters, the film rearticulates the familiar opposition between religion and modernity. When it becomes obvious that Bernadette's visions actually bring a newfound prosperity to the town, it is these same government officials—and not the Church or the faithful peasant folk—who seek to cash in on the grotto's popularity. In one scene, the mayor of Lourdes is seen secretly designing logos for bottled Lourdes water that he hopes to ship around the world.

At the end of the film, the viewer's attention is drawn momentarily to the newfound prosperity of the pilgrimage town. The former imperial prosecutor has come back to visit Lourdes, only to find his once-beloved town overrun by thousands of pilgrims seeking the Virgin's help. As the prosecutor, in a pivotal scene, debates the reality of the cures with the town doctor and village priest, the viewer sees behind them the many souvenir shops and peddlers that line the city streets. Unwilling to give up his rational skepticism, the prosecutor, now cancer-ridden and dying, continues to dismiss Lourdes as a bastion of superstition and exploitation; his lack of faith allows him to see only the profane Lourdes. Yet the film quickly cuts to a new scene—the grotto candlelit at night—and the camera follows the prosecutor as he makes his way through the crowds of pilgrims who, seemingly far from the modern sights and sounds of the previous scene, pray before the statue of the Virgin. Here, the prosecutor contemplates the misery of his life and the specter of impending death. Regretting his own unbelief and overwhelmed by loneliness, he kneels before the grotto and asks Bernadette to pray for him. There, in the midst of these simple souls at prayer, he seeks forgiveness and finds the true meaning of the grotto. The simple faith of the people triumphs, and all memory of profane Lourdes is erased. With the resolution of this conflict, the scene shifts to the final days of Bernadette's life at the convent in Nevers. There, the viewer sees the visionary, weak from years of ill health, still insisting from her deathbed that she really did see the beautiful lady of her visions. Then, at the moment of her death, Bernadette again experiences a vision of the lady hovering above her, like a Saint-Sulpice image of the Virgin Mary, and she dies in peace.

The Song of Bernadette thus reasserts quite emphatically a separation between religious devotion and modern commercial life. The irony, of course, is that this presentation of the shrine as a symbol of simple faith triumphing over the forces of secularism and modernity was itself the product of the very best tools of the commercial motion-picture industry. The film's narrative structure and visual imagery work together to present a carefully crafted image of Lourdes as a realm beyond the forces of the modern world, even as the movie reinscribes an already modern shrine within the more recent forms of mass culture offered up by the Hollywood dream factory. In this sense, *The Song of Bernadette* reflects, and pretends to resolve, the inescapable tensions of public religious expression in the modern era. Seeking to reconcile the religious with the modern, the film asserts an arbitrary opposition between sacred and profane that, like so many commentaries throughout the history of Lourdes, only imperfectly erases the more complicated nature of the shrine. In the process, Lourdes—from its earliest development as a nineteenth-century French pilgrimage destination to its more recent status as a global signifier of religious devotion—remains visible as a modern site where key contradictions of modernity itself are produced, contested, and obscured.

Acknowledgments

Someone once said that psychoanalysis terminates when the patient realizes that it could go on forever. The same could be said about writing a book. The product of a long gestation, this book gives me the opportunity to thank numerous individuals and institutions: some for enabling me to carry out the project and others for having the wisdom to tell me it was done.

I would like to express profound gratitude to Bonnie Smith and Joan Scott, whose support I initially experienced while a graduate student at Rutgers University. Bonnie Smith not only provided insightful criticism but her wide-ranging imagination helped me conceptualize a first project about Lourdes. Years later, she continued to offer creativity, thoughtful critique, and needed humor. She has my enormous appreciation for her willingness to read and criticize the manuscript in its revised form. I owe Joan Scott an equal debt of gratitude. Joan's interest and enthusiasm have spurred this project onward through its long journey. Her incisive criticisms, the result of careful reading of multiple drafts, have done much to sharpen the argument (and the prose) of this book. At crucial moments, her well-timed encouragement and advice kept the project on track. Together, Bonnie and Joan have been exemplary mentors and models of feminist scholarship.

Rutgers University was a very special place to be a graduate student, offering a stimulating intellectual community shared by professors and students alike. From the many remarkable members of this community, several deserve special mention. John Gillis ignited my initial interest in the subject of popular religion and later became an enthusiastic reader of the dissertation. Philip Nord, down the road at Princeton, made thoughtful suggestions on the dissertation. Special thanks to Carol Helstosky and Scott Sandage for intellectual comradeship and more. I am also very grateful to Brian Roberts for close readings of my early work and for pushing me to take seriously the commercial culture of the Lourdes shrine. Our many conversations about what it means to write history had a profound influence on this book.

At various stages of this project, I was helped out with crucial financial support. A Bourse Chateaubriand and a fellowship from the National Endowment for the Humanities enabled me to research and write the dissertation that represented a first effort to come to grips with Lourdes. Summer research grants from the NEH and Loyola University as well as a fellowship from the American Council of Learned Societies made possible several uninterrupted stints of postdoctoral research and writing. A faculty fellowship from the Ann Ida Gannon Center for Women and Leadership at Loyola University gave me a needed semester's leave to finish a final revision of the book.

My profound appreciation goes to the archivists and staff at the Archives de l'Œuvre de la Grotte in Lourdes. The late Père Rîme, who opened the Lourdes archives to me when I was just beginning my research, brought me countless boxes of dusty documents and patiently answered many questions about the workings of the shrine. When I returned to Lourdes some years later, Thérèse Franque and her assistant Roselyne de Boisséson gave me access to a variety of visual sources not yet cataloged and allowed me to photograph them for the book. Roselyne even gave up her days off to keep the archives open so that I could make full use of my time at the shrine. I would also like to thank Père Cerfontaine of the Lourdes Sanctuary in Oostakker, Belgium, who, along with the entire Jesuit community there, extended me a very warm welcome while I used the shrine's archives. Similarly helpful was the staff at the Marian Library at the University of Dayton, where Cecilia Mushenheim gave me free rein to consult the library's Clugnet Collection of printed materials (the largest on Lourdes in the United States) and the late Marjorie Yefchak took several photographs that appear in this book. Finally, a general thanks to the staffs at the Bibliothèque Nationale, the Archives Nationales, the Archives Départementales des Hautes-Pyrénées, the Musée Pyrénéen, the New York Public Library, the Library of Congress, and the New York Academy of Medicine, along with the interlibrary-loan staff at Loyola University Chicago for locating hundreds of obscure books and articles.

Over the years of this project, I have received support from numerous other friends and colleagues in academia. Among a long list of people who read, listened to, and commented on various parts of the book, I want especially to thank Shelley Baranowski, Joshua Cole (and his fellow members of the Faculty Seminar on French History and Culture in Athens, Georgia), Seth Fein, Ellen Furlough, Hilary Jewett, Susan Rosenbaum, Paul Seeley, Aaron Segal, Greg Shaya, Todd Shepard, Steve Soper, Susan Whitney, and Judith Zinsser. I would also like to thank Thomas Kselman, whose expert knowledge of French popular Catholicism led to a number of very helpful criticisms and suggestions. A source of encouragement since the earliest stages of this project, Vanessa Schwartz read the entire manuscript and offered invaluable advice for the final revisions. My colleagues at Loyola University were very helpful while I was finishing this work, with Barbara Rosenwein and Tim Gilfoyle offering sage advice on the many challenges of writing and publishing a book. The comments and suggestions of the anonymous readers for Cornell University Press helped to clarify my argument and produce a better book.

Friends in France also provided vital assistance. Jean-Pierre Dieterlen, Pascale Girard, and Lea Nash housed me, fed me, and entertained me on several research trips; their generosity made me feel at home in Paris. At Lourdes, I had the great fortune to meet Marie-Jo Legathe at the sanctuary's archives, a chance encounter that sparked a wonderful friendship. Marie-Jo and her husband Roland opened their home to me and shared their vast knowledge of the region's rich history and their deep love of the Pyrenees. My understanding of Lourdes—both town and shrine—was immeasurably enhanced by them.

I am grateful to John Ackerman at Cornell University Press for his confidence in the manuscript and to Sheri Englund and Ange Romeo-Hall for their editorial oversight. Thomas Greene, Deborah Kimmey, and Camille Robcis helped prepare the manuscript, and Andrea Gohl took photographs of my collection of Lourdes memorabilia. Portions of chapters 1 and 2 appeared as "Selling Lourdes: Pilgrimage, Tourism, and the Mass-Marketing of the Sacred in Nineteenth-Century France," in *Being Elsewhere: Tourism, Consumer Culture and Identity in Modern Europe and North America*, edited by Shelley Baranowski and Ellen Furlough (Ann Arbor, Mich.: University of Michigan Press, 2001). I thank the University of Michigan Press for permission to use this material.

To my mother, Marilyn Kaufman, and to my sister, Lori Kaufman, I can only say thanks for having learned when to ask and when not to ask how the book was going. Their good humor and forbearance have been much appreciated. My deepest gratitude goes to Bill Sites, who has read this book more closely than anyone (even me) and has applied his extraordinary talents as a thinker, writer, and editor to make it better. For this and so much more, I thank him. Finally, our daughter Isabelle Kaufman-Sites arrived just as I was making the final revisions to the manuscript. The joy and chaos that she brought to our lives made me realize, more than anything else, that the book was finished and new projects lay ahead. I dedicate this book to her.

Notes

Introduction: *Religious and Modern*

1. Many historians have interpreted this Marian lay piety as the expression of a larger femi-
nization of Catholic practice that was already underway by the late eighteenth century. Not only
were the seers women and children but the faithful who flocked to these new places of pilgrimage
were also disproportionately female. In nineteenth-century France, women predominated in devotional activities such as pilgrimage; they also outnumbered men in church attendance and in
commitment to religious orders. For discussions of Marian lay piety and the role of women and
children, see David Blackbourn, *Marpingen: Apparitions of the Virgin Mary in Nineteenth-Century
Germany* (New York, 1993), chap. 1; Barbara Corrado Pope, "Immaculate and Powerful: The Marian Revival in the Nineteenth Century," in *Immaculate and Powerful: The Female in Sacred Image
and Social Reality,* ed. Clarissa W. Atkinson, Constance H. Buchanan, and Margaret R. Miles
(Boston, 1985), 173–200; Thomas A. Kselman, *Miracles and Prophecies in Nineteenth-Century
France* (New Brunswick, N.J., 1983); and Sandra L. Zimdars-Swartz, *Encountering Mary: From
La Salette to Medjugorje* (Princeton, 1991). Also see Ralph Gibson, *A Social History of French
Catholicism, 1789–1914* (London, 1989); Claude Langlois, *Le Catholicisme au féminin: Les Congré-
gations françaises à supérieure générale au XIXe siècle* (Paris, 1984); and Bonnie G. Smith, *Ladies of
the Leisure Class: The Bourgeoises of Northern France in the Nineteenth Century* (Princeton, 1981).

2. Of the hundreds of proclaimed Marian apparitions in nineteenth-century France, the Catholic
Church recognized only three others as authentic. They were the visions of Catherine Labouré in
Paris (1830), those of Mélanie Calvat and Maximin Giraud at La Salette (1846), and those of five
peasant children in Pontmain (1871). The Church was often reluctant to accept popular visions because they threatened the hierarchy and doctrine of the male-dominated faith. However, persistent
displays of popular piety, combined with favorable outcomes of ecclesiastical investigations, sometimes led the Church to incorporate these visions into mainstream Catholic thought.

3. In accordance with customary French usage, I employ the term *les miraculés* (plural of the
masculine noun *le miraculé*) to refer generally to devout believers who claimed to be healed through
the intervention of the Virgin of Lourdes. The terms *la miraculée* and *les miraculées* will be used
when discussing the women who made such claims.

4. For a more comprehensive account of the apparitions of Bernadette Soubirous and the

early history of the grotto, see Suzanne K. Kaufman, "Miracles, Medicine, and the Spectacle of Lourdes: Popular Religion and Modernity in Fin-de-Siècle France," Ph.D. diss., Rutgers University, 1996, chaps. 1–2; and Ruth Harris, *Lourdes: Body and Spirit in the Secular Age* (London, 1999), chaps. 1–5. Also see the compilation of documents concerning the apparitions and later development of the pilgrimage site, edited and annotated by René Laurentin and Bernard Billet, *Lourdes: Dossier des documents authentiques,* 7 vols. (Paris, 1957–1962). The Archives de l'Œuvre de la Grotte, the private archives of the Lourdes sanctuary, house many of the key documents compiled by Laurentin and Billet. See Archives de l'Œuvre de la Grotte (hereafter AG) A2, Apparitions de Lourdes; AG A8, Sur les apparitions; AG A12, Sur les fausses visionnaires; AG 6H1, Rapport sur les premières guérisons opérées par l'usage de l'eau de la grotte de Lourdes (1858–1859).

5. In this view, the French Revolution of 1789 fatally undermined the power of the Catholic Church over public life, ushering in the slow but steady march of secularization. Subsequent declines in church attendance, especially among urbanites and male citizens, have been understood by such scholars as evidence of an increasingly secularized public sphere. For a summary of these studies, see Gibson, *Social History of French Catholicism,* chaps. 6 and 7. Gibson himself complicates this secularization thesis, pointing out that certain regions in France maintained high levels of religious practice late into the nineteenth century. Also see Gérard Cholvy and Yves-Marie Hilaire, *Histoire religieuse de la France contemporaine,* vol. 2 (Toulouse, 1986), chaps. 1–5.

6. Émile Durkheim, *The Elementary Forms of the Religious Life,* trans. Joseph Ward Swain (New York, 1915), 54–55.

7. See Max Weber, "Science as a Vocation," in *From Max Weber: Essays in Sociology,* ed. H. H. Gerth and C. Wright Mills (New York, 1946), 129–56. Weber's famous phrase appears on page 155: "The fate of our times is characterized by rationalization and intellectualization and, above all, by the 'disenchantment of the world.'" For Marx's discussion of the "fetishism of the commodity and its secret," see *Capital,* vol. 1, trans. Ben Fowkes (New York, 1976), 163–77.

8. See Kselman, *Miracles and Prophecies;* Blackbourn, *Marpingen;* Raymond Jonas, *France and the Cult of the Sacred Heart: An Epic Tale for Modern Times* (Berkeley, 2000); Philippe Boutry and Michel Cinquin, *Deux Pèlerinages au XIXe siècle: Ars et Paray-le-Monial* (Paris, 1980); Gérard Cholvy and Yves-Marie Hilaire, *Histoire religieuse de la France contemporaine,* vol. 1 (Toulouse, 1985), chap. 5; and Michel Lagrée, *La Bénédiction de Prométhée: Religion et technologie, XIXe–XXe siècle* (Paris, 1999).

9. See Jonas, *France and the Cult of the Sacred Heart.* In his analysis of the cult of the Sacred Heart as a key symbol of nineteenth-century counterrevolutionary Church politics, Jonas shows that clerical authorities often packaged their conservative messages in new and even democratic forms of worship.

10. See Harris, *Lourdes,* chaps. 7–10.

11. An interesting exception is Thomas A. Kselman's *Death and the Afterlife in Modern France* (Princeton, 1993), which argues that increasingly commercialized and homogenized funeral practices led to new rituals with respect to death and mourning. Also see Raymond Jonas, "Sacred Tourism and Secular Pilgrimage: Montmartre and the Basilica of Sacré-Coeur," in *Montmartre and the Making of Mass Culture,* ed. Gabriel P. Weisberg (New Brunswick, N.J., 2001), 94–119.

12. Harris's analysis of Lourdes, for example, begins: "At first glance Lourdes seems to epitomize packaged piety and rampant consumerism, the mass mobilization of crowds and new techniques of indoctrination. From this perspective it appears as a vibrant manifestation of 'modernity.' The concept, however, hardly does justice to the complex reality of the pilgrimage phenomenon," which instead is centered on "the lure of the miraculous and the individual encounter with the supernatural, a vision of community and of selfhood entirely at odds with secular creeds." Harris, *Lourdes,* 11.

13. See Colleen McDannell, *Material Christianity: Religion and Popular Culture in America*

(New Haven, 1995), 4–13. McDannell's discussion of religion and materiality has helped to shape my own approach to these questions.

14. Max Horkheimer and Theodor W. Adorno, "The Culture Industry: Enlightenment as Mass Deception," in *Dialectic of Enlightenment*, trans. John Cumming (New York, 1972), 120–67.

15. See, for instance, Neil McKendrick, John Brewer, and J. H. Plumb, eds., *The Birth of Consumer Society: The Commercialization of Eighteenth-Century England* (Bloomington, Ind., 1982); Victoria de Grazia, ed., with Ellen Furlough, *The Sex of Things: Gender and Consumption in Historical Perspective* (Berkeley, 1996); and Rudy Koshar, ed., *Histories of Leisure* (New York, 2002).

16. See Rosalind H. Williams, *Dream Worlds: Mass Consumption in Late Nineteenth-Century France* (Berkeley, 1982); and Michael B. Miller, *The Bon Marché: Bourgeois Culture and the Department Store, 1869–1920* (Princeton, 1981).

17. See Douglas Peter Mackaman, *Leisure Settings: Bourgeois Culture, Medicine, and the Spa in Modern France* (Chicago, 1998); Vanessa R. Schwartz, *Spectacular Realities: Early Mass Culture in Fin-de-Siècle Paris* (Berkeley, 1998); and Patrick Young, "*La Vieille France* as Object of Bourgeois Desire: The Touring Club de France and the French Regions, 1890–1918," in *Histories of Leisure*, ed. Koshar, 169–89.

18. Walter Benjamin, "Paris, the Capital of the Nineteenth Century," in *The Arcades Project*, trans. Howard Eiland and Kevin McLaughlin (Cambridge, Mass., 2002), 7. As Susan Buck-Morss has noted, "Benjamin's central argument in the *Passagen-Werk* was that under conditions of capitalism, industrialization had brought about a *re*enchantment of the social world, and through it, a 'reactivation of mythic powers.'" See Susan Buck-Morss, *The Dialectics of Seeing: Walter Benjamin and the Arcades Project* (Cambridge, Mass., 1989), 253–54.

19. See Williams, *Dream Worlds;* Miller, *Bon Marché;* Schwartz, *Spectacular Realities;* Leora Auslander, *Taste and Power: Furnishing Modern France* (Berkeley, 1996); Lisa Tiersten, *Marianne in the Market: Envisioning Consumer Society in Fin-de-Siècle France* (Berkeley, 2001); and Aaron J. Segal, "The Republic of Goods: Advertising and National Identity in France, 1875–1918," Ph.D. diss., University of California at Los Angeles, 1995. See also Thomas Richards, *The Commodity Culture of Victorian England: Advertising and Spectacle, 1851–1914* (Stanford, 1990).

20. Two works have been especially helpful in shaping my understanding of modernity and modern religious experience: Marshall Berman, *All That Is Solid Melts into Air: The Experience of Modernity* (New York, 1982); and Mica Nava and Alan O'Shea, eds., *Modern Times: Reflections on a Century of English Modernity* (London, 1996). Also see de Grazia, ed., *Sex of Things;* Richards, *Commodity Culture of Victorian England;* and Schwartz, *Spectacular Realities.* For Baudelaire's well-known pronouncement, see Charles Baudelaire, *The Painter of Modern Life and Other Essays*, trans. Jonathan Mayne (London, 1964), 13.

21. Here, I wish to distinguish between popular culture—which comprises beliefs, practices, and objects that are locally produced and shared—and mass culture, in which producers and consumers typically are distinct and in which cultural forms reflect and construct urban social life while also being shared by large numbers of people outside of urban centers. See David Morgan, *Protestants and Pictures: Religion, Visual Culture, and the Age of American Mass Production* (New York, 1999), chap. 1. Morgan suggests that "what transforms human experience from local to mass culture is not the quantities of production but the socioeconomic apparatus of circulation, which occurs at the regional level no less than at the national"; see pages 350–51, note 11.

22. Berman, *All That Is Solid Melts into Air,* 15.

23. See Patrick Verley, *Nouvelle histoire économique de la France contemporaine,* vol. 2 (Paris, 1989); and Jean-Pierre Daviet, *La Société industrielle en France, 1814–1914: Productions, èchanges, rep-rèsentations* (Paris, 1997). Also see Judith Coffin, "Credit, Consumption, and Images of Women's Desires: Selling the Sewing Machine in Late-Nineteenth-Century France," *French Historical Studies* 18 (1994): 749–83. See also works cited in note 19.

24. Eugen Weber, *France, Fin de Siècle* (Cambridge, Mass., 1986), 179–80.

25. As the numbers of pilgrims and the diversity of represented regions grew, organized pilgrimages from the southwest continued to predominate, followed by dioceses in Bretagne and the Nord. Shrine records also indicate that women outnumbered men in organized pilgrimages to Lourdes from the start of Church-run pilgrimages in the 1870s through the outbreak of World War I. For a list of pilgrimages according to region, see AG 12 E2, Liste des localités venues en pèlerinage à Lourdes (1868–1887); and AG 1HD1, Processions, guérisons, et pèlerinages divers (1866–1950), Journal du Sanctuaire de Notre-Dame de Lourdes. For data on women and men, see AG 18E4, Statistiques générales (1893–1977), Statistiques fournies par l'hospitalité.

26. Geoffrey Chaucer, *The Canterbury Tales*, trans. Nevill Coghill (London, 1974), 261.

27. Scholars of premodern Christian pilgrimage have shown that shrine tenders, at both local and international sites, traded in sacred relics and specialized in the selling of medals, badges, and printed broadsheets. Itinerant peddlers also hawked religious and secular goods at shrines. This commerce not only satisfied the religious desires of pilgrims but also acted as religious publicity for holy destinations. See, for example, William A. Christian Jr., *Apparitions in Late Medieval and Renaissance Spain* (Princeton, 1981); William A. Christian Jr., *Local Religion in Sixteenth-Century Spain* (Princeton, 1981); Jean Chelini and Henry Branthomme, *Les Chemins de Dieu: Histoire des pèlerinages chrétiens des origines à nos jours* (Paris, 1982); Alphonse Dupront, *Du sacré: Croisades et pèlerinages, images et langages* (Paris, 1987); and Ronald C. Finucane, *Miracles and Pilgrims: Popular Beliefs in Medieval England* (London, 1977), especially chaps. 2 and 3.

28. For a discussion of the Miraculous Medal in the context of other French nineteenth-century popular devotions, see Kselman, *Miracles and Prophecies*, 78 and 153. Also see Boutry and Cinquin, *Deux Pèlerinages au XIXe siècle*.

29. See Walter Benjamin, "The Work of Art in the Age of Mechanical Reproduction," in *Illuminations*, ed. Hannah Arendt, trans. Harry Zohn (New York, 1969), 217–52. For a discussion of Adorno and Horkheimer versus Benjamin on this question, see Fredric Jameson, *Late Marxism: Adorno, or, the Persistence of the Dialectic* (New York, 1990), 106–7.

30. Among a very large literature, see Morgan, *Protestants and Pictures;* Laurence Moore, *Selling God: American Religion in the Marketplace of Culture* (New York, 1994); Leigh Eric Schmidt, *Consumer Rites: The Buying and Selling of American Holidays* (Princeton, 1995); Diane Winston, *Red-Hot and Righteous: The Urban Religion of the Salvation Army* (Cambridge, Mass., 1999); and John M. Giggie and Diane Winston, eds., *Faith in the Market: Religion and the Rise of Urban Commercial Culture* (New Brunswick, N.J., 2002). Despite the innovative nature of this scholarship, it has generated surprisingly few such studies outside of North America. For one exception, see Pamela Walker, *Pulling the Devil's Kingdom Down: The Salvation Army in Victorian Britain* (Berkeley, 2001).

31. McDannell, *Material Christianity*, 14–15. Vanessa Schwartz's analysis of early mass cultural forms in fin-de-siècle Paris makes a similar point about the interdependence of word and image in an era of near universal literacy. See Schwartz, *Spectacular Realities*, 2.

32. Robert Orsi, *Thank You, St. Jude: Women's Devotion to the Patron Saint of Hopeless Causes* (New Haven, 1996), 211.

33. Recent scholarship on women and consumer culture has been particularly useful for my own interpretation of the role that commercialized devotional practices played in the lives of female pilgrims, especially Lourdes *miraculées*. Certain nineteenth-century women learned to use the production of commercialized feminine images to shape different, and sometimes radical, selves. See, for example, Judith Walkowitz, *City of Dreadful Delight: Narratives of Sexual Danger in Late-Victorian London* (Chicago, 1992); and Mary Louise Roberts, *Disruptive Acts: The New Woman in Fin-de-Siècle France* (Chicago, 2002). For an overview of this literature, see Mary Louise Roberts, "Gender, Consumption, and Commodity Culture," *American Historical Review* 103, no. 3 (June 1998): 817–44.

34. On the modern public sphere and commercialization, see Jürgen Habermas, *The Structural Transformation of the Public Sphere: An Inquiry into a Category of Bourgeois Society*, trans. Thomas Burger (Cambridge, Mass., 1991); see also Craig Calhoun, ed., *Habermas and the Public Sphere* (Cambridge, Mass., 1992).

1. Remaking Lourdes: Catholic Pilgrimage as Modern Spectacle

1. Louis Veuillot, *L'Univers*, 28 August 1858, quoted in René Laurentin and Bernard Billet, *Lourdes: Dossier des documents authentiques* (hereafter *LDA*), vol. 4 (Paris, 1958), 87; and "De L'Avenir de Lourdes," *Le Lavedan*, 5 June 1866, quoted in Laurentin and Billet, *LDA*, vol. 7 (Paris, 1962), 14–15. (All translations are my own, unless otherwise noted.) See Archives de l'Œuvre de la Grotte (hereafter AG) 18E3, Listes des pèlerinages, Journal des chapelains, 1903–1909, statistique envoyée à M. le Chanoine Berengers. Also see Archives Nationales (hereafter AN) F7 12734, Rapport du préfet des Hautes-Pyrénées au ministère de l'intérieur, Tarbes, 15 November 1908, 1–5.

2. See Thomas A. Kselman, *Miracles and Prophecies in Nineteenth-Century France* (New Brunswick, N.J., 1983), 198; and Ruth Harris, *Lourdes: Body and Spirit in the Secular Age* (London, 1999), 247. Raymond Jonas makes a similar argument about the Catholic Church's promotion of the cult of the Sacred Heart of Jesus in nineteenth-century France; see *France and the Cult of the Sacred Heart: An Epic Tale for Modern Times* (Berkeley, 2000). On the invention of tradition, see Eric Hobsbawm and Terence Ranger, eds., *The Invention of Tradition* (Cambridge, 1983).

3. Crucial for my argument in this chapter is the fact that, by the late nineteenth century, there was near-universal literacy in France; the mass production of popular reading material, reaching both women and peasants, made it possible for clerical authorities at Lourdes to cater to them. See Martyn Lyons, *Readers and Society in Nineteenth-Century France: Workers, Women, Peasants* (New York, 2001); Raymond Grew and Patrick J. Harrigan, *School, State, and Society: The Growth of Elementary Schooling in Nineteenth-Century France: A Quantitative Analysis* (Ann Arbor, Mich., 1991); and François Furet and Jacques Ozouf, *Reading and Writing: Literacy in France from Calvin to Jules Ferry* (Cambridge, 1982).

4. See René Laurentin, *Lourdes: Histoire authentique des apparitions*, vol. 3 (Paris, 1962), 57–80. Also see Thérèse Taylor, "'So Many Extraordinary Things to Tell': Letters from Lourdes, 1858," *Journal of Ecclesiastical History* 46, no. 3 (July 1995): 457–81.

5. On 28 July 1858, the same day that Veuillot visited the grotto, Bishop Laurence announced his plan to convene a commission to investigate the apparitions and miracle cures; see AN F19 2374, Apparitions, ordonnance de Monseigneur, l'évêque de Tarbes, July 1858. Also see the bishop's letter to the minister of the interior, dated 7 August 1858, in which he justified his decision to intervene in the affair. For more on Veuillot, see Pierre Pierrard, *Louis Veuillot* (Paris, 1998).

6. On the first pilgrimages to Lourdes and the popular cult surrounding Bernadette, see Harris, *Lourdes*, chaps. 3–5.

7. See Harris, *Lourdes*, 169–76; and Amélie Gravrand, "L'Impact géographique du tourisme de pèlerinage sur la ville de Lourdes," Thèse, Université de Bretagne Occidentale, 1997, chap. 3. On the Church's efforts to institutionalize popular expressions of religiosity, see Ralph Gibson, *A Social History of French Catholicism, 1789–1914* (London 1989), chap. 5; and Kselman, *Miracles and Prophecies*, chap. 6.

8. See Laurentin and Billet, *LDA*, vol. 7, 11; "De L'Avenir de Lourdes," *Le Lavedan*, 5 June 1866. For the railway's impact on local and regional pilgrimages in nineteenth-century France, see Michel Lagrée, *La Bénédiction de Prométhée: Religion et technologie, XIXe–XXe siècle* (Paris, 1999), 231–39; and Michael R. Marrus, "Cultures on the Move: Pilgrims and Pilgrimages in Nineteenth-Century France," *Stanford French Review* 1 (1977): 205–20.

9. The two visionaries of La Salette had proved difficult to control and found themselves at

odds with the local clergy, who did not fully believe their claims. See Sandra L. Zimdars-Swartz, *Encountering Mary: From La Salette to Medjugorje* (Princeton, 1991), 25–92, 165–90.

10. Bernadette remained at the Convent of Saint-Gildard until her death in 1879. See René Laurentin, *Visage de Bernadette*, vols. 1 and 2 (Paris, 1992); Claude Langlois, "La Photographie comme preuve, entre médecine et religion," *Histoire des Sciences Médicales* 28, no. 4 (1994): 325–36; and Claude Langlois, "Photographier des saintes: De Bernadette Soubirous à Thérèse de Lisieux," in *Histoire, images, imaginaires: Fin XVe siècle–début XXe siècle,* ed. Michèle Ménard and Annie Duprat (Le Mans, 1998), 261–71.

11. See Henri Lasserre, *Notre-Dame de Lourdes* (Paris, 1870 [1869]).

12. Ultramontanism, from the Latin for "beyond the mountains," was a nineteenth-century intellectual and political movement in countries such as France, Germany, Spain, and England whose adherents believed in the supremacy of the papacy in Italy (that is, beyond the Alps) as a bulwark against political liberalism and modern scientific beliefs. In France, the Assumptionists, along with a number of other ultramontane orders, sought to reshape Catholic religious practice by promoting popular devotions and orchestrating elaborate—even flamboyant—ceremonies that appealed to large numbers of believers. According to René Rémond, the Assumptionists were particularly successful in these endeavors and played a significant role in France's religious revival of the 1870s and 1880s. Important lay supporters of the Lourdes shrine also embraced ultramontane Catholicism, including Louis Veuillot and Henri Lasserre. See René Rémond, *The Right Wing in France from 1815 to de Gaulle,* trans. James M. Laux (Philadelphia, 1966), 184–88. Also see Austin Gough, *Paris and Rome: The Gallican Church and the Ultramontane Campaign, 1848–1853* (Oxford, 1986); and Gérard Cholvy and Yves-Marie Hilarie, *Histoire religieuse de la France contemporaine,* vol. 1 (Toulouse, 1985), chap. 5.

13. See Marrus, "Cultures on the Move," 216–18; and Harris, *Lourdes,* 251–55.

14. Church records show that the numbers of sick pilgrims who came to Lourdes on the national pilgrimage increased each decade during the period from 1874 to 1914. See AG 18E4, Statistiques générales, les malades pauvres à Lourdes: 1874–1914.

15. See Cholvy and Hilaire, *Histoire religieuse de la France contemporaine,* vol. 1, 194–95; Kselman, *Miracles and Prophecies,* 163–64; and Marrus, "Cultures on the Move," 216–18. The success of the national pilgrimage to Lourdes also translated into large numbers of regional pilgrimages to the site as well. For Church and government statistics on the numbers of pilgrims and visitors to the shrine during the first decade of the twentieth century (roughly one hundred and fifty thousand to three hundred thousand each year), see AG 18E3, Listes des pèlerinages, Journal des chapelains, 1903–1909, statistique envoyée à M. le Chanoine Berengers; and AN F7 12734, Rapport du préfet des Hautes-Pyrénées au ministère de l'intérieur, Tarbes, 15 November 1908, 1–5.

16. See Cholvy and Hilaire, *Histoire religieuse de la France contemporaine,* vol. 1, 167. On the Touring Club de France, see Patrick Young, "*La Vieille France* as Object of Bourgeois Desire: The Touring Club de France and the French Regions, 1890–1918," in *Histories of Leisure,* ed. Rudy Koshar (New York, 2002), 169–89.

17. In building its own press empire, the Assumptionist order drew on earlier religious models of commercial publishing in France, most importantly the Abbé Jacques-Paul Migne's Ateliers Catholiques. See R. Howard Bloch, *God's Plagiarist: Being an Account of the Fabulous Industry and Irregular Commerce of the Abbé Migne* (Chicago, 1994). *La Croix,* in particular, was produced with the explicit goal of countering the secular mass press. With its low price, simple page layout, and editorial cartoons, the newspaper imitated the design and style of secular mass dailies and proved successful in capturing a large Catholic readership. See René Rémond and Émile Poulat, *Cent ans d'histoire de La Croix* (Paris, 1988); and Jacqueline Godfrin and Philippe Godfrin, *Une Centrale de presse catholique: La Maison de la Bonne Presse et ses publications* (Paris, 1965). Also see Lagrée, *La Bénédiction de Prométhée,* chap. 7.

18. These manuals and guides were intended as tools for overworked clergy, who might not have

the time to instruct large numbers of parishioners about the goals of the new national pilgrimage to Lourdes. See Abbé Chaudé, *De Lourdes au Cirque de Gavarnie (Hautes-Pyrénées), guide pratique du pèlerin et du touriste* (Versailles and Lourdes, 1875); and Abbé Le Cointe, *Le Guide du pèlerin de Coutances et de Bayeux à Notre-Dame de Lourdes* (Caen, 1883).

19. Later Lourdes guidebooks included *Guide du pèlerin et du touriste à Lourdes, aux environs et vers la montagne* (Tarbes, 1888); Abbé Martin, *Guide de Lourdes et ses environs à l'usage des pèlerins* (Saumur, 1893); J. Couret, *Guide-Almanach de Notre-Dame de Lourdes, 1900* (Bordeaux, 1900); and *Lourdes en deux jours: Guide religieux, historique, pittoresque et documentaire* (Tarbes, 1914). On the Guides Joanne, see Daniel Nordman, "Les Guides-Joanne," in *Les Lieux de mémoire: La Nation*, vol. 2, ed. Pierre Nora (Paris, 1997), 1035–72.

20. There were two major periods of land acquisition by the bishopric of Tarbes. During the first, from 1861 through 1874, the Church bought the grotto property and the surrounding territory to build the shrine; in the second, from 1875 through 1882, the bishopric bought property in the city of Lourdes to build the boulevard de la Grotte. See AN BB18 1589, Administration de la mense épiscopale de Tarbes: Rapport de M. Monsourat, Commissaire-Administrateur, 27 December 1899, 63–85. Also see AG A16, Rapports avec la maire de Lourdes et surveillance de la grotte, carton 1, dossier 4, letter from Père Sempé to the Mayor of Lourdes, Lourdes, 23 March 1881; and AG 1E1, État comparatif des avantages procurés à la ville de Lourdes par la mouvement des pèlerins (1860–1906).

21. On nineteenth-century spa and resort towns, see Eugen Weber, *France, Fin de Siècle* (Cambridge, Mass., 1986), chap. 9; Douglas Peter Mackaman, *Leisure Settings: Bourgeois Culture, Medicine, and the Spa in Modern France* (Chicago, 1998); and Alain Corbin, *The Lure of the Sea: The Discovery of the Seaside in the Western World, 1750–1840*, trans. Jocelyn Phelps (Berkeley, 1994).

22. Although the plan to connect the national route to the town was approved by the central government in August 1875, protests by some Lourdes inhabitants stalled construction until 1880. Many shopkeepers feared a loss of revenue if pilgrims were rerouted away from the inner city to the sanctuary below. A compromise was reached by linking the new route to the city via two adjoining streets, the new boulevard de la Grotte and the rue de la Grotte. See AN BB18 1589, Administration de la mense épiscopale de Tarbes: Rapport de M. Monsourat, Commissaire-Administrateur, 27 December 1899, 76–84. Also see Archives Départmentales des Hautes-Pyrénées 17J7, Surveillance des pèlerins (1875); and AG A16, Rapports avec la maire de Lourdes et surveillance de la grotte, carton 1, dossier 4.

23. In 1888 the Assumptionist leader, François Picard, instituted the Procession of the Blessed Sacrament as a regular ritual at Lourdes. During these Eucharistic processions, the Blessed Sacrament was paraded before sick pilgrims, who prayed to be cured by its power. Picard also instituted a nightly procession at the shrine, in which thousands of pilgrims carried candles as they prayed, sang, and marched around the esplanade, basilica, and grotto. See chap. 3.

24. For further discussion of these construction projects, see Gravrand, "L'Impact géographique du tourisme de pèlerinage," 32–36. Another important project (discussed in chap. 3) was the building of the Medical Bureau in 1884.

25. AN BB18 1589, Administration de la mense épiscopale de Tarbes: Rapport de M. Monsourat, Commissaire-Administrateur, 27 December 1899, 12–14, 44. According to this report, subscription revenues of the two periodicals were some twenty thousand francs in 1899; the shrine made another fifteen thousand francs from newsstand sales.

26. The Grotto fathers did not charge for the water itself but did impose a fee to cover the cost of the bottles, corks, carpentry, labor, and transport. The same government report estimated that the year's sale of candles at the boutique generated an additional one hundred thousand francs. See AN BB18 1589, Administration de la mense épiscopale de Tarbes: Rapport de M. Monsourat, Commissaire-Administrateur, 27 December 1899, 14, 40–45, 87.

214   *Notes to Pages 31–44*

27. For statistics on the amount of water shipped from late nineteenth-century thermal spas, see Weber, *France, Fin de Siècle,* 183.

28. See AG 1E1, État comparatif des avantages procurés à la ville de Lourdes, secs. 2 and 3; see sec. 13 for data on thermal spas in the region. Also see AN F7 12734, Rapport du préfet des Hautes-Pyrénées au ministère de l'intérieur, Tarbes, 15 November 1908, 5, 9–13. Emphasis in original.

29. See Rudy Koshar, "Seeing, Traveling, and Consuming: An Introduction," in Koshar, ed., *Histories of Leisure* (New York, 2002), 7; and Vanessa R. Schwartz, *Spectacular Realities: Early Mass Culture in Fin-de-Siècle Paris* (Berkeley, 1998), 2–3.

30. Beyond practical information, Lourdes guidebooks also offered religious instruction on topics such as the Immaculate Conception, presented condensed versions of the authorized account of Bernadette's apparitions, and explained the shrine's processions and rituals. See, for example, Bernard Dauberive, *Lourdes et ses environs: Guide du pèlerin et du touriste* (Poitiers, 1896), 9–23; Martin, *Guide de Lourdes,* 13–15; and *Lourdes en deux jours,* 93–94, 139–60.

31. See Nordman, "Les Guides-Joanne"; Young, "*La Vieille France* as Object of Bourgeois Desire"; and Jan Palmowski, "Travels with Baedeker: The Guidebook and the Middle Classes in Victorian and Edwardian England," in *Histories of Leisure,* ed. Koshar, 105–31.

32. *Guide du pèlerin et du touriste à Lourdes,* 35; Dauberive, *Lourdes et ses environs,* 63–64 (emphasis in original); and *Souvenir guide du pèlerin, cinquantenaire de l'Immaculée-Conception, livre d'or de Notre-Dame de Lourdes* (Toulouse, 1909), 27.

33. Martin, *Guide de Lourdes,* 3; Dauberive, *Lourdes et ses environs,* 88; *Guide du pèlerin et du touriste à Lourdes,* 32–33; and *Lourdes en deux jours,* 9–10, 79. See also Couret, *Guide-Almanach de Notre-Dame de Lourdes.*

34. Young, "*La Vieille France* as Object of Bourgeois Desire," 184.

35. Chaudé, *De Lourdes au Cirque de Gavarnie (Hautes-Pyrénées),* 40–41, 43; and Couret, *Guide-Almanach de Notre-Dame de Lourdes,* 65.

36. See *Lourdes en deux jours,* 73, and front page; Dauberive, *Lourdes et ses environs,* 82.

37. The earliest picture postcards mass produced in France were created for the 1889 Universal Exposition in Paris. Postcards, however, did not become a means of mass communication or souvenir items until the first decade of the twentieth century—often called the golden age of postcard collecting. See Frank Staff, *The Picture Postcard and Its Origins* (London, 1966); and Aline Ripert and Claude Frère, *La Carte postale: Son Histoire, sa fonction sociale* (Paris, 1983). Also see Naomi Schor, "*Cartes Postales:* Representing Paris 1900," *Critical Inquiry* 18 (winter 1992): 188–244.

38. See René Laurentin, *Lourdes: Cartes postales d'hier* (Paris, 1979). The book is a comprehensive compilation of Lourdes postcards with no commentary on their imagery or their use in the devotional life of the pilgrimage.

39. A number of postcards analyzed in this chapter are part of the vast postcard collection that is housed (but not yet catalogued) at the Archives de l'Œuvre de la Grotte; others are from my private collection.

40. Marcel Jouhandeau, *Mémorial,* vol. 2 (Paris, 1951), 51, originally cited in Weber, *France, Fin de Siècle,* 189–90. See also Cholvy and Hilaire, *Histoire religieuse de la France contemporaine,* vol. 1, 167.

41. See Bertile Ségalas, "Huit jours à Lourdes," *Revue de Bretagne, de Vendée et d'Anjou* 23 (January–March 1900); this account was also published as a pamphlet called *Huit jours à Lourdes* (Vannes, 1900). In addition, see Bertile Ségalas, "Mon sixième voyage à Lourdes," *La Femme et la Famille* (1904); and Madeleine D., *Mon Pèlerinage de Lourdes* (Blois, 1912).

42. Ségalas, "Huit jours à Lourdes," *Revue de Bretagne* 23 (January): 47–49; and Madeleine D., *Mon Pèlerinage de Lourdes,* 1–2.

43. Ségalas, "Huit jours à Lourdes," *Revue de Bretagne* 23 (February): 130; and 23 (March): 195.

44. The postcards referred to here are from my private collection of some twenty Lourdes postcards.

45. Government and Church records confirm that these women were not unusual in merging pilgrimage and tourist activities. During the period of national pilgrimages to Lourdes, there were huge increases in visits to nearby towns such as Pau as well as to neighboring thermal spas. For statistics on visitors to Pau, see AN F7 12734, Rapport du préfet des Hautes-Pyrénées au ministère de l'intérieur, Tarbes, 15 November 1908, 5. For information on thermal spas in the region, see AG 1E1, État comparatif des avantages procurés à la ville de Lourdes, sec. 13.

46. One indication of the popularity of Lourdes postcards is the extraordinary revenue made by the state from the sale of stamps at Lourdes. The prefect of the Hautes-Pyrénées claimed revenues of over one hundred thousand francs in 1907 and double that amount in 1908; see AN F7 12734, Rapport du préfet des Hautes-Pyrénées au ministère de l'intérieur, Tarbes, 15 November 1908, 6–7.

47. Couret, *Guide-Almanach de Notre-Dame de Lourdes*, 3–4.

48. See Michael B. Miller, *The Bon Marché: Bourgeois Culture and the Department Store, 1869–1920* (Princeton, 1981), chaps. 5 and 6. On the emergence of an advertising industry in French provincial towns and cities, see Aaron J. Segal, "The Republic of Goods: Advertising and National Identity in France, 1875–1918," Ph.D. diss., University of California at Los Angeles, 1995. Also see Marc Martin, *Trois siècles de publicité en France* (Paris, 1992).

49. Advertisements for the Grands Magasins des Galeries Catholiques appeared regularly on the back page of the shrine's *Journal de la Grotte de Lourdes*. For a sampling, see the issues dated 11 July 1909, 24 July 1910, and 10 December 1911. A copy of a catalog for the Grands Magasins de l'Alliance Catholique is part of the Clugnet Collection housed at the Marian Library at the University of Dayton; see *Cantiques de Lourdes, Offerts par les Magasins de l'Alliance Catholique* (Lourdes, 1911?), 4, for its advertising copy: "Vendre beaucoup pour vendre bon marché / Vendre bon marché pour vendre beaucoup!"

50. See Miller, *Bon Marché*, 174–75.

51. The term "Saint-Sulpice art" refers to the mass-produced religious objects and images manufactured and sold in the Parisian neighborhood surrounding the Church of Saint-Sulpice. See Claude Savart, "À la recherche de l' 'art' dit de Saint-Sulpice," *Revue d'Histoire de la Spiritualité* 52 (1976): 265–82. Also see Lagrée, *La Bénédiction de Prométhée*, chap. 7.

52. *Cantiques de Lourdes*, 11 and 15.

53. AG, 7P3, Affaire vente d'eau de la grotte (1879–1888), dossier 1, advertising brochure for Pastilles à l'Eau de Lourdes, F. Valette & Co., 1888.

54. *Cantiques de Lourdes*, 4. Emphasis in original.

55. See Couret, *Guide-Almanach de Notre-Dame de Lourdes*, 44–45.

56. See *Cantiques de Lourdes*.

57. See Schwartz, *Spectacular Realities*, chaps. 3 and 4. Schwartz links these entertainments to an emerging mass urban culture that put extraordinary value on viewing spectacles that recreated reality.

58. Martin, *Guide de Lourdes et ses environs*, 37.

59. *Guide du pèlerin et du touriste à Lourdes* declared that the panorama re-created the miracle of the candle with "natural grandeur"; see p. 31. *Lourdes en deux jours*, 153, commented on the "absolute authenticity" of the scene. Also see Couret, *Guide-Almanach de Notre-Dame de Lourdes*, 134–35; *Guide du pèlerin de Saint-Brieuc à Lourdes* (Saint-Brieuc, 1922), 85; *Manuel du pèlerinage interdiocésain de la Suisse Française à Notre-Dame de Lourdes* (Belley, 1913), 213.

60. Advertisements for the "Panorama de Notre-Dame de Lourdes, Seule au Monde" ran in the *Journal de la Grotte de Lourdes* in every issue from 1899 to 1902.

61. *Lourdes en deux jours*, 153.

62. See David Freedberg, *The Power of Images: Studies in the History and Theory of Response*

(Chicago, 1989), chap. 9, especially 192–201. The tradition of religious replication underwent a significant renaissance with the production of replica Lourdes grottos. These replicas became extremely popular after 1870, when hundreds were constructed in France and its colonies as well as in other countries. Two especially well-known replicas are the grotto of Oostakker, Belgium, site of a Church-sanctioned miraculous cure attributed to Our Lady of Lourdes (completed in 1871) and the grotto at the University of Notre Dame in Indiana (built in 1896). In 1904–5, Pope Pius X built a replica grotto in the Vatican gardens. Replica grottos enabled even the poorest pilgrims to have access to the shrine and its healing powers, as was the case with the Belgian worker Pierre de Rudder, whose cure at Oostakker is treated in chap. 5. See Lagrée, *La Bénédiction de Prométhée,* 197–99; and Colleen McDannell, *Material Christianity: Religion and Popular Culture in America* (New Haven, 1995), chap. 5.

63. Madeleine D., *Mon Pèlerinage de Lourdes,* 3 and 7.

64. It seems probable that postcard writing and collecting at Lourdes were generally women's activities. The postcards housed at the Archives de l'Œuvre de la Grotte were written mostly by women and typically were addressed to other women or to male family members. Postcards in my own collection were written almost entirely by female pilgrims. Naomi Schor has also noted that early twentieth-century postcard writing and collecting were seen as feminine preoccupations; indeed, commentators often labeled them feminine vices. See Schor, *"Cartes Postales,"* 211–12.

65. All cards are from my private collection.

66. See, for example, Schwarz, *Spectacular Realities;* and T. J. Clark, *The Painting of Modern Life: Paris in the Art of Manet and His Followers* (Princeton, 1984).

67. Thirty-five-millimeter prints of these short films are preserved in the Motion Picture and Television Reading Room of the Library of Congress. The three frame enlargements presented here are from the Pathé Frères title: "Lourdes" (1904?), LoC call number FEA 3128, in the Library of Congress AFI—Dorothy M. Taylor Collection.

68. See Miriam Hansen, "Early Cinema, Late Cinema: Transformations of the Public Sphere," in *Viewing Positions: Ways of Seeing Film,* ed. Linda Williams (New Brunswick, N.J., 1995), 137–38; and Tom Gunning, "An Aesthetic of Astonishment: Early Film and the (In)Credulous Spectator," in *Viewing Positions,* 121.

69. The films of Lourdes made by the Lumière brothers and by Charles Pathé were similar in both form and content to their other actualités of the period. On early film in France, see Richard Abel, *The Ciné Goes to Town: French Cinema, 1896–1914* (Berkeley, 1994), chaps. 1–3; and Alan Williams, *Republic of Images: A History of French Filmmaking* (Cambridge, Mass., 1992), chap. 1.

70. See Abel, *Ciné Goes to Town,* 59; and Williams, *Republic of Images,* 52–53. For further discussion of early French cinema and religion, see Roland Cosandey, André Gaudreault, and Tom Gunning, eds., *Une Invention du diable? Cinéma des premiers temps et religion* (Lausanne, 1992).

2. Commercialized Pilgrimage and Religious Debasement

1. During the 1880s the government of the Third Republic passed the Laic laws, which created tax-supported public primary education, reducing Catholic influence over schooling. Further legislation passed in the 1890s and early 1900s sought to regulate all religious orders and outlawed nonauthorized ones, culminating in the separation of Church and state in 1905. See Paul A. Gagnon, *France since 1789* (New York, 1964), 198–238;. For more detailed accounts, see Pierre Sorlin, *Waldeck-Rousseau* (Paris, 1966); and Malcolm O. Partin, *Waldeck-Rousseau, Combes, and the Church: The Politics of Anticlericalism, 1899–1905* (Durham, N.C., 1969).

2. See Rosalind H. Williams, *Dream Worlds: Mass Consumption in Late Nineteenth-Century France* (Berkeley, 1982); and Lisa Tiersten, *Marianne in the Market: Envisioning Consumer Society*

in Fin-de-siècle France (Berkley, 2001). Solidarist republicans, in particular, were concerned to rein in the corrosive effects of the capitalist marketplace, but even liberal republicans worried that modern commerce promoted social unrest among workers, unleashed uncontrolled desires in women, and ultimately undermined civic virtue by promoting self-interest over self-restraint.

3. William Christian, for example, has suggested that sixteenth-century Spain was "plagued by con artists who made their living off the shrines and the pilgrim routes, and who won alms and celebrity status by faking miracles at shrines." See William A. Christian Jr., *Local Religion in Sixteenth-Century Spain* (Princeton, 1981), 104.

4. One guidebook claimed that petty thieves haunted every part of the sanctuary, "in the shops, in the churches, and right up to the communion table." Another guide lamented that "from morning till evening, it is the same congestion that the pickpockets exploit by digging through the pockets of pilgrims in prayer." Pilgrims were advised to "have an inside safety pocket for their valuables, emergency funds, and train tickets, as well as a special change purse for their immediate monetary needs." See *Manuel du pèlerinage interdiocésain de la Suisse Française à Notre-Dame de Lourdes* (Belley, 1913), 51; and G. Marès, *Lourdes et ses environs* (Bordeaux, 1894), 68. Also see *Manuel du pèlerinage dit "Des Malades" à Notre-Dame de Lourdes* (Lyon, 1913).

5. *Manuel du pèlerinage interdiocésain,* 51–52.

6. Emphasis in original. Archives de l'Œuvre de la Grotte (hereafter AG) 7P3, Affaire vente d'eau de la grotte (1879–1888), dossier 1, Mandat de l'évêque de Tarbes, Tarbes, 2 May 1888.

7. See, for example, *Manuel du pèlerinage interdiocésain,* 53–54.

8. "Escroqueries exploitant le culte de Lourdes," *Journal de la Grotte de Lourdes,* 5 February 1899, front page.

9. Lasserre leveled these serious charges only after his own commercial interests had been thwarted. He sought authorization to have his hugely popular *Notre-Dame de Lourdes* sold as the exclusive official account of the grotto at the shrine's piety shop. The bishop refused, and a rift developed between the author and Lourdes authorities that was never repaired. The many public attacks launched by Lasserre were not only embarrassing to the Grotto fathers but led to a dramatic drop in donations to the shrine. See Ruth Harris, *Lourdes: Body and Spirit in the Secular Age* (London, 1999), 187–94.

10. Francisque Sarcey, "Trahi par les siens," *Le XIXe Siècle,* 24 May 1877. See AG 8P1, Attaque du journal "Le XIXe Siècle," which contains an extract of the article by Sarcey, correspondence between *Le XIXe Siècle* and Brother Henri Soubiat, and a copy of the court judgment. Also see AG 7P1, Procès et condamnation pour articles injurieux; lettres (1876–1885), which contains letters and further litigation.

11. See AG 8P1, Attaque du journal "Le XIXe Siècle," Letter from Frère Henri Soubiat to Francisque Sarcey, 14 July 1877, and Arrêt de La Cour d'Appel de Paris condamnant le Journal "Le XIXe Siècle," 25 January 1878.

12. I am grateful to Aaron Segal for bringing the case to my attention. See Aaron J. Segal, "The Republic of Goods: Advertising and National Identity, 1875–1918," Ph.D. diss., University of California at Los Angeles, 1995, p. 192.

13. See AG 6P1, Publicité commerciale, commercialisation de l'eau; this file contains a copy of the flyer for La Bernadette and the correspondence between the Grotto fathers and the Maison Victor Sabatier. See the letter from M. Sabatier-Lavigne to Father Sempé, Pau, 25 May 1887; the letters from Father Carrère to Sabatier-Lavigne, Lourdes, n.d., and 28 May 1887; and the letter from Sabatier-Lavigne to Father Carrère, Pau, 30 May 1887.

14. AG 7P3, Affaire vente d'eau de la grotte (1879–1888), dossier 1, Mandat de l'évêque de Tarbes, Tarbes, 2 May 1888.

15. "Communique de Mgr. l'évêque de Tarbes et Lourdes condamnant l'abus que fait de la dévotion à Notre-Dame de Lourdes," Lourdes, 2 February 1913, reproduced in *Manuel du pèlerinage interdiocésain,* Annexe, 13.

16. AG 6P1, Publicité commerciale, commercialisation de l'eau, letter from Sabatier-Lavigne to Father Carrère, Pau, 30 May 1887.

17. AG 7P3, Affaire vente d'eau de la grotte (1879–1888), dossier 2, letter from Marie Rataboul to the director of the sanctuary of Lourdes, Lauzerte (Tarn-et-Garonne), n.d.

18. AG 7P3, Affaire vente d'eau de la grotte (1879–1888), dossier 2, letter from Madame Émilie Capelle to the director of the sanctuary of Lourdes, Vauvillers, 22 December 1882.

19. AG 7P3, Affaire vente d'eau de la grotte (1879–1888), dossier 2, letter from Jules Robert to the superior of the missionaries of Notre-Dame de Lourdes, 9 January 1888; dossier 2, letter from J. Calibon to the superior of the missionaries of Notre-Dame de Lourdes, Nantes, 8 May 1879; dossier 1, letter from B. Guyot to the director of the sanctuary, 1 February 1882; dossier 2, anonymous letter to the director of the sanctuary of Lourdes, 4 January 1888. See AG 7P3 for other letters that discuss cases of fraud committed against the Lourdes sanctuary and the family of Bernadette.

20. Emphasis in original. AG 7P3, Affaire vente d'eau de la grotte (1879–1888), dossier 1, letter from Louis Baron to Father Sempé, Toulouse, 12 April 1888.

21. AG 7P3, Affaire vente d'eau de la grotte (1879–1888), dossier 1, letter from Z. Heurville to the Fathers of the Grotto, Dordogne, 1 August 1875; AG 8P3, Attaque du Dr. Vachet, letter from Comte de Lupel to the bishop of Tarbes, Autrêches (Oise), July 1889.

22. The major sources for religious goods in the countryside of early modern France were peddlers and the fairs and markets they attended, though the Counter-Reformation Church often condemned these roving dealers for their association with secular forms of popular culture. See Cissie Fairchilds, "Marketing the Counter-Reformation: Religious Objects and Consumerism in Early Modern France," in *Visions and Revisions of Eighteenth-Century France,* ed. Christine Adams, Jack R. Censer, and Lisa Jane Graham (University Park, Penn., 1997), 49–50. Despite such criticism, shrine tenders relied on peddlers to spread word of their sites. See Christian, *Local Religion,* chap. 3.

23. For Zola's decision to write a novel about Lourdes, see Émile Zola, *Mes voyages: Lourdes, Rome, journaux inédits preséntés et annotés par René Ternois,* ed. René Ternois (Paris, 1958), 9–14. Zola's extended visit to Lourdes in 1892 was covered by both the left-wing and right-wing presses; see, for example, "Le Pèlerinage de Lourdes," *Le Gaulois,* 19 August 1892; "Encore M. Zola à Lourdes," *Le Monde,* 28 August 1892; "M. Zola et le pèlerinage de Lourdes," *Le Temps,* 26 August 1892; and "M. Zola à Lourdes," *La Lanterne,* 27 August 1892. *Le Figaro, L'Univers,* and *La Croix* also wrote about Zola's trip; see Zola, *Mes voyages,* 25, for discussion of the press coverage. Also see the introduction by Henri Mitterand in Émile Zola, *Lourdes* (Paris, 1998).

24. Archives Nationales (hereafter AN) F19 2376, Coupures de presse, "La Vierge en actions: Scapulaires, biscuits, bonbons, et bénédictions," *La Lanterne,* 29 May 1893.

25. AN F19 2376, Coupures de presse, "Pieuse mendicité," *La Lanterne,* 5 May 1894.

26. AN F19 2376, Coupures de presse, "Une Réclame bien faite," *Le Journal,* 27 July 1893.

27. See Williams, *Dream Worlds;* Tiersten, *Marianne in the Market;* and Segal, "Republic of Goods," especially chap. 4. Fears of the untutored masses falling prey to the Church's marketing of Lourdes were probably fed by Gustave Le Bon's ideas about the uncontrolled irrationality of the crowd, as well as new psychological theories of suggestion, hypnosis, and hysteria articulated by Hippolyte Bernheim and Jean-Martin Charcot. See Susanna Barrows, *Distorting Mirrors: Visions of the Crowd in Late Nineteenth-Century France* (New Haven, 1981); Jaap van Ginneken, *Crowds, Psychology, and Politics, 1871–1899* (Cambridge, 1992); Henri Ellenberger, *The Discovery of the Unconscious: The History and Evolution of Dynamic Psychiatry* (New York, 1970); and Jan Goldstein, *Console and Classify: The French Psychiatric Profession in the Nineteenth Century* (Cambridge, 1987).

28. AN F19 2376, Coupures de presse, "Pharmacie cléricale chez le marchand d'eau de Lourdes," *Le XIXe Siècle,* 24 September 1890.

29. Zola had already written about crowds in *Germinal*, published in 1885, and had devoted sustained attention to the development of mass consumption in *Au Bonheur des dames* (*The Ladies' Paradise*), published in 1884. See Barrows, *Distorting Mirrors;* Naomi Schor, *Zola's Crowds* (Baltimore, 1978); Williams, *Dream Worlds*, 67–68, 198–99, 315–16; and Tiersten, *Marianne in the Market*, chap. 1. See also the introduction by Kristin Ross in Émile Zola, *The Ladies' Paradise* (Berkeley, 1992).

30. Émile Zola, *The Three Cities: Lourdes*, vol. 2, trans. Ernest A. Vizetelly (New York, 1899), 279–80.

31. Zola was especially interested in Jean-Martin Charcot's theories of hysteria, which sought to reinterpret religious experiences such as visions, possessions, and miracles as pathological phenomena. For Charcot's views on religion, see Goldstein, *Console and Classify.*

32. AN F19 2376, Coupures de presse, "La Boutique de Lourdes," *La Lanterne*, 14 October 1903.

33. Zola suggested that the Grotto fathers were able to blackmail town officials by threatening to close the sanctuary if they did not receive special treatment. See Zola, *Mes voyages*, 66.

34. Secular-minded, even anticlerical, men of the middle class often approved of the religious instruction that their wives provided for their children, including male children. For such men, religion was "naturalized" as a key aspect of bourgeois maternity and an important function of the private realm of middle-class women's lives. See Paul Seeley, "O Sainte Mère: Liberalism and the Socialization of Catholic Men in Nineteenth-Century France," *Journal of Modern History* 70, no. 4 (December 1998): 862–91. Seeley's insight helps explain why men could endorse legislation that severely limited the public power of the Catholic Church while seeking to preserve a private realm for religious practice. I would add that, once religion became relocated within a feminized private sphere, the mixing of religious practice with modern public life came to be seen as a perversion of what was "natural."

35. Thomas A. Kselman, *Death and the Afterlife in Modern France* (Princeton, 1993), 273–90, here 273. Also see Judith F. Stone, "Anticlericals and *Bonnes Sœurs:* The Rhetoric of the 1901 Law of Associations," *French Historical Studies* 23, no. 1 (winter 2000): 103–28; and Katrin Schultheiss, "Gender and the Limits of Anti-Clericalism: The Secularization of Hospital Nursing in France, 1880–1914," *French History* 12, no. 3 (1998): 229–45.

36. M. Meys, "Lourdes," *L'Illustration*, 18 August 1894, 132–34.

37. Zola, *Mes voyages*, 72, 75.

38. Zola, *Mes voyages*, 66–67.

39. See Chanoine Jules Didiot, "Vue de Lourdes," *Revue de Lille* (January 1893): 3–16; here 9–11.

40. Didiot, "Vue de Lourdes," 11–12.

41. Abbé Domenech, *Lourdes, hommes et choses* (Lyon, 1894), 14, 20.

42. Domenech, *Lourdes, hommes et choses*, 121.

43. Domenech, *Lourdes, hommes et choses*, 121–22, 125–26.

44. Produced initially in the Paris neighborhood surrounding the church Saint-Sulpice, "l'art sulpicien" soon came to refer to mass-produced Church art and acquired the derogatory meaning later associated with the term *kitsch*. See Claude Savart, "À la recherche de l' 'art' dit de Saint-Sulpice," *Revue d'Histoire de la Spiritualité* 52 (1976) 265–82.

45. For a discussion of the Catholic literary revival in late nineteenth-century France, see the classic work by Richard M. Griffiths, *The Reactionary Revolution: The Catholic Revival in French Literature, 1870–1914* (London, 1966). Also see Stephen R. Schloesser, "Mystic Realists: Sacramental Modernism in French Catholic Revival, 1918–1928," Ph.D. diss., Stanford University, 1999, chap. 2.

46. See Léon Bloy, *Méditations d'un solitaire en 1916* (Paris, 1917), 151; and Léon Bloy, *Journal*, vol. 1 (Paris, 1956), 150.

47. In 1878, shortly after his reconversion to Catholicism, Bloy made his first pilgrimage to this holy site in the French Alps where the Virgin had appeared to Mélanie Calvat and Maximin Giraud. He was captivated by the remote site, so removed from the disruptions of the secular world. See E. T. Dubois, *Portrait of Léon Bloy* (London, 1951), 57–67; and Sister Mary Rosalie Brady, *Thought and Style in the Works of Léon Bloy* (Washington, D.C., 1946), 101–10, 125–37.

48. Léon Bloy, *Dans les ténèbres* (Paris, 1918), 178–79; and Léon Bloy, *She Who Weeps: Our Lady of La Salette*, trans. Emile LaDouceur (Fresno, Calif., 1956), 141–42.

49. See Schloesser, "Mystic Realists," chap. 2.

50. As early as 1884, Huysmans had attacked the Church in his novel *À Rebours* (*Against the Grain*) for allowing modern market practices to contaminate the faith. For a discussion of *À Rebours*, see Williams, *Dream Worlds*, 126–50.

51. J.-K. Huysmans, *The Cathedral*, trans. Clara Bell (New York, 1922), 8–9. This more forgiving view of religious commerce contrasts sharply with the critique of clerical greed in *À Rebours*.

52. J.-K. Huysmans, *The Crowds of Lourdes*, trans. W. H. Mitchell (New York, 1925), 88.

53. See the letter from J.-K. Huysmans to the Abbé Mugnier reproduced in Robert Baldick, *The Life of J.-K. Huysmans* (Oxford, 1955), 318; the letter from J.-K. Huysmans to Henry Céard, Lourdes, 19 March 1903, in *The Road from Decadence: From Brothel to Cloister, Selected Letters of J.-K. Huysmans*, ed. Barbara Beaumont (London, 1989), 219; and the letter from J.-K. Huysmans to the Abbé Mugnier in Baldick, *Life of J.-K. Huysmans*, 332.

54. A discussion of Henri Lasserre's novel *Notre-Dame de Lourdes* is in chap. 1. Huysmans made clear his contempt for the novels by Lasserre and Zola in chap. 12 of *The Crowds of Lourdes;* see also *The Cathedral*, 9–12.

55. Huysmans, *The Crowds of Lourdes*, 80–82, 99, 178–79.

56. Huysmans, *The Crowds of Lourdes*, 127–28, 37, 141.

57. Huysmans, *The Crowds of Lourdes*, 27–28, 38.

58. Huysmans, *The Crowds of Lourdes*, 95.

59. Huysmans, *The Crowds of Lourdes*, 95, 110–11.

60. Huysmans, *The Crowds of Lourdes*, 186–87.

61. Huysmans, *The Crowds of Lourdes*, 25, 146, 216.

62. Huysmans, *The Crowds of Lourdes*, 156, 246.

63. Amie Virginia Godman, "Positivistic and Catholic Naturalism: A Study of the Role of Lourdes in the Work of Huysmans and Zola," M.A. thesis, George Washington University, 1967, p. 24.

3. Scientific Sensationalism and the Miracle Cure

1. See Thomas A. Kselman, *Miracles and Prophecies in Nineteenth-Century France* (New Brunswick, N.J., 1983), chaps. 2 and 6.

2. See Ruth Harris, *Lourdes: Body and Spirit in the Secular Age* (London, 1999), chaps. 8 and 9. Like Harris, Kselman suggests that the Church was responding to the desires of the laity by adapting traditional beliefs about miracles and healing to fit the mass politics of the era; see Kselman, *Miracles and Prophecies*, chaps. 6 and 7.

3. Although the Church had long relied on medical experts to judge whether a cure defied the known laws of nature, only a bishop or other high-ranking church official could determine whether a cure constituted an act of divine intervention and thus could be called a miracle. This clerical power was confirmed at the Council of Trent (1545–1563), where the Church attempted to codify a coherent set of rules for evaluating claims of private revelation and miraculous healing. The Coun-

cil of Trent made a formal inquiry by a local bishop mandatory for the evaluation and confirmation of supernatural activity. At Lourdes, therefore, the medical bureau was empowered to authenticate cures, but it had no authority to claim these cures as miracles. Its doctors have authenticated thousands of cures, yet, to this date, the Church has only recognized sixty-six Lourdes cures as miracles. Although the distinction between a miracle and a cure has been a central part of church doctrine, this distinction was often obscured in the late nineteenth-century devotional literature about Lourdes. Moreover, faithful Catholics often accepted "authenticated" cures as divine events even when clerical authorities did not recognize them as miracles. For the impact of the Council of Trent on the development of French Catholicism, see René Taveneaux, *Le Catholicisme dans la France classique, 1610–1715* (Paris, 1980), vol. 2, 382–89.

4. See the now-classic work, Michel Foucault, *The Birth of the Clinic: An Archaeology of Medical Perception,* trans. A. M. Sheridan Smith (New York, 1973). An enormous literature has since examined the process of medicalization of French society. See Jan Goldstein, *Console and Classify: The French Psychiatric Profession in the Nineteenth Century* (Cambridge, 1987); Jacques Léonard, *Les Médecins de l'Ouest au XIXe siècle* (Lille, 1978); Jacques Léonard, *La Médecine entre les savoirs et les pouvoirs* (Paris, 1981); Ruth Harris, *Murders and Madness: Medicine, Law, and Society in the Fin de Siècle* (Oxford, 1989). See also Pierre Guillaume, *Médecins, Église et foi depuis deux siècles* (Paris, 1990). On the Church's desire to expunge "superstitious" practices from lay religious worship, see Ralph Gibson, *A Social History of French Catholicism, 1789–1914* (London, 1989), chap. 5.

5. On melodrama in nineteenth-century France, see Peter Brooks, *The Melodramatic Imagination* (New Haven, 1976). Also see Judith Walkowitz, *City of Dreadful Delight: Narratives of Sexual Danger in Late-Victorian London* (Chicago, 1992), chap. 3; Jo Burr Margadant, ed., *The New Biography: Performing Femininity in Nineteenth-Century France* (Berkeley, 2000); and Sarah Maza, "Domestic Melodrama as Political Ideology: The Case of the Comte de Sanois," *American Historical Review* 94, no. 5 (December 1989): 1249–64.

6. Even before the Council of Trent, the Church sought out expert testimony to help verify claims of the miraculous. Throughout the medieval period, for example, clerical officials relied on the eyewitness testimony of priests and "faithful men" to legitimate miraculous cures at local shrines. See Pierre-André Sigal, *L'Homme et le miracle dans la France médiévale, XIe–XIIe siècles* (Paris, 1985); Janet Kay Ryder, "Miracles and Mentality: The Medieval Experience," Ph.D. diss., University of California at Santa Barbara, 1993; Benedicta Ward, *Miracles and the Medieval Mind: Theory, Record, and Event, 1000–1215* (London, 1982); André Vauchez, *La Sainteté en Occident au derniers siècles du Moyen Age: d'après les procès de canonisation et les documents hagiographiques* (Rome, 1981). On oral tradition, see David P. Henige, *The Chronology of Oral Tradition: The Quest for a Chimera* (Oxford, 1974); and Julia M. H. Smith, "Oral and Written: Saints, Miracles, and Relics in Brittany, c. 850–1250," *Speculum* 65, no. 2 (April 1990): 309–43.

7. See Harris, *Lourdes,* 289–93; Alban Bensa, *Les Saints guérisseurs du Perche-Gouët* (Paris, 1978); Brigitte Caulier, *L'Eau et le sacré: Les Cultes thérapeutiques autour des fontaines en France du Moyen Age à nos jours* (Paris, 1990); Henri Charbonneau, *Chapelles et saints guérisseurs basques et béarnais* (Hélette, 1995); and Paul Leproux, *Dévotions et saints guérisseurs* (Paris, 1957). The many thermal spas that dotted the Pyrenees also helped to spread the belief in the therapeutic power of springs and other water sources. See Jean-François Soulet, *Les Pyrénées au XIXe siècle,* vol. 1 (Toulouse, 1987), 84–86.

8. See René Laurentin and Bernard Billet, *Lourdes: Dossier des documents authentiques* (hereafter *LDA*), 7 vols. (Paris, 1957–1962), especially vol. 5.

9. See Archives Nationales (hereafter AN) F19 2374, Apparitions, ordonnance de Monseigneur, l'évêque de Tarbes, July 1858.

10. See Archives de l'Œuvre de la Grotte (hereafter AG) 6H1, Rapport sur les premières guérisons opérées par l'usage de l'eau de la grotte de Lourdes, soit en boisson, soit en lotion, pre-

senté à Monseigneur l'évêque de Tarbes, par la commission instituée par ordonnance de sa Grandeur, du 28 juillet 1858. This same information is also contained in AG A7A, Relations des apparitions et des guérisons servenues à cette époque (1858–1859).

11. Father Sempé, the superior general of the newly appointed Grotto fathers, sent out numerous letters to diocesan priests around France asking for information concerning miracle cures that had occurred before the arrival of his missionary order. The responses to these inquiries can be found in AG 6H4, Enquête Sempé sur les guérisons obtenues en 1858 (1878–1879).

12. See AG 1HD1, Processions, guérisons, et pèlerinages divers (1866–1950), Journal du Sanctuaire de Notre-Dame de Lourdes depuis le 17 mai 1866.

13. For examples of these diverse healing accounts, see AG 1HD1, Processions, guérisons, et pèlerinages divers (1866–1950), Journal du Sanctuaire de Notre-Dame de Lourdes depuis le 17 mai 1866, Juliette Montferaud, 4 July 1866, 2; and Catherine Dupont, 30 May 1866, 2. See also AG 6H4, Enquête Sempé sur les guérisons obtenues en 1858 (1878–1879), letter from Louise Bouvet to Father Sempé, n.d.

14. Harris, *Lourdes*, 293–300.

15. See Smith, "Oral and Written."

16. Henri Lasserre, *Notre-Dame de Lourdes* (Paris, 1870), 135–36, 262.

17. Lasserre, *Notre-Dame de Lourdes*, 135, 171–72.

18. See AG 18E4, Statistiques générales, les malades pauvres à Lourdes: 1874–1914. For an official history of the Association, see AG 3E1A, Pèlerinage National: Rapports, lettres, coupures de presse, etc. (1872–1898), Association de Notre-Dame de Salut, *Jubilé du pèlerinage national à Lourdes* (Paris, 1897), 12–20. Also see Harris, *Lourdes,* 226–45, 258.

19. The Grotto fathers received letters from pilgrims and clergy complaining that these new lay volunteers were insensitive toward the sick at the shrine. See Harris, *Lourdes,* 267–71.

20. Géry Delalleau, "Pèlerinage National à Notre-Dame du Salut à Lourdes," *Le Pèlerin* (1 September 1877), 545–52.

21. Shrine records show that the number of sick pilgrims who came to Lourdes on the national pilgrimage of the sick increased each decade during the period from 1874 to 1914. During the first years of national pilgrimages of the sick (1874–1882), the average number of sick pilgrims who came annually to Lourdes was estimated at 465. This jumped to 1,620 per year for the period 1883 to 1892. By the 1890s over four thousand registered malades were going to Lourdes on annual national pilgrimages, and for the following decade that figure doubled to over eight thousand registered malades. See AG 18E4, Statistiques générales, les malades pauvres à Lourdes: 1874–1914.

22. See Bernard Billet, "L'Histoire médicale de Lourdes et la faculté Catholique de médecine de Lille," *Ensemble* (June 1996): 87–97; and Guillaume, *Médecins, Église et foi,* 62–64.

23. Boissarie attributed the recoveries of his two sons from serious illnesses (one from cholera and the other from meningitis) to the intercession of the Virgin Mary. See the appendix to Gustave Boissarie, *Lourdes: Les Guérisons,* ser. 4 (Paris, 1922), 84–87. Also see Harris, *Lourdes,* 329–31.

24. See Louis Rose, *Faith Healing* (Harmondsworth, 1971), 94. Boissarie later instituted an annual meeting where the cures of the past year were discussed and verified, and where the continued good health of registered cured pilgrims was ascertained.

25. See Amélie Gravrand, "L'Impact géographique du tourisme de pèlerinage sur la ville de Lourdes," Thèse, Université de Bretagne Occidentale, 1997, p. 32.

26. See Alan Neame, *The Happening at Lourdes* (New York, 1968), 126–27. These verses from the New Testament are the entreaties made to Jesus by lepers, cripples, and others.

27. For descriptions of the Procession of the Blessed Sacrament, see AG 3E1A, Pèlerinage National: Rapports, lettres, coupures de presse, etc. (1872–1898), Association de Notre-Dame de Salut, *Jubilé du pèlerinage national,* 26–30; and Gustave Boissarie, *Lourdes: Les Guérisons* ser. 3 (Paris, 1912), 3–11.

28. Kselman, *Miracles and Prophecies,* 48–49. The recitation of the Invocations, with their New Testament verses, further linked the hope of a cure at the shrine to the healings of the sick performed by Jesus.

29. For the impact of Boissarie's *Lourdes: Histoire médicale, 1858–1891* on the secular reading public in France, see Billet, "L'Histore médicale de Lourdes," 88. According to Ruth Harris, some six thousand doctors visited the bureau between 1899 and 1913; see Harris, *Lourdes,* 330. Boissarie's later works include *Lourdes depuis 1858 jusqu'à nos jours* (Paris, 1894); *Les Grandes Guérisons de Lourdes* (Paris, 1900); and *Lourdes: Les Guérisons,* ser. 1–4 (Paris, 1911–1922).

30. See Gustave Boissarie, *Lourdes: Histoire médicale, 1858–1891* (Paris, 1891), 4, 6. See, especially: bk. 2, chaps. 1–3 for efforts to reclassify the first cures; bk. 3, chaps. 1–10 for analysis of the cures found in *Annales de Notre-Dame de Lourdes;* and bk. 4, chaps. 1–8 for analysis of organic disease and cures at Lourdes.

31. See Thomas W. Laqueur, "Bodies, Details, and the Humanitarian Narrative," in *The New Cultural History,* ed. Lynn Hunt (Berkeley, 1989), 176–204. For a discussion of the narrative strategies of melodrama and their use in popular writings of Victorian reformers, see Walkowitz, *City of Dreadful Delight,* 85–102.

32. Boissarie, *Lourdes: Histoire médicale,* 167–68. Pott's disease is a degenerative spine disorder usually associated with tuberculosis.

33. Boissarie, *Lourdes: Histoire médicale,* 168–71. A moxa is a flammable substance or material obtained from the leaves of certain Chinese and Japanese wormwood plants, especially artemisia moxa. This substance is used in traditional Chinese medicine. It is placed on the skin, usually in the form of a cone or a cylinder, and ignited for use as a counterirritant. The results are comparable to acupuncture.

34. On the promotion of patent medicine, see Thomas Richards, *The Commodity Culture of Victorian England: Advertising and Spectacle, 1851–1914* (Stanford, 1990), chap. 4. Douglas Mackaman also notes that promoters of thermal spas used firsthand testimonials to attract middle-class female readers as clients; see Douglas Peter Mackaman, *Leisure Settings: Bourgeois Culture, Medicine, and the Spa in Modern France* (Chicago, 1998), 86–92. The shrine's monthly *Annales de Notre-Dame de Lourdes* also used patient testimonials in its accounts of the cures.

35. Boissarie, *Lourdes: Histoire médicale,* 389–90. See bk. 4, chaps. 9–11 for his discussion of hysteria at Lourdes and the ideas of Charcot and Bernheim. On the nineteenth-century French psychiatric profession and new theories of hysteria, see Goldstein, *Console and Classify;* Georges Didi-Huberman, *Invention de l'hystérie: Charcot et l'iconographie photographique de la Salpêtrière* (Paris, 1982); A. R. G. Owen, *Hysteria, Hypnosis, and Healing: The Work of J.-M. Charcot* (New York, 1971); and Mark S. Micale, *Approaching Hysteria: Disease and Its Interpretations* (Princeton, 1995).

36. See Robert G. Hillman, "A Scientific Study of Mystery: The Role of the Medical and Popular Press in the Nancy-Salpêtrière Controversy on Hypnotism," *Bulletin of the History of Medicine* 39, no. 2 (1965): 163–82; Harris, *Murders and Madness;* Goldstein, *Console and Classify;* and Debora L. Silverman, *Art Nouveau in Fin-de-Siècle France: Politics, Psychology, and Style* (Berkeley, 1989).

37. Boissarie, *Lourdes: Histoire médicale,* 396–97, 407–12, 417.

38. See Gustave Boissarie, *Zola: Conférence du Luxembourg* (Paris, 1895), x, for the decision to combat Zola's novel. The conference was also covered by the medical journal *Le Progrès Médical,* which was known for its anticlerical opinions. See "Les Miracles de Lourdes et la médecine," *Le Progrès Médical,* 19 January 1895.

39. Boissarie, *Zola,* 18–49.

40. Boissarie, *Zola,* 73–74. See pages 61–74 for the description of the presentation of miraculées. The article from *Le Temps,* 23 November, is quoted on page 76 of Boissarie's pamphlet.

41. Boissarie, *Zola,* 9.

42. Mary Louise Roberts, "Acting Up: The Feminist Theatrics of Marguerite Durand," in *The New Biography: Performing Femininity in Nineteenth-Century France,* ed. Jo Burr Margadant (Berkeley, 2000), 194. Also see Eugen Weber, *France, Fin de Siècle* (Cambridge, Mass., 1986), chap. 8; Charles Rearick, *Pleasures of the Belle Époque: Entertainment and Festivity in Turn-of-the-Century France* (New Haven, 1985); Vanessa R. Schwartz, *Spectacular Realities: Early Mass Culture in Fin-de-Siècle Paris* (Berkeley, 1998), especially chap. 1; Edward Berenson, *The Trial of Madame Caillaux* (Berkeley, 1992), chap. 6; and Gregory K. Shaya, "Mayhem for Moderns: The Culture of Sensationalism in France, c. 1900," Ph.D. diss., University of Michigan, 2000.

43. See Boissarie, *Lourdes: Les Guérisons,* ser. 1, 17.

44. Boissarie, *Zola,* xi.

45. Boissarie, *Zola,* 21. See also Boissarie, *Lourdes: Les Guérisons,* ser. 1, 50–51.

46. Boissarie, *Lourdes: Les Guérisons,* ser. 4, 87–88.

47. AN F19 2376, Coupures de presse, "Pèlerinage National," *La Croix,* 23–24 August 1891.

48. See Schwartz, *Spectacular Realities,* chap. 1, especially 34–40; Berenson, *Trial of Madame Caillaux,* chap. 6; and Shaya, "Mayhem for Moderns," chap. 1, 3–4.

49. AN F19 2376, Coupures de presse, Dr. Salles, "Une Grande Guérison de Lourdes," *Journal de la Grotte de Lourdes,* 23 April 1901. These detailed accounts of healing remained a staple of the religious press throughout the early twentieth century. For example, in 1912 the newspaper *La Croix de Lourdes* presented seventy-six accounts of healing in August alone; see *La Croix de Lourdes* in AN F19 2377, La presse religieuse, 1912–1914.

50. Bernard Dauberive, *Lourdes et ses environs: Guide du pèlerin et du touriste* (Poitiers, 1896), 74–75; and J. Couret, *Guide-Almanach de Notre-Dame de Lourdes, 1900* (Bordeaux, 1900), 73–121. The shrine's own *Souvenir guide du pèlerin, cinquantenaire de l'Immaculée-Conception, livre d'or de Notre-Dame de Lourdes* (Toulouse, 1909), 38–40, also devoted a section to the proclaimed cures investigated during the year 1908.

51. On female celebrity and the theater in nineteenth-century France, see Roberts, "Acting Up"; Lenard R. Berlanstein, *Daughters of Eve: A Cultural History of French Theater Women from the Old Regime to the Fin de Siècle* (Cambridge, Mass., 2001); and Rhonda K. Garelick, *Rising Star: Dandyism, Gender, and Performance in the Fin de Siècle* (Princeton, 1998). Also see Irving J. Rein, Philip Kotler, and Martin R. Stoller, *High Visibility* (New York, 1987); and Richard Schickel, *Intimate Strangers: The Culture of Celebrity* (New York, 1985).

52. AG 3E1A, Pèlerinage National: Rapports, lettres, coupures de presse, etc. (1872–1898), Association de Notre-Dame de Salut, *Jubilé du pèlerinage national,* 33–39, 49–56, 71–76; and Boissarie, *Lourdes: Les Guérisons,* ser. 3, 6–9.

53. AG 3E1A, Pèlerinage National: Rapports, lettres, coupures de presse, etc. (1872–1898), Association de Notre-Dame de Salut, *Jubilé du pèlerinage national,* 35, 49, 72–75. Also see Boissarie, *Lourdes: Les Guérisons,* ser. 3, 6–7.

54. L. R. Lynch, "Lourdes and the National Pilgrimage of 1903," *Catholic World* 78, no. 404 (1903): 204–5; Madeleine D., *Mon Pèlerinage de Lourdes* (Blois, 1912), 6; and Bertile Ségalas, "Huit jours à Lourdes," *Revue de Bretagne, de Vendée et d'Anjou* 23 (February): 130–31.

55. See AG 6H23, Relations de guérisons (1873–1897), dossier on Sœur Maire-Eugène Liégeois, 1880, attached letter from M. A. de B. Chateau de Bateng.

56. *Les Merveilles de Lourdes: Gabriel Gargam, son accident de chemin de fer, sa vie d'hôpital, sa guérison* (Toulouse, 1914), 11; and Robert Triger, *Lourdes: 1872–1908, impressions et souvenirs* (Le Mans, 1909), 45.

57. Triger, *Lourdes,* 28–29.

58. These postcards are part of the postcard collection housed (but not yet cataloged) at the Archives de l'Œuvre de la Grotte.

59. On woman as "commodity fetish" in nineteenth-century France, see Abigail Solomon-Godeau, "The Other Side of Venus: The Visual Economy of Feminine Display," in *The Sex of*

Things: Gender and Consumption in Historical Perspective, ed. Victoria de Grazia, with Ellen Furlough (Berkeley, 1996), 113–50.

4. Female Pilgrims and Spiritual Authority

1. There are 127 accounts placed into separate dossiers and arranged chronologically beginning with 1873, the first year of the national pilgrimage to Lourdes. Of these 127 accounts, 117 were written by women. See Archives de l'Œuvre de la Grotte (hereafter AG) 6H23, Relations de guérisons (1873–1897). Although the cures described in the accounts occurred over a long period of time, all of the accounts were written in 1897.

2. Ruth Harris, *Lourdes: Body and Spirit in the Secular Age* (London, 1999), 306–7; see pages 307–19 for her analysis of these healing accounts. Harris incorrectly cites these documents as part of AG 6H22; the correct citation is AG 6H23.

3. My interpretation of these healing testimonials as a type of literary performance has been influenced by recent feminist scholarship that analyzes autobiographical writing and other kinds of written texts by women as opportunities for (re)inventing the self. Much of this work accepts the idea of a "constructed" self and seeks to examine how women (usually of the middle and upper classes) have tried to imagine alternative identities for themselves by remaking, extending, or overtly contesting traditional notions of femininity in their writing as well as their public activities. See, for example, Judith Walkowitz, *City of Dreadful Delight: Narratives of Sexual Danger in Late-Victorian London* (Chicago, 1992), especially chap. 6; Kali Israel, *Names and Stories: Emilia Dilke and Victorian Culture* (New York, 1999); Jo Burr Margadant, ed., *The New Biography: Performing Femininity in Nineteenth-Century France* (Berkeley, 2000); and Mary Louise Roberts, *Disruptive Acts: The New Woman in Fin-de-Siècle France* (Chicago, 2002). Walkowitz's work has been especially helpful in pointing out how emerging forms of commercial culture offered nonelite women opportunities to shape public identities for themselves. Much of this scholarship has drawn insight from the work of Judith Butler; see, for example, *Gender Trouble: Feminism and the Subversion of Identity* (New York, 1990). Also see Joan Scott, "The Evidence of Experience," *Critical Inquiry* 17, no. 4 (1991): 773–97, for a critical analysis of appeals to experiential reality.

4. *The Golden Legend,* a collection of saints' lives, was compiled by the Dominican Jacobus de Voragine in the mid-1260s. The work provided short readings for feast days according to the ecclesiastical calendar. Along with other popular collections of saints' lives, *The Golden Legend* was widely read in nineteenth-century France. Such texts figured prominently in the education and daily reading habits of devout (middle- and upper-class) women. See Bonnie G. Smith, *Ladies of the Leisure Class: The Bourgeoises of Northern France* (Princeton, 1981), chaps. 5 and 7; and Martyn Lyons, *Readers and Society in Nineteenth-Century France: Workers, Women, Peasants* (New York, 2001), chaps. 5 and 6. Lyons notes that published collections of saints' lives were among the few books that peasant families of the period owned and read (or had other people read to them) on a regular basis.

5. My understanding of the rhetoric and structure of Catholic hagiography has been enriched by the work of Michel de Certeau, especially his analysis of the narrative structure of popular devotional literature on saints' lives. It is de Certeau who divides the popular narrative of the saint's life into a time of personal trial followed by a time of public glorification; see Michel de Certeau, *The Writing of History,* trans. Tom Conley (New York, 1988), chap. 7, especially 276–77. I have also found helpful Robert Orsi's analysis of twentieth-century American Catholic devotional culture, especially the argument that Catholics exhibited two distinct ways of interpreting physical suffering in their own lives and the lives of others: as a vehicle to saintliness or as a sign of personal sin. See Robert Orsi, *Thank You, St. Jude: Women's Devotion to the Patron Saint of Hopeless Causes* (New Haven, 1996), chap. 6.

6. See AG 3E1A, Pèlerinage National: Rapports, lettres, coupures de presse, etc. (1872–1898), Association de Notre-Dame de Salut, *Jubilé du pèlerinage national à Lourdes* (Paris, 1897), 33–35. Picard announced his intention to organize a procession of miraculés on 2 July 1897. The jubilee pilgrimage to Lourdes began on 20 August and ended on 24 August 1897; the procession of miraculés took place on 22 August.

7. I have reconstructed these initial recruiting procedures from one of Notre-Dame de Salut's devotional pamphlets about the jubilee; see AG 3E1A, Pèlerinage National: Rapports, lettres, coupures de presse, etc. (1872–1898), Association de Notre-Dame de Salut, *Jubilé du pèlerinage national*, chap. 1, especially 33–36.

8. See AG 6H23, Relations de guérisons (1873–1897), for the testimonial accounts, medical certificates, and a copy of the form letter written by P. Hippolyte, the subdirector of the Council of Pilgrimages, dated 19 August 1897. Based on Hippolyte's letter, I have assumed that there was earlier correspondence between pilgrimage organizers and the chosen cured pilgrims, including the sending of special badges and crosses; however, I have not seen this correspondence. I have also relied on the letter to help reconstruct the timing and conditions under which these final testimonial accounts were written. Hippolyte's letter, asking those chosen to review their dossiers and compose final accounts of the cure, is dated three days before the procession of miraculés occurred on Sunday, 22 August. Almost all the testimonial accounts (or at least those that are both signed and dated) were written between 14 and 24 August. It should also be noted that while the shrine's devotional literature claimed that over 350 pilgrims participated in the jubilee procession of miraculés, only 127 dossiers remain in the Lourdes archives. It is not clear whether other accounts were lost or discarded after the event, or whether the participants failed to write a final account or chose not to leave their dossiers at the shrine. See also AG 3E1A, Pèlerinage National: Rapports, lettres, coupures de presse, etc. (1872–1898), Association de Notre-Dame de Salut, *Jubilé du pèlerinage national*, 54–55 for reproduced excerpts from the testimonial accounts.

9. This information has been compiled from the dossiers kept on the jubilee participants. Each dossier contained a testimonial and certificates of attestation. Also listed on the cover of each dossier were: the name, age, and address of the pilgrim; the type of pilgrimage undertaken; the year the cure took place; and a medical diagnosis. See AG 6H23, Relations de guérisons (1873–1897).

10. Because the testimonials in AG 6H23, Relations de guérisons (1873–1897) were filed chronologically, I will cite each one according to the name of the cured pilgrim and the date of the cure. See AG 6H23, Mme. Rosalie Gouhier, 1888; Mlle. Elisa Fichelle, 1887; Mlle. Hermine Jumeau, 1896; Mme. Le Compte, 1895; Mme. Louise Tanny, femme Lagrange, 1887; Mme. Louise Lecourt; and Vve. Grandelaude, 1887. A number of women thanked the Assumptionists or Notre-Dame de Salut for defraying the cost of the pilgrimage; see AG 6H23, Mlle. Marie Beaudet, 1896; Mlle. Cécile Laffargue, 1890; Mlle. Euphrasie Bourgault, 1890; Mlle. Aréne Millot, 1892; and Mlle. Marguerite Ménard, 1896.

11. AG 6H23, Mlle. Elzire Gronnier, 1890.

12. AG 6H23, Mlle. Léotine Aubain, 1882; and Mlle. Constance Piquet, 1893.

13. Orsi, *Thank You, St. Jude,* 151–52. See also de Certeau, *Writing of History,* chap. 7. Also see Darrell W. Amundsen, "The Medieval Catholic Tradition," in *Caring and Curing: Health and Medicine in the Western Religious Traditions,* ed. Ronald Numbers and Darrell W. Amundsen (New York, 1986), 65–107; and Lisa Silverman, *Tortured Subjects: Pain, Truth, and the Body in Early Modern France* (Chicago, 2001), chap. 4. Women mystics, in particular, adopted the language of suffering and sanctity in their writings; see Michel de Certeau, *The Mystic Fable,* trans. Michael B. Smith (Chicago, 1992). Also see Judith Perkins, *The Suffering Self: Pain and Narrative Representation in the Early Christian Era* (New York, 1995); and Elaine Scarry, *The Body in Pain: The Making and Unmaking of the World* (New York, 1985).

14. Smith, *Ladies of the Leisure Class,* chaps. 5 and 7; and Lyons, *Readers and Society,* chaps. 5 and 6. Also see Jacques Léonard, "Femmes, religion, et médecine: Les Religieuses qui soignent, en

France au XIXe siècle," *Annales: Économies, Sociétés, Civilisations* 32, no. 5 (1977): 887–907; and Katrin Schultheiss, *Bodies and Souls: Politics and the Professionalization of Nursing in France, 1880– 1922* (Cambridge, Mass., 2001).

15. On the Church's emphasis on historical accuracy, see de Certeau, *Writing of History*, 271– 72.

16. AG 6H23, Mlle. Léotine Aubain, 1882; Mlle. Marguerite Lecherpin Descoutures, 1892; Mlle. Jeanne Delesalle,1893; and Mlle. Eugénie Hanceaux, 1893.

17. AG 6H23, Mlle. Léotine Aubain, 1882; Elzire Gronnier, 1890; and Mlle. Marguerite Lecherpin Descoutures, 1892.

18. AG 6H23, Mlle. Hermine Jumeau, 1896.

19. Vesicants or vesicatories were plasters or liquid salves applied to the skin that caused blistering. These blistering plasters, often uncomfortable if not outright painful, were supposed to bring to the surface poisonous substances causing harm to the body.

20. AG 6H23, Mlle. Marie Havard, 1893.

21. AG 6H23, Mlle. Eugénie Hanceaux, 1893; Mlle. Marguerite Ménard, 1896; and Mlle. Eugénie Sédilère, 1896.

22. AG 6H23, Mlle. Elzire Gronnier, 1890.

23. Although not explicitly raised in the testimonials, the threat of sexual danger seems to pervade their descriptions of medical treatment, in which male doctors were consistently portrayed as having access to women's bodies. On the threat of sexual danger as a common trope in nineteenth-century melodrama, see Walkowitz, *City of Dreadful Delight*.

24. AG 6H23, Mlle. Marguerite Ménard, 1896.

25. AG 6H23, Elise Delahaye, 1893; Mlle. Eugénie Hanceaux, 1893; Mlle. Jeanne Delesalle, 1893; and Mlle. Blanche Meurant, 1887.

26. AG 6H23, Marie de Saint Sacrement, 1891; Mlle. Blanche Meurant, 1887; Mlle. Marguerite Ménard, 1896; Mlle. Marie Favraux, 1888; Mlle. Louise Leroux, 1894; and Mlle. Hermine Jumeau, 1896. For testimonials that provide a strict chronology of the cure or that list outside witnesses (including doctors) to the healing event, see Mlle. Léotine Aubain, 1882; Mlle. Marguerite Lecherpin Descoutures, 1892; Mlle. Céline Laffargue, 1890; Mme. Maria Lefebre, 1896; Mlle. Elisa Fichelle, 1887; Mlle. Marie Pilot, 1892; Mlle. Marie Denontés, 1874; and Mlle. Clémentine Ledoux, 1895. The attention to eating perhaps also had religious significance for these women. Their descriptions of renewed appetite and the contents of their first meals may have signified a sense of bodily wholeness. The importance of bodily integrity (a body immune to decay, as with the saint's body after death) has long been a sign of holiness for the Church. See Caroline Walker Bynum, *The Resurrection of the Body in Western Christianity, 200–1336* (New York, 1995).

27. Michel de Certeau has noted two different narrative traditions of the saint's life within popular hagiography. There is the tale of martyrdom, which predominates when a community is marginal or under threat, and the tale of virtue, which reflects the needs of a more established church. See de Certeau, *Writing of History*, 272–73. That Lourdes miraculées adopted a language of martyrdom may reflect not only a personal sense of embattlement but also a larger sense of social and political struggle connected to the Church's conflicts with the government of the Third Republic. For more on the political dimension of this rhetoric of suffering, see Richard D. E. Burton, *Holy Tears, Holy Blood: Women, Catholicism, and the Culture of Suffering in France, 1840–1970* (Ithaca, 2004).

28. On modern celebrity, see Richard Schickel, *Intimate Strangers: The Culture of Celebrity* (New York, 1985).

29. AG 6H23, Mlle. Elzire Gronnier, 1890; Mlle. Mélanie Herrman, 1882; Mlle. Marie Favraux, 1888; Mlle. Hermine Jumeau, 1896; and Mlle. Adéline Guirand, 1895.

30. AG 6H23, Mlle. Léotine Aubain, 1882.

31. AG 6H23, Mlle. Marie Havard, 1893; Mlle. Eugénie Ghisolfi, 1884; and Mme. Hugot, 1890.

Interestingly, the women writers almost never connected their suffering with personal sin. In only one testimonial—that of Mme. Rosalie Gouhier, 1888, who thought her illness helped her atone for past behavior—did a miraculée link her suffering to sin. The other writers presented themselves as virtuous and pious heroines who suffered for the good of others.

32. AG 6H23, Mlle. Aline Desrumaux, 1888.

33. AG 6H23, Mlle. Marie Favraux, 1888; Mlle. Blanche Sergheraert, 1894; Mme. Hugot, 1890; and Mme. Quiriel, 1895.

34. AG 6H23, Mlle. Elise Delahaye, 1893.

35. AG 6H23, Mlle. Constance Piquet, 1893. An account of Constance Piquet's cure and her photograph appeared in Boissarie's later medical studies. See Gustave Boissarie, *Lourdes: Les Guérisons*, ser. 1 (Paris, 1911), 50–55. For requests by cured female pilgrims to remain anonymous, see AG 1HD1, Processions, guérisons, et pèlerinage divers (1866–1950), Journal du Sanctuaire de Notre-Dame de Lourdes depuis le 17 mai 1866, 3, 4, and 9.

36. AG 6H23, Mlle. Marie Aiglehoux, 1879; Mlle. Louise Reutenam, 1896; Mlle. Elise Delahaye, 1893; and Mlle. Angèle Lesbrossart, 1874.

37. AG 6H23, Mlle. Marie Demontés, 1874.

38. See Harris, *Lourdes*, 307–19, which argues that the women preferred their own "subjective certainty" of the cure to Boissarie's demanding verification process. I do not find this interpretation persuasive and, in any event, would question the notion of a "subjective certainty" unmediated by the discursive conditions that construct subjectivity itself.

39. AG 6H23, Mme. Hugot, 1890.

40. AG 6H23, Mlle. Léotine Aubain, 1882; Mlle. Eugénie Hanceaux, 1893; and Mlle. Marie Dout, 1893.

41. AG 6H23, Mlle. Marie Pilot, 1892.

42. AG 6H23, Mlle. Elise Delahaye, 1893.

43. On the instability of the supplement, see Jacques Derrida, *Of Grammatology*, trans. Gayatri Chakravorty Spivak (Baltimore, 1976), 141–64.

44. AG 6H23, Mlle. Elzire Gronnier, 1890; Mlle. Marie Favraux, 1888; and Mlle. Rosalie Gouhier, 1888.

45. AG 6H23, Mlle. Jeanne Delesalle, 1893; and Mlle. Euphrasie Bourgault, 1890.

46. AG 6H23, Mme. Rosalie Gouhier, 1888.

5. Public Wager: Publicity and the Truth of the Cure

1. Artus is quoted in Alfred Deschamps, S. J., *Le Cas Pierre de Rudder et les objections des médecins* (Brussels, 1913), 52. The public challenge was reprinted in Catholic newspapers across Europe, and Artus published an inexpensive brochure that proclaimed the wager. Sent first to well-known freethinkers and critics of the Lourdes miracles, the brochure, sold on the open market, went through some twenty-five editions during the next six years. See E. Artus, *Les Miracles de Notre-Dame de Lourdes: Défi public à la libre pensée: Guérison de Juliette Fournier* (Paris, 1872); E. Artus, *Les Médecins et les miracles de Lourdes* (Paris, 1873); E. Artus, *Les Miracles de Lourdes et la presse* (Paris, 1874); and E. Artus, *Histoire complète du défi public à la libre pensée sur les miracles de Notre-Dame de Lourdes* (Paris, 1877).

2. See Harry W. Paul, *The Edge of Contingency: French Catholic Reaction to Scientific Change from Darwin to Duhem* (Gainesville, Fla., 1979); and Pierre Guillaume, *Médecins, Église et foi depuis deux siècles* (Paris, 1990).

3. See, for example, Mark S. Micale, *Approaching Hysteria: Disease and Its Interpretations* (Princeton, 1995), 260–84; and Ruth Harris, *Lourdes: Body and Spirit in the Secular Age* (London, 1999), chap. 10.

4. See Jason Szabo, "Seeing Is Believing? The Form and Substance of French Medical Debates over Lourdes," *Bulletin of the History of Medicine* 76, no. 2 (2002): 199–230. Szabo also makes the point that the framing of the Lourdes debate as a set of legal challenges and polemics in the popular press intensified the politico-religious divisions between religious and medical authorities.

5. On the mass press and the Dreyfus affair, see Pierre Boussel, *L'Affaire Dreyfus et la presse* (Paris, 1960); Paula Hyman, "The Dreyfus Affair: The Visual and the Historical," *Journal of Modern History* 61, no. 1 (March 1989): 88–109; Nancy Fitch, "Mass Culture, Mass Parliamentary Politics, and Modern Anti-Semitism: The Dreyfus Affair in Rural France," *American Historical Review* 97, no. 1 (February 1992): 55–95; and Mary Louise Roberts, *Disruptive Acts: The New Woman in Fin-de-Siècle France* (Chicago, 2002), chap. 4. For more general discussion of the importance of the mass press in late nineteenth-century France, see Claude Bellanger, *Histoire générale de la presse française*, vol. 3 (Paris, 1969); and Theodore Zeldin, *France, 1848–1945: Taste and Corruption* (Oxford, 1977), chap. 4.

6. Examining the Dreyfus affair and other fin-de-siècle newspaper scandals, a number of historians have recently argued that the mass press effectively turned public life—not just social and cultural events but politics itself—into a "spectacle," a species of ongoing entertainment for readers. See, for example, Edward Berenson, *The Trial of Madame Caillaux* (Berkeley, 1992), especially chap. 6; Vanessa R. Schwartz, *Spectacular Realities: Early Mass Culture in Fin-de-Siècle Paris* (Berkeley, 1998); Roberts, *Disruptive Acts;* and Gregory K. Shaya, "Mayhem for Moderns: The Culture of Sensationalism in France, c. 1900," Ph.D. diss., University of Michigan, 2000, chap. 3.

7. Noting a similar set of oppositions in the case of Dreyfus, Mary Louise Roberts also links these polarities to the growing commodification of public life. See Roberts, *Disruptive Acts*, 140–41.

8. Artus is quoted in Deschamps, *Le Cas Pierre de Rudder,* 51–52. See also Artus, *Histoire complète du défi public.*

9. The newspaper's response is reprinted in Artus, *Les Miracles de Lourdes et la presse,* 7–10.

10. Artus, *Les Miracles de Lourdes et la presse,* 14–15, 17–20.

11. Artus, *Les Miracles de Lourdes et la presse,* 16, 21–22.

12. Artus, *Les Miracles de Lourdes et la presse,* 24–26.

13. Artus, *Les Miracles de Lourdes et la presse,* 26, 28, 33.

14. "Au jour le jour, M. Zola et le pèlerinage de Lourdes," *Le Temps,* 26 August 1892. Zola was not the first person to refer to healing at Lourdes as mind cure. See, for example, Dr. P. Diday, *Examen médical des miracles de Lourdes* (Paris, 1873); and Hippolyte Bernheim, *De la suggestion et de ses applications à la thérapeutique* (Paris, 1886), 213–18. See also Hippolyte Bernheim, *Hypnotisme, suggestion, psychothérapie: Études nouvelles* (Paris, 1891).

15. "Au jour le jour," *Le Temps,* 26 August 1892.

16. By 1892, Dr. Charcot was a distinguished professor at the Paris Faculty of Medicine and the reigning authority on hysteria. The essay was one of his last published works, as he died eight months later. See Jean-Martin Charcot, "La Foi qui guérit," *Revue Hebdomadaire* (3 December 1892): 112–32; Jean-Martin Charcot, "The Faith Cure," *New Review* 8 (January 1893): 18–31; and Jean-Martin Charcot, "La Foi qui guérit," *Archives de neurologie* 25, no. 73 (January 1893): 72–87. My subsequent citations of the essay refer to a reprinted version; see Jean-Martin Charcot, "La Foi qui guérit," in *Bibliothèque diabolique (Collection Bourneville),* ed. Félix Alcan (Paris, 1897), 1–39. Also see Jan Goldstein, *Console and Classify: The French Psychiatric Profession in the Nineteenth Century* (Cambridge, 1987), chap. 9.

17. In the course of doing research for the novel, Zola also interviewed Giles de la Tourrette, one of Charcot's medical protégés and a physician at the Salpêtrière. See Frederick Brown, *Zola, A Life* (New York, 1995), 680.

18. Émile Zola, *The Three Cities: Lourdes,* trans. Ernest A. Vizetelly (New York, 1899), vol. 1, 54–55; and vol. 2, 153–54.

19. Zola, *Three Cities: Lourdes,* vol. 2, 122, 151. See pages 160–66 for the description of Marie's

cure. Zola's presentation of the cure not only drew on Charcot's ideas but also seemed to incorporate the theories of crowd psychology of Gabriel Tarde and Gustave Le Bon. See Susanna Barrows, *Distorting Mirrors: Visions of the Crowd in Late Nineteenth-Century France* (New Haven, 1981); Naomi Schor, *Zola's Crowds* (Baltimore, 1978); Robert Nye, *The Origins of Crowd Psychology: Gustave Le Bon and the Crisis of Mass Democracy in the Third Republic* (London, 1975); and Jaap van Ginneken, *Crowds, Psychology, and Politics, 1871–1899* (Cambridge, 1992).

20. See, for example, Monseigneur Antoine Ricard, *La Vraie Bernadette de Lourdes: Lettres à M. Zola* (Paris, 1894); Dr. Antoine Imbert-Gourbeyre, *La Stigmatisation, l'extase divine et les miracles de Lourdes: Réponse aux libres-penseurs*, 2 vols. (Clermont-Ferrand, 1894); Dr. D. Moncoq, *Réponse complète au Lourdes de M. Zola* (Caen, 1894); and Abbé Paulin Moniquet, *Un Mot à M. Émile Zola et aux détracteurs de Lourdes* (Paris, 1895).

21. See, for example, *Le Gaulois*, 6 August 1894; *Le Figaro*, 18 August 1893; *Le Figaro*, 31 August 1894; and *Le Temps*, 23 November 1894. Also see B. H. Bakker, ed., *Émile Zola: Correspondance*, vol. 8, 1893–1897 (Montreal, 1991), 151–52, 173; and the introduction by Henri Mitterand in Émile Zola, *Lourdes* (Paris, 1998), especially 17–23. Despite lukewarm reviews from critics, the novel was popular with readers and sold very well. Zola gave a public reading of the novel to an audience of four thousand Parisians at the Place du Trocadéro on 27 April 1894. See Brown, *Zola, A Life*, 681–82.

22. "Le Miracle de Lourdes," *Le Progrès Médical*, 17 September 1892 (reprinted from *L'Écho de Paris*). Known for its anticlericalism, *Le Progrès Médical* was founded by Désiré-Magloire Bourneville, a student of Charcot's and a key figure in the political battle to secularize hospitals in the second half of the nineteenth century. For further accounts of the story of the fleeing pilgrims, see Deschamps, *Le Cas Pierre de Rudder*, 64–66.

23. Charcot, "La Foi qui guérit," 23.

24. Marcel Baudouin, "Science et miracles," *Le Progrès Médical*, 10 September 1892. For a similar critique from a liberal Catholic critic of Lourdes, see Félix Lacaze, *Pour le vrai: À Lourdes avec Zola* (Paris, 1894).

25. See Archives de l'Œuvre de la Grotte (hereafter AG) 6H32, Lettres de Boissarie sur les guérisons et sur la suggestion à Lourdes (1898–1908), Mystification du Dr. Dubois de Reims (1901). Although neither party specified which of Boissarie's books was the subject of debate, it seems likely to have been the most recently published work, *Les Grandes Guérisons de Lourdes* (Paris, 1900).

26. AG 6H32, Lettres de Boissarie sur les guérisons et sur la suggestion à Lourdes (1898–1908), Mystification du Dr. Dubois de Reims (1901), letter from Dr. Dubois to Dr. Boissarie, 8 April 1901; and letter from Dr. Boissarie to Dr. Dubois, 11 April 1901.

27. AG 6H32, Lettres de Boissarie sur les guérisons et sur la suggestion à Lourdes (1898–1908), Mystification du Dr. Dubois de Reims (1901), letter from Dr. Dubois to Dr. Boissarie, 15 April 1901; and letter from Dr. Boissarie to Dr. Dubois, 22 April 1901.

28. AG 6H32, Lettres de Boissarie sur les guérisons et sur la suggestion à Lourdes (1898–1908), Mystification du Dr. Dubois de Reims (1901), letter from Dr. Dubois to Dr. Boissarie, 15 April 1901; letter from Dr. Dubois to Dr. Boissarie, 1 May 1901; and letter from the Abbé Bonnaire to Dr. Boissarie, 7 May 1901.

29. Dr. Bernheim, for example, wrote the preface for a popular book about suggestion at Lourdes that was published during the height of the Zola controversy. Charcot, too, was supposed to have written a preface for the same book but died before doing so. For the work in question, see Lacaze, *Pour le vrai*.

30. Dr. A. Vourch, *La Foi qui guérit: Étude médicale sur quelques cas de guérisons de Lourdes* (Bordeaux, 1911), 8–12, 99. Bernheim, for example, had criticized Charcot's findings on hysteria as largely the product of the institutional culture of the Salpêtrière. For critiques of Charcot by Catholic doctors, see Dr. Félix de Backer, *Lourdes et les médecins* (Paris, 1905); Dr. Hubert Lavrand,

La Suggestion et les guérisons de Lourdes (Paris, 1908); and Dr. Jeanne Bon, *Thèse sur quelques guérisons de Lourdes* (Paris, 1913).

31. On this point, see Szabo, "Seeing Is Believing?" 219–25.

32. See, for example, Imbert-Gourbeyre, *La Stigmatisation*, vol. 2, 484–85, 488–90.

33. Szabo makes a similar point, though he does not draw attention to the problem of economic interest; see Szabo, "Seeing Is Believing?" 225–29. Clerical authorities used the findings of Boissarie's medical bureau to compile statistics on the cures; this information was then published in popular devotional works about Lourdes. For example, the Abbé Georges Bertrin, an independent scholar of the shrine, proclaimed 3,962 miraculous cures associated with Lourdes water; see Abbé Georges Bertrin, *Histoire critique des événements de Lourdes: Apparitions et guérisons* (Paris, 1912). The Assumptionists calculated 2,973 cures for the period between 1888 and 1910; see Alan Neame, *The Happening at Lourdes* (New York, 1968), 135.

34. Dr. Terrien, "Les Guérisons miraculeuses et la science," *Le Progrès Médical*, 26 January 1901.

35. The quotations in this paragraph are taken from Dr. Rouby, *La Vérité sur Lourdes* (Paris, 1910), 65–66, 114, 120, and 271. It is worth noting, more generally, that while the medical profession in turn-of-the-century France enjoyed growing power and prestige, many ordinary medical practitioners found this period to be one of insecurity and crisis. For example, doctors routinely complained in the pages of medical journals that, to survive economically in the countryside, they were forced to kowtow to the superstitious beliefs of their patients. See Jacques Léonard, "Femmes, religion, et médecine: Les Religieuses qui soignent, en France au XIXe siècle," *Annales: Économies, Sociétés, Civilisations* 32, no. 5 (1977): 887–907; and Jack D. Ellis, *The Physician-Legislators of France: Medicine and Politics in the Early Third Republic, 1870–1914* (Cambridge, 1990), 65–70.

36. Baudouin, "Science et miracles."

37. By the late nineteenth century, thinkers of all political stripes routinely attacked the secular mass press for exacerbating, if not causing, growing levels of violence, corruption, immorality, and ignorance among its readers. See Berenson, *Trial of Madame Caillaux*, chap. 6; and Shaya, "Mayhem for Moderns," chap. 4.

38. Abbé Domenech, *Lourdes, hommes et choses* (Lyon, 1894), 148, 151.

39. Catholic critics saw the secular mass press as a source of corruption in French society, often presenting the religious press as the antidote to this corruption. For examples, see Joseph Mallat, *La Presse et les lectures populaires* (Paris, 1887); and Abbé S. Coubé, *La Bonne et la mauvaise presse* (Paris, 1905).

40. J.-K. Huysmans, *The Crowds of Lourdes*, trans. W. H. Mitchell (New York, 1925), 69–70, 108.

41. Huysmans, *Crowds of Lourdes*, 75, 107–8.

42. For the earliest published account of this cure, see Abbé Émile Scheerlinck, *Het Vlaamsche Lourdes* (Ghent, 1875); the book was published in French as *Lourdes en Flandre* (Ghent, 1876).

43. For reprinted copies (in French) of Boissarie's letters to Dr. Royer, see Kanunnik A. De Meester, *De Wonderbare genezing van Pieter De Rudder, Het Kanoniek Onderzoek, 1907–1908* (Oostakker, 1957), 99, 102. For Boissarie's address to the Catholic Congress of Paris on 10 June 1900, see *Annales de Notre-Dame de Lourdes* (June 1900), 65–66. Boissarie had included only a brief account of de Rudder's cure in *Lourdes: Histoire médicale, 1858–1891* (Paris, 1891), but gave it greater prominence in *Lourdes depuis 1858 jusqu'à nos jours* (Paris, 1894); see 175–92.

44. It is unclear where the original bones are now held. After the declaration of the miracle, the bones of the miraculé were first housed at the bishopric in Bruges. By 1911, however, the Jesuit shrine tenders at Oostakker were seeking to reclaim the bones because so many pilgrims were requesting to see them. Today the shrine at Oostakker has a copy of the bones on display. For correspondence between the shrine and the bishop, see Archives de Notre-Dame de Lourdes d'Oostakker, Box 450, Correspondance sur Pierre de Rudder.

45. De Rudder died in 1898, and the autopsy of his legs was performed in May of the following year. The findings from the autopsy were first published in *Revue des Questions Scientifiques*, a well-known Belgian medical journal, in October 1899. Deschamps also recounted the medical facts of the case in a later work, *Un Miracle contemporain* (Paris 1903), which was widely translated.

46. Logie's findings are quoted in Alfred Deschamps, *Le Cas Pierre de Rudder*, 74–75. A similar conclusion was reached by a Dr. Nélis, who was one of the three doctors asked by Monseigneur Waffelaert, Bishop of Bruges, to submit a medical analysis for the commission investigating the cure; the other two doctors submitted reports verifying that the cure defied natural explanation. See Deschamps, *Le Cas Pierre de Rudder*, 228.

47. These medical debates are covered in some detail in Deschamps, *Le Cas Pierre de Rudder*, 31–34, 76–110. In each country, debate erupted in response to church-sponsored medical conferences on de Rudder or in reaction to the publication of *Un Miracle contemporain*.

48. Quoted in Deschamps, *Le Cas Pierre de Rudder*, 31–33.

49. The debate in *La Chronique Médicale* lasted from 15 July 1907 to 15 April 1908. For a summary, see Deschamps, *Le Cas Pierre de Rudder*, 79–85.

50. The Milan conference took place on 10–11 January 1910. See Deschamps, *Le Cas Pierre de Rudder*, 87–88.

51. See the comments, respectively, of Dr. Ferrari, Dr. Sigurta, and Dr. Bonardi, quoted in Deschamps, *Le Cas Pierre de Rudder*, 90–96.

52. See the comments of Dr. Sigurta, Dr. Bonardi, and Dr. Bayla, quoted in Deschamps, *Le Cas Pierre de Rudder*, 91, 94–95, 97–98. The following year, the Medical Society of Milan voted unanimously to oust Gemelli. For details, see the comments of Dr. Baruffaldi and Dr. Filippetti, quoted in Deschamps, *Le Cas Pierre de Rudder*, 105–10.

53. Dr. Louis Necchi, quoted in Deschamps, *Le Cas Pierre de Rudder*, 98–99.

54. Dr. Filippetti, quoted in Deschamps, *Le Cas Pierre de Rudder*, 102–3.

55. Rouby claimed that when bone fragments were secretly removed, the fracture healed. See Rouby, *La Vérité sur Lourdes*, 124–29.

56. Saintyves accused Bishop Waffelaert of concealing a damaging medical report from the ecclesiastical commission investigating the cure. See P. Saintyves, *La Simulation du merveilleux* (Paris, 1912), 328–35. P. Saintyves is the pseudonym of Émile Nourry.

57. See F. Verhas, *Un Miracle de Lourdes-Oostakker: La Guérison de Pierre de Rudder, ou la miraculeuse substitution d'une jambe droite à une jambe gauche* (Brussels, 1911).

58. Verhas, *Un Miracle de Lourdes-Oostakker*, 7–10; also see chapter 5 for presentation of the textual discrepancy over the left and right legs, and chapters 6 and 7 for the accusations of a cover-up.

59. Verhas, *Un Miracle de Lourdes-Oostakker*, 14, 68–69, 111. Verhas also accused the Abbé Bertrin, one of the major chroniclers of the Lourdes cures, of outright deception because the priest had omitted all the references to the right leg when he cited previous accounts of the de Rudder cure in his own work, *Histoire critique des événements de Lourdes;* see Verhas, *Un Miracle de Lourdes-Oostakker*, 107–10.

60. Deschamps, *Le Cas Pierre de Rudder*, 145–47. In his defense of the de Rudder cure, Deschamps responded as well to the multiple charges made by doctors at the various medical conferences across Europe and to the polemics in the popular press. See also H. Bolsius, S. J., *Un Miracle de N.-D. de Lourdes: Pierre de Rudder et son récent historien* (Paris, 1913).

61. Deschamps, *Le Cas Pierre de Rudder*, 50–51.

62. For copies of the letters exchanged between Chide and Duplessy, see *La Réponse: Revue Mensuelle d'Apologétique Populaire* 46 (October 1911), 47 (November 1911), and 48 (December 1911). Also see Chanoine E. Duplessy, *Histoire d'un défi aux adversaires de Lourdes sur la guérison de Pierre de Rudder* (Paris, 1929); and Deschamps, *Le Cas Pierre de Rudder*, 62–72. Newspaper articles about Chide's conference and the wager by Duplessy that originally appeared in *Le Progrès*

Gapençais and *Les Alpes Républicaines* have been collected into an album of press clippings now housed at the Marian Library at the University of Dayton; see "Culte Local de la Vierge Marie, Articles de Journaux et de Revues, Lourdes, vol. II."

63. See Deschamps, *Le Cas Pierre de Rudder,* 209–21, for the wager between Royer and Verhas.

64. For Duplessy's anecdote about the lion tamer, see Deschamps, *Le Cas Pierre de Rudder,* 68. The public wager in Germany was issued by the Abbé Van der Bom in 1905. In 1908 a Dr. Aigner accepted the bet but eventually backed out when the two men were unable to agree on a set of experts to judge the case. Aigner sued the cleric for libel after Van der Bom attacked him in the German religious press. See Deschamps, *Le Cas Pierre de Rudder,* 57–62; and Saintyves, *La Simulation du merveilleux,* 357.

Epilogue: Politics and Mass Culture

1. See, for example, Ralph Gibson, *A Social History of French Catholicism, 1789–1914* (London, 1989); Maurice Larkin, *Church and State after the Dreyfus Affair: The Separation Issue in France* (London, 1974); John McManners, *Church and State in France, 1870–1914* (New York, 1970); Mona Ozouf, *L'École, l'Église et la Republique, 1871–1914* (Paris, 1963); René Rémond, *L'Anticléricalisme en France de 1815 à nos jours* (Brussels, 1985); and Frank Tallett and Nicholas Atkin, eds., *Religion, Society, and Politics in France since 1789* (London, 1991), especially the essays by Ralph Gibson, Geoffrey Cubitt, and Nicholas Atkin. A view of intractable conflict has also shaped more recent interpretations of popular Catholicism and Church-state relations. See, for instance, Caroline Ford, *Creating the Nation in Provincial France: Religion and Political Identity in Brittany* (Princeton, 1993); Raymond Jonas, *France and the Cult of the Sacred Heart: An Epic Tale for Modern Times* (Berkeley, 2000); and Judith F. Stone, "Anticlericals and *Bonnes Sœurs:* The Rhetoric of the 1901 Law of Associations," *French Historical Studies* 23, no. 1 (winter, 2000): 103–128.

2. Lourdes remains one of the most visited Catholic shrines in the world today. According to the shrine's own figures, some five million pilgrims and tourists from around the world come to Lourdes each year. Both the shrine and the town have continued to pursue the kinds of innovative technologies and commercial practices that first transformed Lourdes into a mass pilgrimage destination. For example, the shrine has recently installed its own Webcam at the grotto, enabling faithful Catholics throughout the world to keep up with pilgrimages via the Internet. These devout spectators can also e-mail prayers to the site, whereupon the messages are printed out and placed before the grotto's statue of Our Lady of Lourdes. For information on visitors and the Webcam, see the official Lourdes Web page, www.lourdes-france.org. Also see "Des adresses pour prier, envoyer des mails au mur des Lamentations ou faire une cyberetraite . . ." *Le Monde,* 9–10 July 2000, 8.

3. According to the original wording of the bill, these religious orders, if authorized, would have been placed under the legal jurisdiction of a French bishop. For more on the 1901 Law on Associations, see Larkin, *Church and State after the Dreyfus Affair,* chap. 5; Malcolm O. Partin, *Waldeck-Rousseau, Combes, and the Church: The Politics of Anticlericalism, 1899–1905* (Durham, N.C., 1969), chaps. 6–8; and Pierre Sorlin, *Waldeck-Rousseau* (Paris, 1966), chaps. 8–9.

4. See Ford, *Creating the Nation in Provincial France,* especially 135–169; and Stone, "Anticlericals and *Bonnes Sœurs.*"

5. See Archives Nationales (hereafter AN) F19 2375, Fermeture de la grotte de Lourdes, Extrait du registre des délibérations du conseil municipal de la ville de Lourdes en date du 18 Avril, 1903; and letter from the mayor of Lourdes, Lourdes, 18 April 1903. Ninety-three communes in the department of the Hautes-Pyrénées sent formal petitions to Combes protesting the closing of the sanctuary on economic grounds.

6. See AN F19 2375, Fermeture de la grotte de Lourdes, letter from the prefect of the Hautes-Pyrénées to the minister of the interior and cults, 15 March 1904; and Rapport, situation légale de la chapelle de Lourdes, Paris, n.d.

7. AN F19 2376, Coupures de Presse, "Le Miracle de Lourdes!" *Le Temps,* 6 May 1903. For responses by republican journalists, see AN F19 2376, Coupures de Presse, "Marchands d'Eau Bénite," *Le Radical,* 26 April 1903; "La Défense de Lourdes," *La Lanterne,* 6 May 1903; "Il Faut Oser," *La Lanterne,* 23 August 1903; "Lourdes pour les Sots," *La Lanterne,* 28 August 1903; "La Boutique de Lourdes," *La Lanterne,* 14 October 1903; and "La Concurrence à Lourdes," *Le Siècle,* 20 January 1904.

8. See Larkin, *Church and State after the Dreyfus Affair,* chaps. 6–12; and Partin, *Waldeck-Rousseau, Combes, and the Church,* chaps. 9–12. Also see Theodore Zeldin, *France, 1848–1945: Politics and Anger* (Oxford, 1973), 324–334.

9. See Jean de Bonnefon, "Lourdes Actuel: Au-Dessus des Lois," *La Petite République,* 19 September 1905; Jean de Bonnefon, "Lourdes Actuel: La Loi de 1901 et les Congregations de Lourdes," *La Petite République,* 20 September 1905; Jean de Bonnefon, "Faut-il fermer Lourdes? Opinions de médecins," *Les Paroles Françaises et Romaines* (1 July 1906): 1–64; and Jean de Bonnefon, "Faut-il fermer Lourdes? Réponses des médecins à Jean de Bonnefon," *Les Paroles Françaises et Romaines* (1 August 1906): 1–64.

10. See AN F7 12734, Rapport du préfet des Hautes-Pyrénées au ministère de l'intérieur, Tarbes, 15 November 1908, 4–13.

11. AN F7 12734, Rapport du préfet des Hautes-Pyrénées au ministère de l'intérieur, Tarbes, 15 November 1908, 6–7, 13.

12. Pétain also officially transferred legal possession of the shrine back to the bishop of Tarbes in 1940; its status has not changed since that time. See Alan Neame, *The Happening at Lourdes* (New York, 1968), 132.

13. Franz Werfel was an Austrian Jew who escaped the Nazis by fleeing through France en route to the United States. During this journey, he found temporary refuge at Lourdes. In gratitude for the help he received from the inhabitants of Lourdes, he vowed to write a novel about the famed visionary. He published *The Song of Bernadette* in 1942, and it became an immediate best-seller.

14. Max Horkheimer and Theodor W. Adorno, "The Culture Industry: Enlightenment as Mass Deception," in *Dialectic of Enlightenment,* trans. John Cumming (New York, 1972), 129. Horkheimer and Adorno incorrectly attributed the film to producer Darryl Zanuck. William Perlberg is credited as producer of the film, in which Hollywood mogul David O. Selznick cast Jennifer Jones (soon to be his wife) as its lead.

Bibliography

ARCHIVAL SOURCES

Archives Nationales

Série BB18, Correspondance générale de la Division criminelle
  1589, Administration de la mense épiscopale de Tarbes, Rapport de M. Monsourat.
Série F7, Police générale
  12734, Rapport du préfet des Hautes-Pyrénées.
Série F19, Cultes
  2374, Apparitions.
  2375, Fermeture de la grotte de Lourdes.
  2376, La presse, 1883–1906.
  2377, La presse religieuse, 1912–1914.

Archives Départementales des Hautes-Pyrénées

Série J, 17J7, Surveillance des pèlerins (1875).

Archives de l'Œuvre de la Grotte

Série A, Histoire des apparitions
  A2, Apparitions de Lourdes.
  A7A, Relations des apparitions et des guérisons servenues à cette époque (1858–1859).
  A8, Sur les apparitions.
  A12, Sur les fausses visionnaires.
  A16, Rapports avec la maire de Lourdes et surveillance de la grotte (1870s–1890s).
Série E, Pastorale
  1E1, État comparatif des avantages procurés à la ville de Lourdes par le mouvement des pèlerins (1860–1906).

3E1A, Pèlerinage National: Rapports, lettres, coupures de presse, etc. (1872–1898).

12E2, Liste des localités venues en pèlerinage à Lourdes (1868–1887).

18E3, Listes de pèlerinages (1903–1909).

18E4, Statistiques générales (1893–1977).

Série H, Animation pastorale

1HD1, Processions, guérisons, et pèlerinages divers (1866–1950).

6H1, Rapport sur les premières guérisons opérées par l'usage de l'eau de la grotte de Lourdes (1858–1859).

6H4, Enquête Sempé sur les guérisons obtenues en 1858 (1878–1879).

6H23, Relations de guérisons (1873–1897).

6H32, Lettres de Boissarie sur les guérisons et sur la suggestion à Lourdes (1898–1908).

Série P, Relations publiques

6P1, Publicité commerciale, commercialisation de l'eau.

7P1, Procès et condamnation pour articles injurieux; lettres (1876–1885).

7P3, Affaire vente d'eau de la grotte (1879–1888).

8P1, Attaque du journal "Le XIXe Siècle."

8P3, Attaque du Dr. Vachet.

Archives de Notre-Dame de Lourdes d'Oostakker

Box 450, Correspondance sur Pierre de Rudder.

PERIODICAL SOURCES

L'Assiette au Beurre
Annales de Notre-Dame de Lourdes
La Chronique Médicale
La Croix
La Croix de Lourdes
Le XIXe Siècle
L'Écho de Paris
Le Figaro
Le Gaulois
L'Illustration
Le Journal
Journal de la Grotte de Lourdes
La Lanterne
Le Lavedan
Le Monde
Le Pèlerin
La Petite République
Le Progrès Médical
Le Radical
La Réponse: Revue Mensuelle d'Apologétique Populaire
Le Siècle
Le Temps
L'Univers

PRIMARY SOURCES

Artus, E. *Les Miracles de Notre-Dame de Lourdes: Défi public à la libre pensée: Guérison de Juliette Fournier.* Paris, 1872.

——. *Les Médecins et les miracles de Lourdes.* Paris, 1873.

——. *Les Miracles de Lourdes et la presse.* Paris, 1874.

——. *Histoire complète du défi public à la libre pensée sur les miracles de Notre-Dame de Lourdes.* Paris, 1877.

Association de Notre-Dame de Salut. *Jubilé du pèlerinage national à Lourdes.* Paris, 1897.

Bakker, B. H., ed. *Émile Zola: Correspondance.* Vol. 8, 1893–1897. Montreal, 1991.

Beaumont, Barbara, ed. *The Road from Decadence: From Brothel to Cloister, Selected Letters of J.-K. Huysmans.* London, 1989.

Bernheim, Hippolyte. *De la suggestion et de ses applications à la thérapeutique.* Paris, 1886.

——. *Hypnotisme, suggestion, psychothérapie: Études nouelles.* Paris, 1891.

Bertrin, Abbé Georges. *Histoire critique des événements de Lourdes: Apparitions et guérisons.* Paris, 1912.

Bloy, Léon. *Méditations d'un solitaire en 1916.* Paris, 1917.

——. *Dans les ténèbres.* Paris, 1918.

——. *Journal.* Vol. 1. Paris, 1956.

——. *She Who Weeps: Our Lady of La Salette.* Translated by Emile LaDouceur. Fresno, Calif., 1956.

Boissarie, Gustave. *Lourdes: Histoire médicale, 1858–1891.* Paris, 1891.

——. *Lourdes depuis 1858 jusqu'à nos jours.* Paris, 1894.

——. *Zola: Conférence du Luxembourg.* Paris, 1895.

——. *Les Grandes Guérisons de Lourdes.* Paris, 1900.

——. *Lourdes: Les Guérisons.* Series 1–4. Paris, 1911–1922.

Bolsius, H., S. J. *Un Miracle de N.-D. de Lourdes: Pierre de Rudder et son récent historien.* Paris, 1913.

Bon, Dr. Jeanne. *Thèse sur quelques guérisons de Lourdes.* Paris, 1913.

Cantiques de Lourdes, Offerts par les Magasins de l'Alliance Catholique. Lourdes, 1911?

Charcot, Jean-Martin. "La Foi qui guérit." *Revue Hebdomadaire* (3 December 1892): 112–132.

——. "La Foi qui guérit." *Archives de neurologie* 25, no. 73 (January 1893): 72–87.

——. "The Faith Cure." *New Review* 8 (January 1893): 18–31.

——. "La Foi qui guérit." In *Bibliothèque diabolique (Collection Bourneville),* edited by Félix Alcan. Paris, 1897.

Chaucer, Geoffrey. *The Canterbury Tales.* Translated by Nevill Coghill. London, 1974.

Chaudé, Abbé. *De Lourdes au Cirque de Gavarnie (Hautes-Pyrénées), guide pratique du pèlerin et du touriste.* Versailles and Lourdes, 1875.

Coubé, Abbé S. *La Bonne et la mauvaise presse.* Paris, 1905.

Couret, J. *Guide-Almanach de Notre-Dame de Lourdes, 1900.* Bordeaux, 1900.

D., Madeleine. *Mon Pèlerinage de Lourdes.* Blois, 1912.

Dauberive, Bernard. *Lourdes et ses environs: Guide du pèlerin et du touriste.* Poitiers, 1896.

de Backer, Dr. Félix. *Lourdes et les médecins.* Paris, 1905.

de Bonnefon, Jean. "Faut-il fermer Lourdes? Opinions de médecins." *Les Paroles Françaises et Romaines* (1 July 1906): 1–64.

——. "Faut-il fermer Lourdes? Réponses des médecins à Jean de Bonnefon." *Les Paroles Françaises et Romaines* (1 August 1906): 1–64.

De Meester, Kanunnik A. *De Wonderbare genezing van Pieter De Rudder, Het Kanoniek Onderzoek, 1907–1908.* Oostakker, 1957.

Deschamps, Alfred, S.J. *Un Miracle contemporain.* Paris, 1903.

——. *Le Cas Pierre de Rudder et les objections des médecins.* Brussels, 1913.

Diday, Dr. P. *Examen médical des miracles de Lourdes.* Paris, 1873.

Didiot, Chanoine Jules. "Vue de Lourdes." *Revue de Lille* (January 1893): 3–16.

Domenech, Abbé. *Lourdes, hommes et choses.* Lyon, 1894.

Duplessy, Chanoine E. *Histoire d'un défi aux adversaires de Lourdes sur la guérison de Pierre de Rudder.* Paris, 1929.

Guide du pèlerin et du touriste à Lourdes, aux environs et vers la montagne. Tarbes, 1888.

Guide du pèlerin de Saint-Brieuc à Lourdes. Saint-Brieuc, 1922.

Huysmans, J.-K. *The Cathedral.* Translated by Clara Bell. New York, 1922.

——. *The Crowds of Lourdes.* Translated by W. H. Mitchell. New York, 1925.

Imbert-Gourbeyre, Dr. Antoine. *La Stigmatisation, l'extase divine et les miracles de Lourdes: Réponse aux libres-penseurs.* 2 vols. Clermont-Ferrand, 1894.

Jouhandeau, Marcel. *Mémorial.* Vol. 2. Paris, 1951.

Lacaze, Félix. *Pour le vrai: À Lourdes avec Zola.* Paris, 1894.

Lasserre, Henri. *Notre-Dame de Lourdes.* Paris, 1870.

Laurentin, René. *Lourdes: Histoire authentique des apparitions.* 6 vols. Paris, 1961–1986.

——. *Visage de Bernadette.* 2 vols. Paris, 1992.

——. *Lourdes: Cartes postales d'hier.* Paris, 1979.

Laurentin, René, and Bernard Billet. *Lourdes: Dossier des documents authentiques.* 7 vols. Paris, 1957–1962.

Lavrand, Dr. Hubert. *La Suggestion et les guérisons de Lourdes.* Paris, 1908.

Le Cointe, Abbé. *Le Guide du pèlerin de Coutances et de Bayeux à Notre-Dame de Lourdes.* Caen, 1883.

Lourdes en deux jours: Guide religieux, historique, pittoresque et documentaire. Tarbes, 1914.

Lynch, L. R. "Lourdes and the National Pilgrimage of 1903." *Catholic World* 78, no. 404 (1903): 200–201.

Mallat, Joseph. *La Presse et les lectures populaires.* Paris, 1887.

Manuel du pèlerinage dit "Des Malades" à Notre-Dame de Lourdes. Lyon, 1913.

Manuel du pèlerinage interdiocésain de la Suisse Française à Notre-Dame de Lourdes. Belley, 1913.

Marès, G. *Lourdes et ses environs.* Bordeaux, 1894.

Martin, Abbé. *Guide de Lourdes et ses environs à l'usage des pèlerins.* Saumur, 1893.

Merveilles de Lourdes, Les: Gabriel Gargam, son accident de chemin de fer, sa vie d'hôpital, sa guérison. Toulouse, 1914.

Moncoq, Dr. D. *Réponse complète au Lourdes de M. Zola.* Caen, 1894.

Moniquet, Abbé Paulin. *Un Mot à M. Émile Zola et aux détracteurs de Lourdes.* Paris, 1895.

Ricard, Monseigneur Antoine. *La Vraie Bernadette de Lourdes: Lettres à M. Zola.* Paris, 1894.

Rouby, Dr. *La Vérité sur Lourdes.* Paris, 1910.

Saintyves, P. *La Simulation du merveilleux.* Paris, 1912.

Scheerlinck, Abbé Émile. *Het Vlaamsche Lourdes.* Ghent, 1875.

Ségalas, Bertile. *Huit jours à Lourdes.* Vannes, 1900.

——. "Huit jours à Lourdes." *Revue de Bretagne, de Vendée et d'Anjou* 23 (January–March 1900).

——. "Mon sixième voyage à Lourdes." *La Femme et la Famille* (1904).

Souvenir guide du pèlerin, cinquantenaire de l'Immaculée-Conception, livre d'or de Notre-Dame de Lourdes. Toulouse, 1909.

Triger, Robert. *Lourdes: 1872–1908, impressions et souvenirs.* Le Mans, 1909.

Verhas, F. *Un Miracle de Lourdes-Oostakker: La Guérison de Pierre de Rudder, ou la miraculeuse substitution d'une jambe droite à une jambe gauche.* Brussels, 1911.

Vourch, Dr. A. *La Foi qui guérit: Étude médicale sur quelques cas de guérisons de Lourdes.* Bordeaux, 1911.

Zola, Émile. *The Three Cities: Lourdes.* 2 vols. Translated by Ernest A. Vizetelly. New York, 1899.

———. *Mes voyages: Lourdes, Rome, journaux inédits présentés et annotés par René Ternois.* Edited by René Ternois. Paris, 1958.

SECONDARY SOURCES

Abel, Richard. *The Ciné Goes to Town: French Cinema, 1896–1914.* Berkeley, 1994.

Amundsen, Darrell W. "The Medieval Catholic Tradition." In *Caring and Curing: Health and Medicine in the Western Religious Traditions,* edited by Ronald Numbers and Darrell W. Amundsen. New York, 1986.

Auslander, Leora. *Taste and Power: Furnishing Modern France.* Berkeley, 1996.

Baldick, Robert. *The Life of J.-K. Huysmans.* Oxford, 1955.

Barrows, Susanna. *Distorting Mirrors: Visions of the Crowd in Late Nineteenth-Century France.* New Haven, 1981.

Baudelaire, Charles. *The Painter of Modern Life and Other Essays.* Translated by Jonathan Mayne. London, 1964.

Bellanger, Claude. *Histoire générale de la presse française.* Vol. 3. Paris, 1969.

Benjamin, Walter. "The Work of Art in the Age of Mechanical Reproduction." In *Illuminations,* edited by Hannah Arendt. Translated by Harry Zohn. New York, 1969.

———. "Paris, the Capital of the Nineteenth Century." In *The Arcades Project.* Translated by Howard Eiland and Kevin McLaughlin. Cambridge, Mass., 2002.

Bensa, Alban. *Les Saints guérisseurs du Perche-Gouët.* Paris, 1978.

Berenson, Edward. *The Trial of Madame Caillaux.* Berkeley, 1992.

Berlanstein, Lenard R. *Daughters of Eve: A Cultural History of French Theater Women from the Old Regime to the Fin de Siècle.* Cambridge, Mass., 2001.

Berman, Marshall. *All That Is Solid Melts into Air: The Experience of Modernity.* New York, 1982.

Billet, Bernard. "L'Histoire médicale de Lourdes et la faculté Catholique de médecine de Lille." *Ensemble* (June 1996): 87–97.

Blackbourn, David. *Marpingen: Apparitions of the Virgin Mary in Nineteenth-Century Germany.* New York, 1993.

Bloch, R. Howard. *God's Plagiarist: Being an Account of the Fabulous Industry and Irregular Commerce of the Abbé Migne.* Chicago, 1994.

Boussel, Pierre. *L'Affaire Dreyfus et la presse.* Paris, 1960.

Boutry, Philippe, and Michel Cinquin. *Deux Pèlerinages au XIXe siècle: Ars et Paray-le-Monial.* Paris, 1980.

Brady, Sister Mary Rosalie. *Thought and Style in the Works of Léon Bloy.* Washington, D.C., 1946.

Brooks, Peter. *The Melodramatic Imagination.* New Haven, 1976.

Brown, Frederick. *Zola, A Life.* New York, 1995.

Buck-Morss, Susan. *The Dialectics of Seeing: Walter Benjamin and the Arcades Project.* Cambridge, Mass., 1989.

Burton, Richard D. E. *Holy Tears, Holy Blood: Women, Catholicism, and the Culture of Suffering in France, 1840–1970.* Ithaca, 2004.

Butler, Judith. *Gender Trouble: Feminism and the Subversion of Identity.* New York, 1990.

Bynum, Caroline Walker. *The Resurrection of the Body in Western Christianity, 200–1336.* New York, 1995.

Calhoun, Craig, ed. *Habermas and the Public Sphere.* Cambridge, Mass., 1992.

Caulier, Brigitte. *L'Eau et le sacré: Les Cultes thérapeutiques autour des fontaines en France du Moyen Age à nos jours.* Paris, 1990.

Charbonneau, Henri. *Chapelles et saints guérisseurs basques et béarnais.* Hélette, 1995.

Chelini, Jean, and Henry Branthomme. *Les Chemins de Dieu: Histoire des pèlerinages chrétiens des origines à nos jours.* Paris, 1982.

Cholvy, Gérard, and Yves-Marie Hilaire. *Histoire religieuse de la France contemporaine.* 2 vols. Toulouse, 1985–1986.

Christian, William A., Jr. *Apparitions in Late Medieval and Renaissance Spain.* Princeton, 1981.

———. *Local Religion in Sixteenth-Century Spain.* Princeton, 1981.

———. *Visionaries: The Spanish Republic and the Reign of Christ.* Berkeley, 1996.

Clark, T. J. *The Painting of Modern Life: Paris in the Art of Manet and His Followers.* Princeton, 1984.

Coffin, Judith. "Credit, Consumption, and Images of Women's Desires: Selling the Sewing Machine in Late-Nineteenth-Century France." *French Historical Studies* 18 (1994): 749–83.

Corbin, Alain. *The Lure of the Sea: The Discovery of the Seaside in the Western World, 1750–1840.* Translated by Jocelyn Phelps. Berkeley, 1994.

Cosandey, Roland, André Gaudreault, and Tom Gunning, eds. *Une Invention du diable? Cinéma des premiers temps et religion.* Lausanne, 1992.

Daviet, Jean-Pierre. *La Société industrielle en France, 1814–1914: Productions, èchanges, reprèsentations.* Paris, 1997.

de Certeau, Michel. *The Writing of History.* Translated by Tom Conley. New York, 1988.

———. *The Mystic Fable.* Translated by Michael B. Smith. Chicago, 1992.

de Grazia, Victoria, ed. *The Sex of Things: Gender and Consumption in Historical Perspective.* With Ellen Furlough. Berkeley, 1996.

Derrida, Jacques. *Of Grammatology.* Translated by Gayatri Chakravorty Spivak. Baltimore, 1976.

Didi-Huberman, Georges. *Invention de l'hystérie: Charcot et l'iconographie photographique de la Saltpêtrière.* Paris, 1982.

Dubois, E. T. *Portrait of Léon Bloy.* London, 1951.

Dupront, Alphonse. *Du sacré: Croisades et pèlerinages, images et langages.* Paris, 1987.

Durkheim, Émile. *The Elementary Forms of the Religious Life.* Translated by Joseph Ward Swain. New York, 1915.

Ellenberger, Henri. *The Discovery of the Unconscious: The History and Evolution of Dynamic Psychiatry.* New York, 1970.

Ellis, Jack D. *The Physician-Legislators of France: Medicine and Politics in the Early Third Republic, 1870–1914.* Cambridge, 1990.

Fairchilds, Cissie. "Marketing the Counter-Reformation: Religious Objects and Consumerism in Early Modern France." In *Visions and Revisions of Eighteenth-Century France,* edited by Christine Adams, Jack R. Censer, and Lisa Jane Graham. University Park, Penn., 1997.

Finucane, Ronald C. *Miracles and Pilgrims: Popular Beliefs in Medieval England.* London, 1977.

Fitch, Nancy. "Mass Culture, Mass Parliamentary Politics, and Modern Anti-Semitism: The Dreyfus Affair in Rural France." *American Historical Review* 97, no. 1 (February 1992): 55–95.

Ford, Caroline. *Creating the Nation in Provincial France: Religion and Political Identity in Brittany.* Princeton, 1993.

Foucault, Michel. *The Birth of the Clinic: An Archaeology of Medical Perception.* Translated by A. M. Sheridan Smith. New York, 1973.

Freedberg, David. *The Power of Images: Studies in the History and Theory of Response.* Chicago, 1989.

Furet, François, and Jacques Ozouf. *Reading and Writing: Literacy in France from Calvin to Jules Ferry.* Cambridge, 1982.

Gagnon, Paul A. *France since 1789.* New York, 1964.

Garelick, Rhonda K. *Rising Star: Dandyism, Gender, and Performance in the Fin de Siècle.* Princeton, 1998.

Gibson, Ralph. *A Social History of French Catholicism, 1789–1914.* London, 1989.

Giggie, John M., and Diane Winston, eds. *Faith in the Market: Religion and the Rise of Urban Commercial Culture.* New Brunswick, N.J., 2002.

Godfrin, Jacqueline, and Philippe Godfrin. *Une Centrale de presse catholique: La Maison de la Bonne Presse et ses publications.* Paris, 1965.

Godman, Amie Virginia. "Positivistic and Catholic Naturalism: A Study of the Role of Lourdes in the Work of Huysmans and Zola." M.A. thesis, George Washington University, 1967.

Goldstein, Jan. *Console and Classify: The French Psychiatric Profession in the Nineteenth Century.* Cambridge, 1987.

Gough, Austin. *Paris and Rome: The Gallican Church and the Ultramontane Campaign, 1848–1853.* Oxford, 1986.

Gravrand, Amélie. "L'Impact géographique du tourisme de pèlerinage sur la ville de Lourdes." Thèse, Université de Bretagne Occidentale, 1997.

Grew, Raymond, and Patrick J. Harrigan. *School, State, and Society: The Growth of Elementary Schooling in Nineteenth-Century France: A Quantitative Analysis.* Ann Arbor, Mich., 1991.

Griffiths, Richard M. *The Reactionary Revolution: The Catholic Revival in French Literature, 1870–1914.* London, 1966.

Guillaume, Pierre. *Médecins, Église et foi depuis deux siècles.* Paris, 1990.

Gunning, Tom. "An Aesthetic of Astonishment: Early Film and the (In)Credulous Spectator." In *Viewing Positions: Ways of Seeing Film,* edited by Linda Williams. New Brunswick, N.J., 1995.

Habermas, Jürgen. *The Structural Transformation of the Public Sphere: An Inquiry into a Category of Bourgeois Society.* Translated by Thomas Burger. Cambridge, Mass., 1991.

Hansen, Miriam. "Early Cinema, Late Cinema: Transformations of the Public Sphere." In *Viewing Positions: Ways of Seeing Film,* edited by Linda Williams. New Brunswick, N.J., 1995.

Harris, Ruth. *Murders and Madness: Medicine, Law, and Society in the Fin de Siècle.* Oxford, 1989.

——. *Lourdes: Body and Spirit in the Secular Age.* London, 1999.

Henige, David P. *The Chronology of Oral Tradition: The Quest for a Chimera.* Oxford, 1974.

Hillman, Robert G. "A Scientific Study of Mystery: The Role of the Medical and Popular Press in the Nancy-Saltpêtrière Controversy on Hypnotism." *Bulletin of the History of Medicine* 39, no. 2 (1965): 163–82.

Hobsbawm, Eric, and Terence Ranger, eds. *The Invention of Tradition.* Cambridge, 1983.

Horkheimer, Max, and Theodor W. Adorno. "The Culture Industry: Enlightenment as Mass Deception." In *Dialectic of Enlightenment.* Translated by John Cumming. New York, 1972.

Hyman, Paula. "The Dreyfus Affair: The Visual and the Historical." *Journal of Modern History* 61, no. 1 (March 1989): 88–109.

Israel, Kali. *Names and Stories: Emilia Dilke and Victorian Culture.* New York, 1999.

Jameson, Fredric. *Late Marxism: Adorno, or, the Persistence of the Dialectic.* New York, 1990.

Jonas, Raymond. *France and the Cult of the Sacred Heart: An Epic Tale for Modern Times.* Berkeley, 2000.

——. "Sacred Tourism and Secular Pilgrimage: Montmartre and the Basilica of Sacré-Coeur." In *Montmartre and the Making of Mass Culture,* edited by Gabriel P. Weisberg. New Brunswick, N.J., 2001.

Kaufman, Suzanne K. "Miracles, Medicine, and the Spectacle of Lourdes: Popular Religion and Modernity in Fin-de-Siècle France." Ph.D. diss., Rutgers University, 1996.

Koshar, Rudy, ed. *Histories of Leisure.* New York, 2002.

Kselman, Thomas A. *Miracles and Prophecies in Nineteenth-Century France.* New Brunswick, N.J., 1983.

——. *Death and the Afterlife in Modern France.* Princeton, 1993.

Lagrée, Michel. *La Bénédiction de Prométhée: Religion et technologie, XIXe–XXe siècle.* Paris, 1999.

Langlois, Claude. *Le Catholicisme au féminin: Les Congrégations françaises à supérieure générale au XIXe siècle.* Paris, 1984.

——. "La Photographie comme preuve, entre médicine et religion." *Histoire des Sciences Médicales* 28, no. 4 (1994): 325–36.

——. "Photographier des saintes: De Bernadette Soubirous à Thérèse de Lisieux." In *Histoire, images, imaginaires: Fin XVe siècle–début XXe siècle,* edited by Michèle Ménard and Annie Duprat. Le Mans, 1998.

Laqueur, Thomas W. "Bodies, Details, and the Humanitarian Narrative." In *The New Cultural History,* edited by Lynn Hunt. Berkeley, 1989.

Larkin, Maurice. *Church and State after the Dreyfus Affair: The Separation Issue in France.* London, 1974.

Léonard, Jacques. "Femmes, religion, et médecine: Les Religieuses qui soigent, en France au XIXe siècle." *Annales: Économies, Sociétés, Civilisations* 32, no. 5 (1977): 887–907.

——. *Les Médecins de l'Ouest au XIXe siècle.* Lille, 1978.

——. *La Médecine entre les savoirs et les pouvoirs.* Paris, 1981.

Leproux, Paul. *Dévotions et saints guérisseurs.* Paris, 1957.

Lyons, Martyn. *Readers and Society in Nineteenth-Century France: Workers, Women, Peasants.* New York, 2001.

Mackaman, Douglas Peter. *Leisure Settings: Bourgeois Culture, Medicine, and the Spa in Modern France.* Chicago, 1998.

Margadant, Jo Burr, ed. *The New Biography: Performing Femininity in Nineteenth-Century France.* Berkeley, 2000.

Marrus, Michael R. "Cultures on the Move: Pilgrims and Pilgrimages in Nineteenth-Century France." *Stanford French Review* 1 (1977): 205–20.

Martin, Marc. *Trois siècles de publicité en France.* Paris, 1992.

Marx, Karl. *Capital.* Vol. 1. Translated by Ben Fowkes. New York, 1976.

Maza, Sarah. "Domestic Melodrama as Political Ideology: The Case of the Comte de Sanois." *American Historical Review* 94, no. 5 (December 1989): 1249–64.

McDannell, Colleen. *Material Christianity: Religion and Popular Culture in America.* New Haven, 1995.

McKendrick, Neil, John Brewer, and J. H. Plumb, eds. *The Birth of Consumer Society: The Commercialization of Eighteenth-Century England.* Bloomington, Ind., 1982.

McLeod, Hugh. "Women's Piety and Men's Unbelief." In *Bürgerinnen und bürger,* edited by Ute Frevert. Göttingen, 1988.

McManners, John. *Church and State in France, 1870–1914.* New York, 1970.

Micale, Mark S. *Approaching Hysteria: Disease and Its Interpretations.* Princeton, 1995.

Miller, Michael B. *The Bon Marché: Bourgeois Culture and the Department Store, 1869–1920.* Princeton, 1981.

Mitterand, Henri. Introduction to *Lourdes,* by Émile Zola. Paris, 1998.

Moore, Laurence. *Selling God: American Religion in the Marketplace of Culture.* New York, 1994.

Morgan, David. *Protestants and Pictures: Religion, Visual Culture, and the Age of American Mass Production.* New York, 1999.

Nava, Mica, and Alan O'Shea, eds. *Modern Times: Reflections on a Century of English Modernity.* London, 1996.

Neame, Alan. *The Happening at Lourdes.* New York, 1968.

Nordman, Daniel. "Les Guides-Joanne." In *Les Lieux de mémoire: La Nation.* Vol. 2, edited by Pierre Nora. Paris, 1997.

Nye, Robert. *The Origins of Crowd Psychology: Gustave Le Bon and the Crisis of Mass Democracy in the Third Republic.* London, 1975.

Orsi, Robert. *Thank You, St. Jude: Women's Devotion to the Patron Saint of Hopeless Causes.* New Haven, 1996.

Owen, A. R. G. *Hysteria, Hypnosis, and Healing: The Work of J.-M. Charcot.* New York, 1971.

Ozouf, Mona. *L'École, l'Église et la République, 1871–1914.* Paris, 1963.

Palmowski, Jan. "Travels with Baedeker: The Guidebook and the Middle Classes in Victorian and Edwardian England." In *Histories of Leisure,* edited by Rudy Koshar. New York, 2002.

Partin, Malcolm O. *Waldeck-Rousseau, Combes, and the Church: The Politics of Anticlericalism, 1899–1905.* Durham, N.C., 1969.

Paul, Harry W. *The Edge of Contingency: French Catholic Reaction to Scientific Change from Darwin to Duhem.* Gainesville, Fla., 1979.

Perkins, Judith. *The Suffering Self: Pain and Narrative Representation in the Early Christian Era.* New York, 1995.

Pierrard, Pierre. *Louis Veuillot.* Paris, 1998.

Pope, Barbara Corrado. "Immaculate and Powerful: The Marian Revival in the Nineteenth Century." In *Immaculate and Powerful: The Female in Sacred Image and Social Reality,* edited by Clarissa W. Atkinson, Constance H. Buchanan, and Margaret R. Miles. Boston, 1985.

Rearick, Charles. *Pleasures of the Belle Époque: Entertainment and Festivity in Turn-of-the-Century France.* New Haven, 1985.

Rein, Irving J., Philip Kotler, and Martin R. Stoller. *High Visibility.* New York, 1987.

Rémond, René. *The Right Wing in France from 1815 to de Gaulle.* Translated by James M. Laux. Philadelphia, 1966.

——. *L'Anticléricalisme en France de 1815 à nos jours.* Brussels, 1985.

Rémond, René, and Émile Poulat. *Cent ans d'histoire de La Croix.* Paris, 1988.

Richards, Thomas. *The Commodity Culture of Victorian England: Advertising and Spectacle, 1851–1914.* Stanford, 1990.

Ripert, Aline, and Claude Frère. *La Carte postale: Son Histoire, sa fonction sociale.* Paris, 1983.

Roberts, Mary Louise. "Gender, Consumption, and Commodity Culture." *American Historical Review* 103, no. 3 (June 1998): 817–44.

——. "Acting Up: The Feminist Theatrics of Marguerite Durand." In *The New Biography: Performing Femininity in Nineteenth-Century France,* edited by Jo Burr Margadant. Berkeley, 2000.

——. *Disruptive Acts: The New Woman in Fin-de-Siècle France.* Chicago, 2002.

Rose, Louis. *Faith Healing.* Harmondsworth, 1971.

Ross, Kristin. Introduction to *The Ladies' Paradise,* by Émile Zola. Berkeley, 1992.

Ryder, Janet Kay. "Miracles and Mentality: The Medieval Experience." Ph.D. diss., University of California at Santa Barbara, 1993.

Savart, Claude. "À la recherche de l' 'art' dit de Saint-Sulpice." *Revue d'Histoire de la Spiritualité* 52 (1976): 265–82.

Scarry, Elaine. *The Body in Pain: The Making and Unmaking of the World.* New York, 1985.

Schickel, Richard. *Intimate Strangers: The Culture of Celebrity.* New York, 1985.

Schloesser, Stephen R. "Mystic Realists: Sacramental Modernism in French Catholic Revival, 1918–1928." Ph.D. diss., Stanford University, 1999.

Schmidt, Leigh Eric. *Consumer Rites: The Buying and Selling of American Holidays.* Princeton, 1995.

Schor, Naomi. *Zola's Crowds.* Baltimore, 1978.

——. "*Cartes Postales:* Representing Paris 1900." *Critical Inquiry* 18 (winter 1992): 188–244.

Schultheiss, Katrin. "Gender and the Limits of Anti-Clericalism: The Secularization of Hospital Nursing in France, 1880–1914." *French History* 12, no. 3 (1998): 229–45.

——. *Bodies and Souls: Politics and the Professionalization of Nursing in France, 1880–1922.* Cambridge, Mass., 2001.

Schwartz, Vanessa R. *Spectacular Realities: Early Mass Culture in Fin-de-Siècle Paris.* Berkeley, 1998.

Scott, Joan. "The Evidence of Experience." *Critical Inquiry* 17, no. 4 (1991): 773–97.

Seeley, Paul. "O Sainte Mère: Liberalism and the Socialization of Catholic Men in Nineteenth-Century France." *Journal of Modern History* 70, no. 4 (December 1998): 862–91.

Segal, Aaron J. "The Republic of Goods: Advertising and National Identity in France, 1875–1918." Ph.D. diss., University of California at Los Angeles, 1995.

Shaya, Gregory K. "Mayhem for Moderns: The Culture of Sensationalism in France, c. 1900." Ph.D. diss., University of Michigan, 2000.

Sigal, Pierre-André. *L'Homme et le miracle dans la France médiévale, XIe–XIIe siècles.* Paris, 1985.

Silverman, Debora L. *Art Nouveau in Fin-de-Siècle France: Politics, Psychology, and Style.* Berkeley, 1989.

Silverman, Lisa. *Tortured Subjects: Pain, Truth, and the Body in Early Modern France.* Chicago, 2001.

Smith, Bonnie G. *Ladies of the Leisure Class: The Bourgeoises of Northern France in the Nineteenth Century.* Princeton, 1981.

Smith, Julia M. H. "Oral and Written: Saints, Miracles, and Relics in Brittany, c. 850–1250." *Speculum* 65, no. 2 (April 1990): 309–43.

Solomon-Godeau, Abigail. "The Other Side of Venus: The Visual Economy of Feminine Display." In *The Sex of Things: Gender and Consumption in Historical Perspective,* edited by Victoria de Grazia, with Ellen Furlough. Berkeley, 1996.

Sorlin, Pierre. *Waldeck-Rousseau.* Paris, 1966.

Soulet, Jean-François. *Les Pyrénées au XIXe siècle.* Vol. 1. Toulouse, 1987.

Staff, Frank. *The Picture Postcard and Its Origins.* London, 1966.

Stone, Judith F. "Anticlericals and *Bonnes Sœurs:* The Rhetoric of the 1901 Law of Associations." *French Historical Studies* 23, no. 1 (winter 2000): 103–28.

Szabo, Jason. "Seeing Is Believing? The Form and Substance of French Medical Debates over Lourdes." *Bulletin of the History of Medicine* 76, no. 2 (2002): 199–230.

Tallett, Frank, and Nicholas Atkin, eds. *Religion, Society, and Politics in France since 1789.* London, 1991.

Taveneaux, René. *Le Catholicisme dans la France classique, 1610–1715.* Vol. 2. Paris, 1980.

Taylor, Thérèse. "'So Many Extraordinary Things to Tell': Letters from Lourdes, 1858." *Journal of Ecclesiastical History* 46, no. 3 (July 1995): 457–81.

Tiersten, Lisa. *Marianne in the Market: Envisioning Consumer Society in Fin-de-Siècle France.* Berkeley, 2001.

Verley, Patrick. *Nouvelle histoire économique de la France contemporaine.* Vol. 2. Paris, 1989.

van Ginneken, Jaap. *Crowds, Psychology, and Politics, 1871–1899.* Cambridge, 1992.

Vauchez, André. *La Sainteté en Occident au derniers siècles du Moyen Age: d'après les procès de canonisation et les documents hagiographiques.* Rome, 1981.

Walker, Pamela. *Pulling the Devil's Kingdom Down: The Salvation Army in Victorian Britain.* Berkeley, 2001.

Walkowitz, Judith. *City of Dreadful Delight: Narratives of Sexual Danger in Late-Victorian London.* Chicago, 1992.

Ward, Benedicta. *Miracles and the Medieval Mind: Theory, Record and Event, 1000–1215.* London, 1982.

Weber, Eugen. *France, Fin de Siècle.* Cambridge, Mass., 1986.

Weber, Max. "Science as a Vocation." In *From Max Weber: Essays in Sociology,* edited by H. H. Gerth and C. Wright Mills. New York, 1946.

Williams, Alan. *Republic of Images: A History of French Filmmaking.* Cambridge, Mass., 1992.

Williams, Rosalind H. *Dream Worlds: Mass Consumption in Late Nineteenth-Century France.* Berkeley, 1982.

Winston, Diane. *Red-Hot and Righteous: The Urban Religion of the Salvation Army.* Cambridge, Mass., 1999.

Young, Patrick. "*La Vieille France* as Object of Bourgeois Desire: The Touring Club de France and the French Regions, 1890–1918." In *Histories of Leisure,* edited by Rudy Koshar. New York, 2002.

Zeldin, Theodore. *France, 1848–1945: Politics and Anger.* Oxford, 1973.

——. *France, 1848–1945: Taste and Corruption.* Oxford, 1977.

Zimdars-Swartz, Sandra L. *Encountering Mary: From La Salette to Medjugorje.* Princeton, 1991.